SOVIET POLITICS
AND THE UKRAINE
1917-1957

Soviet Politics and the Ukraine

1917-1957

BY ROBERT S. SULLIVANT

 1962

Columbia University Press

NEW YORK AND LONDON

*To My Mother
and Father*

PREFACE

This book is an effort to place in some perspective the rather uncertain problem posed by the Soviet system as it functions at the regional level. There is little need to justify a regional study of this kind. Despite its modest dramatic impact when contrasted with political studies at the Union level, it offers compensations of its own. Because of the centralized nature of the Soviet federal system, ties between republic and Union politics are much closer than in the American system, and study of the first provides suggestions useful to studies of the second. Moreover, the political process—again unlike the American system—appears remarkably similar at the two levels, and generalizations can be applied appropriately to both. Further, the circumspect fashion in which political events at the center have characteristically been reported in most periods has been less typical in areas removed from Moscow and at regional and local levels; instructive material and interpretations may be found in these places which would not, because of more careful scrutiny, be released at the center. And finally, the regional and nationality attitudes of the people living in the Soviet border areas have posed peculiar problems for Soviet leaders and forced significant modifications of Soviet practices; these special problems and modifications alike are of considerable interest to the West.

Of the Soviet border regions, the Ukraine has played, historically as well as politically, the most important role. Its population is largest and its economic level is highest in the Soviet Union outside the Russian core. Apart from the Georgian republic it has developed perhaps the richest national literature and strongest national movement. Although its party organization has never assumed a central, dominating role as have the Moscow and Leningrad organizations, it has grown to be the largest subdivision of the Communist Party of the Soviet Union and has been linked increasingly with Moscow and Leningrad as a principal basis of political power and support. Because of Khrushchev's personal identification with the Ukraine, the region has become a reservoir supplying highest leadership to the center. In the future the Ukraine may lose importance in the eyes of new Soviet leaders who will be less closely tied to it as a region. But it seems likely to continue to play a major role in Soviet political life.

The scope of the study is broad, covering the whole of the Soviet period until 1957. It is intended, therefore, to serve as an introduction to the problem rather than as a definitive statement. The treatment too is uneven, chiefly because Soviet sources—on which the study is principally based—are rich in some years, lean in others. Without question, the best source material has encompassed the periods of the Revolution and the twenties: in these years there is an abundant literature both in the form of works published at the time and, more recently, in the form of excellent Soviet monographs—many of them unpublished dissertations—based on archival materials not yet available directly in the West. Less complete information is available for the periods of World War II and the years after Stalin's death. The leanest years are those of the purges, 1934 to 1941, and the last of the Stalin years, 1945 to 1952.

The list of those who have influenced and supported and molded the direction of this study is long. Among those who have read and offered suggestions on the manuscript are Quincy Wright, Hans Morgenthau, Leopold Haimson, and Richard Pipes. John Armstrong of the University of Wisconsin provided especially valuable assistance through comments and discussion. A grant from the Inter-University Committee on Travel Grants supported a six-month stay at Moscow State University where materials not available in the United States were found. Publication was subsidized by a generous subvention from the Social Science Research Council. My most grateful thanks go also to the staff of the Columbia University Press, and to my wife whose assistance left its impress on the work at every stage.

June, 1962   ROBERT S. SULLIVANT

NOTE ON TRANSLITERATION

The Library of Congress transliteration system for Russian and Ukrainian words is used throughout this study, but diacritical marks and ligatures are omitted. Certain Russian words such as *kolkhoz* (collective farm), *oblast'* (region), and *raion* (district) are treated as though they were English words.

Place names are given their commonly accepted English spellings which, in most cases, are derived from Russian rather than Ukrainian names. The names of personages are spelled according to the preferred listing in the Library of Congress catalog. For the sake of uniformity and consistency, certain errors which result, snch as the Russian spelling Grin'ko for the Ukrainian name Hryn'ko, are not corrected.

CONTENTS

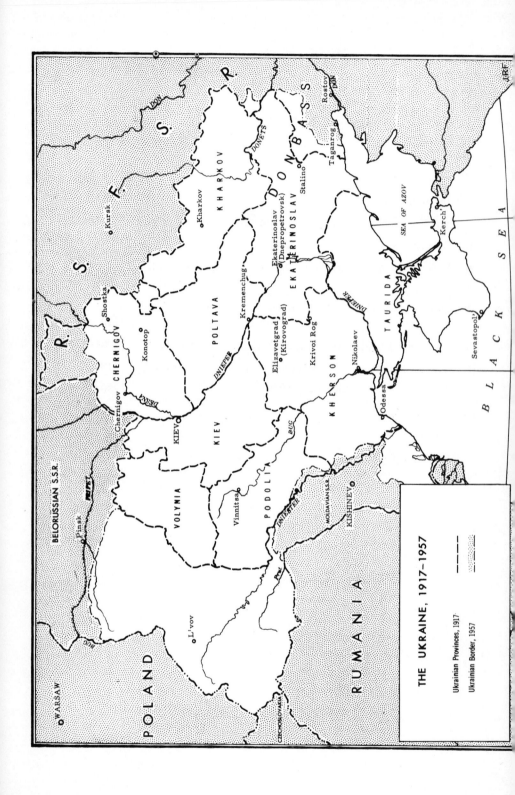

THE UKRAINE, 1917–1957

Ukrainian Provinces, 1917
Ukrainian Border, 1957

INTRODUCTION

Implicit in most discussions of state authority is a general acceptance of the state as an organism unique in the broad independence it displays in the face of other communities. As noted by
one observer, the state is distinguished by its overwhelming superiority over other groups in the territory it controls. "It issues
orders to all men and all associations within that area; it receives
orders from none of them. Its will is subject to no limitation of
any kind. What it purposes is right by the mere announcement
of intention."[1] The essence of political society, it is suggested, is
the authority or ultimate power wielded by some members of society to control or direct other members.

To emphasize in this way the self-determining and self-interpret-
ing aspects of political authority is to affirm the importance of
leadership roles in the formation and execution of public policy.
Yet it is clear that state authority, even in the most docile and
effectively organized societies, is not independent of other-group
pressures. At times the state may appear as a separate force—
as an independent giant dispensing orders and resolutions to its
citizens. But at other moments it is clear that state authority,
even when the state appears to define its rules and regulations
with precision and finality, "is not final or precise socially unless
it is acceptable to the society."[2] The wielder of political power
may exercise authority only when the authority in some measure
serves the common values of the community. Thus the essence of
political society is not the superior-dependent structure which political societies display so persistently and strikingly, but is the rather
uncertain and fluid relationship which develops informally between
the wielders of political power, on the one hand, and the communities, individuals, and groups comprising the state, on the other.

The importance of this concept of the social acceptability of authority is most obvious in societies in which there are one or more

large "out" groups with distinct feelings of apartness. A band of immigrants, a religious sect, an ethnic minority, an embittered class—all challenge the authority of the state to the extent that they reject the behavior patterns officially established as norms. In some instances the members of these groups may conceal their rejection behind a façade of loyalty—a loyalty which the whole political environment prompts them to avow—but on occasion they may see with acute consciousness that there is little in state-prescribed traditions and aims with which they can identify. "The bonds that bind other men to the inclusive community no longer hold them. The basis of their law-abidingness is undermined."[3] Their willingness to oppose the requirements of the state grows to the point of violence, and state authority is challenged.

Where a dissenting group issues such a challenge to the state, political leaders may adopt any of three policies to reweave the community fabric and reassert state authority. They may adopt a policy of repression, countering each measure of rebellion with a greater measure of restriction. If the policy is successful, the dissenters are destroyed or their effectiveness is limited during the interval when group values are modified. Or state leaders may accommodate group values by permitting local expressions of deviation in particular areas in return for acceptance of state values in others. Conflict is not ended—merely transferred to the difficult question of defining areas subject to official control and areas in which deviation is permitted—but state authority and the habit of law-abidingness are preserved, for deviation is exercised in accordance with state directive rather than in opposition. Or, finally, state authorities may work to re-form unacceptable beliefs and aims, drawing them into harmony with official values. Through the school, the community, through mass-action groups and the media of communications, the dissenting group may be weaned from its traditional views to an acceptance of official policies. Where successful, the policy becomes the most effective of all, for with the development of agreement conflict wholly disappears.

In Marxist and Leninist writings the opposition between authority and leadership, on the one hand, mass aspirations and values on the other, is much discussed but never reconciled. In a general way, Marxism minimizes leadership as a rationalizing force by emphasizing historical determinism and materialism. The march of events is a natural and inexorable process in which the progressive flowering of varying modes of production rather than ideas or leadership determines the form of social and political relationships. Man plays in the process no greater role than that of implementing developments otherwise predetermined. And even so, he participates not as an individual but as an exponent of a social class.[4] Where leadership seems to exercise a determinant role, the appearance is deceptive; the charism is no more than a reflection of class relationships.

Yet Marxism allows also for a more generous interpretation of the leadership role. Although progressive class movements are accepted as appearing inevitably in each stage of historical development, Marxism suggests that progressive movements mature only as the class with which they are identified becomes conscious of contemporary class structures and of the new social relationships toward which the forces of history are impelling the community. The proletariat can succeed only as it acquires class consciousness. And such class consciousness, in the Marxist view, is equated with an understanding of Marxist ideas. Leadership can therefore become a positive element by devoting itself to the task of building proletarian awareness, proletarian pride, and proletarian opposition to exploiting classes. Leadership and Marxist ideas—elements of no intrinsic value in the historical process—become significant as elements contributing to class consciousness.

For Marx, this latter element seemed of relatively little importance. Neither leadership nor Marxist ideas seemed likely to play a critical role in the revolutionary movement; the development of class antagonisms and proletarian revolutionary sentiment would proceed inevitably, with or without Marx, with or without revolutionary leaders. But for the Russian Bolsheviks, particularly Lenin, the proletariat offered a less solid revolutionary foundation. The working class of itself could not develop a broad class consciousness, Lenin felt, only a spontaneous feeling of opposition toward the oppressing classes. And this spontaneous element, although an adequate stimulus to revolution, was not sufficient for the revolutionary movement in its broadest aspects. It could become sufficient only with the addition of "conscious" elements from the bourgeois intelligentsia. Hence Lenin rejected the confidence expressed by Marxism in the adequacy of the working masses and demanded the formation of an elite capable of understanding the complexities of the historical process and of guiding the proletariat to fulfill its "historical mission."

Further, Lenin adopted from the beginning a rigorous, even inflexible attitude toward questions of organization and the scope of the leadership role. Having rejected Marx's thesis that the proletariat was capable of developing an adequately broad revolutionary consciousness, he rejected also Marx's implicit conclusion that the leadership function was exclusively educational, involving merely the stimulation of proletarian and revolutionary attitudes. The educational role was essential, Lenin agreed, for without the masses leadership was a powerless shadow. But the organizational and determinative roles were equally important, since an undirected, disorganized proletarian mass, no matter how instinctively prepared and ideally inspired, was incapable of conducting a determined struggle. Only with the formation of a small, disciplined party organization, tightly knit, wholly committed to an elite core, and functioning as the conscious force motivating nd directing the working class—only with such a leadership could the proletarian revolution be accomplished.

Leninism represents, therefore, a conspicuous effort to accommodate the principle of centralized authority and leadership with the principle of mass consciousness and mass activity. On the one hand, revolutionary movements are pictured as reflections of broad class interests, historically determined; on the other hand, the proletarian class is defined as incapable of revolutionary success without organization and militant leadership. In terms of broad historical perspectives the first element is considered determinant as an indispensable precondition. Once established, however, the second element becomes primary, as the practical task of building and safeguarding the revolution comes to demand precise direction and thorough integration. Mass demands—even of a non-Marxist character—are not to be ignored, for the proletariat has a wisdom of

its own and, in any event, can be molded and directed only by
a leadership which adjusts to local situations and to the temper
of the times. But mass demands are not to be accepted automatically, for the proletariat lacks a revolutionary perspective, and
the deficiency can be remedied only by a dedicated, organized
vanguard.

In a practical way, the leader-follower dichotomy became a very
serious one for the Bolsheviks once the Revolution had thrust them
into power. Entering the Russian scene with a full-blown conception of the goals of Soviet society and with a firmly held tradition of a small and close-knit leadership guiding the masses along
paths not open for discussion, the Bolsheviks were little prepared to
adjust to the demands of dissenting groups despite Lenin's conviction that support from many of the groups was essential. As
the Bolshevik program emerged, it developed as a comprehensive
and absolute program in which few areas of public or private life
were left free of state control and in which striking changes from
pre-revolutionary patterns were required. The Bolshevik call was
for a monolithic society, a broad reversal of traditions and customs,
and a strict acceptance of an absolute and all-embracing state authority. The demands were so severe that many elements of Soviet society refused to accept them.

Among the opposition groups confronting the Bolsheviks were the
non-Russian nationalities. Adding ethnic differences to other objections to Bolshevik rule, the minorities became among the most
important of anti-Soviet groups. The problem was particularly
complex because the minorities were traditionally set apart from
the Russians not only in ethnic identity—language, traditions, religion, etc.—but also in economic, social, and culture patterns.
And the differences in patterns were differences Bolsheviks could
not easily accept. In the border areas, for example, the local nationalities were overwhelmingly peasant while the city dwellers
were predominantly Russian and Jewish. The Bolshevik program
with its bias in favor of urban industrial workers inevitably made
it difficult for Soviet leaders to accommodate to the rural attitudes and values of the non-Russian peoples. As a result, the Soviet program became discriminatory against the minorities on a

class if not always on a distinctly national basis. The minorities in turn were prompted to opposition because of economic and social identification as well as ethnic loyalties.

It would have been surprising, therefore, if the Bolsheviks had not experienced difficulty in applying their program to the border areas. Fortified though they were by Lenin's flexible and generally tolerant approach toward the national minorities, they found that the process of applying a program so strongly oriented toward a single class—the urban proletariat—led naturally to oppositions from non-Russians who were predominantly from another class. Although the Bolsheviks endeavored to broaden their appeal to the peasantry, ultimately accepting it as one segment of the proletariat, their effort was never wholly successful. That they were unable also, despite early efforts, to prevent their program from assuming a pro-Russian bias served merely to aggravate a problem already created by other factors.

The present study is broadly a case study of the difficulties rising in a political society where state authority is expressed in absolute terms which are widely conceived but where an important minority group, resisting pressures for conformity, offers oppositions. It is with the policies Soviet leaders have adopted toward the Ukraine and with the efforts they have made to achieve them that the study is principally concerned. Because Soviet politics has not been static but has shifted with the times and in response to local reactions, the story is a developing one. Two threads are emphasized throughout the study: 1) the maturing of Soviet nationality policy from a vague and lenient program of national cooperation to a comprehensive and stern program of national conformity in almost every area of public life; 2) the development by Soviet leaders of legal structures and political techniques for controlling and coordinating republic policies in the face of opposition. In the story woven by these threads lie not only indications of the strengths and weaknesses of Soviet policy toward the USSR's national republics but also suggestions regarding Soviet objectives in vast areas of the world where problems of nationalism and national independence are of critical importance.

I. THE BOLSHEVIK APPROACH
TO NATIONALISM AND THE UKRAINE

The earliest Bolshevik answer to the problem of nationalism and to the problem of the relationship between the various linguistic and racial groups within Russia was a complex one. It was based on three principles which in a sense were contradictory and which were variously emphasized as they were applied to different national areas under different historical conditions. The most basic of the principles and the only one consistently applied and universally affirmed held that the national question was but one part of the general question of the proletarian revolution, a part of the question of proletarian dictatorship. Even as early as 1904, at a time when it was most expedient for the Party to attack national inequities, Stalin urged the subordinate position of the national question:

In [its program the Party] has clearly pointed out to us that so-called "national interests" and "national demands" do not have any particular value *in themselves*, that these interests and demands deserve attention only in as much as they advance or can advance the class consciousness of the proletariat, its class development.[1]

In the pre-revolutionary period it was expected that the national question would serve the interests of the proletarian revolution and would be subordinated specifically to the agrarian question.

The hub of the political life of Russia is not the national but the agrarian problem. Consequently, the fate of the Russian problem, and accordingly the "liberation" of nations, too, is bound up in Russia with the solution of the agrarian problem, i.e., with the destruction of the relics of serfdom, i.e., with the democratisation of the country. This explains why in Russia the national problem is not an independent and decisive problem, but a part of the general and more important problem of the emancipation of the country. . . .
It is not the national, but the agrarian question that will decide

the fate of progress in Russia; the national question is a subordinate question.[2]

In the post-revolutionary period the standards according to which the national question was to be resolved were the success of the world revolution and the consolidation of the dictatorship of the proletariat.

The national question is part and parcel of the general question of the proletarian revolution, part and parcel of the question of the dictatorship of the proletariat. . . .

The rights of nations are not an isolated and self-contained question, but part of the general question of the proletarian revolution, a part which is subordinate to the whole and which must be dealt with from the point of view of the whole.[3]

The belief that all aspects of the national question could and should be sacrificed if necessary to the requirements of the dictatorship of the proletariat was directly expressed by Lenin:

The different demands of democracy, including self-determination, are not an absolute, but are *particles* of the general democratic (at present, general socialist) *world* movement. It is possible that in individual concrete cases, a particle may contradict the whole, in which case it must be rejected. [4]

The second principle of the Bolshevik answer to the national problem declared that national movements, regardless of their motivations, could rightly be used and supported in the pre-revolutionary era as long as they served to weaken the existing social and political conditions of bourgeois societies. There was no requirement that the movements be either proletarian in origin or proletarian in goal. It was enough that they be revolutionary in character.

The important thing is not that the struggle in the East and even in the West has not yet succeeded in shedding its bourgeois-nationalist superstrata; the important thing is that the struggle against imperialism *has begun*, that it is continuing and that it is inevitably bound to arrive at its logical goal.[5]

It is natural that the principle was directed primarily at colonial areas dependent upon the "imperial" powers of the West; such areas offered the Bolsheviks exceptionally promising possibilities for stimulating revolutionary movements. The principle was not to be applied only to colonial areas, however. The Irish question, the minorities of the Austro-Hungarian Empire, even the nationalist movements within pre-revolutionary Russia—in the Ukraine, in Poland, in Finland—were examined and treated with the principle firmly in mind.

The Bolsheviks emphasized that the principle applied only to the *pre-revolutionary* struggle against bourgeois societies. The Bolsheviks saw nothing inherently valuable in national movements, recognizing that they were frequently bourgeois in character and hostile to the dictatorship of the proletariat.

The struggle is usually conducted by the urban petty bourgeoisie of the oppressed nation against the big bourgeoisie of the dominant nation (Czechs and Germans), or by the rural bourgeoisie of the oppressed nation against the landlords of the dominant nation (Ukrainians in Poland), or by the whole "national" bourgeoisie of the oppressed nations against the ruling nobility of the dominant nation (Poland, Lithuania and the Ukraine in Russia).[6]

National sentiments were to be cultivated and used as tools for the destruction of bourgeois societies and for the establishment of the dictatorship of the proletariat. Once the task was accomplished, as in post-revolutionary Russia, the nationalism of minority groups was no longer to be stimulated.

How then were the national movements to be understood and handled in Soviet societies—that is, in multi-national areas where the revolution had been accomplished? The answer was given in the most complex third principle of Bolshevik national policy. Stalin stated it as follows:

The Russian proletariat for a long time has talked about battle. As is known, the sole aim of battle is victory. But for the victory of the proletariat a union of *all* the workers *without distinction of nationality* is necessary. It is clear that the destruction of national barriers and the close solidarity of the Russian, Georgian, Armenian, Polish, Jewish, and other proletariat are necessary conditions for the victory of the Russian proletariat.

Such are the interests of the Russian proletariat.

But the Russian autocracy, as the worst enemy of the Russian proletariat, ever presents resistance to the task of unification of the proletariat. It ruthlessly persecutes the national culture, language, customs, and institutions of the "foreign" nationalities of Russia. The autocracy deprives them of their necessary citizen's rights, it oppresses them on every side, it hypocritically fosters distrust and hostility among them, it incites them to bloody conflicts, thereby indicating that the sole aim of the Russian autocracy is to set the nations and peoples of Russia against one another, to aggravate the national difference between them, to strengthen national barriers, and in this manner to disunite the proletariat more successfully, with greater success to disperse all the Russian proletariat into petty national groups and thereby destroy the class consciousness of the workers, their class unity.[7]

Beginning with the basic premise that the establishment of the dictatorship of the proletariat was the highest goal, the Bolsheviks declared that the goal could not be achieved without the unification of the proletariat and that the national differences which stood in the way of unification could not be eliminated by repressive measures.

Thus it can be seen that Bolshevik hostility to national repression rested not on any fundamental opposition to national repression itself but on a conviction that repression of national sentiments, even when the sentiments were bourgeois in character, would not serve the interests of the Revolution. A two-fold explanation was given. First, national repression retarded the development of the proletariat of minority groups, thereby checking the growth of revolutionary forces: "there can be no possibility of a full development of the intellectual faculties of the Tatar or Jewish worker if he is not allowed to use his native language at meetings and lectures, and if his schools are closed down."[8] Secondly, national repression was dangerous to the cause of the proletariat, inasmuch as it led to an emphasis on the national question in opposition to an emphasis on the class struggle. "It diverts the attention of large strata of the population from social questions, questions of the class struggle, to national questions, questions 'common' to the proletariat and the bourgeoisie."[9] National repression blurred class distinctions and exaggerated the "harmony of interests" of each national group. Under such conditions unification of the proletariat of all nationalities was made difficult.

The hostility of the Bolsheviks to the repression of national minorities was of great importance, for it led them to search for a framework in which minorities could be controlled and utilized in the interests of the dictatorship of the proletariat without the use of repressive measures. Part of the framework was sketched as early as 1903 in the Program adopted by the Second Congress of the Russian Social Democratic Workers Party.[10] Four basic rights for minority groups were here demanded: 1) the right of extensive local self-government—"regional (oblast) self-government for those local areas which are distinguished by their social customs and the composition of their people"; 2) "full equality for all citizens regardless of sex, religion, race, and nationality"; 3) the right of each nationality to use its native language in its schools, in public meetings, and in all institutions of local government; 4) the "right to self-determination for all nations which enter into the composition of the state."[11] The demands were radical, for the Bolsheviks were revolutionaries. Nevertheless, as theoretic principles they have never been repudiated.

The task of amplifying and applying their demands was a difficult one for the Bolsheviks. In particular there was much disagreement over the meaning of the phrase "the right to self-determination."[12] The first serious attempt to clarify the phrase was made by Stalin in his article "Marxism and the National Question," published in 1913 in Vienna.[13] He began by proclaiming the absolute right of all nations to self-determination—a right subject to no limitations.

> The right of self-determination means that only the nation itself has the right to determine its destiny, that no one has the right *forcibly* to interfere in the life of the nation, to destroy its schools and other institutions, to violate its habits and customs, to *repress* its language, or *curtail* its rights....
>
> The right of self-determination means that a nation can arrange its life according to its own will. It has the right to arrange its life on the basis of autonomy. It has the right to enter into federal relations with other nations. It has the right to complete secession. Nations are sovereign and all nations are equal.[14]

It is only by proclaiming the absolute right of self-determination, Stalin asserted, that the aim of the Social Democrats—"to put an end to the policy of national oppression, to render it impossible, and thereby to remove the grounds of hostility between nations, to take the edge off that hostility and reduce it to a minimum"[15] —can be achieved.

To declare the unconditional *right* of nations to self-determination, however, was not to agree to every form in which the right might be exercised.

[The right of self-determination] does not mean that Social-Democrats will support every custom and institution of a nation. While combating the exercise of violence against any nation, they will only support the right of the *nation* to determine its own destiny, at the same time agitating against the noxious customs and institutions of that nation in order to enable the toiling strata of the nation to emancipate themselves from them. . . .

[The right of self-determination] does not mean that Social-Democrats will support every demand of a nation. A nation has the right even to return to the old order of things; but this does not mean that Social-Democrats will subscribe to such a decision if taken by any institution of the said nation. *The obligations of Social-Democrats, who defend the interests of the proletariat, and the rights of a nation, which consists of various classes, are two different things.*[16]

Later Stalin asserted:

Nations have the right to arrange their affairs as they please; they have the right to preserve any of their national institutions, whether beneficial or pernicious—nobody can (nobody has the right to!) *forcibly* interfere in the life of a nation. But that does not mean that Social-Democrats will not combat and agitate against the pernicious institutions of nations and against the inexpedient demands of nations. On the contrary, it is the duty of Social-Democrats to conduct such agitation and to endeavour to influence the will of nations so that the nations may arrange their affairs in the way that will best suit the interests of the proletariat. For this reason Social-Democrats, while fighting for the right of nations to self-determination, will at the same time agitate, for instance, against the secession of the Tatars, or against national cultural autonomy for the Caucasian nations; for both, while not contrary to the *rights* of these nations, are contrary *"to the precise meaning"* of the programme, i.e., to the interests of the Caucasian proletariat.[17]

A nation has the right to secede: it may declare its right to autonomy, or federation, or separation; but Social-Democrats, while accepting and defending the right, are under no obligation to support actual secession, federation, or autonomy. They may do so if such support seems "compatible with the interests of the toiling masses."[18] But if not—and the answer must be sought in the concrete historical conditions in which any nation finds itself—they may interfere and work to influence the will of the nation.

Again it should be noted that Stalin took cover under the phrase "concrete historical conditions." The right to self-determination is an absolute, but the exercise of the right is conditional upon the development and status of the nation.

The solution of the national problem can be arrived at only if due consideration is paid to historical conditions in their development.

The economic, political and cultural conditions of a given nation constitute the only key to the question of *how* a particular nation ought to arrange its life and *what forms* its future constitution ought to take. It is possible that a specific solution of the problem will be required for each nation. If, indeed, a dialectical approach to a question is required anywhere it is required here, in the national question.[19]

Stalin's view was incorporated in the Party program in 1913 when the Central Committee adopted its first comprehensive resolution on the national question. The fifth paragraph of the resolution stated:

The question of the right of a nation to self-determination (that is, the guaranteeing of a state constitution with full freedom and a democratic method of deciding the question of separation) is inextricably tied with the question of the expediency of the separation of one nation from another. The Social Democratic Party must decide this last question in each separate case completely independently, taking as its point of view the interests of the development of the whole society and the interest of the class battle of the proletariat for socialism.[20]

In 1917 the resolution of the Central Committee was confirmed by the Seventh All-Russian Conference of the Party. In a report to the Conference on the national question, Stalin declared:

The question of the *right* of nations freely to secede must not be confused with the question that a nation must *necessarily* secede at any given moment. This latter question must be settled by the party of the proletariat in each particular case independently, according to circumstances. When we recognize the right of oppressed peoples to secede, the *right* to determine their political destiny, we do not thereby settle the question of whether particular nations *should* secede from the Russian state at the given moment. I may

recognize the right of a nation to secede, but that does not mean
that I compel it to secede. A people has a right to secede, but it
may or may not exercise that right, according to circumstances.
Thus we are at liberty to agitate for or against secession, according
to the interests of the proletariat, of the proletarian revolution. Hence,
the question of secession must be determined in each particular case
independently, in accordance with existing circumstances, and for this
reason the question of the recognition of the right to secession must
not be confused with the expediency of secession in any given circumstances.[21]

The resolution made it abundantly clear that the "right to self-
determination" must ever serve the interests of the proletariat.

Nevertheless, the Bolsheviks did not abandon the principle of the
right to self-determination, nor did they limit its absoluteness. On
the contrary, while they urged ever more strongly the necessity of
reconciling the interests of the proletariat with the practical expression of self-determination, they also urged more resolutely the
unlimited nature of the principle. The issue was fought out in the
period from 1914 to 1920. Under the leadership of Piatakov and
Bukharin the Left Wing Communist group and the Polish Social
Democrats denied the "right of a nation to self-determination" and
urged instead the formula of "self-determination for the *working
classes* of each nationality."[22] Only the proletariat of any national
group, stated Bukharin, has the right to secede or to demand federation or autonomy. If the Polish workers do not wish to join
with the Russians in a single state, the Russian Communists must
accept the will of the Polish proletariat. But Russian Bolsheviks
must absolutely refuse Polish demands for separation if the demands are expressed and urged by the Polish bourgeoisie.[23]

Lenin and Stalin refused to accept any such limitations.[24] They
pointed out that if only the working classes of a nation possess the
right to self-determination then only Russia can exercise such a
right, since it is the only country in which the working classes are
in control. This, they said, is obviously absurd. Furthermore,
they insisted, such a limitation weakens the positive role which
the right to self-determination plays in leading national groups to
a speedier establishment of a Soviet state. Thus, in Finland, which
is "more developed, more cultured, than we," the process of dif-

ferentiation into proletariat and bourgeoisie is aided by the independence Finland has been given.

The Finns have tried a German dictator, now they are trying an
Entente dictator, but thanks to the fact that we recognized the
right of a nation to self-determination, the process of differentiation
has thereby been facilitated. . . . [The independence of Finland] was
not desirable. But it was necessary to grant it because otherwise
the bourgeoisie would have deceived the people, would have deceived
the working masses into believing that the Muscovites, the chauvinists, the Great Russians wished to stifle the Finns. It was necessary to recognize their independence.[25]

At no time did the dispute concern itself with the relative importance of the national question as opposed to the socialist revolution. There was complete agreement that the true liberation of a
nation was possible only under a socialist regime, and that,
therefore, the slogan of national liberation had to be subordinated
to the slogan of the dictatorship of the proletariat. The disagreement centered upon two questions. 1) Was the slogan, "the right
to self-determination," of value in promoting the proletarian revolution? 2) Could the practical exercise of the right of self-determination ever serve the interests of the dictatorship of the proletariat? Lenin and Stalin resolutely answered in the affirmative.
Only by declaring the right to self-determination could Bolsheviks
unmask the falseness of bourgeois nationalist slogans and destroy
them as counter revolutionary weapons. And where class differentiation was weak and national feeling strong it was only by granting the complete right to self-determination that the basis for
the future establishment of the dictatorship of the proletariat
could be laid.[26]

The Leninist-Stalinist interpretation of the national question gave
the Bolsheviks considerable flexibility in approaching the Ukraine.
They could urge separation and unconditional independence, or
complete integration within a centralized Russian state, or a federalist compromise. Justification for each position could be found
in Bolshevik nationality principles. As a result, the particular position adopted by the Bolsheviks at any moment seemed to emerge
largely from their estimate of the best method of winning and

holding power in Russia rather than from any logical deduction from a rigorous ideology.

It is not surprising, therefore, that the solutions to the Ukrainian problem posed by the Bolsheviks before their rise to power were radical ones. Under Tsarist rule, as well as under the Provisional Government, the Bolsheviks had no responsibility for government decisions. The task of preserving order and stability within Russia was not theirs. On the contrary, the Bolsheviks understood they could achieve political power only through the creation and stimulation of unrest and dissatisfaction. The national movements of the Ukraine, Poland, and Finland were ready sources of such unrest. Furthermore, the Communists hoped to identify the aims of Ukrainian nationalists with their own objectives in such a way that Ukrainian support for Bolshevik aspirations would be assured. By championing Ukrainian nationalist demands for autonomy or independence, the Bolsheviks could secure the assistance of non-Bolshevik Ukrainians and at the same time contribute to a movement which was divisive and hostile to the old Russian state.

Accordingly, Stalin proposed in 1913 that the Bolsheviks support demands for autonomy and independence as the answer to the Ukrainian problem. In "Marxism and the National Question" he stated:

> It is quite possible that a combination of internal and external factors may arise in which one or another nationality in Russia may find it necessary to raise and settle the question of its independence. And, of course, it is not for Marxists to create obstacles in such cases.
> It follows from this that Russian Marxists cannot do without the right of nations to self-determination.
> Thus *the right of self-determination is an essential element* in the solution of the national problem.
> Further. What must be our attitude towards nations which for one reason or another will prefer to remain within the general framework? . . .
> The only real solution is regional autonomy, autonomy for such crystallised units as Poland, Lithuania, the Ukraine, the Caucasus, etc.[27]

After the February Revolution, as nationalist sentiment in the Ukraine grew stronger, the Bolsheviks supported demands for au-

tonomy or independence more firmly. At the April Conference of
the Party in 1917 Lenin asserted:

Why should we Great Russians who have been oppressing a greater
number of nations than any other people, why should we refuse to
recognize right of secession for Poland, the Ukraine, Finland? ...
We are for the fraternal union of all nations. If there is a Ukrainian republic and a Russian republic, there will be closer ties, more
confidence between them. If the Ukrainians see that we have a
Soviet republic, they will not break away. But if we retain a Miliu-
kov republic, they will break away.[28]

At the All-Russian Military Conference in June an even more resolute position was taken. In an address before the Conference
Stalin severely attacked the Provisional Government for its failure
to deal adequately with the national probem:

The Provisional Government, hypocritically granting the right of self-
determination to the Poles, has refused this right to the Finns and
Ukrainians. This, of course, is stimulating the agitation for a national battle. Formerly Finland did not think at all of separation
from Russia, but now our comrades, the Finnish Social Democrats,
as they return from Finland, are forced to admit the appearance
and development of an extreme separatist tendency in Finland. So
it will also be in the Ukraine.[29]

The resolution on the national question adopted by the Conference
was clear indeed. It urged that "the people of Russia have the
full right to self-determination and to the independent determination of their future even to separation, and that the Ukraine in
particular has the absolute right to realize its independence without waiting for a Constituent Assembly." Further the Conference
expressed its conviction "that only a decisive and irreversible recognition of the right of a nation to self-determination, a recognition
put into action not merely into words, can strengthen the brotherly friendship between the peoples of Russia, and can lay a strong
road for their union, a voluntary not compulsory union, into one
single state."[30]

At the same time, however, the Conference emphasized that the
fundamental objectives of the Bolsheviks had not been forgotten
and that the Communists had no intention of permitting the disintegration of the Russian empire. "The right of a nation to self-

determination does not absolutely require it to separate itself but, on the contrary, it must seek unity in the voluntary principles and decisions ... [of] brotherly agreement between the peoples of Russia."[31] On the specific question of separate armed forces for the Ukraine, the Conference took the same position.

The Conference is convinced that the formation of national regiments in general is not in the interests of the working masses, although the Conference does not deny the right of each nationality to the formation of such regiments, and the Conference expresses its complete assurance that the proletariat of the Ukraine together with the proletariat of all Russia, interested in the substitution of an all-peoples militia for the regular army, will fight against the establishment of national regiments of the Ukraine completely separated from the peoples army.[32]

Thus the Bolshevik attitude toward the Ukraine was crystallized before the November Revolution. The aim of the Bolsheviks was to hold the Ukraine as an integral part of Russia and to ensure its control by Soviet forces. But difficulties were to be expected because of the obvious development in the activity of Ukrainian nationalists. The Bolsheviks saw the Ukrainian Central Rada, the Ukrainian Army Councils, the publication of Universals, the formation of separate armed groups as expressions of a strong Ukrainian sentiment for independence or autonomy.[33] And, in accordance with their theoretic position, the Bolsheviks attributed the growth of Ukrainian nationalism to the "oppressive relationship" established by the Tsarist and Provisional governments in their dealings with the Ukraine. To press immediately for unity and integration, they feared, would be to align themselves with their Russian enemies and further stimulate the nationalist movement. Rather they should combat the growing nationalism by re-emphasizing the independence of the Ukraine and the right of the Ukrainian people to determine their future status. Only by a complete recognition of the right of peoples to independence could national feeling be controlled and the brotherly relationship between the proletariat of Russia and the Ukraine strengthened.[34] So strongly did the Bolsheviks hold this view that they were willing to sacrifice certain immediate goals and grant certain limited measures of autonomy in order that they—as champions of self-determination—might gain Ukrainian support. Yet they were aware of the dangers of such a policy. They were willing to urge it only to the extent that it marked Bolsheviks as Ukrainian sympathizers, but not to the point that it might threaten the unity of Russia and the Ukraine. National autonomy in the border areas was a necessary concession to local sentiment, but Bolshevik leaders hoped to limit it to as few areas as possible and to bring these areas quickly under the control of local Soviet sympathizers.

II. BOLSHEVIKS AND THE REVOLUTION, 1917-1920

In the first flush of enthusiasm following the November Revolution, the Bolsheviks reaffirmed their faith in absolute self-determination. In a "Declaration of the Rights of the Peoples of Russia" the Council of People's Commissars adopted four liberal principles as the foundation for its national policy:

1) The equality and sovereignty of the peoples of Russia.
2) The right of the peoples of Russia to free self-determination even to the point of separation and the formation of an independent state.
3) The abolition of all national and national-religious privileges and limitations.
4) The free development of national minorities and ethnographic groups living on Russian territory.[1]

But with the Revolution the position of the Bolsheviks had changed radically. No longer were they revolutionaries, irresponsibly fomenting dissension and unrest. Now they were wielders of power, and the change brought with it the necessity of modifying these general and vague principles as they were applied to the particular situations in the border areas.

RUSSIAN BOLSHEVIKS AND NOVEMBER IN THE UKRAINE

The most serious difficulty confronting the Bolsheviks was that of the possible separation of the minority areas. Bukharin and Piatakov demanded that the principle of self-determination now be abandoned lest it weaken the "international solidarity of the proletariat."[2] For Lenin, however, the solution was to be found in a new and more radical affirmation of the right of self-determination coupled with a forceful campaign aimed at the preservation and development of the unity of the proletariat of all nationality

groups—in short, the two-fold program he had propounded in
1914.[3] Insistence on self-determination, Lenin declared, would lessen
the hostility of the minority groups toward the Great Russians,
since that hostility had been based on Great-Russian persecution.
And effective Communist world unity could be built, if self-determination were accompanied by an unyielding "battle against the
nationalism of all nations, in all forms." By adopting both programs together, Lenin argued, Bolsheviks could guarantee an eventual amalgamation of the proletariat "into an international community, in spite of the bourgeois efforts for national division."[4]
There need be no fear that minority areas would separate from
the Russian empire even under the tolerant conditions which would
follow the proletarian revolution. Instead there would develop a
free and natural process of union. As each minority group matured
in its proletarian character, it would in its turn establish a dictatorship of the proletariat; it would then voluntarily ally itself
with other proletarian countries throughout the world.[5] The principle of self-determination would destroy the basis for national
hostility; the principle of proletarian unity would guarantee the
eventual solidarity of all workers regardless of nationality.

At the time Lenin presented his two-fold program he was aware
—though only vaguely--of its principal difficulty. Under his program he had assumed that proletarian revolutions would develop
simultaneously, or nearly simultaneously, in all the border regions
of the Russian empire. Or, at least, he had assumed that revolutions
could be stimulated among each of the nationalities if the proletariat of all ethnic groups were mutually supporting. It was obvious, however, that social and economic conditions differed widely
in each of the minority areas. In Central Asia and the Caucasus
there were primitive tribes with an economy based on nomadic
pasturage. In the Russian and Ukrainian steppes there was extensive and well-developed agriculture, little industrialization. In
the urban areas of Moscow, St. Petersburg, and the Donbass there
were important industries and a city proletariat. The differences
were so great that it would seem improbable that the "development of Marxist revolutionary forces" would proceed simultaneously in each of the nationality groups. It was conceivable that

at the time of the revolution in the industrial areas of Russia the minority areas would not have developed industrially to the point where they could carry through their own proletarian revolutions. Led by bourgeois governments, these areas might refuse to unite with a Bolshevik Russia and insist on separation and independence.

This difficulty was not seriously considered by Lenin in his early writings, for it seemed less important than other revolutionary problems. After February, 1917, however, he briefly sketched his answer. The principle of self-determination, he affirmed, was the primary principle. While Bolsheviks should strive for the unity of the proletariat of all national groups and the establishment of a proletarian dictatorship in each minority area, they should not identify themselves inflexibly with preservation of the territorial integrity of Russia and should emphasize the right of separation for those nationalities which could not be led to proletarian revolutions and which insisted on establishing themselves as independent bourgeois states.[6] The friendship of the minorities for the Russian proletariat would thereby be assured and the way paved for their amalgamation with Russia once they had developed an important proletarian class of their own. If a coercive policy were followed, the border areas would be alienated and strong anti-Bolshevik forces stimulated not only to press for independence but also to oppose the Revolution inside Russia.

By ascribing such importance to the principle of self-determination, Lenin came close to establishing it as the ultimate guiding rule in the national question. He did not quite do so, however, for he refused to view as serious the problem of national minorities desiring to separate. Even as late as the November Revolution neither he nor Stalin anticipated that many areas would break away or that these areas would be important or even decisive to the success of the Russian Revolution.[7] Conflict between the national and proletarian questions would appear—if indeed it arose at all—only in scattered districts. Hence Lenin's generous support for self-determination promised to cost the Bolsheviks little.

In the period after the November Revolution it became clear that Lenin's optimism was not justified. On the contrary, the

Revolution seemed only to stimulate the minorities to press more strongly for autonomy or independence. In Belorussia and the Ukraine, in the Caucasus and Central Asia, the national governments which had appeared following the February Revolution showed themselves less willing to accept the Bolsheviks than the Provisional Government;[8] in none of the border areas were stable Soviet governments formed. Moreover, as military opposition to the Bolsheviks developed, it became clear that the national governments in certain areas were anxious not only to maintain their own independence but also to support the anti-Bolshevik campaign. The national movements became centers of opposition to Bolshevism as well as separatist movements striving to out off large regions from Russia. As it became increasingly difficult to distinguish between the national movements as expressions of local nationalism and expressions of anti-Bolshevik sentiment, Soviet leaders found themselves forced to re-examine their liberal answer to the national question.

In the Ukraine, the problem confronting the Bolsheviks was further complicated by the character and unique distribution of the region's population. Two factors were important. The first was the striking concentration of the Ukraine's heavy industry in the easternmost districts—in the Donbass and near Kharkov, and to a lesser extent near Ekaterinoslav (Dnepropetrovsk) and the iron mines at Krivoi Rog.[9] Here were the Ukraine's great mines and factories, and here too were the principal concentrations of the Ukraine's industrial proletariat. Elsewhere, scattered urban centers were to be found—along the Black Sea littoral and along the banks of the Dnieper River—but these centers owed their importance to trade and commerce or to the services and cultural facilities they provided. Odessa, for example, although a cosmopolitan center with a heterogeneous population, included only a handful of factory workers. The capital city, Kiev, had no enterprises employing more than one and one-half or two thousand workers and, according to Bolshevik observers, was largely rural in position and outlook: "the majority of workers," the complaint ran, "still maintain their character as industrial artisans."[10] As a result, there had developed important differences in the character and attitudes of the people living in the eastern industrial districts and those living elsewhere. In the former, city workers found Bolshevik slogans appealing and generally supported Bolshevik programs for socialization of industry and worker control of factories. In the latter, it was the peasant who predominated, and his primary interest was land reform and, specifically, land redistribution. Both the factory worker and the peasant found elements of the Bolshevik program which they could endorse, but it was apparent to both that the Party was primarily for the industrial worker. Hence the peasants, except in the areas of Russian influence in Chernigov province, refused to join with the Bolsheviks and gravitated instead to those parties which emphasized most strongly the demands of the farmers.[11] At the time the Bolsheviks assumed power in Petrograd it was only in the eastern districts of the Ukraine that Communists controlled important Party organizations, and it was only in the east that the Party was able to develop even limited popular support.[12]

The second important factor was the pattern of ethnic settlement in the Ukraine. Although ethnic Ukrainians formed a majority in almost every district, they were predominantly a rural group. Over 90 percent of them lived in the countryside and less than 10 percent in the cities. On the other hand the Russians living in the Ukraine were largely urban and, although only a small minority of the total population, formed the dominant ethnic group in the cities. Altogether they made up 44 percent of the urban population while Ukrainians constituted only 36 percent. In the big, industrial cities in the eastern Ukraine Russian predominance was even more striking, reaching in some cases as high as 70 to 80 percent.[13] As a result the division of the Ukraine into an eastern industrial section and an agricultural section was paralled by an ethnic division which found the eastern city population predominantly Russian, or Russified-Ukrainian, and the rural population almost exclusively non-Russian and largely Ukrainian. The antagonism between the urban industrial workers and the rural peasants was increased by the conflict between Russians and Ukrainians, and the Ukrainian demand for national autonomy was colored by the largely agrarian interests of the Ukrainians who were suspicious of the Bolshevik program with its emphasis on the cities.[14] The result was a sharp schism in political attitudes in the two regions. As the conflict for control of the Ukraine developed in the weeks following the November Revolution, the differences in political attitudes became important, influencing Russian Bolsheviks considerably as they worked to formulate a program for the area.[15]

Three policies were considered by Soviet leaders. The first, and most desirable from the viewpoint of the Bolsheviks, called for transformation of the Ukrainian national government—the Central Rada and its General Secretariat—into a Bolshevik-controlled government. This solution provided the only practical possibility of reconciling the "national" and "proletarian" questions in the Ukraine. It would enable the Bolsheviks to stress the right of the Ukraine to self-determination, thereby affirming their national slogans and stimulating nationalist support; at the same time, it would guarantee that the Ukraine would remain an integral part of the new Soviet Russia and would support Bolshevik programs.

A second possibility was open recognition of the predominantly agrarian and nonindustrial character of the Ukraine and of the importance of national feelings and a consequent acceptance of the Central Rada as a non-Bolshevik government of an independent or autonomous state. This solution was consistent with Leninist theory on the national question and, indeed, with Leninist practice in the case of Finland; but it was particularly unsatisfactory in that it meant the separation from Russia of the important industrial regions in the eastern Ukraine. The possibility of losing control of such a critical area made it difficult for the Bolsheviks to consider such a policy. Apparently only Lenin, and he with great uncertainty, saw it as a real alternative.

A third solution called for the formation of a separate Soviet government in the Ukraine based on the Russian industrial proletariat in the east. This Soviet government would be prompted to oppose the Central Rada and would be given whatever support was needed to establish itself. The policy was not in agreement with Bolshevik declarations for self-determination and the right of separation, but it came to be regarded as the only solution which could guarantee a measure of Bolshevik authority over the Ukraine. It was favored by the majority of Russian leaders.

In the weeks immediately following the November Revolution there was much confusion both in the Ukraine and in Petrograd, and the Bolsheviks were unable to agree on a clear program. In part, their indecision resulted from their uncertainty about the Central Rada. And the Ukrainian government, on its side, adopted an ambivalent position by both attacking and supporting the Bolsheviks: at the moment of the November Revolution the Rada denounced the Bolshevik uprising[16] but in other actions, both before and after the Revolution, took steps suggesting that elements within the Ukrainian government were sympathetic.[17] In any event, the Russian Bolsheviks in November and the first weeks of December determined to explore possibilities of an understanding with the Rada and in this direction approved a number of conciliatory gestures. In official statements the Bolsheviks recognized the authority of the Rada and the right of Ukrainians to decide their own future without outside interference. Early in December Trotsky invited the Rada to name a representative to join his delegation at Brest-Litovsk in negotiations with the Germans.[18] As late as December 12 Stalin, while denouncing the Ukrainian government for refusing to adopt policies urged by the Bolsheviks, repeated Russian recognition of the government's legitimacy.[19] Even later in December discussions between representatives of the Central Rada and the Russian government continued both in Petrograd and in Kiev.[20] In general, however, no positive results were achieved, and it became obvious to Russian leaders that the Central Rada did not intend to follow central direction in matters affecting the Revolution. Sometime before December 17 the Bolsheviks abandoned their policy of accepting the Rada and began to consider seriously the sponsoring of a rival, Soviet government.

The principal difficulty of the new policy was that it appeared to violate the rights Bolsheviks had earlier promised the border areas. Mindful of the difficulty and hoping to avoid its consequences, the Bolsheviks sought a formula which would justify intervention within the framework of self-determination. Such a formula was outlined by Trotsky on December 8:

The Ukrainian laboring masses must understand that All-Russian Soviet power will place no obstacles in the way of the Ukraine's self-determination.... [But] although we do not intend to impose our will upon the Ukrainian people, we are prepared, nevertheless, with all means, to support the Soviets of Ukrainian soldiers, workers and poor peasants in their struggle against the bourgeois policy of the leaders of the present Central Rada.[21]

The formula was officially presented to the Central Rada in an ultimatum adopted by the Council of People's Commissars on December 17, 1917. The ultimatum began with an impressive recognition of the independence of the Ukraine:

Having regard to the fraternal kinship and community of interests of the working classes in their struggle to realise Socialism, and also to the principles constantly proclaimed in the resolutions of the democratic revolutionary organizations—of the Soviets, and particularly of the Second All-Russian Congress of Soviets, the socialist government of Russia—the Council of People's Commissars—yet again affirms the right of self-determination for all nations who have been oppressed by Tsarism and by the Great-Russian bourgeoisie, even to the right of these nations to separate from Russia. Therefore, we, the Council of People's Commissars, recognize the Ukrainian People's Republic, its right to separate completely from Russia or to enter into negotiations with the Russian Republic with a view to establishing federal or other relations with it. Everything concerning the national rights and national freedoms of the Ukrainian people is recognized by us, the Council of People's Commissars, completely without limitation and without condition.[22]

However, the note continued, the Central Rada has adopted a "deceptive, bourgeois policy." It has refused to call a Congress of Ukrainian Soviets; it has disorganized the front by recalling Ukrainian army groups from the battle lines; it has disarmed Soviet troops found on Ukrainian soil; it has rendered support to the Cadet, Kaledin forces battling Soviet power in the Don-Kuban area; it has given permission to the Kaledin troops to pass through Ukrainian territory while denying such permission to the Bolshevik armies. Altogether it has shown itself hostile to Soviet power and the demands of the workers and has allied itself with the Cadet, bourgeois groups. The errors of the Rada must be corrected immediately, the note concluded. "In the event that completely satisfactory answers to these demands are not received within forty-eight hours, the Council of People's Commissars will count the Rada in a state of open war against Soviet power in Russia and in the Ukraine."[23]

The ultimatum was not a satisfactory answer for the Bolsheviks because it lent credence to arguments by Ukrainian nationalists that their struggle with the Bolsheviks was part of the continuing battle of the Ukrainian people against Russian oppression. The argument was a convincing one and was used by the Central Rada with considerable effectiveness.[24] Hence, the Bolsheviks were forced, on the one hand, to affirm in stronger language their recognition of Ukrainian independence and, on the other hand, to excuse their armed intervention in the Ukraine as a defense of the Ukrainian people—the workers and toilers—against the Ukrainian oppressors—the landlords and imperialists of the Central Rada. Stalin, on December 25, 1917, summarized the Bolshevik position as follows:

The Council of People's Commissars from the very beginning has adopted and continues to adopt the principle of free self-determination. It has never opposed the right of the Ukrainian people to separate into an independent state. It has spoken on this officially several times. . . . It is prepared to recognize as a republic any national region of Russia at the wish of the working populaton of that region. It is prepared to recognize a federative structure for the political life of our country if the working people of the regions of Russia so desire. . . . But when self-determination of a people is identified with the tyranny of Kaledin, when the General Secretariat of the Rada attempts to represent the counter-revolutionary turmoil of the Cossack generals as an expression of people's self-determination—the Council of People's Commissars cannot but remark that the General Secretariat is playing with self-determination, concealing with this game its union with Kaledin and Rodzianko.[25]

Plainly, Bolshevik leaders had concluded that the Ukrainian national movement threatened to destroy all Bolshevik control over the Ukraine, that Bolshevik slogans for the right of self-determination were not of themselves sufficient to guarantee Ukrainian cooperation, and that firm military measures on the part of the Bolsheviks might enable them to hold power without producing excessive national hostilities. Accordingly they were willing to abandon their broad affirmations of support for those regions which desired to separate under nationalist governments, and to insist instead on the formation of Bolshevik regimes. The Russians did not abandon the principle of self-determination; but by insisting that it be subordinated to whatever best served the interests of the proletariat, they reduced the principle, as a practical matter, to little more than a slogan.

UKRAINIAN BOLSHEVIKS AND NOVEMBER IN THE UKRAINE

In shifting their support from the government of the Central Rada, Russian leaders turned first to the Bolshevik Party organizations that existed in the Ukraine and secondly to the local soviets that had developed in the principal cities. Russian leaders were confident that both groups would support them in opposing the Central Rada. Already Russian Party leaders had played a considerable role in building Bolshevik organizations in the Ukraine and in providing them with direction and leadership. Immediately following the February Revolution, K. E. Voroshilov and L. M. Kaganovich (Boris Kosherovich) had been sent to the Donbass to direct Party work there; somewhat later H. I. Petrovs'kyi had been sent to Ekaterinoslav (Dnepropetrovsk) and F. A. Artem (Sergeev) to Kharkov;[26] in March G. Piatakov and E. Bosh had been dispatched to Kiev.[27] With these leaders had gone money, weapons, and literature. Under their direction the weak Social Democratic Party groups in these cities had been strengthened and control over them placed firmly in the hands of the Bolsheviks.[28] In November and December, 1917, following the decision taken by Russian leaders to abandon support of the Central Rada, additional stimulation and assistance were given these groups. On December 1 nearly five regiments of troops were sent from Petrograd to the eastern Ukraine, and shortly thereafter an additional detachment was sent from Moscow and another, from Voronezh.[29] The troops were to be used along the Don against the forces of Kaledin rather than against the Ukrainian Central Rada, but they strengthened the Bolsheviks in the eastern Ukraine and supported the area's independence from the Ukrainian government. In view of the military vacuum which existed in the area, the presence of the troops was decisive, and by December 25 the Bolshevik position in the eastern Ukraine was solidly established.

In contrast, Bolshevik organizations in the western parts of the Ukraine were poorly organized and ill-supported. All were young and handicapped by a lack of leadership and local interest. The most influential of the western Party groups, the Kiev organization, as late as April, 1917, consisted of only 200 members.[30] Although it grew steadily in size and importance in the following months, it was considerably weakened by internal disagreements over policy and particularly over the thorny question of the attitude to be taken toward the Central Rada. A majority of the Kiev Party Committee—a right group headed first by Piatakov and later by Gamarnik—favored a moderate policy toward the Rada with recognition of its position and authority: the power of the bourgeoisie was yet too strong to be challenged, it was insisted, and the Bolsheviks could gain most by participating in a modest way in the national government while, at the same time, developing their own organization and strength. A left group, on the other hand, urged a more vigorous policy. The group took the position that the Revolution was in its final phase and that the bourgeois Central Rada, as the last obstacle to the establishment of a dictatorship of the proletariat, should be attacked actively and openly.[31] The left and right groups were unable to reconcile their differences even after the November Revolution, and the disagreements continued to plague the Party organization until the end of December. Not only did they weaken the Bolsheviks in their opposition to the Central Rada, but they also led to quarrels with other Party groups in the western Ukraine and retarded the development of a unified Party organization throughout the area.

Outside Kiev the Bolsheviks were less divided within their own organizations but, in most cases, were less numerous and influential. Of the six nonindustrial administrative regions of the Ukraine, strong and independent Party groups existed in only one, the Chernigov province.[32] In the two westernmost provinces, Volynia and Podolia, there were virtually no important Party organizations even at the time of the November Revolution.[33] In the Kherson and Poltava provinces active Bolshevik groups were to be found, but they were united with and to a certain extent dominated by other parties (the Socialist Revolutionary Party and the Internationalists or Borotbists).[34] The general picture of Bolshevik organization was not encouraging even in the cities, and in the smaller towns and villages, with only few exceptions, the Bolsheviks exerted little if any influence over the peasants and local population.

Not only were the separate local Party groups small and weak, but their effectiveness was limited also by their inability to unite into a single All-Ukrainian organization. Throughout 1917 attempts were made by the Kiev Party Committee to establish a Party center for the eight provinces of the Ukraine (excluding the Taurida and Don areas), but the Committee could not win support from either the eastern or southern regions and was forced to confine its activities, for the time being, to a much smaller area in the northwestern Ukraine—a section that came to be known as the Southwestern Region.[35] In part the failure of the Kiev Committee may be attributed to the vagueness with which the area of the Ukraine had historically been defined: since the Ukraine had achieved in modern times neither independence nor recognition as a single political subdivision within the Russian empire, its area was without definite limits, and there was disagreement over its natural boundaries. Of greater importance, however, was the real division of opinion between Party leaders in the south, east, and west and the major differences in the development of Party work in the three areas. In the east Bolshevik Party organizations had appeared earlier than in the west and south and had already joined-together in their own area organization—the Donets-Krivoi Rog Region. The leaders of the region were more closely tied to Russian leaders in Petrograd and more hostile to the government of the Central Rada in Kiev than were their western counterparts. Suspicious that the newly established Southwestern Region might subordinate them to the Kiev City Committee, they refused to participate.[36]

Party groups in the south, though less well-organized than those in the east, were also reluctant to accept the leadership of the Kiev

Bolsheviks. Guided by the Odessa Party Committee, they resisted efforts to draw them into the Southwestern Region and laid plans for the establishment of a separate Southern organization. Although their plans were never realized, it was not until the November Revolution that they united with the Kiev Bolsheviks. The strong Odessa organization refused even then to join with other groups and remained separate throughout 1917.

In the light of the divisions among Bolsheviks in the Ukraine and the relative weakness of Party groups in the western areas, it is surprising that Russian leaders did not intervene in the closing months of 1917 or at the beginning of 1918 to unify, stabilize, and strengthen Party work. As conflicts over policy arose among Ukrainian Bolsheviks, central leaders refused to support one group against another or to adopt and urge a clear position of their own. As early as July, 1917, they had agreed to the formation of separate east-west regional organizations but had opposed a separate southern group. [37] In November a representative of the Kiev Bolsheviks, I. Kulik, apparently had won Lenin's support for a single, unified Ukrainian Party,[38] but when separate east-west conferences had been held in the Ukraine in early December, there had been no central opposition. It was only in mid-March, 1918, that a plenum of the Russian Central Committee declared firmly in favor of a single Ukrainian government which would include the Donbass. So it was also with factional conflicts. Perhaps the difficulty was a result of the confusion of the times which made it difficult to evaluate the situation in the Ukraine. As a Soviet source has noted, the Party Central Committee was occupied with All-Russian questions and "was not always able to take sufficient account of the peculiar conditions in the Ukraine."[39] Apparently, too, there was concern lest it appear Russians were interfering in Ukrainian affairs or attempting to dominate Urainian Bolshevik organizations. Although the Russian Sovnarkom named Sergei Ordzhonikidze temporary, extraordinary commissar of the Ukraine on December 19, 1917, in a number of statements central leaders declared themselves in favor of autonomy for the Ukraine, and in early 1918 Lenin stated flatly to the commander of Red troops in Kharkov that "on the whole, our interference in the internal affairs of the Ukraine, except as it is imperative for military reasons, is undesirable. It is more convenient to put various measures into effect through organs of local government, and in general, it would be best if all misunderstandings were solved on the spot."[40] Apparently Russian leaders hoped, by adopting a cautious policy, to avoid antagonizing Ukrainian Bolsheviks and alienating Ukrainian nationalists. In any event there was little central direction of Party work in the months following the Revolution, and local Party organizations worked as best they could without assistance.[41]

The disorganized character of Party work in the Ukraine and the weaknesses of local Party groups were reflected in the position held by the Bolsheviks in the many soviets which had sprung up in the Ukraine. One of the principal objectives of the Bolsheviks throughout 1917 had been to gain control of these bodies and to use them to provide a broader foundation for opposition to the Central Rada. On the whole the Bolsheviks had been unsuccessful. Only in the strongest Bolshevik centers had they been able to win control, and often only through uncertain coalitions with other party groups.[42] Outside the Bolshevik strongholds it was the Mensheviks and Socialist Revolutionaries who were able to form dominant majorities in most soviets. In the important centers of Kharkov and Kiev the Bolsheviks were influential but, except for brief periods, did not win clear control of either city soviet until the end of December.[43] In the Southwestern Region the Bolsheviks, in concert with the Left Socialist Revolutionaries, succeeded in forming a Regional Soviet early in September. It became one of the most active of the Ukrainian soviets and was used by the Bolsheviks who controlled it to extend Bolshevik influence among groups who were otherwise hostile. In the village and rural areas, however, and especially in the soviets of peasants' deputies the Bolsheviks were rarely more than a small minority faction.

The position of the Bolsheviks in the Ukraine in the weeks immediately following the November Revolution has been set forth in some detail because it established the conditions under which the relationship between Russian and Ukrainian Communists was to develop in the succeeding months and years. In the Ukraine the Bolshevik Party began as a weak and divided organization. The Party groups which appeared in the cities were not large, and they differed from one another in membership and political attitudes. The strongest Bolshevik centers were in the eastern Ukraine where there was little sympathy for Ukrainian nationalism or interest in the Ukrainian peasant. Party leaders there identified themselves more closely with Russian Bolsheviks than with their comrades to the west and were indifferent to efforts to build a united Ukraine or Ukrainian Party. In the west Bolshevik groups were more Ukrainian in composition and identification but were divided and weak. The Kiev organization, which might have provided leadership in unifying and directing Party work, was limited by the internal disagreements which plagued it throughout 1917 and by its inability to win support from other Bolshevik centers, especially in the southern Ukraine. The failure of eastern and western Party groups to form a single joint organization was critical, for it forced Ukrainian Bolsheviks to meet the difficult period following the Revolution without centralized leadership other than that originating in Petrograd. The possibilities of developing a Ukrainian Bolshevik Party, independent and separate from the Russian, were therefore compromised in part from the beginning, even before the Bolsheviks won control of the area.

THE BOLSHEVIK BID FOR POWER

The problem of seizing power in the Ukraine was one which perplexed the Ukrainian Bolsheviks for a large part of 1917. From the middle of the year until the November Revolution there were frequent discussions and much disagreement on the question of "state power." One group urged acceptance of the government of the Central Rada, another advocated immediate seizure of power by the Ukrainian soviets, and a moderate group suggested that recognition be withheld from the Rada but that no efforts be made to replace it. Following the November Revolution the most conservative Bolsheviks—those favoring acceptance of the Rada—

were for a brief period the dominant group, at least in Kiev. Their position was strengthened by the apparent willingness of the Russian Bolsheviks to treat with the Rada. Subsequently, however, as relations between the Kiev Bolsheviks and the Rada deteriorated, agitation for the establishment of a new Soviet Ukrainian government increased. By the end of November there was general agreement among the Bolsheviks and their allies—including a majority of the Kiev organization—that active measures should be taken.

Two suggestions for seizing power were presented. The first urged simply that the Executive Committee of the Kiev Soviet denounce the Central Rada and declare itself the legitimate government of the Ukraine. The Soviet would then appoint its own commissars who would take steps to rid Kiev of its nationalist government. The second proposal urged that the authority of the Central Rada be accepted temporarily but that an All-Ukrainian Congress of Soviets be convened immediately to reorganize the government or possibly to replace it. This solution had an important advantage, inasmuch as a government established by a Congress of Soviets would have a broader base of representation than one established by the Kiev Soviet alone and could describe itself more convincingly as an All-Ukrainian institution. Furthermore, the proposal promised to attract greater support from non-Bolshevik groups[44] and especially from soviets in the Ukraine which hitherto had upheld the Rada. Consequently, when the Russian Council of People's Commissars gave the proposal its blessing,[45] the Ukrainian Bolsheviks issued a call for an All-Ukranian Congress of Soviets.[46] The date for the first meeting of the Congress was December 16.

It seems clear that the Bolsheviks conceived of the Congress not as a representative body reflecting the composition and attitudes of the Ukrainian soviets but rather as a selected group of men hostile to the Rada —a group which would provide a measure of legitimacy for the government the Bolsheviks intended to establish. In this they were at first assisted unwittingly by the Rada which refused to participate in the calling of the Congress and which indicated that its supporting groups would not send delegates. Before the Congress convened, however, the Rada reversed itself

and issued instructions to its local organizations to dispatch as
many representatives as possible to Kiev. As a result, the selected
group of fifty-four Bolshevik delegates which met to open the
Congress was overwhelmed by the nearly 2,500 representatives
from other parties—most of whom were sympathetic to the Rada.
For a brief period the Bolsheviks tried to dominate the Congress,
first by refusing seats to the Rada's delegates and then by tightly
managing the organization of the Congress. In neither effort were
they successful. By the second day supporters of the Rada were
in clear control, and their authority was backed by friendly military
units which dominated the city. With no possibility of attacking
the Rada's position, the Bolsheviks and a small group of allies from
other parties stalked out of the Congress and proceeded to Kharkov,
where the presence of Russian Bolshevik troops assured them a
monopoly of authority. There they joined with Bolsheviks from
the Donets-Krivoi Rog Region in the convocation of a second,
rival All-Ukrainian Congress of Soviets. On December 24, 1917,
this Bolshevik Congress met, declared itself the only legitimate
representative of the Ukrainian people, and selected a Central
Executive Committee to serve as the first government of the new
Soviet Ukrainian Republic.[47] The Bolsheviks thereby established,
albeit under somewhat inauspicious circumstances, a political body
which could lay claim to a measure of support from the Ukrainian
soviets and in whose name direct action could be taken against
the nationalists.

The reaction of Russian leaders to the formation of the Ukrainian
Soviet Republic was immediate and enthusiastic. Whatever reservations they may have entertained about the effectiveness and
vitality of its political organization they did not express. Here
was a Ukrainian government which could be recognized as the
head of an independent state, which could be given all the freedoms of absolute self-determination, but which could be expected,
nonetheless, to pursue policies laid down by Moscow. The Council
of People's Commissars hailed the Soviet government and pledged
its full support:

Greeting the formation in Kharkov of a genuinely popular Soviet
authority in the Ukraine and regarding this workers' and peasants'

Rada as the real goverment of the Ukrainian People's Republic, the council of People's Commissars pledges to the new government of our brother republic absolute and complete support in the cause of peace, and also in the task of transferring all lands, factories, enterprises, and banks to the laboring peoples of the Ukraine.[48]

Specifically, the Russian Bolsheviks were prepared to provide military support to the new government to assist it in wresting control from the Central Rada. For a brief period they hoped that control of the Rada would pass without violence into the hands of the Bolsheviks or that the Rada would be overthrown directly by the Kiev Soviet;[49] no immediate active measures against the government were taken. By mid-January, however, hopes for a peaceful transfer of authority were abandoned. On January 18 a part of the military units in Kharkov, joined by detachments from Moscow, Minsk, the Baltic fleet, and the first and second air squadrons of the Moscow revolutionary aviation detachment, were dispatched to Kiev to overthrow the Rada and to occupy the city. Only limited resistance was encountered, and within a few weeks the city was occupied and the Ukrainian Soviet government established with Kiev as its capital.

THE GERMAN OCCUPATION

The Russian success in establishing a Soviet Ukrainian government was only temporary. The dominant military force in Eastern Europe in 1918 was the German Army and, for a variety of reasons, the Germans were unwilling to allow the Bolsheviks to consolidate their hold on the whole of the Russian empire. In negotiations at Brest-Litovsk German spokesmen, despite Russian objections, admitted representatives from the Central Rada as the official delegation from the Ukraine and insisted, as a basic condition of any armistice, that the Bolsheviks recognize the independence and authority of the nationalist government.[50] The Bolsheviks were extremely reluctant to accept these conditions[51] but were convinced that an armistice was essential if the Bolshevik position in Russia was to be maintained. After some delay they accepted the German demand which was incorporated in Article Six of the Treaty of Brest-Litovsk:

Russia undertakes to conclude peace at once with the Ukrainian people's republic and to recognize the treaty of peace between that state and the powers of the Quadruple Alliance. The territory of the Ukraine must be, at once, cleared of Russian troops and of the Russian Red Guard. Russia ceases all agitation or propaganda against the government or the public institutions of the Ukrainian People's Republic.[52]

The government of the Central Rada, now supported by the German army, was re-established in the Ukraine, and the Soviet Ukrainian government, only a few weeks after its arrival in Kiev, was forced to withdraw first to Kharkov and subsequently to Russian territory and the protection of Russian troops.

This new and somewhat unexpected development confronted Russian leaders with a situation which was unacceptable, but apparently unavoidable. Strongest opposition came from the "left Communists," led by Bukharin, who denounced the whole Peace Treaty with Germany as a betrayal of international socialism. On the question of the Ukraine, the left Communists were joined by others, especially Stalin, who denounced the occupation in uncompromising terms, declaring it a temporary one. Despite the Treaty provisions, these groups called on the Ukrainian people to resist the advancing German armies and to oppose the re-established government of the Central Rada. On February 24, 1918, Stalin noted in a wire to the Ukrainian Soviet government: "We must have the courage to face the facts and recognize that we have temporarily fallen into the clutches of German imperialism. . . . Meanwhile we must prepare, and thoroughly prepare, for the organization of a sacred war against German imperialism."[53]

But there was no possibility of preventing the German occupation, and in the following weeks Lenin and the more moderate and flexible Bolsheviks urged acceptance of the new situation and indicated a willingness to accept a peace treaty with the German-supported Ukrainian government. On March 8, 1918, Lenin stated to the Seventh Congress of the Russian Bolshevik Party:

When comrade Trotsky puts forward a new demand: "Promise that you will not conclude peace with Vinnichenko," I say that under no circumstances will I give such a pledge. If the Congress gave such a pledge, neither I, nor a single one of those who think with me would accept any responsibility for it. It would mean that instead of having a clear line of manoeuvering—retreating, when it is possible sometimes attacking—we would tie our hands again with a formal decision.[54]

There was no serious suggestion, however, that the German occupation should be considered more than a temporary one, and, in the months that followed, Bolshevik opposition to the Ukrainian government hardened. Only after persistent German representations[55] did the Russians dispatch a preliminary peace delegation to negotiate with the Ukrainian Rada, and the delegation showed itself interested primarily in the conclusion of an armistice which would stabilize the Bolsheviks' southern frontier.[56] As the German occupation continued, it became clear that the Ukrainian government was completely dependent on the German Army, and German military reverses in the west made it doubtful that the occupation would long continue. Gradually, the early willingness of Russian leaders to accept the Ukrainian government disappeared.

The attitude of Ukrainian Bolsheviks to the German occupation was also uncertain and divided. As has been noted previously, a basic split had developed between eastern and western Bolsheviks even before the November Revolution. The division had assumed major proportions in December when the western Bolsheviks had fled to Kharkov following the abortive opening meetings of the Congress of Soviets in Kiev. The presence of the two factions in the same city had not strengthened Party unity. On the contrary, jealousies and disagreements had developed to the point where there was almost continuous petty bickering, and the smallest questions were blown up into major issues.[57] So serious in fact did the division become that an appeal for adjudication was sent to Bolshevik leaders in Petrograd, and Ordzhonikidze was dispatched to Kharkov to reconcile the factions.[58] Nevertheless, the disagreements continued. When the western Bolsheviks left Kharkov in January, 1918, and returned to Kiev following its occupation by Russian forces, the split between the two groups sharpened. Subsequently it was solidified at the Fourth Congress of Soviets of the Donets-Krivoi Rog Region (February 9, 1918), when the eastern Bolsheviks declared the separation of the eastern territories from the Ukraine and the establishment of a separate Donets-Krivoi Rog Soviet Republic.[59] At the moment of the German occupation there was division in the Ukraine, not only within its Bolshevik Party groups, but also in its governmental structure. It was this division which served as a foundation for the disputes which continued among the Ukrainian Bolsheviks throughout the German occupation.

Superimposed on the east-west split was disagreement over the policy to be adopted toward the occupation. As in Russia itself, a powerful faction—the left Communists—led by G. Piatakov, A. Bubnov, and S. Kosior urged strongest opposition to the German army and the Ukrainian nationalist government: the occupation was not to be accepted, and peasant and other likely revolutionary groups were to be encouraged and armed against it. The faction was strongest in Kiev, Ekaterinoslav, Kharkov, and Odessa and, according to a Soviet source, was admittedly anti-Leninist, hoping to destroy the peace settlement with Germany. Initially a minority faction, it was defeated first in March, 1918, at the Second All-Ukrainian Congress of Soviets, which voted its support of the Brest Treaty, and again at the Taganrog Party Conference (April, 1918), where the faction won only 23 of 69 votes [60].

The majority position at these meetings was that of the right Communists headed by M. Boguslavskii, E. Kviring, and V. Lipshits. The socialist revolution in the Ukraine was dead, they urged, and there would now be a long period of state reaction in which revolutionary measures would not succeed and opposition to the Germans and Ukrainian Central Rada should be dropped. Until a German revolution would make possible a new uprising, stress should be placed only on bourgeois parliamentary tactics, agitation and propaganda.

Until July, 1918, the rightists dominated Ukrainian meetings, in part, perhaps, because Bolsheviks of the Donets-Krivoi Rog region refused to participate. During March and April the westerners, despite the German occupation, proceeded with resolution to clarify their position. At a meeting in Poltava on March 7, shortly before the arrival of the German occupation army, a resolution was adopted calling for a single, united Ukraine and denouncing proposals for creation of several separate Soviet republics on Ukrainian soil.[61] Ten days later, at the Second All-Ukrainian Congress of Soviets at Ekaterinoslav, the resolution was reaffirmed. The Donets-Krivoi Rog Soviet Republic took no notice of the resolutions which were not implemented.[62] But they suggested the emergence among western Bolsheviks of a distinct Ukrainian regional consciousness.

On the matter of Russian-Ukrainian state relations, the western Bolsheviks followed the official pattern outlined by Lenin. They admitted with proper reluctance that, as a result of the Brest Treaty, the Ukraine was now independent. It should be reunited with Russia, however, once liberated from the Germans.[63] The only point at which disagreement with Lenin was suggested was the statement that future ties would be "federative" rather than centralized.

In the area of Party relations, the western Bolsheviks moved gradually toward a sharply autonomous position. The problem had already been discussed in Moscow. In December, 1917, the Russian Central Committee had considered two proposals for the Ukraine, one, to form an independent Ukrainian Party organization, and two, to view the Ukrainian Party as no more than a regional subdivision of the Russian. On December 17, Sverdlov, in a letter to the Bolsheviks of the Southwestern Region, gave the opinion of Lenin that the first solution would be "undesirable." Apparently Lenin's view was adopted by the Russian Central Committee and the decision communicated to the Southwestern Region as well as to the Poltava Bolsheviks.

Ukrainian Bolsheviks were of three minds. An influential group headed by Bosh, Kreisberg, and Aussem was wholly opposed to an autonomous Ukraine and refused to consider a separate Party center for the Ukraine no matter how tightly controlled from Moscow. At the other extreme was a group headed by Lapchyns'kyi and apparently Skrypnik that supported a completely independent Party. Kulik and a smaller group urged a kind of federated compromise [64].

Gradually the left Communists, particularly Piatakov, began also to support an independent Party in the Ukraine, perhaps chiefly because of their opposition to Lenin and their hope to win control of a Party machine of their own, separate from Moscow. In any case at the Taganrog Conference (April 19 and 20, 1918) the leftist and nationalist factions of the western Bolsheviks joined together and pushed through a radical proposal suggested by Skrypnik, "to form an independent Communist Party with its own Central Committee and Party congresses and joined to the Russian Communist Party through the international commission (the Third International)."[65] In view of the recently expressed opposition of Russian leaders, the resolution was surprising. More surprising, the resolution was apparently subsequently approved by the Russian Central Committee itself.[66] Perhaps it was felt the resolution maintained an appearance of independence which would win support from non-Bolshevik nationalist groups, particularly during the occupation.[67] For the moment the influence of nationalists and regionalists among Ukrainian Bolsheviks seemed decisive.

The declarations by western Bolsheviks of the independence of the Ukraine from Russia and of the separation of the new Communist Party (Bolshevik) of the Ukraine (CP[b]U)[68] from its parent body represented the maximum achievements of the nationalists. Almost at once the political pendulum reversed its swing, and the influence of centralists and anti-nationalists began to grow. Several factors contributed to the change, above all the German occupation itself. As long as Bolshevik leaders had been established in Kiev or even in the eastern parts of the Ukraine, they had been able to maintain at least modest ties with Ukrainians and with political groups representing the nationalist movement. At the Second All-Ukrainian Congress of Soviets, for example, the majority of the delegates had been representatives of the nationalist and agrarian parties rather than Bolsheviks.[69] The association of nationalists with Bolsheviks had encouraged the Soviet government to follow a policy at least moderately tolerant of nationalist feelings. With the arrival of the German army and the evacuation of the Bolshevik government to Moscow, however, the situation had changed radically. The government now was far removed from the center of Ukrainian national consciousness, and contacts were virtually broken.[75] A number of the most active nationalist Bolsheviks remained inside the Ukraine to organize underground opposition and hence could not participate in the work of Ukrainian Bolsheviks in Moscow. Many Communists from the eastern Ukraine who had not been present at the Poltava and Taganrog meetings now fled to Moscow and augmented the ranks of those opposing an autonomous Ukraine. Above all, the forced emigration of Ukrainian Bolsheviks to sanctuary inside Russia made it inevitable that Russian leaders would play a more dominant role in Ukrainian Party affairs. As Russian influence expanded, the role of the nationalist Bolsheviks diminished.

It was in this new political climate that the First Congress of the CP(b)U convened on July 5, 1918, in Moscow. Nearly half the Congress delegates (49.3 percent) came from the Donets-Krivoi Rog Region and only a third (34.8 percent) from the Ukraine's Right Bank.[71] At once the Congress was broken by sharp factional dispute. The left group headed by Piatakov and Bubnov and including most of the Kiev delegation was in a slight majority. However, the rightists represented by Kviring and Iakovlev seemed to have the confidence of Russian leaders, and a center group dominated by Skrypnik and Zatons'kyi held an important balancing position.[72] On the question of the organization of the Party the leftists were in clear control and were able to elect a Party Central Committee consisting almost exclusively of leftist representatives. The question of partisan warfare against the German occupation of the Ukraine was similarly resolved in favor of the leftist group: it was decided to sponsor an active underground movement and, with the agreement of Lenin, a Central Revolutionary Committee was created to stimulate and supervise partisan activities in the Ukraine. On the most important question, however—the question of the relationship of the Ukrainian and Russian Communist Parties—the leftists were defeated. At the insistence of Lenin and other Russian Bolsheviks, the decision of the Taganrog Conference that the two parties were separate and equal was reversed, and it was agreed instead that the CP(b)U was to be amalgamated as an integral and subordinate section of the Russian Party, subject to its control and supervision.[73] The

Congress thereby recognized the dependence of Ukrainian Bolsheviks on Russian support and the importance of Russian aid if
control over the Ukraine were to be re-established. More significantly, the Congress decision halted the gradual process of autonomization which in previous months had increased the independence of Ukrainian Bolsheviks. Instead there was established
a centralized, hierarchical Party structure which was to be a permanent feature of Party relationships between the two areas.

Immediately following the Congress, the Ukrainian Central Committee, dominated by leftists and nationalists, sought to limit
Russian influence in Party affairs. In a plenary session on July 16,
the Committee adopted a resolution proposed by Bubnov, restating
its independence in local matters.

The Central Committee of the Russian Communist Party, in accordance with the decision of the First Congress of the Communist
Party of the Ukraine, has the right to interfere in the work of the
Communist Party of the Ukraine only over questions of a program-
matic and general political character; questions of internal affairs
are the exclusive concern of the Central Committee of the Communist
Party of the Ukraine, the decisions of which can be appealed only
to congresses of the Communist Party of the Ukraine.[74]

But in the following weeks the Central Committee suffered
critical reverses. A general call for an uprising against the Germans
went largely unheeded, and efforts to stimulate an underground
movement were unsuccessful.[75] Leftist prestige and leftist representation among the *emigré* Bolsheviks fell. At a September
plenum of the Central Committee, Piatakov was ousted as secretary and the decision taken to abandon anti-German revolutionary work. By the time the Second Congress of the CP(b)U met
(October, 1918), the leftist majority was completely gone. The
Central Committee chosen by the Congress was dominated by
rightists such as Kviring, Artem, and Iakovlev. To expand Russian
influence, Stalin was elected a permanent member. The old leftist
demand for an active underground struggle with the German occupation was completely rejected, the Congress agreeing that
future uprisings would be sponsored only with the permission of
the Russian Central Committee. The Revolutionary Committee
which had been appointed to direct the partisan movement was

abolished, and the Committee's undergound military units were shifted outside the Ukraine to battle against anti-Bolshevik forces in the Don region.[76] On every point the more independence-minded, leftist Ukrainians were defeated, and their leadership posts were taken over by pro-Russian centralists. The CP(b)U, which at its First Congress had been made subordinate in principle to the Russian Communist Party, was drawn at its Second Congress under the firm, practical control of Russian Bolsheviks. The decisions were doubly significant, for they came on the eve of German withdrawal from the Ukraine and only shortly before Soviet power was again established in the area. As the CP(b)U returned to the Ukraine, it did so recognizing that it was to function only as an arm of the Russian Communist Party, with the particular responsibility of strengthening Bolshevik groups in the Ukraine, but with no independent concern for the Ukrainian character or nationalist aspirations of these groups.

In March, 1919, the subordinate character of the CP(b)U was confirmed by a decision of the Eighth Congress of the Russian Communist Party. In two resolutions the Congress formally adopted the principle of a single, centralized Party structure for all Soviet republics:

5) At the present time the Ukraine, Latvia, Lithuania and Belorussia exist as separate Soviet republics. Thus there is settled at the present moment the question of the formation of a state union.

But this does not at all mean that the Russian Communist Party for its part must organize itself on the basis of a federation of independent communist parties.

The Eighth Congress of the Russian Communist Party resolves that: there must be created a single centralized Communist Party with a single Central Committee leading all Party work in all parts of the RSFSR. All decisions of the Russian Communist Party and its directing institutions are absolutely compulsory for all Party groups, independently of their national composition. The central committees of the Ukrainian, Lithuanian, and Latvian Communists enjoy the rights of district committees of the Party *and are completely subordinate to the Central Committee of the Russian Communist Party.*

. . . .

7) The Party finds itself in such a situation that the most rigid centralism and most severe discipline are absolutely compulsory for

all. Each decision must be executed first of all, and only afterward will an appeal to the responsible Party organ be permitted.[77]

The consequence of these resolutions was critical indeed. Henceforth each Party organization in the republics allied with Russia was to be joined to the parent body not as an equal group to be coordinated through an international organ—the Third International—nor as an autonomous unit under the general supervision of Russian leaders, but as a subordinate section of a single Party structure with no greater measure of freedom or independence than that exercised by lower levels of the Russian Communist Party itself.

RE-ESTABLISHMENT OF UKRAINIAN SOVIET INSTITUTIONS

In November, 1918, German troops were withdrawn from the Ukraine, and the Ukrainian puppet government, in the person of the discredited Hetman Skoropadskii, was forced to flee from Kiev. With the German evacuation, Russian leaders were once again given the opportunity to expand Soviet authority into the Ukraine. For a moment they hesitated, however, vacillating in a manner reminiscent of their indecision in November of the preceding year. And again, as in 1917, their confusion was rooted in basic disagreements present within both Russian and Ukrainian Party leadership.

For Lenin and the right faction of the Ukrainian Bolsheviks the important consideration was the imminence of the final triumph of international Communism. The world revolution was at hand, it was believed, and again and again in many statements Lenin and others expressed their confidence that the time had come when the proletariat of the world would overthrow their bourgeois, imperialist governments and replace them with Communist regimes.[78] Specifically, Lenin was hopeful that Germany would experience its proletarian revolution. With such optimism, he was able to view the problem of the Ukraine in a relaxed and flexible manner and to consider the task of consolidating Soviet power in Russia and its borderlands as a less urgent one in view of the importance of encouraging socialist revolutions elsewhere.

In addition, Lenin's broad vision of the world revolution guided him to a more tolerant attitude toward other socialist parties and to a greater willingness to accept local differences within Russia itself. Conditions everywhere were not the same, he asserted, and consequently the world revolution would "not be established in so uniform a fashion that everywhere, in all countries, it [would] follow a single path." Where conditions demanded, Bolsheviks should be willing to adapt to local peculiarities and, mindful of the importance of winning support, should compromise with local groups even if non-Bolshevik in character.

Thus Lenin was encouraged to view Ukrainian nationalists with moderation and even to explore the possibilities of recognizing a nationalist Ukrainian government—albeit a socialist one. In the closing months of the German occupation, secret negotiations with non-Bolshevik Ukrainian socialist parties were carried on, and ultimately a preliminary agreement was reached pledging the Russians to support a non-Bolshevik socialist government, with the single condition that Ukrainian Bolsheviks be permitted to organize openly and actively.[79] For a brief period, it appeared that this agreement would form the basis for Russian policy toward the Ukraine.

In opposition to Lenin's moderate policy, however, were powerful groups among both Ukrainian and Russian Bolsheviks. Under Stalin's leadership these groups adopted a position of inflexible hostility to any non-Bolshevik, nationalist government. In a number of statements Stalin attacked the socialist governments which had appeared in the border areas, insisting that only Bolshevik rule could ensure the establishment of Communist societies and the development of the national minorities.[80] Furthermore he encouraged the left faction of the Ukrainian Bolsheviks, urging them to organize opposition to the Ukrainian nationalists despite the agreement recently reached between the nationalists and Russian representatives. Under the leadership of Piatakov and Zatons'kyi there was organized at Kursk a new Soviet government for the Ukraine which was prompted to follow an active policy of encouraging Bolshevik undergound groups and of preparing military units for an invasion from Russia. Thus, Russian Bolsheviks found themselves in the somewhat anamolous position of simultaneously recognizing, if only informally, two governments: a Soviet government selected by the Russians and identifying itself closely with Bolshevik objectives but nevertheless an *emigré* government with but limited influence inside the Ukraine; and a nationalist government, the Directory, accepting Bolshevik policies only in part and showing evidence of a disquieting independent spirit, yet a government which had established itself in Kiev and had gained considerable support from peasant and other groups.

At the end of November the decision was taken to abandon the agreement negotiated with the Directory and to assist the *emigré* Ukrainian Bolsheviks. It is not clear how the decision was reached nor what the principal considerations were. It has been suggested the choice was made by Stalin on his own authority and in the face of opposition from Lenin and other Russian leaders.[81] In any event, on November 28 the Soviet government headed by Piatakov was formally recognized and given permission to invade the Ukraine with the military units under its control. With Red Army assistance Kharkov was occupied on January 3, 1919, and by early February Kiev and a large part of the Ukraine were taken. For the next seven months the Piatakov group governed the area with as much stability as the Red Army supporting it was able to ensure.

The relationship which developed in these months between the new Ukrainian government and the Russian Bolsheviks was ambiguous. To a remarkable degree Ukrainian reliance on Russian support was concealed beneath a facade of independence. The circumstances under which the government had been established militated against any genuine expressions of autonomy: the Ukrainians were dependent on the Red Army for the territory they governed; they had been selected by Russian leaders and in practice retained their posts only at the sufferance of the Russians. Furthermore, there was a close identity of interest between the two groups, since the Ukrainian leaders were in most instances centralist and pro-Russian. At the Third Congress of the CP(b)U held in early March, 1919, it was agreed by the Ukrainians that Russian experience should provide the basis for Ukrainian policy and that the closest ties between the two republics should be maintained.[82]

Nevertheless, as the new government took control of the Ukraine it made no reference to its close identification with Russia but insisted on the Ukraine's absolute independence. In a manifesto issued on January 26, 1919, the government declared itself the sole political authority in the Ukraine and called upon the Ukrainian people to support Soviet rule and to affirm their freedom from foreign influence.[83] In the constitution adopted by the Third All-Ukrainian Congress of Soviets (March 18, 1919) there was no suggestion that Soviet Russia was to play a role in Ukrainian affairs. All authority for governing the Ukraine was placed in the hands of Ukrainian governing bodies, and no provision was made for special consultation with Russian Bolsheviks. The only mention of Russia was the proviso that the inscription on the Ukrainian flag be printed in both the Russian and Ukrainian languages.[84] In legal theory if not in practice, the Ukraine was established as an independent Soviet republic.

There are two explanations for the semblance of independence and separation so carefully maintained. First, the policy was viewed as a means of emphasizing Bolshevik concern for the rights of the national minorities. If national slogans were appealing, as they obviously were to at least a segment of the Ukrainian population, it seemed only sensible to stimulate local support by fastening on the most radical of the nationalist demands—complete independence—and adopting it as a Bolshevik program. Russian leaders were more resolute on this point than were the Ukrainian Bolsheviks themselves.[85]

Secondly, there are indications that Ukrainian leaders shared Lenin's optimistic hope that Communist revolutions would develop in other countries. The question of unity or separation for Russia and the Ukraine was therefore less important than the question of unity with all the proletariat everywhere. If Germany, Russia, Hungary, the Ukraine, and other countries were soon to be drawn into an international union of proletarian states, it seemed unnecessary and somewhat unreasonable to insist that the Ukraine now be held as an integral part of Soviet Russia. In its first manifesto the Ukrainian government indicated its position by declaring:

In complete unity with revolutionary Russia, with the workers of Germany, and with the Soviet areas of the former Austro-Hungarian state there must be organized a defense including all united as one in the ranks of the socialist army of the Ukraine. The final and decisive battle of capital with the world proletariat is at hand.[86]

Subsequently, the government amplified its position, first, by inviting the Soviet republics of Russia, Latvia, Estonia, Belorussia, and Lithuania "to enter into defensive alliances against all groups having for their object the destruction of the power of the workers and peasants,"[87] and, secondly, by declaring somewhat later its intention of entering ultimately into the composition of a single "International Socialist Soviet Republic."[88] In this manner the Ukrainian government avoided the difficult question of state union with Russia and, while accommodating to the nationalist demand for separation, prepared the way for later federation with other proletarian states including Soviet Russia.

The process of establishing federal ties with Russia began almost from the moment Ukrainian independence was declared. It was first apparent in the field of foreign affairs. Ostensibly the Ukrainian Commissariat of Foreign Affairs, headed by Khristian Rakovskii, was separate from its Russian counterpart. Diplomatic envoys were exchanged with several countries;[89] formal diplomatic correspondence was carried on between the Ukraine and Soviet Russia;[90] in some cases diplomatic notes were exchanged directly between the Ukraine and non-Soviet governments. There is no question, however, that Ukrainian policies were those approved by Moscow, and little effort was made to conceal Russia's influence. In March, 1919, it was openly recognized by Rakovskii. In a note to the French Foreign Minister he pointed out that the Ukrainian Soviet government could only conclude from French actions "that the French Government recognizes in the Government of the Soviets of Russia the right to represent all the Soviet Republics regardless of nationality. The Ukrainian Government of Workers and Peasants has no objection to this procedure."[91]

In the field of military affairs a more formal agreement was considered necessary. Throughout 1919 vigorous fighting was in progress in the Ukraine, involving not only the military forces of Denikin and the Ukrainian and Russian Bolsheviks, but also many peasant bands and the troops of the Directory. The Ukrainian question had become but one aspect of the civil war then covering large parts of Russia, and Russian leaders recognized that a defeat for the Ukrainian Bolsheviks would seriously jeopardize the Revolution in Russia itself. From the beginning of the Bolshevik occupation of the Ukraine, centralized control over Red military units had been provided through the person of Antonov-Ovseenko, who was both a member of the Russian Commissariat of Military Affairs and Commander-in-Chief of Soviet forces in the Ukraine. In practice, military matters were controlled increasingly by the highest Russian military body, the Council of Workers' and Peasants' Defense. On February 11, 1919, a Ukrainian military order extended to Ukrainian territory all military rules then in force in Russia. In April, 1919, the Ukrainian Commissariat of Military Affairs was ordered informally to subordinate itself to its Russian counterpart, and in May all separate Ukrainian Soviet military units were merged with the Russian Red Army. Subsequently, the Ukrainian government requested the other Soviet republics to join with it "to work out the concrete forms of organization of a single front of revolutionary battle."[92] On the first of June, 1919, the Russian Central Executive Committee approved the Ukrainian request and broadened its scope.[93] Cooperation was not to be limited to the military field. A close union was to be established in five areas: 1) military organization and military command; 2) national economy; 3) railway administration; 4) finance; and 5) labor. Leadership in each of the areas was to be vested in a single college seated at Moscow. The decisions and orders of the colleges were to be valid for both Russia and the Ukraine. Under the provisions of this decree the Russian Revolutionary War Soviet assumed complete control over military activities in the Ukraine. In an order adopted on June 19, 1919, the Soviet announced that henceforth all decrees, statutes, and ordinances concerning the Red Army and the Commissariat for Military Affairs would be equally valid and effective for all troops operating on Ukrainian territory.[94]

In the months that followed, the Bolshevik position in the Ukraine deteriorated rapidly. Soviet troops were defeated by

the White Armies, and much of the local support the Bolsheviks
had won as they had first entered the Ukraine evaporated: a
number of the supporting partisan bands withdrew, joining the
opposition. By the end of August, 1919, the Reds were pushed out
of most of the Ukraine, and the Ukrainian Bolsheviks and their
Soviet government found themselves forced once again to seek
refuge in Moscow.

The new set-back was a major one for the fledgling government.
Not only did it compel the government to recognize once again
its dependence on Russian support, but also—and this was of
greater importance to Russian leaders—it suggested that the government had been negligent in failing to build enthusiasm for the
Communist cause among the majority of Ukrainians. In fact,
there was considerable evidence that the government had alienated
potentially sympathetic elements by its harsh policies on the
national and farm questions.[95] For a moment, therefore, Russian
leaders abandoned their policy of encouraging a separate Ukrainian
government and, in a decision taken on October 2, 1919, dissolved
the Central Committee of the CP(b)U and suspended the work of
republic officials.[96] For the next several months the only body
concerning itself with the Ukraine, apart from the regular organs
of the Russian Party and government, was a small secretariat with
headquarters in Moscow.[97]

By the end of 1919 it was apparent to Russian leaders that
a re-evaluation of policy was necessary. Plainly they had a-
chieved no successes in the Ukraine either in forcefully suppressing
opposition elements or in winning over non-Communist Ukrainians. Their decision to dissolve Ukrainian Party and government organs was under attack by Ukrainian Bolsheviks, who insisted that regional autonomy for the Ukraine was important.[98]
On the other hand, a group of Russian and Ukrainian Bolsheviks
was critical of the concessions to Ukrainian nationalism which
had been urged by some leaders. Yet again there was the immediate need to establish some form of political authority over the
republic as it was once more occupied by Bolshevik troops. At
the Eighth Conference of the Russian Communist Party (December
2-4, 1919) the Ukrainian question was reopened and discussed

with considerable frankness. A comprehensive resolution was adopted, reformulating Soviet policy.[99]

The new policy was little changed from the program urged by Lenin in the preceding two years. Certain aspects were given greater emphasis and presented in greater detail. Three basic propositions emerged. The first was a reiteration of Bolshevik insistence that the right of the Ukraine to self-determination was fully recognized as was the fact of the Ukraine's independence from Russia. The principle was qualified by the declaration that the closest union of all Soviet forces was essential and that until "Ukrainian workers and peasants had finally decided the forms of this union," the Ukraine and Russia would be considered federated states under the May and June decisions of their governments.[100] The second proposition was the recognition that the importance of Ukrainian nationalism had been completely missed by Ukrainian Bolsheviks and that in the future it was the solemn obligation of all Communists to remove every obstacle to the free development of the Ukrainian language and culture and to oppose every attempt to reduce Ukrainian institutions to a secondary plane. The Conference proceedings attributed responsibility for the failure of Bolshevik rule in the Ukraine in 1919 to the unwillingness of the Bolsheviks to "conduct themselves . . . with the greatest toleration and prudence" toward the Ukrainian nationalist movement. Finally, the Conference insisted on building the closest possible contact between Ukrainian peasants and Communists. The Conference noted that the peasantry made up the overwhelming majority of the population in the Ukraine. It was necessary that peasant representatives be drawn into all Soviet institutions in order that a "decisive influence" over peasant groups might be secured.

It is noteworthy that the Conference decisions called for two changes in Bolshevik policy. First, the propositions spoke quite specifically of union of the Ukraine with Russia rather than with a generic proletariat of the world. The optimism of the preceding year that the world revolution was imminent and a world union of proletarian states possible was gone. Future emphasis was to be placed on Russian unity and on the consolidation of the revolution in Russia and in its borderlands. Secondly, the new policy admitted a shift in the emphasis to be given the principle of self-determination. Lenin now insisted—as indeed he had suggested in the previous year—that a vague declaration of the right of national groups to secession and independence was not sufficient, but that in any given situation national rights needed to be given concrete form by a genuine recognition of the peculiarities of each ethnic group. In the Ukraine, the Conference resolutions declared, these peculiarities consisted primarily of the Ukrainian language and cultural heritage and of the Ukraine's dominantly rural character. Hence, it was essential for Bolsheviks to give special regard to the farm and national questions and to encourage peasants and ethnic Ukrainians to participate in Bolshevik activities and to develop their uniqueness within an accepted Bolshevik framework. The right to self-determination was thereby broadened to include the right to local development in accordance with local institutions and local peculiarities.

Results of the new policy were apparent in the period following the Conference. Within two weeks a new Soviet Ukrainian government—an All-Ukrainian Revolutionary Committee—was created, as was a new "Party center."[101] As the Red Army moved once again into the Ukraine, the new *emigré* government and Party organs accompanied it and were established in Kharkov. Almost at once they sought to develop ties with local Ukrainian groups, with Ukrainian peasants, and with other socialist parties which had come to represent more closely than the Bolsheviks the attitudes of Ukrainians. In a manifesto of December 15, 1919, the Ukrainian Bolsheviks criticized the mass exodus of Bolsheviks from the Ukraine during its occupation by the White Armies and admitted that Party forces inside the country had lost much of their influence and had been replaced by other parties which had remained active.[102] At the same time, the Bolsheviks moved toward an agreement with the most sympathetic of the left-wing socialist parties—the Ukrainian Communist Party (Borotbist).

The position of the Borotbists in the Ukraine in 1920 requires some elaboration in view of the influence they exerted on the development of the CP(b)U in succeeding years. The Borotbist Party

was not an old one, having been formed only in May, 1918, by a
left faction (the Internationalist wing) of the established Ukrainian
Socialist Revolutionary Party.[103] Just as the Socialist Revolutionaries had developed their greatest strength in the rural and
more distinctly Ukrainian areas, so also had the Borotbists. Consequently, they represented an important segment of the Ukraine
and one which Lenin had consistently insisted had to be brought
in to support the revolution. Moreover, the Borotbists had disagreed from the moment of their formation with other less radical
socialist groups, insisting on their complete unity with Russian
Bolsheviks on all questions concerning the class war and the proletarian revolution. Their disagreement with the Bolsheviks centered
on the national problem and, specifically, on the question of the
areas of autonomy to be permitted the Ukraine. In the period
before the Eighth Conference of the Russian Communist Party
(December, 1919) the Bolsheviks had viewed Borotbist activities
with considerable misgivings.[104] However, the inability of the Bolsheviks to maintain their hold on the Ukraine had been a sobering
experience and had led them to moderate their hostility toward
the Borotbists in the hope that greater local support might be
achieved. At the Eighth Conference of the Russian Communist
Party Lenin emphasized the "need for a bloc with the peasantry
of the Ukraine" and suggested that "in order to realize this bloc
we should not conduct the dispute with the Borotbists in the way
in which it is being conducted."[105] Somewhat later he assumed
a more resolute position, insisting that the Bolsheviks adopt a
conciliatory attitude toward the Borotbists and especially toward
the Borotbist approach to the national problem. In a "Letter to
the Workers and Peasants of the Ukraine" he stated:

> The Borotbists differ from the Bolsheviks among other things in
> that they stand for the unconditional independence of the Ukraine.
> The Bolsheviks do not make *of this* an issue of disagreement and
> disunity; *in this* they do not see any obstacle to friendly prole-
> tarian work. Let there be unity in the struggle against capital-
> ist oppression and for the dictatorship of the proletariat, and over
> the question of national borders and federal or other ties between
> states Communists must not disagree. . . .

Therefore, we Great-Russian Communists must be ready to make concessions in our differences with the Ukrainian Communist-Bolsheviks and Borotbists if our differences concern state independence for the Ukraine, the form of its union with Russia, or the national question in general.[106]

Yet it is obvious that Lenin did not mean to strengthen the Borotbists or to allow them to grow as an independent Communist force. His objectives in adopting a conciliatory tone were to prevent them from falling away into a completely hostile position and to absorb them, with their supporting elements, into the Bolshevik pattern.[107] Consequently, in the first months of 1920 each Borotbist effort to strengthen the Party's position was resisted,[108] while the Party was encouraged to merge with the CP(b)U. By March, 1920, it had become apparent to Borotbist leaders that their Party could play no independent role in the Ukraine and, in a difficult decision taken with considerable reluctance, the Party dissolved itself. Subsequently, under an agreement with the Bolsheviks, many of the Borotbists and almost all their leaders were reregistered as members of the CP(b)U, and a number were quickly given positions of leadership.

Whatever significance the dissolution of the Borotbist Party may have had as an early example of Bolshevik unwillingness to accept independent nationalist socialist parties in the border areas, the merger was immediately important because of the influence Borotbist elements were to exert on the development of Ukrainian Bolshevism. As the leading Borotbists entered the CP(b)U, they formed a cohesive group of Communists who were distinctly Ukrainian, who had never been subjected to the dependence-producing humiliation of forced exile under the protection of the Russian armies, and who, as a result, were neither hand-picked by Russian leaders nor particularly subservient to them. Furthermore, the Borotbists had earlier made plain their strong disagreement with the Bolsheviks over the national question and over the question of central versus local authority. The disagreement was deliberately minimized at the time of the merger and in the months immediately following. But it remained, nonetheless, and was absorbed into the CP(b)U and its leadership organs. If the CP(b)U had been a strong and firmly based political organization, the Borotbists would doubtless have been quickly amalgamated and their influence kept within narrow limits. But the CP(b)U was neither strong nor broadly based. It was little larger than the Borotbist Party and consisted principally of a small group of *emigré* leaders and of a mass of newly admitted Party members, many of whom were Russians and many of whom were anxious to exploit their membership in the Party rather than to join actively in its work.[109] As a result, the impact of the Borotbists was considerable. Undoubtedly the merger of the two parties strengthened the CP(b)U by providing, as a Soviet source has noted, "cadres of workers that not only knew the Ukrainian language, but also were tied with the Ukrainian masses."[110] Of greater importance, however, was the influence exerted by the Borotbists in modifying the attitudes of Ukrainian Bolsheviks and in encouraging a Party shift toward greater emphasis on the national question and greater resistance to central control.

RUSSIAN INTERVENTION IN THE CP(b)U AND STATE ALLIANCE

Despite the agitation which accompanied the incorporation of the Borotbists within the CP(b)U and the difficulty which the merger portended for future relations between Russian and Ukrainian Bolsheviks, it was not from the Borotbists but from a different quarter that the first challenge to Russian control over the CP(b)U appeared. The challenge was made not by Ukrainians at all but by a group of Russian Bolsheviks who had been sent to the Ukraine from Moscow to strengthen Party work there and who were indifferent or even hostile to the Ukrainian national movement. The challenge came in a dramatic way at the Fourth Conference of the CP(b)U[111] which met at Kharkov on March 17-23, 1920, as the first All-Ukrainian Party meeting following the re-entry of the Bolsheviks into the Ukraine. At the Conference it became apparent that among rank and file Party members there was wide-spread dissatisfaction with Party leadership and especially, it seems, with Rakovskii. In a number of resolutions introduced at the beginning of the Conference, Party leadership was denounced in vigorous terms. It was noted that control of the CP(b)U was vested completely in the hands of a small group of its Central Committee, that the composition of the group was changed arbitrarily, and that it exhibited no independence in developing Party and Soviet work in the Ukraine. The Central Committee was accused of failing to provide effective guidance for the Party during the period of the Ukraine's occupation and of showing itself unable, since its return, to cope with the difficult problems of Party organization or to direct all aspects of Party work.[112] Rakovskii, on his part, was apparently equally critical of the mass of Party workers. At one point during the Conference he stated bluntly: "We do not have a proletarian party in the Ukraine. We have an intelligentsia, petty-bourgeois party, that is afraid to go to the frontlines."[113] In part as a result of these exchanges, a large majority of the Conference membership refused to support Rakovskii and joined with an opposition group which had developed under the leadership of one of the Russian Bolsheviks—T. V. Sapronov—who had but recently arrived in the Ukraine.[114]

The principal issue on which the Sapronov opposition challenged Party leadership was the question of the organization of the state apparatus of the Ukraine. Stalin, who was present at the Conference as a representative of the Russian Central Committee, presented the official position, urging that the principle of "one-man control" be adopted for all industrial and state organizations. In opposition, the Sapronov group supported the principle of "democratic centralism," declaring in favor of considerable local autonomy in political and economic affairs and the vesting of control over each level of administration in local rather than central Party and Soviet bodies. When the Stalin resolution was put to a vote, it was defeated by the Conference, and the Sapronov proposal was adopted by a large majority. Then, in a move astonishing in its brashness, the Conference selected for the new Central Committee of the CP(b)U a majority from the opposition and, in a direct affront to both Russian and Ukrainian Party leaders, excluded from official posts the three most important Bolsheviks sent to guide the CP(b)U: Rakovskii, Manuilskii, and Kosior.[115] The Conference, as a final measure of rebellion, chose to represent the Ukraine at the Ninth Congress of the Russian Communist Party a delegation packed with opposition members. By the time the Conference finally adjourned the old leaders of the Ukrainian Bolsheviks found themselves defeated on almost every point and their dominant position assumed by Sapronov and his adherents.

The reaction of Russian leaders to the decisions of the Ukrainian Conference was immediate and determined. In a resolution adopted at once by the Politburo the Conference proceedings were denounced and declared irregular. It was agreed that the question of Ukrainian Party organization should be examined by the Russian Communist Party, but it was decided not to present the question to the Party Congress which was shortly to convene,[116] but to refer it to the first plenary session of the Central Committee. Consequently, in early April the Central Committee discussed the decisions of the Ukrainian Conference and, in a strongly worded resolution, reversed them completely. The Ukrainian leadership chosen by the Conference was rejected, and in its place a new Central Committee was selected arbitrarily. From the Committee were excluded the Sapronov opposition members and into it were incorporated the regular Bolsheviks defeated by the Conference.[117] Further, in a statement to all branches of the CP(b)U, the Russian Central Committee repeated its insistence that the primary task of the Bolshevik parties in the border republics was to guarantee the execution of Soviet and Party policy. In a directive to the Ukrainian Central Committee, Russian leaders ordered it to purge the CP(b)U and to remove from its ranks "adventurers" and "demagogic elements" who were "not schooled in Party traditions and discipline" and who had "demoralized the Party, . . . battled Soviet power, opposed Party control, and interfered with Soviet construction and with Party work."[118] These decisions were absolute, and in the following months Ukrainian Party organizations were reconstructed and opposition elements largely excluded. By the end of the year only small remnants remained as a faction, and they were no longer able to enlist the support of other Party members.[119] The unity and discipline of the CP(b)U were thereby restored and the principle of Russian control over Ukrainian Party organizations established more firmly than before. Never again were Ukrainian Bolsheviks to challenge so openly and so forcefully central direction of Party affairs.

In the same manner, Russian leaders, assisted by the Ukrainian Bolsheviks they had boosted into power, moved in 1920 to tighten state relationships between Russia and the Ukraine. At the Fourth All-Ukrainian Congress of Soviets (May, 1920) a clear position was adopted favoring the closest possible ties between the two Soviet republics and speaking of the two as though they were in fact joined in a federal union. Under Rakovskii's direction, resolutions were passed endorsing the intimate union constructed between Russia and the Ukraine, and calling upon the Ukrainian government to unite the republics even more closely.[120] In the following months the Russian government for its part took steps to strengthen ties. In a resolution of June 19, 1920, the Russian Central Executive Committee authorized the Ukrainian government to appoint thirty representatives from the Ukraine to join as members of the Russian Central Executive Committee.[121] The Ukraine was thereby placed on a par with subordinate regions of the RSFSR. Subsequently (December 20, 1920), a Treaty of Alliance between the UkSSR and the RSFSR was concluded.[122] The treaty restated agreements previously made, but presented them in more formal style, broadening the scope of central authority. The independence and sovereignty of the contracting parties was ostentatiously recognized, but a close military and economic alliance was formed. The alliance provided for unification of seven Russian and Ukrainian commissariats: military and maritime affairs, foreign trade, finance, labor, communications, the councils of national economy, and posts and telegraph. The heads of the unified commissariats were to sit as members of the Russian Council of People's Commissars and were to report to it. Each commissariat was to appoint a representative to the Ukrainian Council of People's Commissars, and in theory the representatives were to be "confirmed and directed by the Ukrainian Central Executive Committee and Congress of Soviets." In practice, however, it became clear that the work of the unified commissariats was to be directed and controlled by the All-Russian Central Executive Committee. The presence of Ukrainian representatives within the Committee assured the Ukraine a voice, although a voice which was to be dominated by a host of others.

It should be noted that the Treaty of Alliance left under Ukrainian jurisdiction four important areas: foreign affairs, agriculture, justice, and education. There was no reason for Russian leaders to fear local control, for state activities in the Ukraine were to be dominated by the CP(b)U, and there was no question of the Party's subordination to central leadership. Nevertheless, it seems clear that the four areas were viewed in a different light than other government functions. In the case of agriculture, justice, and education a measure of local autonomy was apparently anticipated, and in the period following the alliance extensive local authority was exercised. In the field of foreign affairs, however, other considerations were primary. Russian leaders hoped to maintain the appearance of independence for the Ukraine, and a foreign ministry with embassies abroad contributed to the illusion. At the same time, there was no danger that the Ukrainian Commissariat of Foreign Affairs would diverge from Russian policy, for the ministry was headed by Kh. Rakovskii, and he had made plain on many occasions his identification with Russian policies and his strong belief in centralization—a belief exceeding that of many Russian leaders.[123] On the eve of the signing of the Treaty of Alliance he expressed his centralist convictions once again:

The tendency of Socialistic revolution is political and economic centralization, provisionally taking the form of international federation. Of course, the creation of this federation cannot be effected by the stroke of the pen, but is the result of a more or less extended process of elimination of particularism, provincialism, democratic and national bourgeois prejudices.[124]

In the period following the conclusion of the alliance the role of the Ukraine in foreign affairs steadily diminished. The last foreign representatives in the Ukraine—a Polish delegation—were withdrawn shortly after the signing of the Treaty of Riga. Authority was given Russian diplomats abroad to act directly for the Ukraine. By 1922 the inactivity of the Ukrainian ministry was officially recognized:

The foreign policy of the Ukraine has not and cannot have any interests different from Russia, which is just such a proletarian state as the Ukraine. The heroic struggle of Russia in full union with the Ukraine, on all fronts against domestic and foreign imperialists, is now giving place to an equally united diplomatic front. The Ukraine is independent in her foreign policy where the specific interests of the Ukraine are concerned. But in questions which have political and economic importance for all Soviet republics, the Russian as well as the Ukrainian Commissariats for Foreign Affairs act as joint representatives of the united federal power.[125]

By December, 1920, the revolutionary forces which had dominated the Russian scene for nearly four years were spent, the exegesis of revolutionary doctrine on the national question was completed, and the first attempts were made to regularize relationships between Russia and its border areas. Despite the instability which was the primary characteristic of the period, a considerable legacy of practices and beliefs was constructed, serving as a foundation on which relationships between Russia and the national republics were to be built. In the case of the Ukraine the legacy was a major force in the decade which was to follow, and many of its basic elements remained unchanged even in later years.

During the revolutionary period three elements seemed most significant in the development of Russian-Ukrainian relationships. The first was the composition of the Ukraine as an area, particularly the rural and non-Russian character of its population. Both attributes prompted opposition to the Bolsheviks, the first because of the Bolshevik anti-peasant bias and the second because of the Bolshevik identification with Great Russians. There was therefore little enthusiasm for Bolshevism in the Ukraine, particularly in the western provinces—less local support than in any other area of the Russian empire.

The second element was the attitude of Russian Bolsheviks toward the Ukraine. Two convictions dominated Soviet thinking: 1) an unwillingness to lose control of the Ukraine either to non-Bolshevik forces or to anti-centralist Bolsheviks; 2) a strong conviction, upheld primarily by Lenin but accepted by others, that the Bolsheviks could not succeed without local support, particularly from rural elements. The two convictions encouraged Bolshevik leaders to grant concessions to Ukrainian nationalists and agrarians, but not so far as to jeopardize central control. The third element was the progress of the Revolution in the Ukraine and the influence of the many waves of occupation forces which surged back and forth across the area. The struggle for the Ukraine was in part a national struggle, and Ukrainian nationalists and peasant bands fought against Russians and their allies, the Ukrainian Bolsheviks. But the struggle was also much broader, involving German, Polish, and French troops and the Russian White Armies, all of which were interested in the Ukraine only as a segment of the Russian empire. Nevertheless, they, too, contributed to the pattern, for the instability they created made it difficult for local groups, Bolshevik or nationalist, to develop independently and therefore encouraged repeated and increasingly severe Russian intervention.

With these conditions in mind it is not surprising that there developed neither a strong and independent local Bolshevik movement nor a powerful political center able to resist Russian efforts to draw the Ukraine into a close and subordinate alliance. In the early phase of the Revolution Ukrainian Bolsheviks were unable to build local support and maintained themselves only with Russian assistance. They became mere appendages of the Russian Communist movement with few ties to their local environment. Subsequently, as membership increased, distinctly Ukrainian elements entered the Party, which assumed a more nationalist aspect. In the middle phase of the revolutionary period, however, this aspect was destroyed as successive waves of occupation troops forced Bolshevik leaders to flee to Russia, severing ties with local groups. Russian control over the emigrant leaders increased, and on each occasion as they returned to the Ukraine they did so under closer supervision. By 1920 the CP(b)U had become an island with few links joining it to the Ukraine and with support generally limited to Russian Bolsheviks and the Red Army. Although central leaders favored Russian control of the CP(b)U, they were disturbed by the Party's lack of local support. Consequently, in the final phase of the revolutionary period, they encouraged Ukrainian nationalists to join with the Bolsheviks and, in a mass registration, accepted Borotbists into the Party. The CP(b)U became a two-layered structure with a Russian-dominated leadership group at the top—strong in its centralist views—and a strange, amorphous collection of nationalists and proletarians, opportunists and agrarians at the bottom. Control by the leadership group was guaranteed by Russian support and, under its direction, preliminary arrangements were made for a close union of the two Soviet republics. Nevertheless, opposition elements remained in the Party, and their activity came to dominate relations between Russia and the Ukraine in the following years.

III. FEDERALISM AND UKRAINIAN CULTURAL NATIONALISM, 1921-1927

Although the treaty of alliance negotiated between Soviet Russia and the Ukraine in the closing months of 1920 provided a legal framework for the close ties which had developed between the two republics, it was apparently expected to serve simply as a wayhouse on the path toward full amalgamation. Soviet leaders favored, in theory and practice alike, the closest union of all Soviet societies and viewed treaty relationships between independent states as inadequate to meet the unusually rigorous demands which the new Soviet world was to prescribe. The Ukrainian-Russian alliance was only shortly established before it and the alliances with the other Soviet republics were denounced and new unifying steps were taken.

FORMATION OF THE SOVIET UNION

The obvious vehicle for unification was a close constitutional union, and at the Tenth Congress of the Russian Communist Party (March, 1921) Stalin called for its creation:

The campaign [for unification] means that the old compact relationships—the convention relationships between the RSFSR and the other Soviet republics—have exhausted themselves, have shown themselves to be inadequate. The campaign means that we must inevitably pass from old compact relationships to relationships of closer unification. . . . In brief, it is proposed, in the course of the campaign, to form as something permanent what has hitherto been decided spasmodically within the framework of convention relationships.[1]

In a resolution the Tenth Congress accepted Stalin's report:

The isolated existence of separate Soviet republics is unstable and impermanent in view of the threats to their existence presented by the capitalist states. The general interests of defence of the Soviet republics on the one hand, and the necessity of restoring productive facilities destroyed by the war on the other, and the necessity of supplying assistance to the grainless Soviet republics as a third factor, all demand imperatively a state union of the separate Soviet republics as the sole road of salvation from imperialist serfdom and national oppression. Freeing themselves from their own and from foreign bourgeoisie, the national Soviet republics can safeguard their independence and can conquer the united strength of imperialism only when joined together in an intimate state union.[2]

Among Ukrainian leaders the call for an "intimate state union" was accepted as a natural and inevitable forward step. The heads of the CP(b)U had come to regard the independence of the Ukraine from Russia as a temporary political aberration— a concession to Ukrainian nationalist spirit—and had repeatedly emphasized the "full solidarity of interests" between Russia and the Ukraine, insisting that their commonality of purpose transcended any momentary separation and required no treaties or constitutions to give it expression.[3] Such a view had been expressed forcefully by the Fourth All-Ukrainian Congress of Soviets in May, 1920,[4] and had become even more widely accepted in the following months with the expulsion from the Party of nationalist and Sapronov oppositionist elements.[5] By the time of the Tenth Party Congress in March, 1921, the CP(b)U was completely dominated by centralists. The task of governing the Ukraine was viewed as an exercise in regional administration, and the principal function of the CP(b)U was conceived to be the interpretation and elaboration to the Ukraine of central directives. Without sympathy for Ukrainian independence and strongly identified with Russian Bolshevism by background and interest, Party leaders in the Ukraine favored a close and firm relationship between the two republics.

At the same time, the opposition to unification which might have developed among some Ukrainian leaders was forestalled by the belief that the new union would require no fundamental changes in Ukrainian-Russian relations. Throughout the period from 1920 to 1922 Ukrainians had witnessed in the day-to-day conduct of government affairs a steady trend toward the centralization in Russian administrative bodies of functions involving the Ukraine. The trend had been accelerated after December, 1920, following the signing of the Ukrainian-Russian alliance, but it had been obvious many months before and was largely independent of the alliance or of any formal ties between the republics. To Ukrainian leaders it seemed clear that, for all practical purposes, an "intimate state union" already existed and that no greater degree of centralization would result from a merging of the separate republics. On the contrary, there was speculation that a new arrangement might decrease Russian influence. Unification, it was argued, would ensure a greater measure of equality among the republics, for all would be mutually joined together rather than joined only with Russia as under the system of alliances. Furthermore, a union agreement, by defining more concretely the general terms of the Russian-Ukrainian alliance, might halt the growth among Russian administrators of a confusion of their role in the alliance with their role in exclusively Russian affairs.[6] The establishment of union organs of government and administration would ensure, it was hoped, the development of a more broadly representative leadership and bureaucracy. These arguments appealed especially to those who supported an international rather than Russian union of Soviet republics and encouraged them to join with the centralists in support of unification.

Nevertheless, agreement within the CP(b)U was not unanimous. An important group opposed unification, urging in its stead a decentralization of authority under which many of the powers absorbed by Russia would be returned to the Ukraine. Leader of this group was Nikolai Skrypnik, a Bolshevik highly regarded in both Russia and the Ukraine who had been active among Ukrainian Communists during the Revolution and now held the posts of Commissar of Justice and Procurator for the Ukraine. At the Eleventh Congress of the Russian Communist Party (March, 1922) Skrypnik presented a stern indictment of the tendency to centralize government authority in Russia. A group of comrades, he noted, had lost sight of the crucial significance for Bolshevik success of the independence of the national republics and had sub-

verted the national policy of Lenin, attempting to establish a united and undivided Russia. So far had the efforts of these comrades
been successful, he declared, that the separate government administrations of the republics had been virtually poisoned and the ground-
work laid for their ultimate, complete liquidation. In certain instances it was clear that the very existence of the Ukrainian state
was being questioned. These efforts must all be resolutely opposed, Skrypnik announced. "A single unified Russia is not our
slogan. We can never adopt such a slogan."[7]

It is difficult to determine the extent of the support given Skrypnik by others within the CP(b)U. It seems doubtful that the question of unification was discussed at either of the general meetings
of the CP(b)U held in 1921.[8] In the fall of 1922 the problem was
discussed in local Party meetings where, according to Stalin, the
principle of union was given an "extraordinarily favorable response."[9] When Skrypnik challenged unification at the Eleventh
Party Congress, he was disavowed by other Ukrainian delegates:
Dmitrii Manuil'skii, speaking on behalf of eighty members of the
Ukrainian delegation, declared that while all recognized Skrypnik
as an old, faithful revolutionary, all further recognized that he
held his own "peculiar" viewpoint.[10] Undoubtedly there were members of the CP(b)U who agreed with and supported Skrypnik, but
the group was a minority in 1922, and the Eleventh Congress seemed
not to be the place nor the time appropriate for a challenge to
central leadership. Throughout 1922 Ukrainian Party leaders guided the CP(b)U along the lines of a full acceptance of unification:
in December the Ukrainian government dutifully called for union
with Russia,[11] approving a group of proposals which closely followed the pattern outlined by central leaders.[12]

But the misgivings Skrypnik had expressed did not disappear,
and in the early months of 1923 other Ukrainian leaders began to
withdraw their support from unification and to attack Russian centralization. The circumstances which led these men to reverse
themselves are obscure. Undoubtedly, they were much influenced
by the open discontent which had burst forth among Georgian
Bolsheviks in the fall of 1922. In October of that year the entire
Central Committee of the Georgian Communist Party had resigned

in protest against central interference in local affairs and against the lack of concern shown by central authorities for the wishes of the local population. To study the protests of the Georgian Bolsheviks and to investigate the general situation in the Caucasus a commission including the Ukrainian leader D. Z. Manuil'skii had been appointed by Lenin and dispatched to the area to report on local conditions.[13] Although the findings of the commission were unsympathetic to the Georgian nationalists, and although Manuil'-skii himself adopted a firm anti-nationalist position, it seems likely that other Ukrainians were impressed by the Georgians' stand and by their opposition to measures which also weighed heavily in the Ukraine. At the same time, Ukrainian leaders were encouraged by suggestions that Lenin himself had become concerned with the dangers of centralization and Great-Russian chauvinism: in December, 1922, he had taken the strongest stand against bureaucratic centralism and Russian nationalism, urging a resolute battle against both forms of deviationism within the Party.[14] With support from so powerful a quarter Ukrainian leaders felt there was now a possibility of challenging the extent to which republic affairs had come to be dominated by the RSFSR.[15]

Foremost among Ukrainian leaders who had formerly supported but now opposed unification was Khristian Rakovskii, head of the Ukrainian government and long a firm advocate of close ties between Russia and the Ukraine. Bulgarian by birth, Rakovskii had been appointed by Lenin in January, 1919, to establish a Soviet government on Ukrainian soil. From the beginning he had made clear his opposition to nationalist movements and his enthusiasm for an international union of the proletariat. In 1920 he had declared that nationalism was an ideology of bourgeois states and that state frontiers had been transformed by the Revolution into mere administrative boundary lines.[16] When Lenin had urged concessions to the nationalities at the Eighth Conference of the Russian Communist Party (December, 1919), Rakovskii had opposed him, taking a strong centralist stand.[17] In his activities in the Ukraine Rakovskii had seized every opportunity to build closer relations with Russia and to discourage Ukrainian nationalists.[18] According to his own statements, however, he opposed Ukrainian nationalism only because it was counterrevolutionary and supported Ukrainian union with Russia because that country represented the only revolutionary center anywhere firmly established.[19]

In the period from 1920 to 1923 Rakovskii's enthusiasm for centralization waned. He continued to denounce Ukrainian separatism and to defend an international union of Soviet republics: only such a union, he insisted, could guarantee the preservation and development of the revolution.[20] But by 1923 he was suggesting that a Russian-dominated union was not the same as an international union and that "the concentration of power in the hands of one central organ and the transformation of all the masses of the population into obedient instruments for the execution of the orders of the central power" was counterrevolutionary.[21] Perhaps Rakovskii's shift in emphasis was influenced by his experience in the Ukraine where the centralist Russian hand had begun to weigh heavily on local administrators.[22] Of greater importance was his awareness that Lenin no longer dominated the Bolshevik movement and that factions opposed to Rakovskii were gaining control of the Party. By fighting against centralization he hoped, perhaps, to strike at these factions and, at the same time, to increase his own independent strength in the Ukraine.[23] In any event, in the early months of 1923 he dropped his support for Russian centralist policies and assumed leadership of the Ukrainian Bolsheviks urging republic autonomy.

Meanwhile, events inside Russia were moving rapidly forward toward the formation of a Union of Soviet republics. On December 29, 1922, representatives of the four Soviet republics (the RSFSR, the Transcaucasian Federation, the Ukraine, and Belorussia) signed a Treaty of Union which on the following day was ratified by the First Congress of Soviets of the USSR.[24] On January 10, 1923, a Central Executive Committee, chosen to serve temporarily as the government of the Union, appointed a commission of fifteen representatives to prepare a draft constitution.[25] The time-table adopted for the commission suggested that it was to complete its work within one or two months. In a second decision, adopted also on January 10, the Central Executive Committee instructed the governments of the separate republics to examine carefully the constitutional provisions included in the Treaty of Union and to present whatever changes they wished to recommend. The recommendations were to be submitted by the first of March.[26] Apparently it was expected that the recommendations would be few and could be quickly rejected or, if acceptable, quickly incorporated into the commission's draft constitution. If so, a final constitution could be prepared by the end of March, and its ratification accomplished by an early meeting of the Second Congress of Soviets.

Almost from the moment the constitutional commission began its work, however, disagreements over major questions appeared. The first and most difficult problem developed over the question of whether the legislative authority—the Central Executive Committee —should be a unicameral or bicameral body, and in the latter case how the upper chamber should be composed and what its powers should be. Several months earlier (November, 1922) Stalin had stated clearly his opposition to a two-chamber legislature, asserting that "the existence of an upper chamber is not compatible with the Soviet government, at any rate, at the present stage of its development."[27] Accordingly, the December Treaty of Union had recommended a single-house legislature. On February 4, 1923, however, Stalin had reversed himself and in a proposal submitted to the Russian Politburo had urged that a second chamber—a Council of Nationalities—be created.[28] Whether Stalin was motivated chiefly by a desire to enhance his personal authority in the new legislature, as has been suggested,[29] or was hoping to lessen the opposition to union which had developed among the republics is not clear. In any case, his new recommendation was decisive, and the commission agreed to provide in the draft constitution for a two-chamber Central Executive Committee. When the commission tried to define the composition and authority of the new body, however, it reached a hopeless deadlock and was forced finally to adjourn without completing its work.[30] The entire problem of the constitution was placed in the hands of Party leaders, and it was not until four months later, when all important questions had been decided in Party meetings, that the constitutional commission was again convened.[31]

It was within Party circles, therefore, that the opposition of republic representatives to the form of unification urged by Stalin
was expressed. The opposition appeared openly at the Twelfth
Congress of the Russian Communist Party (April, 1923), behind
closed doors at meetings of the Party's Central Committee and
Politburo, and in sessions of a special Party commission appointed
to draw up proposals for the constitution.[32] The opposition was
expressed most forcefully by Rakovskii, but was expressed also
by other Ukrainian representatives such as Skrypnik and Grin'ko,[33]
by Belorussian and Georgian spokesmen, and even by Russian
leaders, notably Bukharin.

The core of the opposition arguments rested on the long accepted principle that Communism should be built, not within
the framework of a single state structure, but on the basis of
an international union of workers and peasants. Lenin's thesis
that the Bolshevik revolution could succeed only with the establishment of the closest ties between the Russian proletariat and
non-Russian peasantry was repeated by Rakovskii, who suggested
that civil war would result if the Party failed to show the necessary sensitivity in the question of "the union of the revolutionary Russian proletariat with the sixty million non-Russian
peasants who under a national flag present their demands for a
share in the economic and political life of the Soviet Union."[34]
That this sensitivity had not been shown in the past, Rakovskii
declared, was amply demonstrated by the centralist policy of the
Bolshevik bureaucracy. Again and again the administrative machinery of the Soviet Union had by-passed and overruled the government apparatus of the separate republics, and Party leadership
had not only failed to control these excesses of centralism but had
even encouraged them by interpreting central authority as broadly
as possible. As a result, the possibility of building a close union
joining the Russian proletariat with the non-Russian peasants under
international Communism had been jeopardized. To correct this
dangerous perversion of Party policy, the opposition asserted, would
require sympathetic attention to the national development of the
separate regions of the Soviet Union and a reformulation of the
principles on which the union itself was being constructed.[35]

Specifically, the opposition urged two modifications in Union construction. The first called for incorporation into the constitution of provisions increasing the role of the republics in choosing Union governing bodies. Several recommendations were suggested, but chief stress was placed on the necessity of guaranteeing that the second chamber of the legislature—the Council of Nationalities—would represent the republics and would not merely duplicate the Council of Union with its decisive Russian majority. Under the draft proposal each independent and autonomous republic, as well as each national region, was to have four representatives in the Council of Nationalities. Inasmuch as the RSFSR consisted of a large number of autonomous republics and regions, its representation would number sixty-four while the Ukraine, without such subdivisions, would have but four seats. At the February Plenum of the Russian Central Committee Ukrainians protested that the provision destroyed the independence of the Ukraine; at the Twelfth Party Congress (April, 1923) Rakovskii insisted that it violated the very purpose of a two-chamber legislature, which was to guarantee the rights of the separate units against the central body or dominant group.[36] The Ukrainian protest was successful in part, and a compromise was adopted allowing each independent and autonomous republic five representatives while the regions were allowed only one. But a Ukrainian proposal that no single republic (e.g., the RSFSR) be given more that two-fifths of the seats was rejected,[37] as was a suggestion that the republics be represented according to population with a maximum of five delegates from any one republic.[38] Party leaders flatly refused to permit Russian domination of the Council of Nationalities to be challenged.

The second modification demanded by Ukrainians was an increase in the authority of the republic governments as opposed to the center. The demand was expressed initially by Rakovskii and Grin'ko to the Twelfth Party Congress[39] but was given in complete form only in May, 1923, when an elaborate draft constitution, prepared by the Ukrainian government in response to the invitation of the Union Central Executive Committee, was presented.[40]

The draft constitution recommended sweeping changes in the distribution of authority between the central government and the republics. First, it took away from the center many of the powers included in the official draft, providing that in matters such as the conduct of foreign affairs, the determination of re-public boundaries, the establishment of local taxes and rules for local trade, local concession agreements, education, health and welfare, local economic planning, etc. republic control and administration would be limited only by the authority of the Union government to establish general guiding principles. Secondly, the Ukrainian draft decreased the number of central commissariats provided by the official constitution and increased the number to be established by the republics.[41] Commissariats of labor, food, and workers'-peasants' inspection were transformed into exclusively re-public commissariats; commissariats of military and naval affairs, foreign trade, foreign affairs, posts and telegraph, and transportation—all established as exclusively Union administrative bodies under the official draft constitution—were shifted to Union-republic commissariats. The changes were far-reaching and, if adopted, would have materially altered the character of the federation. Stalin and other leaders agreed that the changes would destroy the Union as a single federal state and establish it as a "conglomeration of republics."[42]

By the time the Ukrainian draft was presented for discusion (May, 1923), however, there was no longer any serious question about the form the union was to take. The Twelfth Congress of the Party, by rejecting Rakovskii's suggested change in representation on the Council of Nationalities, had decided that the Union was to be a "centralized federation" with Russian control carefully guaranteed. This decision was not to be changed. At the time of the Congress, Ukrainian leaders—encouraged by the concessions to the nationalities made in the area of cultural affairs—failed to interpret correctly the defeat they suffered in the political field.[43] Consequently, they continued to press for decentralization, and the Ukrainian draft was presented for discussion at Party and government meetings in May and June, 1923. At the June 4 meeting of the Russian Politburo Rakovskii and Skrypnik tried as a last effort to write into the constitution provisions for republic commissariats of foreign affairs and foreign trade.[44] The Ukrainian arguments were rejected, however, as they had been earlier, and no important changes in the official draft were made before its final adoption in July by the USSR Central Executive Committee.

The failure of the Ukrainians to achieve liberalization of the constitution in favor of the republics was both a political and an ideological failure. From the beginning the Ukrainians had faced an insurmountable obstacle in the solid array of Party members and leaders who not only lacked sympathy for the nationalist movements but viewed them with little interest or concern except as they challenged or interfered with the stabilization of Bolshevik power in Russia. This attitude was common not only among the members of the Russian Communist Party but also, to a surprising degree, within the national Communist parties where Russian elements were generally a decisive majority and were frequently less sympathetic to the minority problem than were Bolsheviks from the RSFSR.[45] To the great majority of Bolshevik leaders the most logical form of political society was a centralized one, and the decision to establish a federal system was in itself viewed as an unfortunate though possibly necessary concession to the nationalities.[46] There was no eagerness to support measures which would further weaken central authority and stimulate greater independence among the minority groups. When the plea for modification of the constitution was presented to the Twelfth Party Congress and to other Party meetings, it was presented to groups dominated by centralist-minded Great Russians, and they refused to accept it.

At the same time, Ukrainians were hampered by ideological difficulties they could not resolve satisfactorily. Marxian socialism as interpreted by Lenin was a centralist dogma resting on the authority of the Communist Party and on the complete acceptance of the principle of economic, political, and social planning for Russia and its border republics as a necessary preliminary stage in their preparation for Communist life. The purpose of Soviet society was not the preservation of national differences or the development of local institutions and individual peculiarities. In

his most generous moments Lenin agreed to accept national independence and local autonomy but only as requisites for the development of the solidarity of the working classes of all the republics and as examples to be used in appeals to the nationalism
of the colonies of capitalist countries. For Ukrainians to have
urged the supremacy of the national over the proletarian question
would have required them to challenge the basic premises of the
Communist Party, and this they were unwilling to do. They were
forced, therefore, to argue only that the centralization of the constitution was inefficient, or that it was offensive in and of itself
to the minorities, or that the new federal arrangement failed to
provide sufficient guarantees for the separate republics.[47] Excellent though such arguments were, they were not sufficient to produce any important change in Party policy or in the structure
of the constitution. Stalin could dismiss them as exaggerations
or could accept them as valid criticisms but as criticisms which
should best be handled within a centralized Communist framework.[48] Whatever corrective work was needed, Stalin declared,
should be developed within the Party and within the administrative agencies of the central government. Stalin's argument was
impressively supported by the resolution of the Twelfth Congress
on the national question which called for a firm recognition by
the Party of the rights of the minorities, for a resolute attack on
survivals of Great-Russian chauvinism, and for corrective work to
eliminate the excessively centralizing practices of a number of government agencies.[49] Armed with Communist dogma, on the one
hand, and with these liberal concessions to the nationalities, on
the other, Stalin's position was strong and appealing. His leadership on the national question was accepted at every point.

THE 1924 CONSTITUTION

The centralist principle was incorporated in the 1924 constitution in a number of provisions.[50] Foremost was Article 1 which
granted the Union an overwhelming share of governmental powers
including not only the functions carried on previously by the

RSFSR under its alliance with the Ukraine but also a whole group of new powers. Under the Russian-Ukrainian alliance the RSFSR had exercised the following: control over the armed forces of the USSR and authority to declare war and conclude peace; control over the "whole national economy of the Union," including the power to regulate both foreign and domestic trade; power to establish the monetary system of the Union and to approve both Union and republic budgets; authority to establish "fundamental labor laws"; control over transportation and communications. Among the powers added by the constitution to the central government were: authority to lay down general principles controlling education, justice, and health; control over the exploitation of natural resources, including the "development and use of land"; power to annul decisions of the Union republics in conflict with the constitution; authority to admit new republics into the Union; authority to handle foreign affairs on behalf of the republics as well as for the Union. The only important areas on which the constitution was silent and which were left to the jurisdiction of the republics were the areas of elections and civil rights.[51]

The central government's authority was enlarged also by a broad change in the system of commissariats. Under the 1920 alliance two categories of commissariats had been established— joint Russian-Ukrainian commissariats functioning in seven areas of common concern and republic commissariats acting separately in each republic in other fields. According to the new constitution a third, wholly centralized category of commissariats was added. These were to be known as Union commissariats and were to function exclusively under Union control. They were to comprise five of the old, joint commissariats—foreign affairs, foreign trade, transportation, communications, and military affairs. A similar upgrading was accomplished in the areas of national economy, food, and workers'-peasants' inspection which were removed from exclusive republic control and established as Union-republic commissariats. Left solely to the administration of the republics were agriculture, internal trade, internal affairs, justice, education, health, social welfare, and national minorities.[52] All commissariats were specifically enumerated in the constitution and were not to be altered by the republics. In most instances, including the republic commissariats, the Union government retained the right to provide general policy direction.

The constitution also improved the mechanisms by which the Union government controlled the work of the republics. First, the constitution declared that any republic decision could be suspended or repealed by the USSR Central Executive Committee (Article 20).[53] The reason for rejection was to be the unconstitutionality of the local decision, but no provision for appealing the ruling of the Committee was included. In addition, "questions concerning mutual relations between the Council of People's Commissars of the USSR and the people's commissars of the USSR, on the one hand, and the central executive committees of the Union republics and their presidia, on the other," were to be decided by the Presidium of the USSR Central Executive Committee (Article 35). Again, there was no appeal.

Secondly, the constitution provided that all decisions of USSR governing bodies were binding on the republics and were to be carried out immediately throughout the whole territory of the Union (Articles 19 and 38). The central executive committees of the republics were empowered to protest Union decisions they considered unconstitutional to the Presidium of the USSR Central Executive Committee, but the republics could neither suspend nor annul the decisions (Article 42).

Thirdly, the USSR Supreme Court was given certain specific powers to regulate the work of the republics. The court was authorized to "give . . . guiding interpretations on questions of the general legislation of the Union" to the supreme courts of the republics; it was allowed to protest to the USSR Central Executive Committee the decisions of republic supreme courts; it was empowered to decide legal conflicts between republics and to hand down opinions on the constitutionality of actions of the republics when requested to do so by the USSR Central Executive Committee (Article 43).

Fourthly, the constitution included provisions designed to guarantee that administrative decisions of the Union and Union-republic commissariats would be carried out in the republics. Each Union commissariat was authorized to send representatives to the republics to sit as members of the republic councils of people's commissars and ensure that the work of the councils conformed to central policies (Article 53). In the case of the Union-republic commissariats no such representatives were authorized, but the constitution required republic administrators to "put into effect in their work the general directions of the corresponding people's commissariats of the USSR" (Article 68).

Finally, the constitution provided for the establishment of a separate administrative organization to carry on the fight with "political and economic counterrevolution, espionage, and banditism." The organization was to be known as the Unified State Political Administration (OGPU). The Administration was to work through local organs in each of the republics, but in practice republic authority was limited, for the local organs were directed not by the republic governments, but by agents of the OGPU attached to the republic councils of people's commissars. The work of the OGPU was defined so broadly by the constitution that it was able to exercise supervision in all areas of republic administration (Articles 61 and 62).

The centralizing features incorporated into the 1924 constitution provided clearly for the subordination of the republics to the Union. The USSR was empowered to determine general legislative policy in most government fields; it was empowered to administer policy exclusively in five areas and concurrently in five others; it was enabled to guarantee the conformance of the republics through a system of checks and controls. Only slight guarantees were given the republics, and they were little more than vague and unsubstantial declarations. The republics were declared sovereign in all matters not falling under the competence of the Union (Article 3) and were assured of their unlimited right of free withdrawal from the Union (Article 4). No method of implementing these rights was provided and, in practice, each served only as a reassurance to the republics. The republics were guaranteed the inviolability of their borders (Article 6) and were empowered to suspend ordinances of USSR commissariats (Article

59). Again the rights were meant to serve only as reassurances and were never invoked against the Union.

Significant areas of activity were left the republics in the six fields administered by republic commissariats. Even here local authority was limited, since the commissariats were to operate in accordance with general policies set forth by the Union; in practice a number of the commissariats were to become little more than regional offices of the central government. Yet the existence of regional offices of republic subordination was in itself an important concession. In fields such as education, justice, and minority problems the republics were to attract capable people to administrative posts and were to develop unique and comprehensive programs. It was the opportunity to elaborate such programs which encouraged nationalist leaders in the Ukraine to accept the constitution despite their misgivings about its centralist features. To the extent that the constitution permitted the development of local programs it represented a compromise by Russian centralists. Yet the compromise was one which centralists and localists viewed in different ways, and almost from the moment the constitution was adopted disagreements arose over its interpretation.

THE STRUGGLE OVER CENTRALIZATION

As the new constitution was applied, Union agencies began at once to interpret its broad grants of power in the most liberal fashion. And republic leaders, viewing with dismay the widening of central authority, were led to opposition. Guided by Ukrainian Bolsheviks, they spoke out again and again at meetings of the Union parliament, urging concessions to the localities and limitations on the powers of the central government.

The clearest expressions of republic views were those of Skrypnik and the Ukrainian Premier Vlas Chubar'. It was their conviction that the strength of the Soviet Union lay in its separate republics and that the Union would grow powerful as it encouraged wide independence at the local level. In January, 1924, Skrypnik declared: "The Union of Soviet republics will be strong and powerful to the extent that the Union republics which have formed the Union are strong and powerful. . . . That is why . . . it is necessary to think about the strengthening and development of each member entering into the Union."[54] In May, 1925, Chubar' emphasized the necessity of expanding activities on the local level.

The building of our Union has followed, is following, and will continue to follow along the path of broad, independent activity for the separate national republics, will continue to follow along the path of broad, independent activity for the wide masses of workers and peasants in each *raion*, in each *oblast*, in each republic. This is our basic policy, and it is essential for the Union government to heed it so that in the process of its work, this independent activity will not be limited, will not be destroyed, will not be hindered.

Further, we must say openly before the Congress of Soviets that in the work of our Union institutions there still is apparent a tendency toward bureaucracy which remains as a legacy from Tsarist days. Bureaucratic perversions in certain institutions, certain parts of our apparatus are still to be felt. This danger is not yet destroyed, it is still necessary to battle with it, remembering what Lenin said about the weakness of our state apparatus.[55]

Specifically, Ukrainian leaders adopted the role of champions of the federal principle in the Union constitution. At the October, 1924, session of the USSR Central Executive Committee Skrypnik suggested that the most important element in the constitution was its provision for a federal system and urged that the constitution itself was a weapon defending the rights of the republics against centralizing tendencies.

Our Constitution is not simply a formality, something insignificant that we can lightly change, but is the foundation of our life, the formulation of those aspirations out of which have been forged the Soviet republics by the workers and peasants. . . .

Two aspects appear in the foundations of our Constitution. . . . Above all is the firm principle of the union of all peoples and of the Union republics into a single force, a defensive union against world capital. And, secondly, that which our Union has given new in the area of state construction—a union on the principle of the sovereignty of each people, liberated from power of capital. . . .

We have evolved a new theory and have incorporated it into our Constitution: a single Union, a single sovereign state, guaranteeing at the same time in full measure the sovereignty of each republic entering into the Union. Within the limits of the Constitution the Union is sovereign, within the limits of the Constitution each republic also is sovereign. With deep abhorrence, with contempt we recall the ancient time of the Tsarist empire, a single, indivisible state. For us there is no single, indivisible state.[56]

Unfortunately, Skrypnik continued, many proposals had been recommended which, if adopted, would destroy the federal system and amalgamate the USSR into a "single, indivisible state." How was it possible, he queried, to avoid a centralized government if, as had been suggested, citizenship was to be solely a Union matter, or if the territory of the republics was to belong exclusively to the federal government, or if questions of the internal life of the republics including the most detailed and specific problems were to be decided by central authorities? Again and again, he observed, bureaucrats and centralists had endeavored to impose their anti-Leninist views on the Party and on Soviet institutions, declaring the Union the sole source of authority and policy and the republics no more than local agents of central administrators. Refusing to accept the limitation imposed by the constitution on the federal government to determine only general, guiding rules, they had encouraged Union officials to prepare elaborate and minute orders and to supervise their administration in the closest way. If the Soviet Union was to be preserved as a union of Soviet republics, it was necessary to curb the tendency toward centralization and to oppose each centralizing measure as it was presented.[57]

Accordingly, Ukrainian leaders attacked a wide variety of centralizing measures. In November, 1923, they denounced the "Statute on Central Organs of Power" drawn up to amplify provisions of the Union constitution dealing with the powers of central governing bodies.[58] Skrypnik complained that the "Statute" expressed a strong centralist position in the authority it granted the Union Council of People's Commissars and in the limitations it placed on the republics. In October, 1924, the draft statute on the budget authority of the USSR and of the republics was similarly opposed. Chubar', Skrypnik, and Butsenko noted that the draft gave the Union control over the smallest republic expenditures and allowed the Union to regulate in a detailed way the special taxes to be established by the republics.[59] On the questions of court structure, criminal court procedure, and criminal legislation the Ukrainian leaders Blakytnyi and Grin'ko joined Skrypnik in denouncing Union efforts to establish uniform codes for the whole USSR.[60] In each case the Ukrainian protests were successful in part, and anti-centralist amendments were adopted at many points.

The Ukrainian successes were small, however, and were overshadowed by the larger powers gradually acquired by central bodies. Under Union resolutions the fiscal and budgetary rights of the Union were emphasized almost to the exclusion of the republics; a strong, controlling position was taken by the center over the court structure and legal proceedings of the republics as well as of the Union; the powers of the Union Council of People's Commissars were liberally interpreted to the disadvantage of the republics.[61] In May, 1924, one of the republic commissariats—the Commissariat of Internal Trade—was transformed into a Union-republic body and its opportunities for local independence correspondingly lessened.[62] In 1926, under a decision of the Fourteenth Party Congress, a new program of "socialist industrialization" was inaugurated and with it a greater degree of central control over industrial enterprises.[63] The gains made by the Union government were considerably greater than the rights reserved to the republics, and the net balance of the early years of constitutional application suggested that the unifying rather than federalist principles of the constitution were to be given emphasis.

It seems unlikely that the centralizing trend was the result of a deliberate effort by Russian leaders to weaken the republics and enlarge the Union. On the contrary, many factors inclined the Bolsheviks toward decentralization: they were eager to gain approval in the border regions; they retained, as a legacy of Lenin's leadership, a hostility toward government bureaucracy and excessive concentrations of power; they were not yet embarked on the intensive programs of state industrialization, farm collectivization, and comprehensive planning that were later to demand such enlargements of central authority. As a result, Union officials accepted criticisms and recommendations from the republics and declared their hostility to bureaucratic centralization, agreeing with Ukrainian leaders that "the tendency of our central adminstrators

and of our regulating and planning organs to examine scrupulously every detail . . . deprives local organizations of their individuality, takes responsibility away from them."[64]

Yet Russian leaders remained convinced that Soviet life could
be fostered only through close unification of the republics and
a high degree of centralization in political and economic life.
While accepting decentralizing modifications sponsored by the
republics, they allowed no major limitations on Union authority
and refused to admit, as Ukrainian leaders urged, that strengthening of the republics was an important aim in itself. Bureaucratic practices should be opposed and allowance for local differences made in carrying out programs among the minority nationalities. But neither concession was to alter the basically centralist
nature of the constitution or the general tendency of Russian
leaders to absorb authority wherever they felt authority was
needed.

THE DRIVE FOR UKRAINIZATION

More important than the disagreement over constitutional issues
were Russian-Ukrainian disagreements over internal policy. And
chief among these disagreements was the question of the degree
to which Ukrainian as opposed to Russian institutions would be
stimulated in the Ukraine and the extent to which ethnic Ukrainians would be encouraged to replace Russians in public and private organizations. This entire process of localization of institutions
was described by the term "Ukrainization" and at the simplest
level signified merely the substitution of the Ukrainian language
for Russian in schools, government agencies, and public organizations. At a higher level, it implied also the deliberate stimulation
of ethnic Ukrainians, including those from rural areas, to play a
larger role in political, scientific, and cultural affairs. To Ukrainians
it suggested even the forceful conversion of Russian into Ukrainian institutions and the fostering of a political and cultural independence which might develop anti-Russian or anti-centralist tendencies. The problem was particularly critical because it involved
not only the thorny question of local versus central authority

but also the question of the degree to which the Bolsheviks meant
in practice to grant the Soviet Union's ethnic minorities the independence they had been promised. The period from 1923 to
1927 was a period characterized by Russian and Ukrainian efforts to establish the limits of Ukrainization, by a steady but limited growth in the authority and independence of Ukrainian leaders,
and by a mounting disagreement within both the Ukrainian and
All-Union Communist Parties over the scope and extent of Ukrainian autonomy.

Russian Bolsheviks and Ukrainization

At an early period Russian Bolsheviks had expressed themselves
in the strongest way as favoring a broad Ukrainization program.
Their support was a result chiefly of Lenin's consistently stated
internationalism as an approach to national questions and to the
problems posed by national movements. For Lenin it was axio-
matic that national movements were of no intrinsic merit and
were reactionary and harmful to the revolutionary movement
inasmuch as they drew attention away from the class question
and weakened the development of unity among the proletariat
of separate countries. National movements and a spirit of nationalism, Lenin asserted, had developed as direct products of
the capitalist era when imperial powers subjugated colonial regions and enslaved them to the advantage of the ruling classes.[65]
The nationalism of the oppressing country was a manifestation of
the rivalries engendered by the race for colonial markets and of
the privileges enjoyed against the colonies themselves; the nationalism of the subjegated state was a reaction to the enslaved
status forced upon it. Both forms of nationalism Lenin viewed
as transitory phenomena of the capitalist period; in the proletarian
era both were to be fought against until they disappeared. The
nationalism of the oppressing country was to be especially opposed
for not only did it produce a nationalist opposition within the
subjugated group and thereby weaken international proletarian
unity, but also it brutalized and poisoned political life in the oppressing country itself, strengthening reactionary anti-proletarian
forces.[66] The nationalism of the subjugated country was to be

treated more gently and moderately, for, although it sometimes distorted the perspective of the proletariat of the oppressed nation and prevented cooperation with the proletariat of the imperial power, it necessarily could be eliminated only by a gradual destruction of the suspicions and antagonisms which had given it birth. National forms could on occasion demand support from the proletariat where they were liberal in character, but only because it was essential to separate the national question from the class struggle, and because a separation of the two was possible only if the Bolsheviks supported nationalism where it took the form of a national liberation movement while opposing nationalism wherever it was oppressive.[67]

With specific reference to Russia's multi-national complexion, Lenin made it clear that he considered Great-Russian nationalism oppressive in contrast to the nationalism of the minorities which was directed toward liberation and often included progressive elements. In his most complete statement on the problem, "On the Right of Nations to Self-Determination," Lenin noted in February, 1914, that Great-Russian nationalism:

is now the most formidable [expression of nationalism], it is precisely the one that is less bourgeois and more feudal, it is precisely the one that is the chief brake on democracy and on the proletarian struggle. In the bourgeois nationalism of *every* oppressed nation there is a general democratic content directed *against* oppression, and it is this content that we unconditionally support, strictly distinguishing it from the tendency toward one's own national exclusiveness.[68]

Because of the harsh nature of Great-Russian chauvinism, Lenin urged the proletariat to battle systematically against it.[69] Particularly he urged a battle against those who, under one guise or another, resisted the national demands of Russia's minorities. Such resistance, he suggested, was in itself an expression of Great-Russian chauvinism. "To brush aside the mass national movements once they have arisen and to refuse to support what is progressive in them means in practice to give way to *nationalistic* prejudices, that is to identify 'one's own' nation as the model nation."[70]

Consequently, it was essential for Bolsheviks: 1) to oppose Great-Russian nationalism wherever and in whatever form it appeared;

2) to denounce the suppression of local national movements wherever the suppression was inspired by nationalist rather than proletarian motives; and 3) to accept the national movements and to support their progressive elements with the assurance that local nationalism would thereby diminish in importance and ultimately disappear in the building of an international socialist commonwealth. It was on the basis of these three elements that Russian Bolsheviks determined to support, in a limited way, concessions to the local nationalities.

In the period following the Revolution Lenin repeated his demand for careful accommodation to the peculiarities of minority regions. The unsuccessful experience of Bolshevik leaders in the Ukraine in 1919 convinced him that the Bolsheviks could succeed in the border areas only by adopting the most conciliatory attitude. At the Eighth Conference of the Russian Communist Party (December, 1919) he submitted a resolution calling for the greatest tolerance and understanding of the distinctive features of Ukrainian language and culture.[71] Several elements later to be included under the term Ukrainization appeared in the resolution: the right of the masses of the Ukraine to be educated in their own language and to use it in all Soviet institutions; the necessity of placing workers knowing the Ukrainian language in all Soviet institutions in order that public affairs might be conducted in Ukrainian; the importance of drawing poor and middle-class peasants into local revolutionary committees and soviets; the importance of maintaining Soviet institutions free of urban, petty bourgeois elements which were hostile to the Ukrainian peasants and "often masqueraded as Communists." The resolution said little about Great-Russian nationalism, for in the eyes of the Bolsheviks the Revolution had wiped out the oppressing Russian classes. There was yet little concern that revolutionary leaders might prove equally oppressive in their attitudes toward the nationalities.

By the time of the calling of the Tenth Congress of the Russian Communist Party (March, 1921), however, it was obvious that Great-Russian chauvinism was more than a transitory capitalist phenomenon. Clearly Russian chauvinism had been absorbed into the ranks of the Bolshevik Party and government institutions in

a form scarcely changed from Tsarist days. Not only was the
Russian Communist Party predominantly Great-Russian in composition and attitudes but so also were the Communist parties of
the republics: in the Ukraine only 23 percent of Party members
were Ukrainian while over 50 percent were Great-Russian.[72] Moreover, the majority of Russians holding leadership posts were without sympathy for the national movements and in their work and
public statements expressed a centralist position disturbing to central leaders and to local representatives of the nationalities alike.
Consequently, at the Tenth Party Congress (March, 1921) both
Lenin and Stalin declared their hostility to Great-Russian chauvinism and their support for measures aimed at safeguarding the
position of the minority groups. In the Congress resolution on
the national question the Party condemned "the deviation toward
a great nation, colonizing viewpoint" and expressed its conviction
that "strong, genuinely Communist organizations linked with the
masses and uniting in their ranks the proletarian elements of the
local native and Russian populations on the basis of internationalism" could not be developed in the border regions unless "colonizing and nationalist survivals in the Party ranks [were] overcome."[73]
At the same time, the Party declared that it was essential that
Soviet life in the border regions conform to the national complexion
of each region and that courts, administrative offices, economic
organizations, and organs of power function in the local language,
drawing their personnel from local people "familiar with the customs
and psychology of the local population."[74] Schools, the press, theaters, recreation facilities, cultural and educational institutions
were all to employ the local language. With specific reference
to the Ukraine, Stalin suggested that even the predominantly
Russian cities in the eastern, industrial areas should ultimately be
Ukrainized.

It is clear that a Ukrainian nation exists and that the development
of its culture is an obligation for Communists. It is impossible to
go against history. It is clear that although Russian elements still
predominate in the cities of the Ukraine, in the course of time these
cities will inevitably be Ukrainized.[75]

In the following year Lenin's opposition to Great-Russian chauvinism grew. By the end of 1922 the problem had assumed such magnitude in his eyes that he prepared a special series of notes on the question for consideration by Party leaders.[76] The notes were incomplete and sketchy and suffered from Lenin's tendency to relate the problem of nationalities to the difficult situation which had arisen in the Caucasus. Nevertheless, the burden of his arguments was clear, and his conclusions were striking in their condemnation of Great-Russian chauvinism and in their criticism of the Russian leadership of the Party.

The Party, Lenin declared, had failed in its efforts to cleanse the state apparatus of Russian chauvinists and petty-bourgeois bureaucrats. As a result, the Soviet government had come to be dominated almost to the same degree as had the Tsarist by a centralizing spirit which expressed itself in disdainful attacks on the "social-chauvinism" of the minority nationalities while at the same time displaying within itself a 100 percent Russian attitude representing the most vicious and dangerous form of chauvinism. Party demands for a single state apparatus, for the suppression of local nationalisms, for a unity of state services—all defended as requisites for the establishment of a Bolshevik union—in practice were expressions of a disdainful and crudely imperialistic Russian nationalism. So serious had the problem become, Lenin argued, that it was necessary for the Party to re-examine the whole question of its national policy and to affirm anew with sincerity and goodwill its dedication to the struggle against Great-Russian chauvinism. Specifically, the Party should demand an accounting from three of its leaders—Stalin, Ordzhonikidze, and Dzerzhinskii—for the role they had played in the "Great-Russian nationalistic campaign"; the Party should adopt the strictest rules guaranteeing the use of the local language in the republics; and the Party should discuss again the question of state relationships among the Soviet republics and be prepared to abandon the Union agreements binding the republics together, accepting if necessary the full independence of the republics in all matters but military and foreign affairs. Only in this way, Lenin concluded, would it be possible for the Bolsheviks to avoid falling into a pattern of imperialistic relations toward the minority nationalities; only in this way could the Party retain its clear and challenging call for the liberation of other peoples oppressed by imperialism.

Lenin's notes were not printed, nor were they distributed to the Party as a whole; but their contents were made known to Party leaders and were undoubtedly influential in the preparations for the Twelfth Party Congress (April, 1923) as well as in its proceedings and discussions. The Twelfth Congress was the first after the Revolution which Lenin was unable to attend, and his place in matters involving nationality problems was taken by Stalin. Inasmuch as the Congress adopted a comprehensive resolution on the national question which was to serve as Party policy in the succeeding years, the shift from Lenin's leadership to Stalin's was significant. It was especially important in the area of Union construction where Stalin clearly repudiated Lenin's suggestions for a decentralization of government authority.[77] It was also important in the dispute over Great-Russian nationalism and in the discussion of the concessions to be made to the national minorities, since Stalin, while generally supporting Lenin in these questions, refused to introduce the modifications in emphasis Lenin had recommended.

Nevertheless, for the moment Lenin's insistence on a battle with Great-Russian chauvinism and on the necessity of stimulating national growth within the republics was accepted, and the Congress, in a resolution "On the National Question," called for resolute measures in both areas.[78] On the first point the Congress agreed that the principal obstacle to the development of a brotherly union of all Soviet republics was the survival of great nation chauvinism —a survival of the former privileged position held by Great Russians which persisted in the minds of both central and local Soviet officials as well as in state and public institutions. In practice, the Congress noted, this was expressed by:

a haughtily disdainful and heartlessly bureaucratic attitude on the part of Russian Soviet officials to the needs and wants of the national republics. . . . The situation in some of the national republics (the Ukraine, Belorussia, Azerbaidzhan, Turkestan) is complicated by the fact that an important group of the workers' class, providing fundamental support for Soviet authority, belongs to the Great-Russian nationality. In these regions the development of closer ties between the town and countryside, between the workers' class and the peasants meets a formidable obstacle in the surviving remnants of Great-Russian chauvinism both in Party and Soviet organs. Under these conditions arguments which speak about the superiority of Russian culture and advance ideas about the inevitable victory of the higher Russian culture over the cultures of the more backward peoples (Ukrainians, Azerbaidzhans, Uzbeks, Kirgiz, and others) are nothing more than an attempt to establish the dominance of the Great-Russian nationality. Therefore a decisive battle with these survivals of Great-Russian chauvinism is the first on the list of problems of our Party.[79]

On the second point the Congress repeated the Bolshevik maxim that a union of Soviet states could be established only on the basis of cooperation among all peoples, and that it was consequently necessary to accommodate to "the special needs and requirements of the separate nationalities" as well as to the general needs and wants of the Union as a whole. The Congress agreed that Party and government leaders in the republics who were not from the local nationality should carefully avoid an underevaluation of national peculiarities and should commit themselves to a study of the local language. At the same time, an intensive effort should be made to train local Party workers in the principles of Marxism and to draw them, as they were prepared, into responsible Party work.

The general conclusions of the Twelfth Congress were given greater emphasis at a special meeting of Party leaders summoned in June, 1923. The meeting was labeled the Fourth Conference of the Central Committee of the Party, but it included, in addition to Central Committee members, leaders from the Soviet Union's national republics and regions. The Conference discussed the general problem of national relationships in the minority areas and in a comprehensive resolution established a number of specific programs as guides for Party work.[80] Included in these programs were the following. First, every effort was to be made in the republics to draw representatives of the local nationalities into Party and Soviet work and into the trade unions and cooperatives: each republic was to conduct a cautious purge of its Party and state apparatus, removing all nationalist elements, particularly those

guilty of Great-Russian chauvinism; each republic was to introduce its native language into Party and state institutions and
to establish programs to teach the language to all workers unfamiliar with it; each republic was to work to attract and select
"the more or less loyal elements of the local intelligentsia into
Soviet institutions." Secondly, the republics were to work to
raise the cultural level of the local population: cultural institutions—libraries, clubs, etc.—functioning in the local language
were to be built; the number of schools conducted in the local language was to be increased and additional local teachers, "more
or less loyal," brought into them; general literacy in the native
tongue was to be increased; local publishing houses were to be
established. Thirdly, measures were to be taken to ensure the
growth and development of the economic foundations of each republic. Fourthly, efforts were to be made to prepare local military cadres which could organize national regiments; in a number
of the advanced republics including the Ukraine local military
divisions were to be established at once. Fifthly, the Communist
parties in each of the republics were to emphasize political education work among the local population: schools for political education were to be established in the local language; Marxist literature was to be translated into the native tongue and local political journals established; discussion clubs were to be organized
and special work carried on within the Youth League and among
women's groups. Finally, the resolution recommended that there
be brought into certain departments of the Party's Central Committee a number of representatives from each of the nationalities
who would work with the Committee in its current activities in
the republics to ensure the success of these programs.

The resolutions of the Twelfth Party Congress and of the Fourth
Conference of the Central Committee were striking and far-reaching additions to the Bolshevik nationality program. Although
earlier resolutions had spoken for concessions to the minorities
and for nationalization of Party work within the republics, none
had spoken so clearly, so completely, or in such detail. Moreover
the new resolutions moved a step further toward republic autonomy by suggesting that responsibility for the program should

rest not with central authorities, but with the republics themselves. This suggestion was not only implicit in the resolutions, but was stated directly by Stalin:

The uniqueness of the situation in border areas . . . lies in the fact that our Party organizations in these regions, under the conditions of the development of Soviet power there, can and must organize their forces with the aim of strengthening their ties with the wide masses of the population, utilizing for this purpose the rich experience of our Party during the preceding years. Until recently the Central Committee of the Russian Communist Party has normally functioned directly in the border areas over the heads of the Communist organizations there, sometimes even by-passing these organizations, drawing into the general work of Soviet construction each and every one of the national elements of a more or less loyal character. *Now this work must be carried out by the Party organizations in the border regions themselves.* They can do it and must do it, remembering that this way is the best means of transforming the Marxist cadres among the local people into a genuinely mass Party capable of leading the majority of the population of the region.[81]

The mandate to the Communist parties in the republics was therefore clear and precise. Genuine and comprehensive programs were to be undertaken in each of the nationality areas, directed, first, toward extending Bolshevik principles widely among the local population regardless of ethnic composition or economic status and, secondly, toward drawing into local government and Party posts representatives of the local nationality, even where the representatives were of unproven loyalty. To accomplish these programs, due regard was to be paid to the unique characteristics of each nationality region and, above all, to the local language, which was gradually but definitely to be extended to most areas of public life. At the same time, it was made plain to the republic Communist parties that, in contrast to the situation of previous years, they were themselves to be given responsibility for the program.

In evaluating the elements prompting so liberal a policy, it is important to note the differences in approach separating Lenin from other leaders despite their apparent general agreement. Lenin in his final notes on the national question had suggested in an un-Marxian way that the problem of nationalism was a unique and important one which, in certain respects, defied the neat pattern of answers provided by Bolshevik proletarian theory. He thereby emphasized his previously stated belief that on the national question Bolsheviks needed to adopt a flexible, pragmatic approach and to recognize that, while the proletarian question was in general superior to the national question, there were situations in which national factors were so vital that, for the moment, they demanded precedence. At the same time Lenin took an additional step by implying that not only were there *situations* in which nationalism transcended class interests but that there were also distinct *elements* of nationalism which in and of themselves transcended class elements or at least might do so during an indefinable transition period. Thus he recognized that many Great-Russian Bolsheviks, including a number of the most able proletarian leaders, were guilty of a chauvinism equaling that of earlier Tsarist officials, and he suggested even that it was conceivable that Soviet Russia—a dictatorship of the proletariat—might "give way to imperialist attitudes toward the oppressed nationalities."[82] He thereby approached the point of saying that the interests and outlook of the proletariat of oppressing countries were not identical with the interests and outlook of the proletariat of subjegated states or that at least the two groups might not view their interests in the same light. Lenin made no effort to discuss the problem carefully in his notes. Had he done so, he might have resolved the difficulty by returning to standard Communist explanations about bourgeois survivals and the dangers of the New Economic Policy. In general he avoided such explanations, however, implying that in the forseeable future national problems would require consideration and treatment separate from class problems.

On the other hand, Stalin and the majority of Bolshevik leaders interpreted the national question in an inflexible and doctrinaire manner, avoiding the suggestion that national problems should be treated in any way apart from the proletarian question. In Stalin's reports to the Twelfth Party Congress and the Fourth Conference of the Central Committee he indicated clearly that, while national problems had created difficulties which required great Party effort to resolve, all were but expressions of class hostility and bourgeois remnants and all could be removed through a careful application of Bolshevik principles. Great-Russian chauvinism, he recognized, had penetrated the Party and had steadily grown more pronounced in recent years; but the explanation of its rise lay not in the possibility that proletarian elements might suffer from national prejudices but in the fact that survivals of bourgeois chauvinism had not yet been completely eradicated from the Party and had, in fact, been stimulated by the adoption of the New Economic Policy.[83] At the same time, he emphasized strongly that Great-Russian chauvinism was harmful, not as Lenin had suggested because it was a form of imperialism even when expressed within a proletarian state, but because it threatened to alienate the border regions from Bolshevik Russia and hence endanger the dictatorship of the proletariat.[84] By the same token, Stalin urged the necessity of granting concessions to the minority nationalities and of encouraging them to develop their own unique, institutions and leadership, not from any concern for the peculiarities of the nationalities, but in an effort to develop stronger Communist elements in the republics and to enable these elements to win mass support among the local population.[85]

For Stalin the basic problem in the border regions was one of mass support, and such support, he suggested, could be developed only if Marxist cadres could be established in each national region and if close ties between the cadres and the masses of the local population could be assured. With specific reference to the Ukraine he summarized the problem as follows:

The second weak point of Soviet power is the Ukraine. The situation there in the areas of culture, literacy, and so forth, is the same or almost the same as in Turkestan. The state apparatus there is hardly nearer to the language and customs of the people than in Turkestan. And yet the Ukraine has as great importance for the peoples of the west as Turkestan has for the peoples of the East. The situation in the Ukraine is complicated further by certain peculiarities of the industrial development of the country. The problem lies in the fact that the basic industries, coal and metallurgy, have been established in the Ukraine not from below, not as the result of the natural development of the national economy, but from above, as the result of an imposition artificially implanted from outside. As a result, the composition of the proletariat of these industries is not local, not Ukrainian in language. And this peculiarity leads to the result that the cultural influence of the city over the countryside and the joining of the proletariat with the peasantry has been considerably delayed by these differences in the national composition of the proletariat and peasantry. All these peculiarities must be taken into account in the work of transforming the Ukraine into a model republic. And it necessarily follows to transform her into a model republic, in view of her great importance for the peoples of the West.[86]

It was important, as Lenin had urged, to combat Great-Russian chauvinism in the Ukraine and to develop local institutions staffed by Ukrainian nationals and functioning in the Ukrainian language as transmission links joining the proletarian, Russian, urban culture with the peasant, Ukrainian, rural culture. But Stalin indicated no sympathy for the Ukrainian language and culture and apparently objected to Russification only because it tended to alienate Ukrainians and peasants, interfering with the Bolshevik program for building local support.

Ukrainization: the Beginning (1920-1923)

The earliest practical efforts toward carrying out the Ukrainization policy were made under the most inauspicious of circumstances. At the moment the Eighth Conference of the Russian Communist Party (December, 1919) first declared for Ukrainization, the Ukraine was under occupation by anti-Bolshevik forces, and its government and Party organizations were not only in exile but momentarily dissolved and sharply divided. Moreover, the old Ukrainian government of 1919, dominated as it had been by centralist leaders,[87] had ill prepared the way for Ukrainization by its opposition to the most modest concessions to national feeling. On many occasions Party leaders had spoken openly against the use of the Ukrainian language by government officials, suggesting that the language was unimportant even in the Ukraine's countryside.[88] The government had taken a harsh stand against Ukrainian farmers, driving large numbers into unpopular state farms, viewing all but the poorest as enemies of Soviet power and rejecting Lenin's suggestion for an alliance with middle and poor peasant groups. Little effort had been made to reach an agreement with the non-Bolshevik Ukrainian socialist parties despite their more distinctly Ukrainian composition and attitudes and their closer ties with peasants and workers. The government had followed a definite centralizing policy in which not only government functions but also the activities of public organizations such as the trade unions had been shifted to Moscow.[89] Most seriously, Ukrainian leaders had failed to strengthen the Party, which counted only 36,000 members, the bulk concentrated in eastern industrial centers. The legacy of these policies was one of bitterness and hostility among large parts of the Ukrainian population, and the year 1919 saw a mass exodus of intellectuals from the Ukraine and a growing opposition on the part of peasant groups.

As a result, the new Ukrainian government established in 1920 was faced with a two-fold task: 1) to reverse the unfortunate measures adopted by its predecessor; 2) to form closer bonds with indigenous Ukrainian leaders and with peasant groups. Again, however, the situation was unfavorable. The government had hardly established itself in the Ukraine when it was ousted from Kiev —this time by Polish troops—and forced to move to Kharkov. Throughout 1920 it was harassed by the forces of Wrangel and by numerous peasant bands which loosely controlled extensive rural areas from time to time. In addition, at the head of the government remained Kh. Rakovskii whose earlier opposition to Ukrainization was well known. And the CP(b)U itself was in no position to press Ukrainization: Party organizations were weak and unreliable; Party members were concentrated in the army or in industrial centers in the eastern Ukraine;[90] opposition to Ukrainization was strongly entrenched.

Nevertheless, the government moved forward in several areas to inaugurate Ukrainization. In two popular decisions the government appealed directly for the support of ethnic Ukrainians and poorer peasants: on February 5 an order was issued for the distribution among landless peasants of nearly forty million acres of land which had been previously expropriated;[91] on February 27 a second order established Ukrainian as the republic's official language to be adopted by all public institutions.[92]

In March, 1920, these government measures were matched by the Party which moved to increase participation by ethnic Ukrainians in Party affairs. At the Fourth Conference of the CP(b)U it was agreed to admit Borotbists into the Bolshevik ranks. At once two non-Bolshevik leaders, Terlests'kyi and Grin'ko, were drawn into the government, the latter being given the important post of Commissar of Education. Subsequently, two additional Borotbist leaders, Shums'kyi and Blakytnyi, were named to the thirteen member Central Committee of the CP(b)U.[93] Although the Borotbists formed only a minority in government and Party organizations, their influence was significant. Their entrance into the Party was a major concession to Ukrainian nationalists and nationalist sentiment.

Similarly, in an effort to stimulate support from adherents of other nationalist parties the Bolsheviks made overtures to political leaders who had fled the Ukraine during the previous Bolshevik occupation. The *emigrés* were urged to return to their homeland and accept posts in the Soviet government. Foremost among the *emigrés* was Volodymyr Vynnychenko—one-time leader of the Ukrainian Social Democrats—who was brought, together with a group of *emigré* intellectuals, to Moscow and then to the Ukraine. Vynnychenko was given the posts of Deputy Premier and Commissar of Foreign Affairs and was elected to the Central Committee of the CP(b)U. However, after a brief stay in the Ukraine he refused to accept the posts and, with a dire prediction of future developments in the new Soviet state, rejoined the emigration.[94]

Greater successes were achieved in the areas of language and culture. Throughout 1920 a steady policy of extending the use of the Ukrainian language was pursued. In the elementary schools in the countryside as well as in the rural institutes of political education the language of instruction was shifted gradually from Russian to Ukrainian.[95] New cultural organizations were formed in which the Ukrainian language was used. Many newspapers, including the central organ of the Ukrainian Central Executive Committee (*Izvestiia* or *Visti*), shifted to Ukrainian. As former Borotbists were admitted into the CP(b)U, the number of Party members speaking Ukrainian increased; many of the new workers were assigned to leadership posts in the rural areas. The first steps toward the Ukrainization of the army were made with the establishment of schools for Red Army officers at Kharkov and Kiev.[96] The measures were incomplete, but they represented a first practical effort at reversing the long-established Tsarist policy of Russification. In contrast to the Bolshevik work of 1919, they carried the promise of a new and genuinely liberalizing policy toward the minority nationalities.

Nevertheless, these initial successes were only slowly advanced in the years immediately following. The principal obstacle was the CP(b)U itself, which in 1920 was predominantly Russian rather than Ukrainian and included powerful elements which, by disposition and background, could not accept Ukrainization despite its endorsement by central leaders. The anti-Ukrainian complexion of the Party was made abundantly clear at the Party's Fourth and Fifth Conferences in March and November, 1920. At the Fourth Conference the Party split into three factions. The largest —the Sapronov opposition—consisted chiefly of Russians who were in no way identified with the Ukraine. The faction included Russians from Party units in the Red Army or from the industrial, Russified areas of the eastern Ukraine, workers sent from outside the Ukraine to help in Party work, and opportunist "philistine elements of the intelligentsia and semi-intelligentsia in the cities and small towns."[97] The attitude of the faction was indicated by its opposition to concessions to Ukrainian peasants and by its completely negative approach to the national question. At the Conference leaders of the faction expressed flatly their belief that 99 percent of the Ukrainian peasants had no interest in the national question and cared neither about political union with Russia nor about independence. The proletarian dictatorship, they declared, could be developed in the Ukraine only in closest union with, or in fact by the Russian proletariat, since the Ukrainian proletariat was petty-bourgeois and lacking in revolutionary consciousness.[98] Although the leaders of the faction were withdrawn from the Ukraine following the Conference, and although the faction was dispersed,[99] the elements comprising it continued to form a large and influential block of Party members. Their views on the national question were expressed again and again at subsequent Party meetings.

The second faction included the regular leaders of the CP(b)U and a large proportion of the Bolsheviks from the established Party centers in Kharkov and the Ukraine's eastern districts. Although the faction was primarily Russian in composition, it included many members who had worked long in the Ukraine and were aware of the problem of Ukrainian nationalism, although not necessarily sympathetic toward it. The faction was closely identified with central leaders and was willing to accept the concessions to the nationalities urged by Lenin: in March the faction prodded the Fourth Conference of the CP(b)U to reaffirm the right of the Ukraine to independence and to admit Borotbists into the Party. Yet the members of the faction were the same ones who had spoken so resolutely against Ukrainization in 1919 and plainly viewed the entire program as no more than a necessary evil. Although accepting the program in principle, they lacked the necessary enthusiasm to enforce it in the face of heavy opposition. In the period between the Fourth and Fifth Party Conferences their hostile indifference increased as elements from the Sapronov opposition drifted into the group. By the end of 1920 the faction was speaking openly against Ukrainization and in favor of an amalgamation of the Ukrainian and Russian cultures.[100]

The third faction comprised a small group from the Kiev and Volynia districts—a remnant of the Federalists who several months earlier had urged independence for the Ukraine.[101] Under the leadership of Lapchyns'kyi the faction completely supported a national program for the Ukraine. The faction was small, however, and exercised little influence in the Party;[102] at the Fourth Conference it was overwhelmed by other groups and in the following months was denounced by Russian leaders and its members purged. Nevertheless, its position on the national question was preserved, for the influx into the CP(b)U of former Borotbists brought into the Party an enthusiasm for Ukrainian institutions which replaced that of the expelled members. In the future it was the Borotbists supported by a small group of nationalist Bosheviks who were to press most strongly for Ukrainization.

At the Fifth Party Conference in November, 1920, the intra-Party disagreement burst forth openly in the Conference debates. The majority position was presented by G. E. Zinoviev, Chairman of the Comintern, who spoke in opposition to Lenin and other central leaders. Zinoviev counseled the greatest moderation in accepting Ukrainian nationalist demands. Although the Party should not hinder the Ukrainian peasant from speaking his own language, he declared, and although the Party should guard against bungling in the national question and avoid the appearance of dictating to Ukrainians on cultural questions, it was clear that the Russian language, as a more cultured, dynamic language, would ultimately prevail. It was important that the Party not go too far in adjusting to the local situation.[103] Specifically, Zinoviev suggested that sufficient Borotbists had been absorbed into the Party and that any further enrollment would serve only to strengthen Ukrainian chauvinism.[104] The task of the Party was to accept nationalist demands only when they were broadly based and were requisites for building mass support. National institutions in themselves were not to be encouraged.[105]

In opposition, the Borotbist faction denounced the CP(b)U for its failure to develop as a truly representative party for the Ukraine and for its excessive dependence on Russian leadership. In a report on "Future Tasks of the Party" Vasyl' Blakytnyi, Borotbist member of the Central Committee, condemned the Party for its domination by bureaucratic, petty-bourgeois elements and by cadres sent from Moscow. The difficulty, he suggested, arose from the fact that the only proletarian forces in the Ukraine were those in the cities and industrial centers where the Ukrainian atmosphere had penetrated but little. These forces were insufficient to develop a real revolutionary spirit and, consequently, the Party and government machines had fallen under the control of bureaucrats, opportunists, and petty-bougeosie who were neither socialist nor Ukrainian.

Filled with conglomerate elements and clever opportunists, the Party was unable to master the revolutionary spirit, it lost its ties with the workers' class and did not develop ties with the rural semi-proletariat, it became incapable of carrying through the fundamental tasks of destroying politically the Petliurists and atamans, of creating a powerful base in the rural areas through class stratification there, and finally it literally and obviously began to decompose.[106]

As a result of the Party's failures, Blakytnyi noted, Soviet leaders had decided to incorporate Borotbists into the Party ranks in order to provide cadres of the revolutionary-agrarian proletariat, including poor peasants, rural intelligentsia, and nationally conscious Ukrainian Workers. This step had clearly strengthened the Party. At the same time, however, cadres from the Russian Communist Party were being assigned in great numbers to work in the Ukraine, and these cadres served as thousands of living threads binding the CP(b)U to Moscow. Consequently, the Party had developed a strong centralizing tendency:

This tendency that we call colonization which is based on the national kinship of the majority of the city proletariat of the Ukraine with the proletariat, anti-proletariat, and petty-bourgeoisie of Russia as well as on the sickness of the industrial proletariat of the Ukraine, expresses itself in the demand that there be constructed a state system within the RSFSR with the restoration of the restrictions of the Russian Empire, . . . and the dissolution of the CP (b) U with its complete absorption into the Russsian Communist Party.[107]

This tendency, Blakytnyi concluded, needed to be sternly opposed if the Party was to remain close to the great mass of the Ukrainian people.

The Fifth Conference failed to resolve the factional dispute, although it showed its support for Zinoviev by refusing to re-elect Blakytnyi to the Central Committee and by suggesting in a resolution that, as a result of the Ukrainization work of 1920, the national question had now lost much of its importance. Central leaders, on the other hand, seemed to favor the Borotbists. Blakytnyi clearly had expressed a stronger nationalist position than they could accept: his condemnation of the assignment of Russian cadres to the Ukraine was a direct attack on a major Soviet policy. Nevertheless, his analysis of the CP(b)U as an opportunist, petty-bourgeois, Russified group was acceptable and expressed the Bolshevik position more closely than had the arguments of Zinoviev. In an instruction to the CP(b)U central officials reaffirmed the 1919 Party decisions favoring Ukrainization and insisted that emphasis be placed on strengthening the socialist Ukrainian state, on building a Ukrainian socialist culture, and on drawing into the work loyal elements of the Ukrainian intelligentsia.[108] At the same time, Zinoviev, who had been working with the CP(b)U for some months, was withdrawn, and Molotov was dispatched to the Ukraine in his stead.[109]

In 1921 the gap between central policies and the programs of the CP(b)U continued to grow. At the Tenth Party Congress (March, 1921) central leaders spoke anew for Ukrainization and denounced the same elements in the Russian Communist Party that Blakytnyi had censored in the Ukraine. In July a verification of Party membership throughout Russia was ordered, and Lenin made plain that the purge was to be applied most rigorously to these same elements—the opportunists, former Mensheviks, bourgeoisie, etc. The CP(b)U officially accepted both the purge and the Ukrainization program[110] but, as a practical matter, refused to carry out either program as central leaders had intended. The purge—particularly in the Ukraine's western districts—was applied primarily to Ukrainian nationalists, including rural Ukrainian elements and former Borotbists.[111] In the eastern districts a number of anti-Ukrainian oppositionists were removed in accordance with the purge program, but others were rapidly admitted into the CP(b)U and soon were exerting again great influence in the direction of Great-Russian chauvinism.[112] At the Sixth Party Conference (December, 1921) Oleksandr Shums'kyi, the last Borotbist holding high Party office, was dropped from the Central Committee.[113] By 1922 the position of the anti-Ukrainian faction in the Party was stronger than it had been at the Fifth Conference.

In the following months, under the influence of the anti-Ukrainian faction, a series of steps was taken which halted Ukrainization work and even reversed parts of the program. The most important changes were made in the fields of publishing and education. Support was withdrawn from many of the newspapers which in 1920 and 1921 had begun to publish in Ukrainian rather than Russian, and by mid-1922 the majority of the papers were suspended. The Ukrainian Publishing House, established initially to work in the Ukrainian language, began shifting to the publication of

Russian materials. A definite campaign was mounted against the
work of the new Ukrainian schools. They were accused of teaching in a Petliurist spirit, of failing to develop proletarian views,
and of falling below the standards set in Russian-language schools.
In a circular distributed by the Central Committee of the CP(b)U
in the spring of 1922 it was announced that henceforth all plans
for the extension of education work in rural areas in the Ukrainian language would be considered "critically."[114] Subsequently, the
Ukrainian Commissariat of Education was denounced, and in the
fall its head, the Borotbist G. F. Grin'ko, was dismissed from his
post "for his excessive haste in carrying out Ukrainization."[115]

At the same time, a number of the leaders of the CP(b)U began
speaking directly against the whole policy of Ukrainization, urging that it had become a program of the Ukrainian nationalists
and had been transformed into a "whetstone on which the counter-
revolution can sharpen its arms against Soviet power."[116] Principal spokesman for these leaders was Dmitrii Lebed', a secretary
of the CP(b)U and an influential figure in Party affairs. In the
early months of 1923, Lebed' stated his views openly, presenting
what came to be known as the "Theory of the Struggle of Two
Cultures." The most striking characteristic of the Ukraine's sociological structure, Lebed' declared, was the sharp cleavage between
its urban and rural areas. As a result of historical circumstances,
the Ukraine's cities had developed as proletarian and Russian centers, while the countryside had remained peasant and Ukrainian.
Because the city culture was proletarian, it was more advanced
than the culture of the countryside. And because the Russian culture was that of the cities, it followed that it was more progressive,
higher in its historical perspective than the Ukrainian. Therefore,
the Russian culture would inevitably win in the battle which the
two cultures were waging, one with the other. And of course it
was the duty of the Bolsheviks to support the advanced culture
and to oppose that which was reactionary.[117] Ukrainization could
be defended, Lebed' concluded, only where it was defined as the
mastering by the Party of the Ukrainian language and culture and
only where it was used as a means of extending proletarian culture among the Ukrainian masses. "Our Party must determine

whether in the Ukrainian atmosphere the Ukrainian language can hasten the cultural process in the Ukrainian people, especially a- mong the peasantry as the most backward people, or whether it slows down this process, not aiding the advance of culture, but retarding it."[118] In Lebed's view it was clear that Ukrainization retarded and did not advance proletarian culture.

There was much sympathy within the CP(b)U for Lebed's pro-Russian stand. But already central leaders had endorsed Ukrain- ization on several occasions, and early in 1923, as the Union con- stitution was being prepared, they endorsed it once again. At the moment Lebed's arguments were being presented in the Ukraine, a central Party commission was incorporating into the resolutions to be discussed by the forthcoming Twelfth Party Congress de- mands for a cultivation of local institutions and "a decisive battle with Great-Russian chauvinism."[119] In the face of this opposition from central officials the anti-Ukrainization faction had no choice but to abandon its stand. At the Seventh Conference of the CP(b)U (April, 1923), where the question was discussed in preparation for the Twelfth All-Union Congress, the faction collapsed completely. Lebed' refused even to speak on the question, suggesting that a discussion was now untimely.[120] The Conference unanimously ac- cepted the recommendations of central leaders.[121] The members of the anti-Ukrainization faction did not change their opinions, and Ukrainian nationalists complained at the Twelfth Congress that the faction had accepted the recommendations only formally and that "a large number of comrades who might have objected did not object and did not attempt to understand the present trend of the national policy."[122] But the strictures of Party dis- cipline were sufficient to silence opposition for the time. Under strong central pressure the way was opened once again for prac- tical forward steps in the direction of Ukrainization.

Ukrainization: the Program (1923-1925)

The decision to press again toward Ukrainization was taken at a time when the program seemed urgently needed in the Ukraine. As Stalin suggested to the Fourth Conference of the Russian Cen- tral Committee (June, 1923), the state of affairs in the Ukraine as regards culture, literacy, etc. was as bad or almost as bad as in the most remote parts of Russia. "The state apparatus," he noted, "is hardly nearer to the language and customs of the people than in Turkestan."[123] For Ukrainian leaders the chief problem was the failure of government and Party institutions to transform themselves into Ukrainian bodies.[124] Rakovskii announced that of all government employees less than 35 percent were ethnic Ukrainians, while in the central organs of the Ukrainian government the percentage was even smaller. In the CP(b)U Russian influence was especially strong, Ukrainians numbering only 24 percent of Party membership. Grin'ko pointed out that the Russian language was almost universally used in government work and that with the exception of the rural cooperatives, where 40 to 50 percent of the staff were Ukrainian, the predominance of Russians was overwhelming. Skrypnik noted that progress in Ukrainization of the trade unions had been completely unsatisfactory. The general picture which emerged in 1923 indicated that, apart from the work done in local rural schools and the publication on a limited scale of Ukrainian materials, the policy of nationalization of Ukrainian life had made little progress.

The new leadership   As a first step toward the acceleration of the Ukrainization program several changes were made in Ukrainian leadership. In July, 1923, Rakovskii, who had served so long as Chairman of the Ukrainian Council of People's Commissars, was appointed ambassador to Great Britain, and his place in the Ukraine was taken by Vlas Chubar'.[125] Undoubtedly the principal factor in the decision to remove Rakovskii was the strong opposition to Stalin he had expressed at Party meetings in the first half of 1923.[126] In addition, however, Rakovskii's lack of sympathy for Ukrainian nationalism was well-known and, despite his recent defense of the constitutional rights of the Ukraine, he had come to be identified by nationalists as a foreigner and an enemy of Ukrainian institutions. The new premier, Vlas Chubar', was a native Ukrainian and the son of a poor peasant.[121] It was to be expected that he would show greater concern for Ukrainian institutions and would serve more faithfully as a symbol of the policy of nationality concessions.

A similar change was made in Party leadership. The principal secretary of the CP(b)U in 1922 had been Dmitrii Lebed', who had made no effort to conceal his hostility to the Ukrainian language and customs and, specifically, to Ukrainization. Although he was not removed from his post, an additional secretary was appointed in the person of Emmanuil Kviring, and Kviring quickly replaced Lebed' as Party leader. Kviring had a less favorable background than Chubar', for he was not Ukrainian and had worked chiefly in the Ukraine's industrial centers.[128] Furthermore, in opposition to other Ukrainian leaders, he had supported the centralizing features of the constitution in the debates of 1923[129] and was now unwilling to speak of the Ukrainization program as a new Bolshevik approach to the national question.[130] Nevertheless, he declared his support for Ukrainization and, as a reliable Party worker, was committed to promotion of the program.

A second shift in Party leadership was the appointment of Oleksandr Shums'kyi to the post of Director of the Agitation and Propaganda Section of the Central Committee of the CP(b)U. Shums'kyi had been removed from Party work in 1921 and sent as ambassador to Poland. His return to active work in the Ukraine added once again a Borotbist to high Party circles and to a post responsible for guiding education work within the Party as well as general political training.

Two additional government posts were held by advocates of Ukrainization. The post of Commissar of Justice was held by Nikolai Skrypnik, who on many occasions had expressed his opposition to centralization and Russian nationalism. At the Twelfth Congress of the Russian Communist Party (April, 1923) he restated his views, attacking the tendency toward Russification which had developed in the preceding years. Ukrainian institutions, he declared, should be fostered not only in the Ukraine, but in all parts of the USSR where large Ukrainian populations were to be found. He denounced the Red Army for adopting a policy of Russification toward Ukrainians and other minority peoples. He criticized the Party for its failure to draw Ukrainians into Party work and for its negative attitude toward nationalists who had become Party members. It was essential, he asserted, to adopt measures for stimulating the use of the Ukrainian language, for preventing the army from becoming a "tool of Russification," for increasing the number of Ukrainians in the Party and in active Party work, and for destroying finally and decisively all remnants of Great-Russian chauvinism in Soviet life.[131]

A more questionable figure was the Commissar of Education, Volodymyr Zatons'kyi, appointed to replace Grin'ko in the fall of 1922. Before 1917 Zatons'kyi had been active in revolutionary work in the Ukraine, but as a Ukrainian Socialist Revolutionary not a Bolshevik. Although a native of the Ukraine, he had refused to associate with Ukrainian nationalists and had been drawn toward Russian and Jewish revolutionary circles;[132] in later years he spoke of himself as one who had come from Russia and hence needed to exercise caution to avoid appearing as a foreigner.[133] In February, 1917, he had joined the Russian Communist Party and become a leader in the Kiev organization, rising quickly to the highest posts among the Ukrainian Bolsheviks. Throughout the revolutionary years he had affirmed the necessity of close ties between Russia and the Ukraine but had also insisted on the importance of separate Ukrainian government and Party organizations. At the Tenth Congress of the Russian Communist Party (March, 1921) he had attacked Russian chauvinism: "It is necessary to distinguish in fact between indispensable centralization and simple Russian chauvinism. . . . Comrades must get out of their heads the idea that the Soviet federation is nothing more than a Russian federation, because the important fact is not that it is Russian, but that it is Soviet."[134]

Two years later, however, at the Seventh Conference of the CP(b)U (April 1923) he had emphasized the dangers of Ukrainian nationalism:

When we came under the influence of Ukrainian culture, a number of us were influenced not by our Ukrainian culture, but by a Petliurist spirit and by Petliurist elements within our Party. I am now the Commissar of Education, I happen to have responsibility for this activity, but I no more than my predecessor am able to guarantee that the Ukrainian schools that make up 95 percent of the schools in the Poltava and Kiev regions, that our people's elementary schools yet give an effective proletarian spirit. Our schools in general are far from perfect, and especially the Ukrainian.[135]

Yet Zatons'kyi favored Ukrainization, and his selection to replace Grin'ko as Commissar of Education apparently represented a compromise between the enthusiastic demands for Ukrainization made by the nationalists within the CP(b)U and the confirmed opposition of the pro-Russian faction.

The language program Under the new leadership steps were taken to advance Ukrainization. On August 1, 1923, the Ukrainian Central Executive Committee, in a resolution adopted jointly with the Council of Peoples' Commissars, announced the first group of Ukrainization measures—a group aimed at expanding use of the Ukrainian language. The resolution declared in part:

[Although Soviet power in the Ukraine has carried on great work in the last years for the development of Ukrainian cluture,] it has not been able to destroy the inequality of cultures produced as a result of centuries of oppression.

To assure the destruction of this inequality is the most pressing task of Government in the area of national culture. . . . The Workers'-Peasants' Government of the Ukraine declares it to be essential to center the attention of the state on the extension of knowledge of the Ukrainian language. The equality, recognized until now, of the two most widely used languages in the Ukraine—Ukrainian and Russian—is not sufficient. As a result of the very weak development of Ukrainian schools and Ukrainian culture in general, the shortage of required school books and equipment, the lack of suitably-trained personnel, experience has proven that the Russian language has in fact become the dominant one.

In order to destroy this inequality the Workers'-Peasants' Government hereby adopts a number of practical measures which, while affirming the equality of languages of all nationalities on Ukrainian territory, will guarantee a place for the Ukrainian language corresponding to the numerical superiority of the Ukrainian people on the territory of the Ukrainian SSR.[136]

The resolution continued by insisting that Ukrainian be adopted as the offical language in all state institutions, although Russian, because of its prevalence, also was to be accepted. Courses in Ukrainian were to be established for government workers in the commissariats, and workers failing to learn the language were to be discharged; government correspondence and decrees were gradually to be published in Ukrainian as well as Russian; public forms, stamps, signs, etc. were to be printed in Ukrainian, although Russian or other languages could also be used locally. In order to follow the progress of government agencies in complying with these demands a Ukrainization commission was established on August 7 and empowered to verify the work of state institutions and to report directly on results to the Ukrainian government.[137] Subsequently, additional requirements were established: newspapers and the official Ukrainian news agency were ordered shifted to Ukrainian;[138] a series of commissions were created to supervise Ukrainian work in each government agency; a deadline of January 1, 1926, was set as a final date for achievement of the program.[139] Under the terms of the resolutions it was made plain that all state institutions, newspapers, and state-owned trade and industrial organizations were to abandon Russian as a working language and to adopt Ukrainian. They were to do so quickly and with few exceptions. The program was an ambitious one and indicated that leadership of the CP(b)U was in the hands of those who, however reluctantly, accepted the urgency of nationality concessions.

A second campaign was pressed in the field of education, where an effort was made to complete the conversion of schools to the language of the majority of students. The task was not as difficult as the conversion of government agencies, for much progress had been made earlier during the first period of Ukrainization, and by October, 1923, 61 percent of the schools were teaching exclusively in Ukrainian and 11 percent in both Russian and Ukrainian.[140] Nevertheless, much work remained to be done since a majority of the Ukrainian-language schools were found in the western and rural districts and at the lowest levels, while eastern and urban schools as well as the higher schools were conducted generally in Russian. Thus, of a total of 597 higher schools in the Ukraine in the fall of 1923 (institutes and technical and professional schools), only 43 percent taught solely in Ukrainian while over 36 percent conducted no courses whatever in the national language.[141] Efforts to stimulate the use of Ukrainian in the higher schools had been blocked by the large numbers of non-Ukrainian students attending them: nearly 50 percent of the students were of other nationalities, and in the institutes the figure was almost 70 percent.[142] Consequently, the program for Ukrainization of the schools required not only the conversion of courses, textbooks, and faculty to the Ukrainian language, but also the stimulation of Ukrainian students to continue their education at higher levels and the teaching of Ukrainian to Russian students and students of other nationalities.

Finally, the Ukrainian language program was applied to the CP(b)U, which was ordered to increase the role played by ethnic Ukrainians and to transform Party work from Russian to Ukrainian. In a resolution adopted in April, 1925, the Central Committee of the CP(b)U emphasized that the Party remained far removed from the masses of the Ukrainian people and that closer relations could be built and the masses educated in Marxist principles and Party policy only if the Party shifted to the Ukrainian language and began drawing a larger number of Ukrainians into its ranks.[143] It was necessary to send additional Party cadres into the rural areas, to teach the Ukrainian language to all Party workers and to introduce it into Party schools, to print Party literature and official publications in Ukrainian, to adopt Ukrainian rather than Russian as the language for Party meetings at all levels. Moreover, the Party was obligated to play a direct role in stimulating Ukrainization work in other organizations—in government agencies, in the Red Army, and especially in the trade unions.

The cultural program   A second broad field for Ukrainization was the cultural field where steps were taken to ensure the growth of Ukrainian literature, art, historiography, and science. The program was remarkable not only in its intention to stimulate the use of the Ukrainian language, but also in its willingness to accept cultural expressions which were distinctly Ukrainian and which were not always in agreement with central dogma. Two concepts underlay the liberal policy. The first was the recognition that in a number of areas no inflexible Bolshevik position to which conformity would be required had yet been established and that in certain areas no Marxist or Bolshevik dogma would be needed. The recognition was clearest in the field of languages where at-

tempts to define Russian as the Bolshevik tongue had been rejected and agreement reached that the proletariat could speak as effectively and forcefully in Ukrainian, Polish, or English. Because
the matter was so clearly put, it was here that greatest efforts
toward localization were directed and greatest successes achieved.
But before 1926 Bolsheviks also tolerated variations in other cultural fields and, as a result, accepted differences in the interpretation of questions of history and literature as being disagreements
outside the compass of Bolshevik thought and permissible even
to Party members and government leaders.

The second concept prompting Ukrainization in cultural fields
was the conviction expressed by both Lenin and Stalin that in the
period of Bolshevik weakness assistance should be sought from
non-Bolshevik quarters, and concessions or compromises made as
long as no vital question of authority or principle was involved.
During the years from 1919 to 1925 Bolshevik leaders regarded
their almost complete lack of support among the local nationalities in the border regions as a critical failure. Hence, they agreed
to accept and encourage local non-Bolshevik groups, even where
their loyalty could not be assured. The Fourth Conference of the
Central Committee of the Russian Communist Party (June, 1923)
declared:

> In an effort to win the support of the working masses of the local
> population it is necessary to a greater degree than in the central
> regions to meet halfway either revolutionary-democratic elements or
> even those merely loyal in their attitude to Soviet power. . . .
> The border regions are so poor in local intellectual workers that
> each of them through all efforts must be drawn to the side of So-
> viet power.
>
> A Communist in the border regions must remember: I am a Com-
> munist, *therefore* I must, in accordance with local conditions, make
> compromises with local national elements which wish and are able
> to work loyally within the framework of the Soviet system.[144]

There was no pretense that the policy was a permanent one or
that concessions would continue to be made once the position of
the Bolsheviks had been solidified in the border regions. Rather,
like the New Economic Policy, the concessions were regarded as
momentary setbacks which would be overcome at the appropriate

time. Nonetheless, the concessions were real ones, and their consequences for the Ukraine were considerable.

The first result of the enlarged freedom in cultural fields was a new influx of Ukrainian *emigrés* returning from exile outside the Soviet Union. In 1923 and 1924 a number of Ukrainian Socialist Revolutionaries including former leaders such as Mykhailo Hrushevs'kyi, Pavlo Khrystiuk, Mykola Chechel', Mykola Shrah, and others were admitted to the Ukraine "to continue their scientific work." Given seats in the Ukrainian Academy of Sciences, they worked in its historical section where Hrushevs'kyi was appointed director and where an elaborate program of studies in various aspects of Ukrainian history was developed.

Subsequently, the CP(b)U, guided by resolutions of the Russian Communist Party, declared its general policy toward Ukrainization in the cultural field. The policy was based on an acceptance of the distinctiveness of the Ukraine as a region, not only in its language, historical background, and cultural development, but also in the problems it posed for the building of a socialist state —problems which set it apart from other regions in the USSR. In the Ukraine, for example, the peasant was more important for the success of the Soviet program than in the central industrial districts of Russia. Hence, in the development of Ukrainian culture, it was essential not only that greater emphasis be placed on rural aspects of culture than in Russia but also that Ukrainian cultural forms be expressed in such a way as to strengthen ties between workers and farmers and to facilitate the union of the proletariat with the peasantry. Great efforts were to be made to avoid setting Ukrainian culture in opposition to the culture of other socialist states, and there was no question that Ukrainian culture was ultimately to be merged in a single international proletarian culture. But in the indeterminate period of national separateness cultural expressions in the Ukraine were to develop distinctly, albeit cooperatively, and were not to be subordinated to other national forms. In a comprehensive resolution adopted in June, 1926, the Central Committee of the CP(b)U declared:

The Party stands for the independent development of Ukrainian culture, for an expression of all the creative forces of the Ukrainian people. The Party stands for the wide utilization by the Ukrainian socialist culture now under construction of all the heritages of world culture, for a decisive break with the traditions of provincial narrowness, for the creation of new cultural values adequate for the creativeness of a great class. But the Party declares this cannot be done by opposing Ukrainian culture to the culture of other peoples, but by a brotherly cooperation of the working and toiling masses of all nationalities in the task of constructing an international proletarian culture, in which the Ukrainian working class will be able to contribute its share.[145]

Programs for the army, urban proletariat, and territorial-administrative structure   Ukrainization programs of a limited character were developed also for three more critical areas: the Red Army, the urban proletariat including the trade union organizations, and the local territorial-administrative structure. These programs were of special significance because they did not involve simple matters of form as did the language and cultural programs but offered the possibility that elements on which the Bolsheviks relied for fundamental support would be shifted away from central toward regional control. Ukrainization of the army and urban proletariat promised to increase the regional attachments of these important groups and to diminish their identification with the Union as a whole. Localization of the territorial-administrative structure meant that central officials would be forced to work to a greater extent through the Ukrainian government rather than directly in each lower district. To the extent that the programs were accomplished, they promised to lessen both central authority and Russian influence in the Ukraine.

The drive for Ukrainization of the Red Army was rooted in early statements and decisions by Bolshevik authorities. At the time of the November Revolution the Russian government had declared officially its support for "nationalization" of the army.[146] Subsequently, as a first step toward Ukrainization, military schools for Red Army officers had been established at Kiev and Kharkov.[147] At the Fourth Conference of the Russian Central Committee (June, 1923) there was adopted, on the recommendation of Stalin, a resolution which noted that in order to strengthen the defensive forces of the Soviet Union it was desirable to organize national military units in the border republics, beginning with the creation of military schools and small cadres of national officers, and creating ultimately military units of division size or larger.[148] In the Ukraine, the resolution noted, conditions were suitable for the immediate establishment of one division of militia.

Early in 1924 the Red Army underwent a major reorganization. The army was shifted to a territorial system which provided for the division of the USSR into a number of military districts in each of which was to be located a relatively small cadre of regular army troops operating in conjunction with larger reserve units.[149] Because the reserve units were to be composed of local inhabitants only, they were to be shifted gradually from the Russian language to the language predominating in each district.

Under the new system, the Ukraine was formed as a single military district in January, 1924,[150] and in the next months efforts were made to increase use of the Ukrainian language. Political lectures in Ukrainian were given to army units in the Kiev and Kharkov regions, and by June, 1924, courses in Ukrainian were being offered in sixty-nine of the district's regiments.[151] In May, 1925, the Central Committee of the CP(b)U resolved to enlarge the program.[152] The two military publications *Red Army* and *Red Fleet* were to be published in Ukrainian; all political work in army units as well as the work of the army schools and institutes was to be conducted in Ukrainian; ultimately, it was implied, all military forces were to abandon Russian in favor of Ukrainian. The changes were not to modify in any way the centralized system of conscription, training, and command of the army which existed. But it was made clear that distinct Ukrainian units were to be formed, and that they were to be trained in the Ukrainian language, commanded by Ukrainian officers, and based on Ukrainian territory.

In the matter of Ukrainization of the urban proletariat Ukrainians were also encouraged by central leaders. At the Tenth Congress of the Russian Communist Party (March, 1921) Stalin declared for the nationalization of life throughout the Ukraine, even in the predominantly Russian centers in the east. "It is clear," he stated, "that although Russian elements still predominate in the cities of the Ukraine, in the course of time these cities will inevitably be Ukrainized."[153] But the CP(b)U, dominated by Russian Bolsheviks from the urban centers of the eastern Ukraine, opposed Stalin, insisting that such a step was reactionary and counter-revolutionary.[154] As a result, no progress was made in the period from 1921 to 1923.

Under central pressure, however, the CP(b)U reversed itself early in 1923. At the Party's Seventh Conference (April, 1923) M. Frunze, speaking on the new program, called for a real effort for the Ukrainization of the city proletariat and the Party organizations.[155] Subsequently, the Party denounced the slow pace by which the proletarian masses were being drawn to Ukrainian ways and emphasized that the failure of the program was interfering seriously with the development of closer relations between the peasants and workers.[156] An editorial in *Visti* declared that Soviet construction could not be carried through unless not only the Party and Soviet apparatus was Ukrainized but also the broad masses of the people, especially the workers. Many of the proletariat, the editorial observed, were Ukrainians who had been Russified under Tsarist and bourgeois oppression and should now be redrawn to their Ukrainian heritage. In the future, as Ukrainian industry grew stronger, more and more Ukrainian peasants would be attracted to the cities, and it was essential that they be met by a Ukrainian culture. Consequently, the Party was obligated to Ukrainize the trade union organizations and to convert workers' schools and training courses, workers' literature, and workers' newspapers to Ukrainian.[157]

It is noteworthy that the program as set forth by *Visti* was never completely endorsed by Ukrainian Party or government organs. There remained strong opposition in the Party to the possibility implicit in the program that Russian workers would be forcibly Ukrainized. Nevertheless, as a minimum, Party leaders envisioned the transformation of the cities from Russian to Ukrainian centers and the conversion of workers' organizations, if not the workers themselves, to the Ukrainian language.

The third Ukrainization program—modificaton of the Ukraine's territorial-administrative structure—was proposed as a corrective for an anachronism carried over from Tsarist days. Under Tsarist rule the area of the Ukraine had been divided into nine guberniias or administrative provinces reporting directly to the government at St. Petersburg.[158] Following the Revolution these provinces had been retained despite the formation of the Ukrainian Republic. And, inasmuch as each province possessed its own administrative and Party organizations as well as its established communications links with the central government, the practice had developed within central Soviet and Party organs of by-passing Ukrainian agencies and working directly with the provinces. In June, 1923, Stalin denounced the practice. Henceforth, he declared, Russian officials should work immediately with the republics rather than the guberniias, and the republics themselves should assume responsibility for "the general work of Soviet construction" within their borders.[159] Accordingly, the provinces of the Ukraine lost much of their importance.

In May, 1925, the Ninth Ukrainian Congress of Soviets agreed to revise the republic's whole administrative structure. The guberniias were abolished, and in their place a three-tiered administrative system was established: the republic at the top, forty-two okrugs at the second level, and 523 raions at the bottom.[160] The reform was significant in two respects. First, the elimination of the guberniias increased the authority of Ukrainian republic leadership, since a part of the functions previously exercised by the provinces was shifted to the republic level. Although other functions were assumed by the okrugs, which were strengthened and carefully reorganized, the increase in republic prerogatives was more important. Secondly, the reform altered the pattern of relationships between central and Ukrainian officials. No longer was it easy for central leaders to work directly with local officials: the okrugs were too numerous for efficient central control, and the effective links formerly established with the guberniias were broken. Instead, in both the Party and government, republic agencies became cardinal transmission belts for central resolutions requiring local application. At the Fourteenth Congress of the All-Union Communist Party (December, 1925) Kaganovich noted that whereas "formerly the Central Committee of the Russian Communist

Party tied itself directly to all guberniia committees, . . . now the Central Committee of the Russian Communist Party has no direct ties with the forty-two okrugs of the Ukraine; the Central Committee has relinquished its previous rights."[161] The shift in administrative units was a critical one and increased the influence of republic organizations, particularly of Party organs in Kharkov, over the administration of local programs.

Ukrainization: the Struggle (1925-1927)

By the end of 1925 the policy of Ukrainization had been well-defined and a specific and thoroughgoing program adopted, aimed at establishing the supremacy of Ukrainian institutions and the localization of leadership and program administration. The successes achieved in the program had been uneven, and in organizations such as the trade unions and the Red Army only modest progress had been made. On the other hand, much had been accomplished in areas such as Ukrainian literature and history, primary education in the rural districts, and use of the Ukrainian language in Ukrainian commissariats, and there was a promise of more to be accomplished in the following years. In the most fundamental demands of the program, such as the demand for conversion of the schools, newspapers, and government services to the Ukrainian language, there had been little open opposition, although much resistance had been encountered as the program had been actually applied. Where the program had called for more sensitive changes, such as the conversion of the urban proletariat to Ukrainian ways, opposition had appeared almost at once and had grown steadily stronger. By 1925 it had begun to challenge even the basic postulates of the program. It was the contention over the scope and timing of the program which dominated discussions over the national question in the period from 1925 to 1927.

Even before 1925 there had appeared disquieting signs that neither central leaders nor the majority of Ukrainian Bolsheviks interpreted the localization and nationalist aspects of Ukrainization in as complete a way as did Ukrainian nationalists. The latter hoped that the Ukraine would be allowed to develop not only as a national unit with its own language, cultural forms, and historical traditions but also as a distinct element within the Soviet federation, possessing limited but genuine authority in significant areas of public policy and the opportunity to elaborate a unique form of national socialism, not in opposition to Russian Bolshevism, but as a somewhat variant type. On this question nationalists within the CP(b)U disagreed with nationalists outside the Party only in the extent to which they were willing to see socialist programs modified and Ukrainian life oriented away from Russian. Stalin's statements to Party meetings in 1923 as well as Party resolutions of that year indicated that Bolshevik leaders accepted the nationalist position at least generally. It was these statements and resolutions that encouraged Ukrainians and Russians alike to anticipate a relaxation of central controls in the Ukraine. Bolshevik support for the Ukrainization program in the years from 1923 to 1925 served to stengthen these expectations. In 1925, however, opposition to the program began to reach considerable proportions, and there were indications that Bolshevik leaders did not accept the nationalist position and were prepared under certain conditions to reverse the localization trend.

The Ukrainian Communist Party The earliest sign of official opposition appeared in discussions over the status of a unique political faction in the Ukraine—the Ukrainian Communist Party. The Party was remarkable inasmuch as it was a Communist albeit non-Bolshevik party which, nevertheless, had been allowed to function openly in the Ukraine as the only political party apart from the CP(b)U permitted to organize legally. It represented, therefore, a vestige of the pre-revolutionary period as well as a challenge to the Bolshevik policy of exclusiveness implicit in the doctrine of the dictatorship of the proletariat. The Party had been created early in 1920 by a group of "independents" among the Ukrainian Social Democrats. The "independents" favored establishing the Ukraine as a Soviet republic and hence advocated cooperation with the Bosheviks but, at the same time, placed great emphasis on the national question and hence refused to merge with them. In the tolerant atmosphere which prevailed in 1920 under the Bolshevik policy of stimulating support from Ukrainian national elements, the Ukrainian Communist Party had been ac-

cepted as a legal political group.[162] In July the Party was recognized
by the Communist International,[163] although it was not admitted
to the Comintern's Second Congress (July-August, 1920) ostensibly
on the grounds that it was too small a group to carry on "effective
Communist work."[164]

In the following years the Ukrainian Communist Party supported the Bolshevik program, although it grew steadily more critical of the New Economic Policy as well as of Russia's "colonization" activities in the Ukraine.[165] The Party was unable to attract a mass following and remained a small group of intellectual
leaders which, under Bolshevik pressure, gradually diminished in
importance. At the end of 1921 a number of Party leaders (Iurii
Mazurenko, Iavors'kyi, and others) withdrew to join the CP(b)U.
In 1923 a second group—a leftist segment headed by Kornievs'-
kyi—broke away to form the the "Left Fraction of the Ukrainian Communist Party."[167] Efforts were made by the Party in 1922
and 1923 to amalgamate with the CP(b)U under favorable conditions, but the efforts were unsuccessful.

By mid-1924 Russian Bolsheviks were convinced that the Party's
legal position could no longer be tolerated.[168] Leaders of the Ukrainian Communist Party were called to Moscow to discuss the Party's
status with representatives of the Comintern[169] and were told they
must disband. Subsequently, a resolution was adopted by the
Comintern's Executive Committee dissolving the Party and urging
its members to join the CP(b)U.[170] At the Party's Fourth Congress
(March, 1925) the decision of the Comintern was sorrowfully accepted; the Party dissolved itself, and many of its members transferred to the Bolshevik ranks.

In terms of the Party's impact on Ukrainian political life its
liquidation was of minor note. Small and unable to build an independent program acceptable to the Bolsheviks, the Party had
never become significant, and its disappearance left no noticeable
void. Yet the Party had served as a symbol of Bolshevik willingness to accept minor deviations of a nationalist character. Its dissolution was an early indication that the flexible and tolerant
policy prescribed in 1923 was to be modified and a more stringent
attitude taken toward local nationalisms.

Reorganization of the CP(b) U   Also in 1925 Bolshevik leaders
moved to strengthen the organization and structure of the CP(b)U
and to reaffirm its close ties with the Russian Communist Party
and its complete subordination to the center. From the viewpoint
of the Bolsheviks, the situation in the Ukraine as regards Party
structure and Party work was unsatisfactory. In the past the
CP(b)U had failed to develop at the republic level as a guiding
center for Party and governmental activities. Real leadership had
been provided by the guberniia committees which had come to
dominate Party affairs completely in their localities and had adopted the practice of reporting immediately to Party officials in Moscow, receiving only modest direction from CP(b)U leaders in Kharkov. The CP(b)U had become little more than a federation of
guberniia committees[171] with no responsibility for directing Party
work and with its functions limited to providing recommendations
to local Party groups and to representing the Ukraine occasionally
before central officials. In 1925 the guberniia committees were to
be abolished as the Ukraine shifted to a three-tiered system of
administration. Hence it became desirable to strengthen the center
of the CP(b)U in order that it might assume some of the functions
of the guberniia committees and assist in the reorganization of
lower Party groups, particularly at the okrug level. It was to the
task of fortifying the CP(b)U that Russian leaders turned early
in 1925.

The first change to be made was the appointment of Lazar'
M. Kaganovich to replace E. Kviring as Political or First Secretary of the CP(b)U.[172] The Kaganovich appointment installed in
the highest post in the Ukraine a central leader who had demonstrated his ability in matters of organization and administration.
His immediate tasks were to establish the CP(b)U as a powerful
institution throughout the Ukraine, to accomplish the liquidation
of the guberniia Party units, and to reorganize and stabilize Party
organs at the okrug and raion levels. At the same time, it was expected that he would take steps to ensure the loyalty of CP(b)U
leaders to the Russian Communist Party—a task which was to
grow in importance as the authority of the central organs of the
CP(b)U increased.

Specifically, Kaganovich was expected, as one of Stalin's pro-
tégés, to play an active role in the campaign being waged throughout the Soviet Union against Party opposition groups. Traditionally, the eastern sections of the Ukraine had served as major
centers for oppositionists within the Party: the Sapronov Opposition, the Workers' Opposition, groups supporting Piatakov, Rakovskii, and Trotsky.[173] Despite the purge of 1924, opposition elements had remained powerful, and the decentralized structure of
the CP(b)U worked in their favor. In 1925, as Kaganovich reconstructed the Party into a more tightly knit organization, he was
expected to isolate and root out these elements of opposition and
replace them with elements loyal to Stalin.[174] There are no indications that Kaganovich was instructed to include Ukrainian nationalists among the groups to be suppressed. Nor does it appear
that he was sent to the Ukraine to modify the Ukrainization program.[175] On the contrary, Kaganovich spoke consistently in the
early months in favor of Ukrainization, and it seems likely that
he was accepted by Ukrainian nationalists as one who would preserve a flexible policy against the centralist promptings of Zinoviev and others. It may be that Kaganovich tacitly agreed to
support the nationalists in return for their assistance in fighting
oppositionists. In any case, his appointment augured ill for the
nationalist movement, for he was to re-form the CP(b)U into a
disciplined, centralized organization which, as a subordinate section
of the Russian Communist Party, could serve as an effective instrument against nationalists and oppositionists alike.

Soon after the transfer of Kaganovich to the Ukraine, Russian
leaders moved to confirm the subordination of the CP(b)U to
Moscow. As a practical matter, the Communist parties in the republics had been functioning as subordinate organizations for many
years under the decision of the Eighth Party Congress (March,
1919).[176] But considerable confusion arose from the fact that the
Russian Communist Party ostensibly served as the Party organization only for the RSFSR. With the formation of the USSR in
1923 this peculiarity in Party structure had become more pronounced. When it was decided in 1925 to revise the Party rules,
it was decided also to clarify the Russian Communist Party's role

as both the Party organization for the RSFSR and the supreme authority directing the Communist parties in the other republics.

At the Fourteenth Party Congress (December, 1925) it was proposed that the Party be transformed into an All-Union Party.[177] Ukrainian officials urged that for the sake of consistency of organization there be created also a separate Russian Communist Party to function in the RSFSR as did the various parties in the other republics. But central leaders feared that a dual organization would weaken lines of authority. What was needed, they declared, was no substantive change but only a broader name for the Party which would express more clearly its authority throughout the USSR.[178] Accordingly, the Congress adopted for the Party the title All-Union Communist Party (Bolshevik).

On similar grounds the Congress rejected a proposal that the separate parties in the republics be abolished. In the non-Russian republics, it was argued, separate parties served an important function as expressions of national feeling and local autonomy. Yet they were not to be feared, for they were completely subordinate to the center. The Party was centralized and unified; the separate republic parties did not lessen that centralization but served only as important means of accommodation to local sentiment.[179] The Congress incorporated into the Party rules the following statement:

Party organizations serving the territory of national republics (and regions) of the Union of Soviet Socialist Republics and of the Russian Socialist Federative Soviet Republic are on the same plane as regional (or provincial) organizations of the Party; i.e., they are entirely subordinate to the Central Committee of the All-Union Communist Party.[180]

At the same time, the Congress increased the degree of practical control exercised by central officials over local Party workers. In the past, Party members chosen as workers in local Party committees or as editors of local Party newspapers or journals had been confirmed only at the next higher level, by republic or regional officials. The Congress agreed now to require confirmation also by the All-Union Central Committee.[181]

Attacks on the Ukrainization program By 1926 the organizational reform of the CP(b)U was completed and the Party's close ties with the All-Union Communist Party expressed anew.[182] Simultaneously, there appeared new direct attacks on the Ukrainization program. The attacks were the culmination of a long-smoldering resentment within both the Russian Communist Party and the CP(b)U against the privileged position which, it was claimed, the program accorded ethnic Ukrainians. The resentment broke out initially at the Thirteenth Party Congress (May, 1924) when both Zinoviev and Molotov spoke harshly of Ukrainian Bolsheviks. Zinoviev accused them of emphasizing Ukrainization too strongly and of failing to safeguard, as the Party had required, the rights of the Ukraine's minorities—the Germans, Poles, Moldavians, Jews, etc.[183] Molotov attacked them for their failure to recognize the importance of drawing workers into the Party and, specifically, for the decision of the Eighth Conference of the CP(b)U, taken only a few days earlier, that the Party would strive to draw 65 to 70 percent of its members from the workers' class, although the Russian Communist Party had set a goal of 90 percent.[184] These objections were accepted only in part by the Thirteenth Congress. Mild resolutions were adopted on safeguarding minority rights and drawing workers into the Party; but greater emphasis was placed on the continued importance of the peasant question and on the necessity of expanding localization work.[185]

At the Fourteenth Party Congress (December, 1925) Zinoviev renewed his attack, declaring now that the CP(b)U had catered to the wealthy peasants—the kulaks—and ignored the interests of the poor.[186] Zinoviev was no longer influential in the Party, however, and his views were once again rejected.

At the same time, other attacks appeared from within the CP(b)U. There were charges that the Party was accepting the leadership of Ukrainian chauvinists, that it was exaggerating Ukrainization work, that it was forcing citizens of the Ukraine to learn a "non-existent" language.[187] But the charges were made not by official Party spokesmen, but by oppositionists attacking the Party core Stalin had built around himself in the Central Committee. As a result, the charges were easily dismissed by Ukrainian nationalists who apparently came to view Stalin as the most faithful defender of national prerogatives. Throughout the sessions of the Fourteenth Congress, Ukrainian leaders supported Stalin against the opposition.[188]

In 1925 and 1926, however, attacks appeared from a new and more responsible quarter. The first such attack was a general and relatively moderate criticism of the failure of all the Soviet republics, including the RSFSR, to guarantee the rights of the national minorities living within their borders. The criticism was made by Iu. Larin, who noted to the Third Congress of Soviets of the USSR (May, 1925) that the national problem in the Soviet Union had been only partially solved by the creation of separate national republics and that it could be completely solved only if special guarantees were given also to the various minorities within each republic.[189] For example, he explained, the Ukrainian and Russian minorities in the Kirgiz Republic, although comprising over 37 percent of the total popuation, were not guaranteed the right to use their own languages. In parts of the RSFSR Ukrainian minorities were forced to attend Russian schools, and in the UkSSR the policy of Ukrainization was being used to force Russian, Jewish, and Polish groups to learn Ukrainian. As a result, the Soviet policy of localization—correct as a general policy—was being transformed into a device for repressing the separate minorities in the republics just as the majority groups in the border areas had been repressed earlier under Tsarist rule. It was necessary, he concluded, for the majority nationality in each republic to recognize the same rights and guarantees for the minorities of the republic that the majority had demanded for itself from the USSR.

Larin was answered by representatives of the republics who insisted that he had misrepresented the situation and that, although mistakes had been made, the republics were taking active steps to guarantee the rights of their minorities:[190] special administrative units were being formed; special schools had been established; minority languages were being accepted in administrative and judicial proceedings. Yet it was plain that most of the delegates to the Congress of Soviets sympathized with Larin. At the conclusion of its work the Congress called on the USSR Central Executive Committee to take special steps to guarantee the rights of all the minorities in each of the republics.[191]

In April, 1926, the problem was more carefully presented and more fully discussed at the Second Session of the Third Convocation of the USSR Central Executive Committee. The debate was touched off by a report to the Committee given by Vlas Chubar', who spoke on the work of the Ukrainian government in the previous years.[192] Included in his report was a discussion of the Ukrainization program in which Chubar' pointed out that, although much work remained to be done, important successes had been achieved in expanding the use of the Ukrainian language. His statement was moderate and was generally approved in the discussion which followed. Once again, however, Larin took the floor with a long and careful criticism, castigating Ukrainian leaders for failing, in their Ukrainization zeal, to protect the rights of the minorities in the Ukraine—the Germans, Poles, Jews, and above all the Russians who, he declared, were being persecuted both in public life and in community activities.[193] Again Ukrainian leaders defended their work, pointing out that the Russian language was still predominant in the Ukraine, was the primary language at Party and government meetings, and held a privileged position in publications and in the work of the schools.[194] Again, however, it was obvious that many members of the Central Executive Committee endorsed Larin's criticisms. In a concluding report Enukidze directed the Ukrainians to guard more closely against perversions in the Ukrainization program and to guarantee the rights of the Russian and other minorities in the Ukraine as fully as the rights of Ukrainians.[195] No immediate measures against the Ukrainian government were taken by the Central Executive Committee.[196] But the episode was a serious one, first, because it marked a distinct separating point ending an era in which Ukrainization was supported by Russian leaders and beginning a period in which it was criticzed with increasing severity; and, secondly, because it set the theme which later attacks were to develop more fully that the Ukrainization program, though desirable in itself, needed to be restricted in order to safeguard the rights of the Ukraine's minorities.

Stalin and Shums'kyi   At the same time, a more damaging though considerably milder attack appeared from another quarter.

The circumstances preceding the attack are not fully known but can be reconstructed generally as follows. In 1924 Oleksandr Shums'kyi, perhaps the most resolute nationalist among the leaders of the CP(b)U, had been appointed Commissar of Education—a post of major importance for the Ukrainization program. During 1925 he had become impatient with the progress of the program, apparently with some justification, inasmuch as reports in the closing months of 1925 noted that only the most limited successes had been achieved.[197] He had also become disturbed by the strong opposition he had encountered within the CP(b)U and had become convinced that the majority of Party leaders were not seriously working to complete Ukrainization. Early in 1926 he had gone directly to Stalin, appealing to him to intervene in the Ukraine to correct the shortcomings there. He had emphasized: that Ukrainization was being accomplished only reluctantly and very haltingly; that it was necessary, if the program were to succeed, to convert the proletariat quickly to Ukrainian ways and to place Ukrainians rather than Russians in leadership posts, especially in the Party and trade unions; that Kaganovich, whom he accused of emphasizing Party organization work to the exclusion of all else, should be withdrawn from the Ukraine, and the top leadership posts in the government and Party assumed by the Ukrainian nationalists Grin'ko and Chubar'.[198] Stalin replied in a letter sent to Kaganovich and other leaders of the CP(b)U in which he outlined his attitude to the national problem in the Ukraine and presented the first hints of a growing opposition to the Ukrainization program.

The letter was couched in the moderate language Stalin used so frequently to contrast the evils of two extreme positions he opposed with the sensible moderation of his own middle way. He began by agreeing that Shums'kyi had correctly evaluated the importance of the Ukrainian national movement and the importance for the Bosheviks of identifying themselves with Ukrainian culture and Ukrainian growth. He agreed that it was necessary to oppose Party and Soviet cadres who had failed to understand the significance of the Ukrainian national movement and had adopted a sceptical attitude toward Ukrainian culture and life. He affirmed the necessity of building new cadres of workers able to understand the "new movement in the Ukraine." Nevertheless, he refused to accept Shums'kyi's recommendations for correcting these weaknesses because of the accompanying critical errors he declared Shums'kyi had made—errors which were more dangerous for the Bolsheviks than the weaknesses of the Ukrainization program.

First, he noted that Shums'kyi had erred in supporting a speedy and compulsory Ukrainization of the proletarian class—a program which, Stalin claimed, would only develop as a form of oppression against the minorities in the Ukraine and would in practice defeat its own purpose by giving rise to new outbreaks of anti-Ukrainian chauvinism. Stalin restated his opinion, first expressed in 1921, that the proletariat would eventually be Ukrainized, but he insisted that the process would be a "long, spontaneous, natural" one that could not be forced. Secondly, he reproached Shums'kyi for his failure to recognize the "shadowy" side of the Ukrainian national movement—a side which was characterized by a struggle "for the estrangement of Ukrainian culture and Ukrainian life from general Soviet culture and life" and by a struggle "against 'Moscow' in general, against the Russians in general, against the Russian culture and its highest achievement—Leninism." It was clear, Stalin noted, that this form of nationalism had been growing in the Ukraine and that its destruction was essential if Ukrainian culture were to develop and flower as a Soviet culture. Thirdly, Stalin criticized Shums'kyi for his failure to understand the importance of timing in his demand that Ukrainians be drawn into the highest government and Party posts. It was desirable, Stalin recognized, that the top leadership be ethnically Ukrainian, but there was no question that Marxist cadres in the Ukraine were as yet too weak to permit their quick substitution for Russian leaders. Any such replacement would result only in the weakening of general leadership work and a lessening of the prestige of the highest government and Party bodies.[199]

Stalin's letter suggested no revolutionary changes to Ukrainian leaders. The Ukrainization program was to continue with its ultimate objectives the same and its pace officially accepted at the level it had actually achieved in the preceding years. Yet there was a notable shift in emphasis on three points which indicated a turn in Stalin's approach to the nationalization program. The turn was a vital one, first, because it led to a struggle over the Ukrainization program which was to dominate Ukrainian political life in 1926 and 1927 and, secondly and of much greater importance, because it paved the way for a later hardening of Stalin's attitude on the national question and for the eventual suspension of the Ukrainization program.

The first shift involved the question of Bolshevik toleration of variants or differences of expression in areas of public life such as language and culture. In the period from 1923 to 1925 a large measure of toleration had been shown in the Ukraine, especially in the fields of literature and history where independent writing and study had been encouraged.[200] This independence had been carried furthest in the field of literature, and many literary organizations had appeared with numerous Ukrainian writers producing not only controversial writings but also broad statements on the question of the role of national culture in a proletarian society.[201] The most complete and clear-cut of these statements was formulated by a Bolshevik Ukrainian writer, Mykola Khvyl'ovyi, who in April, 1925, presented the first of a series of writings urging the greatest independence of Ukrainian culture from Russian. Russian literature, he suggested, had for centuries enslaved Ukrainian writing, forcing it to follow a Muscovite pattern which had impeded its development. If Ukrainian art forms were to grow, they must look for instruction and guidance away from Moscow and to Europe, where the seeds of a great new socialist culture could be found. That Ukrainian culture was to be socialist, Khvyl'ovyi consistently affirmed, but he also insisted that it was to be distinctly non-Russian in character.[202] Other Ukrainian writers joined Khvyl'ovyi, and by 1926 it was apparent that a large section of the Ukrainian literary movement was moving away from Russian influence. To Stalin and other Russian leaders the difficulties posed by these writers emphasized the importance of clarifying the Bolshevik position toward national cultures and local differences of expression.

The problem had already been examined briefly by Stalin who had been asked in May, 1925, to explain specifically the apparent contradiction between socialist insistence on the achievement of a single *universal* culture and Boshevik slogans for the development of separate *national* cultures.[203] Stalin had refused to explain how the problem would eventually be solved in a world communist society, suggesting merely that separate languages would continue to exist for an indefinite period; but he had outlined his solution for the immediate future. Although the slogan of national culture had been a reactionary bourgeois slogan in the pre-revolutionary period, he noted, under the conditions of Soviet life national culture had become an essential part of the building of a proletarian culture; for, although proletarian culture required a uniform, universal, socialist content, it would assume in practice "different forms and modes of expression among different peoples . . . in accordance with their differences in language, customs, etc."[204] Hence proletarian culture would be marked as one "socialist in content and national in form." Exactly how the concepts "content" and "form" were to be distinguished, Stalin did not explain. Clearly, Boshevik principles on the organization of society were to be considered "content," while the language in which the principles were expressed was to be considered "form"; hence the publication of Lenin's writings in the languages of the border republics would be an example of proletarian culture assuming a national form and a socialist content.[205] However, Stalin intended the expression "national in form" to apply to more than the use of local languages. Although he was not explicit, he suggested that matters such as literary form and style, approaches to aspects of local history, the method of presentation of the peasant-proletarian question, etc., were matters of "form," not "content" and should be given a national complexion.

In his letter of April, 1926, to Ukrainian Bolsheviks, however, Stalin adopted a more rigid view, asserting that the writings of Khvyl'ovyi had gone beyond the limits of national form and were striking at Soviet culture itself. Again he made no effort to distinguish carefully between "form" and "content," but he insisted that literary expressions involved a question of substance if they encouraged Ukrainians to draw on the experience of other areas in opposition to the experience of Russia. Accordingly, he urged

Ukrainian Bolsheviks to adopt a more inflexible position toward literary exclusiveness.

At the same time, Stalin's letter hinted at a shift in emphasis on two other questions which also were to lead to a less tolerant Bolshevik approach to the nationalization program. The first involved the matter of the relationship of politics to culture under Bolshevik leadership or, more broadly, the relationship of politics to wide areas of public and private life. In 1923 Party members had listened to and generally accepted the views of Ukrainian nationalists such as Grin'ko and Skrypnik, who had urged the development of separate national cultures which would be socialist but, nonetheless, distinct from one another.[206] Their arguments had been absorbed by Khvyl'ovyi and other Ukrainians who had urged the separation of politics from culture, affirming that the political union of Russia and the Ukraine in no way affected their cultural development.[207] Stalin refused to accept such a view, declaring flatly to Ukrainian Bolsheviks that Khvyl'ovyi's "attempt to separate culture from politics [is] ludicrous and non-Marxist."[208] Stalin thereby opened the door for an increasingly close scrutiny of all cultural expressions in the Ukraine and for a mounting interference by Bolshevik leaders in all aspects of Ukrainian life.

Finally, Stalin presented in his letter a strong defense of Russia, of Russian leadership, and of Russian institutions which suggested a rebirth under the Soviet banner of the earlier Tsarist identification of its rule with Russian interests.

[The national movement in the Ukraine] may assume in places the form of a battle for the separation of Ukrainian culture and Ukrainian public life from general Soviet culture and public life, the form of a battle against "Moscow" in general, against Russians in general, against the Russian culture and its highest achievement —Leninism. . . . The demand of Khvyl'ovyi for the "immediate de-Russification of the proletariat" in the Ukraine, his opinion that "Ukrainian poetry must separate itself as quickly as possible from Russian literature and from its style," his assertion that "the ideas of the proletariat are known to us without Moscow art," . . . sounds more than strange. At a time when the West European proletariat and its Communist parties are in full sympathy with "Moscow,"

with this citadel of the international revolutionary movement and
of Leninism, at a time when the West European proletariat looks
with admiration at the banner flying over Moscow, the Ukrainian
communist Khvyl'ovyi can say nothing in favor of "Moscow"
except for Ukrainian leaders to run from "Moscow" "as quickly
as possible." [It is] only by combating extremes like Khvyl'ovyi's
within the Communist ranks ... that the rising Ukrainion culture
and public life can be converted into a *Soviet* culture and public
life.[209]

Stalin's defense of Russian superiority was founded on two points:
first, that Russian development in Marxist terms—that is, in the
growth of a proletarian class and in the concentration and opposition of class interests—had proceeded further than the development of the border republics; and, secondly, that Russia was
unique not only within the USSR but throughout the world as
the locus for the first successful proletarian revolution and the
development of Leninism. These points were not original in
Stalin's letter but had been expressed previously by him as well
as other Russian leaders. At the Tenth Party Congress (March,
1921) he had noted that Russia was "politically and industrially
better developed" than the other Soviet republics and that it was
obligated to assist the backward peoples to catch up in political,
cultural, and economic respects.[210] At the Twelfth Party Congress
(April, 1923) he had repeated these views, emphasizing more
strongly than before the advanced level Russia had attained and
its mission to stimulate growth in the border republics.[211] But in
these early statements there had been no suggestion of a deliberate
glorification of Russia or of Russian culture. On the contrary, the
Twelfth Congress had declared in a resolution that "statements
about the superiority of Russian culture, and the presentation of
views urging the inevitable victory of the higher Russian culture
over the cultures of the more backward peoples (Ukrainian, Azerbaidzhan, Uzbek, Kirgiz, etc.) are nothing more than attempts to
fortify the dominance of the Great-Russian nationality."[212] By
1926, however, Stalin was beginning to identify Russia and Russian
institutions with Marxism and Bolshevik rule. As a result, he
refused to accept demands for an independent Ukrainian culture
and signified that the Ukraine could develop a genuine Soviet

society only by borrowing from Russian patterns and Russian practices.[213]

Where the question of Russian versus local influence in the border republics involved the problem of leadership, Stalin also reversed himself. In June, 1923, at the Fourth Conference of the Russian Central Committee he had spoken strongly for local leadership of Party and government institutions in all the Soviet republics. "Local people who know the language and customs of the population must be placed at the head of the state institutions in the republics," he had declared. Specifically, he had noted with approval that in the Kirgiz and Bashkir republics Russians had been removed from the highest government posts and replaced with native leaders. This work, he had declared, should be extended to all government institutions and especially to the Ukraine.[214] In 1926, however, he refused to reaffirm this view. Although he recognized that top leadership in the Ukraine should ultimately be Ukrainian, he insisted that no major shift could be made immediately because of the weakness of Ukrainian Marxist cadres and the necessity of maintaining strong Russian leadership until cadres could be trained.[215]

Underlying all the changes in emphasis found in Stalin's statement of April, 1926, was a growing confidence among Russian leaders that the uncertainties of Bolshevik rule which had prompted concessions to the nationalities had been overcome. Like the New Economic Policy, the policy of nationality concessions had been adopted in large measure as a compromise, openly recognized as a method of winning the support of faltering groups among the border republics. By 1926, the position of the Soviet Union in international affairs had been stabilized, and Bolshevik authority inside the USSR firmly established. Hence the old willingness to accept national deviations, to encourage "more or less loyal" elements of the local population to participate in Soviet rule was gone.

In regard to the intra-Party rivalries which claimed so much of the attention of central leaders throughout the early 1920s, Stalin's letter was doubly significant. Before 1926, in working to strengthen his position in the Party, Stalin had sought the support of the border nationalities by adopting a flexible and tolerant attitude toward local differences. The Ukrainization program was a result, at least in part, of his campaign to build a strong personal following in what was one of the Soviet Union's most important regional Party organizations, the CP(b)U. His task had been simplified by the stern opposition to the nationalities expressed by his principal rivals Trotsky and Zinoviev: Trotsky had consistently shown little sympathy for demands for local autonomy and, in the Ukraine, had looked for support to the eastern, predominantly pro-Russian Party organizations; Zinoviev, in 1920, 1924, and 1925, had taken the lead in denouncing Ukrainian nationalists and in opposing concessions to the USSR's minorities. On the basis of the centralist, Russifying views of these opponents and fortified by the Ukrainization program, Stalin had been able with little difficulty to win the personal allegiance of anti-centralist, anti-Russification Ukrainian Bolsheviks.

By 1926 the struggle within the Party was largely over, and Stalin's position of leadership generally accepted. Personal support from the non-Russian nationalities was no longer of critical importance, and Stalin was able to begin discussing the national question as no more than one aspect of the whole complex of Bolshevik policy. His letter on Shums'kyi was in a sense a declaration of his independence of Ukrainian nationalists and a statement of his intention to abandon the concessions he had made earlier in his drive for Ukrainian support. In so far as Shums'kyi understood the extent of Stalin's shift in policy it must have been with considerable bitterness that he regarded what could only have appeared to him as a dishonest tactical maneuver.

Reaction of the CP(b)U   For the nationalist and moderate members of the CP(b)U, Shums'kyi's appeal to Stalin was unfortunate, for it provided justification for increased attacks on the Ukrainization program both by central leaders and by the extreme anti-nationalist Russian wing of the Ukrainian Party. On May 12, 1926, Stalin's letter and the defense presented by Shums'kyi were discussed at a meeting of the Politburo of the CP(b)U. Efforts were made to convince Shums'kyi to abandon his stand and repudiate Khvyl'ovyi, but he refused, announcing, "I do not disavow anything in my past," and declaring that he regarded Khvyl'ovyi as a "cultured young proletarian, called to carry on a cultural revolution."[216] Party leaders, led as might have been expected by Kaganovich, at once took steps to disassociate themselves from Shums'kyi and, at the same time, to forestall attacks on the Ukrainization program by re-emphasizing its importance. In a letter to the Ukrainian Politburo dated June 4, 1926, Kaganovich and Chubar', as heads of the Ukrainian Party and government, denounced the "irresponsible position" of comrade Shums'kyi and expressed their concern over the conditions which had given rise to such a deviation. Nevertheless, they insisted, it was also necessary to recognize that the problem he had raised could be solved only through a strict adherence to the Ukrainization program which was now even more important than before.

We must anticipate the danger that, as a result of the irresponsible position of comrade Shums'kyi, there may develop a reaction and a certain withdrawal, at first psychological but later practical, against the achievement of the national policy of the Party, namely Ukrainization. This would present the greatest threat for the Party, especially in view of the general Party situation, and we must guard the Central Committee and its entire organization against such a development.[217]

Subsequently, a plenary session of the Central Committee of the CP(b)U, meeting in June, 1926, adopted a comprehensive resolution setting forth the Party's attitude on the national question.[218] The resolution was remarkable, inasmuch as it reflected an approach much different from that suggested in Stalin's letter. The theme repeated again and again was the necessity of overcoming all obstacles to the successful achievement of Ukrainization.

The unique conditions of the historical development of the Ukraine resulting in the Russification of the Ukrainian city and a large part of its proletariat on the one hand, and on the other hand, the harsh battle with the counterrevolution, represented by the Ukrainian socialist-chauvinist parties, and the existence among some comrades leading our Party in the Ukraine in the first years of the civil war of Luxemburgist views on the national question,—all have resulted in the fact that the Ukrainian party organization in the beginning underevaluated the importance of the national question in the revolutionary battle in the Ukraine, and some comrades went so far as to deny even the existence of the Ukrainian nation. From this developed a misunderstanding of the Leninist solution of the national question, an underevaluation of the importance of the Ukrainian language and of the development of the Ukrainian culture as a powerful means for the cultural elevation of the masses, as a basic weapon for strengthening the bond of the workers class with the peasantry and as a necessary condition for the construction of socialism.

The resolution referred to the decisions of the Twelfth Party Congress on localization and emphasized again that Party organizations must master the Ukrainian language and understand Ukrainian social, political, historical, and cultural conditions. Although recognizing that progress had been made in the task of Ukrainization, the resolution noted that much work yet remained to be done.

Great difficulties remain ahead of us. We as yet have achieved no decisive results in the area of Ukrainization of the Party, and without this it will be extraordinarily difficult for the Party to guide all the developing and increasingly complex cultural processes among the Ukrainian masses; hence there is required the maximum concentration of the strength and will of the Party for further efforts for Ukrainization.

In addition, the resolution emphasized the continued importance of battling against Great-Russian chauvinism, quoting—despite Stalin's letter—the decision of the Twelfth Party Congress that "statements about the superiority of the Russian culture are nothing more than attempts to fortify the dominance of the Russian nationality." The resolution declared:

The Party must conduct both within its own ranks and also among the proletarian masses a decisive battle with the prejudices of the Russian and Russified groups of the proletariat, with the perversions of internationalism, with pseudo-internationalist, Russophile chauvinism. The Party must unmask before the proletariat the whole reactionary character of Russian chauvinism, revealing its roots, historical origins, etc. The Party must stubbornly, systematically, and patiently explain to the workers' class its responsibility for strengthening bonds with the Ukrainian village, must guide it to take its active part in Ukrainization by a study of the Ukrainian language, by making itself acquainted with its history, etc.,strengthening proletarian leadership of the growing cultural movement. The Party must see to the creation of favorable conditions for the Ukrainization of the proletariat of the Ukrainian industrial centers.

At only a few points did the resolution take note of Stalin's criticisms. In speaking about Ukrainization of the workers' class and of the Party itself, it was agreed, as Stalin had suggested, that the work must proceed at a moderate tempo, since it was important to avoid alienating workers and Party members from Soviet policy. Similarly, it was recognized that a distinction should be made between Russian workers in the cities, on the one hand, who should be viewed as a minority in the Ukraine and hence excluded from the Ukrainization program, and the formerly Ukrainian but now Russified city workers, on the other hand, who should be redrawn to their native language and culture. The resolution also accepted Stalin's denunciation of Ukrainian chauvinism and particularly of attempts such as Khvyl'ovyi's to separate Ukrainian from Russian cultural development. It was important, the resolution noted, for Ukrainian culture to grow by drawing widely on the experience of many countries; but its growth should not be apart or separate from Russian, as Khvyl'ovyi had urged, but should proceed in "brotherly cooperation."

Although no records of the meetings of the Central Committee at which the resolution was adopted are available, it seems clear that the document was written by the nationalists within the CP(b)U and accepted by the pro-Stalinist Russian group headed by Kaganovich.[219] Specifically, the document seems to have reflected the views of Skrypnik and Chubar' as expressed to the Twelfth Congress of the Russian Communist Party and to Party meetings in Moscow and the Ukraine in 1926.[220] At no point did the resolution contradict Stalin's letter directly, but in its emphasis and approach it was an independent document with different implications. Leaders of the CP(b)U perhaps failed to realize the degree to which Stalin had abandoned his earlier national program and, hence, the extent of their opposition. Had they done so, the resolution might not have been adopted, although some, such as Skrypnik, had freely opposed Stalin in the past and were willing to do so again. In any case, the resolution represented a real protest against the weaknesses of the Ukrainization program as well as an attack on the large group of Party members which resisted its achievement. It was the most complete and sympathetic statement on the national question in the Ukraine to be adopted by the CP(b)U.[221]

Although the resolution was approved by the leaders of the CP(b)U, it was by no means accepted by all Party groups. Throughout 1926 and 1927 the Party comprised three factions holding separate positions on the national question. On one extreme was a small group headed by Shums'kyi, which continued to insist on the broadest interpretation of the Ukrainization program. Specifically, the group urged a quickening of the pace of Ukrainization, the application of the program to the proletariat of the Ukraine, an orientation of Ukrainian culture away from Russia, and a strong campaign against the pro-Russian "colonizing" members of the CP(b)U. In addition, the group defended the work of Ukrainian nationalists in the fields of literature and history. Shums'kyi upheld the writings of Khvyl'ovyi even after the writer himself had publicly recanted,[222] other members of the group supported nationalist historians such as Hrushevs'kyi and Iefremov.[223] The group was generally ineffective, not only because of the attack made upon it by Stalin, but because of the antagonisms within the CP(b)U Shums'kyi had aroused. Nevertheless, it played an important role in the struggle over Ukrainization by keeping before Party leaders a most liberal interpretation of the program and by crystallizing disagreements over the scope the program was to take.

A second position on the national question was taken by a majority of Party leaders including Skrypnik, Chubar', Kaganovich, Petrovs'kyi, and others. The group's position was that of the Central Committee's June resolution with its strong support for Ukrainization and its mild opposition to the urgings of Shums'kyi. Apparently the group opposed Shums'kyi partly because of his position on Ukrainization and partly because of personal hostility but, above all, because of his basic challenge to the dominant position of ethnic Russians within the CP(b)U and to the whole structure of Russian-Ukrainian relations. By urging Ukrainization

of the Russian proletariat and a campaign against the "colonization" tendencies of Russians in both the Ukrainian and Russian
Communist Parties, Shums'kyi was attacking not only the principal base on which Bolshevik authority in the Ukraine was built,
but also the fundamental compromise between Ukrainian and
Russian leaders on which the program of Ukrainization had been
developed. This compromise, undoubtedly unexpressed or even
recognized as such, called for an acceptance by Stalin and Russian
Bolsheviks of a localization program for the Ukraine and a measure
of independence for the CP(b)U, in return for which the CP(b)U
would support Stalin against opposition groups and would accept
central leadership on questions of high policy and on matters of
importance for the Union as a whole. Shums'kyi's opposition
threatened, therefore, not only Russian leaders within the CP(b)U
but also Ukrainian nationalist Bolsheviks, who understood better
than Shums'kyi the limitations set for the Ukrainization program
and who feared reprisals if his challenge were encouraged. The
group supported a strong statement of the Ukrainization program
and its broadest application throughout the Ukraine;[224] but the
group was unwilling to go as far as Shums'kyi in his suggestion
that the Ukraine should develop as a politically independent unit
within the Soviet Union.

The third position on the national question was that of a group
of Russian, anti-Ukrainian members of the CP(b)U. The group
drew chief support from Party organizations in the eastern districts
of the Ukraine where the percentage of Russian members was high,
but it included none of the Party leaders, although some were
undoubtedly sympathetic.[225] The group was weakened because
it had been identified in the past with opposition factions and,
even in 1926 and 1927, included among its leaders oppositionists
such as Lobanov.[226] Its principal spokesman was Iu. Larin, who
had attacked the Ukrainization program in 1925 and in April,
1926, and who restated his views at the June Plenum (1926) of
the Ukrainian Central Committee[227] and again in an article appearing in the official journal of the All-Union Communist Party,
Bol'shevik.[228] His position deserves fuller statement not because

it was accepted at once but because, oracle-like, it foreshadowed many of the points Soviet leaders later were to emphasize.

Larin's chief objection to the Ukrainization program was its forced application to minority groups, especially Russian workers and Russian city-dwellers. The culture of the proletariat and of urban areas, he insisted, was predominantly—almost exclusively— Russian, and efforts to force an artificial acceptance of another culture would serve only to drive loyal adherents of the Party away from the Bolsheviks. This applied not only to ethnic Russians, but also to Ukrainian and Jewish workers who, in moving to the city, had adopted the city culture and relinquished their original ethnic identity. Equally unfortunate results would ensue, Larin predicted, if the state and Party apparatus, schools, and public institutions were Ukrainized in areas where Ukrainians did not predominate. Already, he observed, Russian workers in the Ukraine were complaining that Russian films were no longer being shown and that trade union and Party meetings were meaningless, being conducted in Ukrainian. This did not mean, Larin conceded, that the Ukrainian language should not be accepted as the official language, or even that Russian workers should not be expected to learn it to ensure close ties with the peasants; but it did emphasize the importance of accepting Russian as an equally official language in order to preserve the linguistic freedom of the quarter of the Ukraine's population—including a majority of the inhabitants of the cities—which knew no other. To follow a different course, Larin believed, would be to encourage the "Russophobes" and "Petliurists" who already had been drawn in great numbers into cultural work in the Ukraine and were attempting to weaken Soviet power and increase national hostilities.

The conflict within the CP(b) U   Early in 1927 the conflict among the three factions of the CP(b)U reached a climax. The struggle developed along two separate lines with the center group in the CP(b)U striking first against the Shums'kyi deviation and then against the opposition of Larin. The struggle became a personalized one as Skrypnik became identified as the spokesman of the center group and assumed much of the direction for the campaigns against both Shums'kyi and Larin.

The immediate controversy between Shums'kyi, on the one hand, and the majority of Ukrainian Party leaders, on the other, was quickly decided. Already in December, 1926, Shums'kyi had been replaced, for all practical purposes, as Commissar of Education. In March, 1927, he was formally removed from his post[229] and was ousted, as well, as general editor of the Ukrainian journal *Chervonyi shliakh*. Subsequently, he was withdrawn from the Ukraine —apparently on the advice of the CP(b)U—and assigned to trade union work in Moscow.

More important than Shums'kyi's personal fate was the support he continued to receive, not primarily from Party members inside the UkSSR, but from Ukrainian Bolsheviks in the adjoining districts of Poland, in the region known as Eastern Galicia or the Western Ukraine. There the Communist Party of the Western Ukraine—a branch of the Polish Communist Party—had consistently expressed its agreement with Shums'kyi, defending his position in meetings of the CP(b)U and at sessions of the Executive Committee of the Comintern.[230] The defection of these Bolsheviks was of grave concern for Russian and Ukrainian leaders alike because it challenged Soviet efforts to build the Ukraine as an international showcase depicting the favorable features of Bolshevik national policy. Soviet leaders had hoped through such a display, first, to stimulate unrest in the Ukrainian districts adjoining the Soviet Union in Poland, Rumania, and Czechoslovakia and, secondly, to develop sympathy for Soviet national policy generally among restive minority groups everywhere throughout the world. The opposition of the Communist Party threatened to weaken these efforts. "Shums'kyism" became identified, therefore, as an expression of unwillingness to accept official Party policy and as a focus for opposition outside the Soviet Union to Bolshevik leadership. Its implications challenged the Bolshevik program much more broadly than had Shums'kyi's direct criticisms of Ukrainization work. Throughout 1927 the CP(b)U, the Executive Committee of the Comintern, and leaders of the All-Union Communist Party, in a succession of resolutions, decisions, letters, and investigations, sought to stamp out this deviation in the Western Ukraine.[231] It was hoped that forceful measures against the Party organization would not be required and that local leaders could be persuaded to disavow Shums'kyi and reaffirm their loyalty to the Russian center. The Western Ukrainian Bolsheviks refused to do so, however, and in February, 1928, the Comintern expelled the group from its membership. Although the Party was subsequently reconstructed along acceptable lines,[232] many of its members continued to affirm their support for Shums'kyi. The problem remained a difficult one for central leaders until April, 1930, when Shums'kyi withdrew completely from his position, recognizing his errors and accepting official policy.[233]

The opposition between leaders of the CP(b)U and Larin was a more difficult one. Shums'kyi's views had found support within the Party among only a small group of Ukrainian nationalists; Larin's views, however, were broadly appealing. Despite Party pronouncements attacking Great-Russian chauvinism and despite many declarations that Russian nationalism was the chief obstacle to a solution of the national problem, there was no question that Party members throughout the Soviet Union and the Ukraine were chiefly concerned with local nationalisms. Indicative of the support Larin enjoyed was the publication of his views in the official Party journal *Bol'shevik* and the subsequent dispatch to the Ukraine of a central Party leader Iaroslavskii to investigate Larin's charges.[234] It must have been apparent to Ukrainian leaders that they could not reject these Russian complaints as easily and completely as they had rejected the complaints made by Shums'kyi.

The uncertainty of Ukrainian leaders was indicated in the early months of 1927. At meetings in Kharkov the moderately nationalist leaders Chubar' and Petrovs'kyi attacked Larin's pro-Russian views.[235] Larin's charge that Ukrainization had been sufficiently carried out was rejected by Chubar', who noted that government and Party reports in the Ukraine were still normally given in Russian; Petrovs'kyi declared more broadly that Larin's "scribblings" were completely without foundation.

An opposite position was taken by other Ukrainian leaders. Zatons'kyi, speaking with Petrovs'kyi in Kharkov, referred to many instances in which Ukrainization had taken a repressive form and concluded that greater guarantees for the rights of minorities in the Ukraine, especially the Russian minority, were necessary.[236]

Unfortunately no records are available of Party meetings in which the disagreement over Larin's criticisms was discussed. At the March (1927) Plenum of the Central Committee Kaganovich took a middle stand, denouncing both Ukrainian nationalists and Russian chauvinists; the final resolution of the plenum called for the rooting out of all nationalist deviations, especially the chauvinism of the Russian proletariat in the Ukraine.[237] Nevertheless, it seems clear that Party leaders as a whole, either under pressure from Russian Bolsheviks[238] or from a conviction that a compromise was necessary, were gradually moving to the acceptance of a more limited Ukrainization program. In April, 1927, the Central Committee adopted a new resolution on Ukrainization in which the old declarations for an expanded use of the Ukrainian language were repeated but were accompanied by a new insistence that the rights of the minorities be guaranteed and special care taken to preserve Russian schools as well as general acceptance of the Russian language.[239] In May the decree requiring that all inscriptions in railway, bus, and waterway stations be printed in Ukrainian was amended to require posting in both Russian and Ukrainian.[240] On July 6 the Ukrainian government adopted a new law on language use which modified considerably the Ukrainization program. The law repeated earlier declarations that Ukrainian was the official state language, but it provided in practice for a dual-language system:[241] Russian and Ukrainian were to be compulsory languages in all the schools of the Ukraine; decisions of all government agencies, local as well as central, were to be published in both languages; efforts to draw minority groups, especially the Russian, to the use of the Ukrainian language were to be abandoned; the right of each citizen to use his own language freely and in all his dealings with the state was guaranteed. Ukrainian was given a preferred position only in three requirements: 1) that Ukrainian be used in all routine governmental communications and papers together with any other appropriate minority language; 2) that higher schools be conducted in Ukrainian except where local conditions dictated otherwise; 3) that government workers be required to know Ukrainian as well as the predominant local language. The law marked the abandonment, for all practical purposes, of the principle, accepted earlier, of ultimate Ukrainization of the cities and incorporated many of the changes in the Ukrainization program demanded by Larin.

At the same time, in a general resolution adopted by the Central Committee of the CP(b)U and transmitted to the Executive Committee of the Comintern as a report on nationalist deviations in the Ukraine,[242] Ukrainian leaders declared that their position on Ukrainization was in the future to be a moderate one, avoiding both the nationalist pitfall represented by Shums'kyi, on the one hand, and the Russian chauvinist pitfall typified by Larin, on the other. In an expression which probably originated with Skrypnik, the resolution called for the strengthening of Soviet power in the Ukraine by a "battle on two fronts: against the landlord-bourgeois centralist Russian counter revolution (Denikinism) and against the petty-bourgeois Ukrainian counterrevolution (Petliurism)." In great detail the resolution contrasted the mistakes typifying the two deviations: the first underestimated the importance of the republics, while the second disparaged the Union, prompting Ukrainians to look to Europe rather than to Russia; the first opposed or ignored Ukrainization, particularly in the cities, and exaggerated the rights of the national minorities, while the second favored an excessive tempo for Ukrainization, advocating its forced application to Russians and other ethnic groups; the first insisted on the use of the Russian language and referred contemptuously to Ukrainian as an unknown "Gallician" dialect, while the second exaggerated the importance of Russian chauvinism, denounced Ukrainians who supported the Soviet regime, and refused in general to recognize the importance of the proletariat in the Ukraine and the ability and willingness of Bolsheviks to nationalize Ukrainian life. Both deviations were equally dangerous and equally to be avoided. For the moment, however, the resolution suggested that it was the Ukrainian-nationalist rather than the Russian-centralist deviation which was of greater concern. Temporarily, Larin and his opposition to the work of the CP(b)U were forgotten as the campaign against "Shums'kyism" was pressed.

In the closing months of 1927, however, Ukrainian leaders returned to their denunciations of Larin. Both Kaganovich and Skrypnik accused him of being as great a danger to Soviet national policy as Shums'kyi. In an address to the Tenth Congress of the CP(b)U (November, 1927)[243] Kaganovich declared that Larin, in his arguments, had allied himself with oppositionists such as Zinoviev and had given substance to charges by enemies of the Soviet Union abroad that Soviet national policy was only a sham.[244] At the Fifteenth Congress of the All-Union Communist Party (December, 1927), Skrypnik supported Kaganovich, accusing Larin of challenging basic Soviet tenets which had been approved again and again by Party and Comintern leaders.[245] Yet these statements by Ukrainian leaders undoubtedly sounded hollow to Russian Bolsheviks and numerous members of the CP(b)U. To them it seemed clear that there had been excesses in the Ukrainizatiou program, that Larin had properly called attention to these excesses, and that the CP(b)U had admitted the validity of Larin's criticisisms by modifying the Ukrainization program. In replying to Skrypnik, Larin made what was perhaps a common observation, that Skrypnik seemed excessively nervous over the Ukrainization question and that to Party members unfamiliar with Skrypnik's impulsiveness it must appear that he favored establishing Ukrainization as an infallible dogma which, like Immaculate Conception, could not be challenged.[246]

Yet the differences between Larin and Skrypnik were greater than Larin and most Party members were willing to admit. Skrypnik saw in Larin's attack not merely an objection to particular instances in which the Ukrainization program had been carried to excess, but a fundamental challenge to the program itself. If political life in the Ukraine was to be converted to the Ukrainian language and Ukrainian customs, and if political power in the Ukraine was to remain in the hands of the proletariat, then it was essential that the proletariat be Ukrainized, either by inducing Russian workers to adopt Ukrainian ways or by drawing masses of the rural local population into the industrial centers. By challenging both programs, Larin was insisting in fact that Ukrainian political life remain Russified.[247] It was this suggestion that Skrypnik refused to accept. At the end of 1927 no other Soviet leaders were willing to view the matter in so strong a light,[248] and the quarrel passed over without decision. Yet the disagreement was a real one and provided the seeds for the growth of the serious opposition between Ukrainian nationalists and Soviet leaders which was to develop in the following years.

The development of Soviet national policy in the period from 1921 to 1927 suggested that two conceptions were uppermost in the minds of Soviet leaders. The first was a stern, even stringent interpretation of the Bolshevik premise of the subordination of the national question to the question of the proletarian dictatorship. Because Soviet leaders identified the proletarian dictatorship with Bolshevik rule from Moscow, the premise took the form of a strict requirement for the absolute subordination of the Ukraine and its government and Party organizations to the center. The premise was demonstrated in the Party structure by the precept incorporated into the Party rules that the Communist parties of the republics were completely subordinate to the All-Union Communist Party. The premise was incorporated into the government structure by the provisions of the 1924 constitution, placing the main areas of government authority under the direction of Union bodies. In both Party and government affairs Russian leaders insisted that authority to pass final judgment on critical political questions rest with central agencies.

The second conception was a less clearly defined but nonetheless real assessment of the national question as an important, even decisive question for the success of the Bolshevik regime. In the early years this conception was influenced by Lenin's moderate approach to the national problem and by Soviet recognition of the practical need to build support among the minority nationalities. In 1923, Stalin emphasized the question of support, declaring that close ties could be formed between the Bolsheviks and the peasant-worker masses of the border regions only if local institutions in the republics were accepted and encouraged. At the same time, he insisted that national differences in language and customs did not endanger Bolshevik power and that the differences would long remain or, in any case, could not be removed by forceful measures. In the years after 1923, the element of support took on added importance as Stalin sought to build a personal following among the minorities. Already he had emerged as one of the most stalwart champions of the rights of the border peoples, and nationalists in the republics were now encouraged anew to support him against more centralist and pro-Russian leaders. In return, Stalin adopted a flexible approach to national problems, urging toleration of differences in national development and a stimulation of local growth. Throughout 1927 these elements remained primary, and the localization policy continued to receive official support.

Nevertheless, although there were no obvious shifts in national policy in the period from 1921 to 1927, it is clear that the period was one of transition and that the attitudes with which Bolshevik leaders approached the national question in 1927 were different from the attitudes prevailing in 1921. In the early years appeals to the nationalities were part of an almost desperate effort to broaden support for the regime at a time when neither Bolshevik nor Stalinist leadership was clearly accepted and when demands for economic and political reconstruction eclipsed all others; the national question, as part of the broader question of support, was crucial. In addition, nationality problems were considered in the light of their probable repercussions outside the Soviet Union, and Russian leaders were mindful of the significance for the international revolutionary movement of the policy they adopted toward non-Russian peoples inside the Soviet Union. By 1927, both aspects of the national question were less critical: Stalin and the Bolsheviks were in firm control of the Soviet Union; the Stalinist notion of socialism in one country had lessened interest in revolutionary and nationalist movements abroad. The national question thereby lost its eminence as a crucial factor in Bolshevik success and came to be regarded as no more than a local problem of relatively modest proportions.

Inside the Ukraine the localization policy produced a feeling of uniqueness and independence among republic leaders and a strong interest in developing local forms of expression in government, history, literature, and science. Although greatest efforts were devoted to the relatively mechanical task of expanding the use of the Ukrainian language, at a higher level a sense of political independence emerged, which resulted on occasion in opposition to Soviet policies by both Russian and Ukrainian elements. Initially this opposition was treated in a moderate way, but gradually Soviet policy hardened and deviations became less tolerable. At the same time, the CP(b)U was reconstructed from a rather loose collection of district Party groups into a single republic organization under tight central control. As a result, by 1927 the Ukrainian localism which had grown in part from the stimulation of Soviet policy saw itself confronted with an increasing hostility from central leaders, supported now by an effective Party machine.

IV. CENTRALIZATION AND THE DEMAND FOR UNIFORMITY, 1927-1934

The Bolshevik successes in consolidating their position in the Soviet Union and overcoming opposition within the Party enabled them after 1927 to turn to new tasks—to the tasks of industrialization, collectivization, and national planning. Already some introductory steps had been taken: central planning agencies had been formed; socialist industries had been established on a modest scale. After 1927 these efforts were to be expanded and agriculture added to the list of institutions to be introduced to the Soviet pattern.

The consequences for the republics of the new socialist programs were considerable, not only because the programs were accompanied by a weakening of Russian enthusiasm for the policy of concessions to the border nationalities, but because the programs seemed to require an increase in central prerogatives and activity. As a result, the years after 1927 witnessed a steady accretion by the center of authority over the republics, particularly in economic fields, accompanied by a growing tendency among Russian leaders to view the national movements not as neutral forces to be drawn to the Bolshevik cause, but as centers of opposition to be reconstructed or suppressed.

CENTRALIZATION: ECONOMIC PLANNING AND DEVELOPMENT

The first of the new centralizing courses appeared in the field of agriculture—a field which before 1927 had been regulated chiefly by the republics. Although the 1924 constitution had authorized the Union to lay down general principles for the "development and use of land," it had also provided for local administration of agricultural affairs. In practice Union interest had been limited to the general task of increasing farm production and procurement and to the implications for the Soviet program of the conflict between poor and wealthy peasants.[1] In 1927, however, a Union plan for agricultural production was prepared and the first step taken in supervising agricultural work by the summoning of a conference of republic commissars of agriculture to examine the new production schedules and other farm questions.[2] At about the same time, the collectivization policy was adopted and a series of Union laws promulgated to inaugurate the program and stimulate participation by individual peasants.[3] Subsequently, Union interest rapidly increased. In 1927 and 1928 a number of Union rural organizations were formed: Grain Trust, Cattle Breeder, Sheep Breeder, Agricultural Equipment, etc.[4] In December, 1928, title to all land in the Soviet Union was assumed by the Union government, and regulations for land use and development were adopted.[5] In the spring of 1929, as the first mass movement of individual farmers to the collectives began, Soviet leaders became convinced that closer central direction of agricultural affairs was necessary; in December the republic commissariats of agriculture were abolished as exclusively republic agencies and formed as subordinate divisions of a newly created Union Commissariat of Agriculture.[6]

A second centralizing trend developed around the program for industrialization and national economic planning. In 1927 the authority of the State Planning Commission (*Gosplan*) was widened together with its control over the local planning commissions in each of the republics. After a long period of discussion and preparation, the First Five-Year Plan as an integrated program for the economy of the USSR was defined and, in the fall of 1928, inaugurated. Although certain aspects of the Plan were drafted at the republic level, final Plan requirements were set by central planning agencies, in some cases against the expressed recommendations of republic leaders.

In like manner, actual operating management of industrial plants was brought under closer Union direction. Despite the decision of the Fourth Congress of Soviets of the USSR (April,

1927) for a decentralization of operating functions in industry, an opposite trend developed. The number of industrial establishments of Union subordination increased, and the independent authority of the republics to manage industries of non-Union subordination decreased. In January, 1932, new administrative machinery was provided to direct industrial operations: all heavy industries and forestry and forest-products industries were separated from the republics and brought under the immediate control of Union commissariats; the light industries remaining under republic administration were placed under Union-republic commissariats and hence under general Union supervision.[7]

Similarly, measures were adopted limiting the work of the republics in social and cultural fields. In education republic control over higher institutions was reduced by transferring supervision over technical and scientific schools from the republic commissariats of education to the appropriate functioning commissariats—agriculture, communications, and others. In the field of public health central control was extended over hospitals and sanitaria. In the field of social welfare Union legislation was adopted on questions of housing, medical control, and pensions.[8] In 1930 the republic commissariats of internal affairs were abolished and their functions assumed, subsequently, by a single Union commissariat.[9] The trend after 1927 in all areas of government suggested that the early emphasis on the right of the republics to administer programs within their borders was to be abandoned in favor of centralized planning and Union management of economic and social affairs.

Republic leaders, particularly Ukrainian officials, accepted the new emphasis with no better grace than they had accepted centralizing measures in the past. In Party and government meetings they denounced central interference in local affairs, urging that the basic role accorded the republics by the constitution be preserved. In contrast to their earlier opposition, however, when criticisms had been directed chiefly at centralization itself, Ukrainian leaders now denounced also the content of the Soviet programs, declaring that they discriminated against the Ukraine, exploiting the region and providing inadequately for its future development.

Ukrainian opposition therefore assumed a two-fold form, broader and more comprehensive in its scope.

The first attacks on centralization were a continuation of criticisms expressed earlier and focused on Union efforts to interpret the constitution in its favor. Chief targets of attack were the Union commissariats which were accused of autocratic and aggressive practices. The Ukrainian government questioned both the exclusive manner in which the commissariats handled affairs under their jurisdiction and also their tendency to expand. In numerous petitions the Ukraine called on the Union to alter or suspend centralizing orders and decrees.[10] The commissariats were denounced for assuming control of the sugar industry despite the fact that 80 percent of the Union's sugar came from the Ukraine.[11] They were accused of assuming legislative powers, of failing to make proper allowance for local conditions in the republics, and of refusing to recognize that local programs might better be carried out by republic agencies.[12] They were criticized in their planning work for prescribing even the smallest allocations of funds and materials for industrial plants and for exercising such close control over republic programs and administrators that the officially accepted policy of decentralized administration was seldom enforced.[13]

In 1928, Ukrainian leaders extended their opposition by attacking two new legislative proposals: the "Statute on Budget Rights of the USSR and the Union Republics"; and "General Principles of Land Use Construction." On the question of budget rights, Ukrainians complained that the statute failed to define clearly the limits of Union and republic responsibility and failed to guarantee the budget authority of the republics.[14] On the question of land use, Skrypnik returned to his basic defense of the sovereignty of the republics, insisting that their right of dominion over the land within their boundaries should not be handed over to the Union.

The first clause of the Union law on land use provides that all land will become the property of the USSR. I assert that such a decision is a grave error, because it is contrary to the decisions of the Party on relationships between the Soviet Union and the Union republics.

The new law on land use provides that the land will become the property not of the republics, but of the whole Union. If such a law is to be approved, it will mean that the sovereignty of the separate republics will amount only to this, that they will have their governments, but without any territory. I assert that all such tendencies must be given a decisive rebuff.[15]

Secondly, Ukrainians began to challenge the regional emphasis of the new Union programs. Most strongly attacked were the industrialization programs which were charged with assuming an anti-Ukrainian bias. Development funds were being assigned in a disproportionate way to other parts of the Soviet Union, it was suggested, and insufficient attention was being paid to the economic needs of the Ukraine.

The first such criticisms were made by lower-level Ukrainian officials [16] and were quickly rejected by government leaders. At the Fourth Congress of Soviets of the USSR (April, 1927) the Ukraine's Prime Minisster Vlas Chubar' attacked suggestions that the Ukraine was being exploited as a Soviet colony and insisted that its development was being adequately ensured.

[The evidence clearly refutes] those claiming that the economic possibilities of the Ukraine are being inadequately developed, that up to the present time there still remains in the Ukraine a legacy of Tsarist policy. All the work of recent years has shown that not a trace of such a legacy remains. ... Representatives of Ukrainian workers and peasants can say today with satisfaction that the economic and cultural development of the Ukraine follows the general tempo of development of the whole Union, that the economy of the Ukraine is being developed, in general and on the whole, satisfactorily.[17]

Yet Chubar' himself, at the same meeting, urged that larger investments be poured into Ukrainian industries, and other representatives joined him, demanding greater attention to the Ukraine's economic growth.[18] Two points were especially emphasized : 1) that the tremendous metals complex of the Donbass and Krivoi Rog regions was being slighted in favor of new developments elsewhere; and 2) that the western districts of the Ukraine were being held down as overpopulated, backward, rural areas by the refusal of central planners to establish much-needed industries.

In the following months the problem grew in importance as preliminary drafts for the First Five-Year Plan were prepared.

At the Fifteenth Party Congress (December, 1927), where instructions for the Plan were presented, Ukrainians pleaded for greater
industrial development in the Ukraine. Kaganovich noted that
the Ukraine produced "80 percent of all coal mined in the Union,
70 percent of all mined metals, 85 percent of the ore, etc." and
suggested that because of its mineral wealth the Ukraine was the
logical site for the construction of new plant facilities.

Comrades, do not think that I am speaking here as a provincial—defending the heavy industry of the Ukraine. I affirm the line of our
Party in the upbuilding and developing of heavy industry and
manufacturing in all the areas of our USSR. But in building new
factories, it is necessary to take into consideration the sources of
raw materials and fuels, and together with this, the areas where
industry already has its base.[19]

Kaganovich was joined by Chubar' and Petrovs'kyi, who complained that the metals industries of the Ukraine—"the most important center of metallurgy"—had suffered great hardship because of the lack of investment capital: construction work near
the projected Dnieper Dam had been retarded because of a limited
allocation of funds; farm production had not increased as planned
because too few tractors had been provided.[20] Although Petrovs'kyi
admitted that, from the standpoint of national defense, it might
be desirable to shift industries eastward to the Urals and Siberia,
he insisted that, for the moment, economic development was a
more important consideration, requiring emphasis on new construction near the coal and ore supplies of the Ukraine.[21]

Much stronger than the protests of Ukrainian leaders was the
criticism of an obscure Ukrainian economist, a Bolshevik named
Mykhailo Volobuev. Early in 1928 Volobuev published in the
Ukrainian journal Bil'shovyk Ukrainy an article "On the Problem
of Ukrainian Economics."[22] The article declared itself to be a
criticism of mistakes made by central leaders in carrying out the
Bolshevik policy for economic development of the Soviet Union;
but, as was noted by Bolshevik writers and subsequently by Volobuev himself,[23] the criticism developed into a broad attack on
Soviet economic policy as a whole.

Volobuev's criticism was based on the conviction that the Ukraine
as an entity was an important and independent economic region,

capable of existing apart from other states and of maintaining its own national economy. Unlike the backward regions of the Russian empire such as Turkestan and the Transcaucasus, the Ukraine contained a balanced and well-developed economy and consequently was justified in considering itself an equal partner with Russia within the Soviet Union, rather than a dependent colony. Unfortunately, Volobuev maintained, Soviet leaders viewed the Ukraine—as had Tsarist rulers before them—as a region subordinate to Russia. Hence they continued to direct its economy so as to stimulate Russian development, drawing greater wealth from the Ukraine than was returned, and tying Ukrainian production more and more closely to Russian industrial centers. As a result, the Ukraine was becoming a true Russian colony. If the trend was to be reversed, Volobuev concluded, it was essential that Russian planners begin to view the Ukraine as an economic equal with Russia, that efforts be made to build factories inside the Ukraine to process Ukrainian raw materials, and that a larger proportion of the industrial products required by Ukrainian industry and agriculture be manufactured locally, rather than imported from other republics.

It was obvious at once that Volobuev had gone further in his criticisms than Party leaders, even in the Ukraine, were willing to allow. His identification of Soviet economic policies in the Ukraine with Tsarist policies and his assertion that the Ukraine was in fact a Russian colony were counterrevolutionary views; his suggestion that the economy of the Ukraine should be directed toward capitalist countries somewhat independently of the economy of the Soviet Union was an attack on the unity of the Soviet republics; his implication that the Russian and Ukrainian economies were distinct from one another and, in certain respects, mutually opposed seemed as dangerous as Khvylovyi's deviationist views on the inevitable cultural battle between Russia and the Ukraine. Volobuev was immediately asked to withdraw his charges, and unlike Shums'kyi, with whom he was compared, he hastily did so. He noted that his article had been prepared in the fall of 1927 —when, he hinted, his views were more acceptable—and he admitted that he had been mistaken in attributing to the Soviet system the faults of a few bureaucrats. He did not believe, he declared firmly, that Soviet economic policy was incorrect, nor had he intended to brand it as a colonial policy.[24]

Volobuev's criticisms were officially declared a bourgeois-nationalist deviation and were stigmatized by Bolsheviks alongside the deviations of Khvyl'ovyi and Shums'kyi.[25] Yet, in practice, Ukrainian leaders accepted his arguments in part and continued to press strongly for economic concessions from the Union. Throughout 1928 and 1929 their objections to Union control figures for economic development and to budget allocations grew.[26] At the end of 1929 their dissatisfaction culminated in a concerted attack on the proposed planning and budget programs for the year 1929-1930.

The attack came at the Second Session of the USSR Central Executive Committee. It was introduced by Petrovs'kyi who referred once again to the wealth of the Ukraine and to its possibilities for growth, contrasting its great potential with the inadequate and niggardly investments alloted for its development.[27] With a measure of sharpness he referred to the Ukraine's budget difficulties. As prepared by republic experts, he noted, the Ukrainian budget had called for an expenditure of 650 million rubles. This figure had been rejected by Union authorities, and with much effort the republic had cut its request to 547 million—an irreducible minimum. However, when submitted for inclusion in the Union budget, the request had been reduced further by central officials to 507 million. As a result, expenditures in the Ukraine were to be the lowest in the entire USSR, averaging seventeen rubles per person as opposed to twenty for the RSFSR and forty-eight for Turkmenistan. The amount was completely insufficient, he observed, to guarantee the "achievement of those great plans, those tasks which have been charged to the Ukraine."

Similarly, Petrovs'kyi criticized investment figures for the Ukraine. He referred to the failure to allocate sufficient funds for development of the Donbass, Zaporozh'e, and Krivoi Rog industrial centers; to the lack of funds for reconstruction of the right-bank districts of the Ukraine and the cities of Kiev and Odessa—cities which he declared had become "empty towns"; to the shortage of farm machinery and equipment necessary for increasing agricultural production and achieving collectivization. "Despite the fact that our country, the Ukraine, is rich," he commented, "we live in poverty.... If you do not give us funds, all will be in desolation."[28]

Similar complaints were registered by other Ukrainian representatives in the Central Executive Committee.[29] But in contrast to previous sessions, where delegates from Belorussia and the Caucasus had also opposed centralization, the Ukrainians now stood alone. Their demands were related too specifically to the needs of the Ukraine and were directed in fact in a limited way against the other national regions which the Ukrainians suggested were being favored. Consequently, delegates from the Urals, Central Asia, Belorussia, and the Caucasus spoke against the Ukrainians, urging that the Ukraine was a wealthy country requiring relatively modest development and that the Ukrainians were guilty of a localism which could not advance the general interests of the Soviet Union.[30] Russian delegates joined in opposing the Ukrainian protest, and the Central Executive Committee, in its final decisions, adopted both the budget and economic control figures with only minor changes.[31]

The Ukrainian effort of December, 1929, was the last major drive to win for the Ukraine a greater role in the preparation of plans for the region's economy and a greater share of the resources available for investment. The defeat the Ukrainians suffered in the Central Executive Committee was apparently followed in 1930 by Party pressure from Moscow aimed at convincing Ukrainian leaders that they had gone too far in championing the special interests of the Ukraine and had failed to regard with sufficient seriousness the needs of the Soviet Union as a whole. By the time of the calling of the Eleventh Congress of the CP(b)U and the Sixteenth Congress of the All-Union Communist Party (June-July, 1930), Ukrainian leaders once more were drawn firmly into line. At sessions of the two Party meetings the Ukrainians agreed that the requirements of Union construction should have priority over republic demands. They welcomed the creation of a new metallurgical base in the Urals and West Siberia rivalling the Ukrainian base in the Donbass[32] and supported the view that the Party's

chief obligation was to increase production throughout the USSR
rather than to build up a single area.[33] In the following year, when
the Soviet legislature met to consider new budget and control
figures for the USSR (April, 1931), Ukrainians raised no objections
but praised the proposed figures as tools for carrying out the
socialization of the USSR and as powerful aids in achieving Lenin's
national policy through the assurance of an equal development of
all the peoples of the Union.[34]

Ukrainian inability to prevent centralizing measures or to obtain
a greater share of investment and development funds was a repetition of the situation in 1923, when the republics had been unable
to improve their constitutional status. The failure demonstrated
once again the difficulties under which nationalist Bolsheviks la-
bored in their effort to reconcile localism and national egocentrism
with Bolshevik omnipotence and exclusiveness. It also demonstrated the pattern Soviet leaders had developed as an approach
to the federal system and the standards they had come to apply
as requirements for republic leaders. Neither the pattern nor the
standards were as well-defined as they were later to become, but
the general outlines were drawn, and the trend was clear.

For Russian Bolsheviks the fundamental consideration was the
principle of a centralized union as set forth many years previously
by Stalin. The Soviet republics could survive and develop as
socialist states, Stalin had insisted, only through the closest possible union and most far-reaching direction from the center. In
the matter of union, there had been little disagreement among
Russian Bolsheviks despite their declaration of an uncertain right
to self-determination. In the matter of central direction, Stalin
had come to be opposed by Lenin and by representatives of the
republics. But he had succeeded, nonetheless, during the drafting
of the 1924 constitution, in winning general acceptance of his
views. On two points, however, the early conception of centralization was limited. First, there was a vague understanding that
central direction would not be exercised at all in certain fields and
in others would be limited to the establishment of general directives
to be amplified by the republics. Secondly, it was generally ac-

cepted that republic leaders would play a special role in applying
Soviet programs and would be expected to adopt a moderately
provincial attitude, defending the interests of their own regions
against the interests of other regions and perhaps even against the
interests of the Union. These two limitations had served to render
the constitution palatable to the republics and to moderate the
otherwise centralizing character of the federation.

By 1930 both limitations had come to be disregarded. The first
was lost through the growing supervision by Union officials of
republic affairs and through the sudden increase in areas of Union
interest following the inauguration of economic planning and the
socialization of industry and agriculture. The second was lost as
Bolshevik leaders came to identify Soviet success with Union success and to insist that republic leaders give principal support
to programs strengthening the Union and interpret all republic
measures in terms of their contribution to the whole. The new
attitude did not require republic leaders to abandon their concern for the special needs of their own localities; but in any
conflict of interest they were to support the Union position.[35]

The problem confronting Ukrainian leaders was therefore the
problem of reconciling their special interest in the Ukraine with
the necessity of supporting the Union above all. The problem was
particularly serious for Ukrainian nationalists but concerned also
those who identified with the Ukraine sufficiently in any way to
feel concern about its development. No satisfactory answer to the
problem was found, and it does not seem that any fully acceptable
solution was possible. In their efforts to find a solution, Ukrainians
could not agree among themselves, separating into three groups
each with its own views.

The solution most acceptable to Union leaders was that suggested
by Kaganovich, who attempted to show that Ukrainian interest
was identical with Union interest or, more accurately, that the
well-being of the Union depended on the vigorous development
of the Ukraine. There was no question that Union growth was
paramount. But Union growth could best be assured if the most
richly endowed areas were developed, and the most promising of
all was the Ukraine. Under this argument Ukrainians could press

for local programs without appearing disloyal to the Union. But there was no assurance Ukrainian development would continue to be emphasized once central officials became convinced that from the viewpoint of the Union more promising fields were to be found elsewhere.

The second answer was that suggested by Petrovs'kyi and Chubar' and supported by the majority of Ukrainian Bolsheviks. Provincialism in Soviet affairs was a danger, the group admitted, and Union interests were always to be considered primary. Nevertheless, the Ukraine should be given special attention, not only because it offered the most favorable conditions for economic development,[36] but also because it posed certain unique problems demanding sympathetic attention. Thus, for example, the right-bank districts of the Ukraine were overpopulated and could be properly developed only if their economy was broadened by the construction of new industries—a program that should be adopted regardless of Union requirements.[37] Such an argument easily degenerated into a form of special pleading, and innumerable requests from representatives of all the republics were made, demanding attention to local projects: the workers of Kharkov needed better housing; the cities of the Donbass required an improved water system; the farm districts near Odessa needed to be developed; etc., etc. At a more general level, however, the demands represented a broad petition for modification of the strictures of central planning and for accommodation to local peculiarities. There was no suggestion that local needs be placed ahead of Union needs or that the decision on local programs be made at the local level. Central leaders were therefore willing to accept these petitions, which were regarded as a method of checking on planning work. Where the petitions were approved, they provided a measure of central adaptation to local demands. But, since the final decision on the petitions was always a central one, the compromise was only moderately satisfactory to the republics.

The only adequate answer from the standpoint of republic development was that suggested by Volobuev. It was necessary, he had implied, that the basic postulates underlying Soviet economic planning be challenged and Stalin's maxim of the primacy of

Union interest and of central direction of Soviet life be rejected. The concept of Union interest had come to mean no more than Russian interest and had therefore become identical with Tsarist colonialism, leading inevitably to the exploitation of the Ukraine for the benefit of Russia. The interests of the Ukraine could be preserved and fostered only by placing them on a par with Russian interests and allowing them to develop independently. These suggestions provided the most complete defense for Ukrainian economic development, but Ukrainian leaders could not accept them. To the majority of Bolsheviks there was no question that the Soviet republics needed to work together in the closest way in economic fields and that comprehensive, specific guidance from Moscow was required. Ukrainian leaders were unwilling to challenge these principles and, hence, were forced to abandon independent programs for development of the Ukrainian economy and to rely on the good-will of central officials as the only guarantee of Ukrainian interests.[38]

CENTRALIZATION: TERRITORIAL-ADMINISTRATIVE STRUCTURE

Accompanying the increase in Union authority over economic matters was a growing conviction among central leaders that the republics did not represent the most useful sub-divisions for developing the Union's economy and that the three-tiered system of administration (including in descending order: republics, okrugs, and raions), with its requirement that central administrators work through the republics, should be modified to make possible more direct contact between Moscow and the localities. As early as 1926 it was decided to establish a fourth administrative level—the oblast—to function between the republics and the okrugs and to assume responsibility chiefly for economic affairs. Specifically for the Ukraine, it was recommended that two oblasts be created: a Southwest Oblast to include the agrarian districts of the right-bank Ukraine and a South Mining-Industrial Oblast to include the Donbass and the left-bank districts. The proposal was intended to provide smaller and more compact areas within the Ukraine which, by virtue of their economic homogeneity, could be directed more easily by central planners. To Ukrainian Bolsheviks, however, the proposal sounded disturbingly like the 1918 decision to divide the Ukraine into two or more separate republics and seemed also a step backward toward the old guberniia system with its central interference in local affairs. They consequently opposed the scheme. The Ukraine was small, they argued, in contrast to the RSFSR where oblasts were being formed and hence needed no further division.[39] The proposal itself, they declared, was an effort to weaken the Ukraine by breaking it into separate parts and was no more than an ill-considered expression of Great-Russian chauvinism.[40] How influential Ukrainian objections were is not known but, in any case, the proposal was abandoned.

Apparently central leaders then made an effort to draw the okrug level of administration in the Ukraine more closely under central direction. Throughout 1928 Party committees in the okrugs were required to report directly on their work to the Central Committee of the All-Union Communist Party and to receive in return criticisms and instructions.[41] The requirement seemed to suggest a lack of confidence in republic Party leadership, but for this there is no other evidence. More probably the requirement was an exploratory effort to determine if the okrugs were an appropriate administrative link for channeling control over the Ukraine's economic life, now to be brought under state management. In December, 1928, the okrugs were strengthened by the adoption of a comprehensive resolution granting them additional supervisory authority at the expense of republic bodies and ordering them to play a more direct role in administering programs in the localities.[42]

In the following months, however, it became clear that the okrugs were not able to carry out instructions from the center in an efficient way.[43] Perhaps the fault lay in their numbers or perhaps in the fragmented way in which they channeled Party and administrative work. Specifically, there was criticism that they blocked closer ties between central economic bodies and local operating organs at the raion level. The okrugs had begun to interfere in the practical work of the raions, it was charged.[44] As a result, the decision was taken early in 1930 to abolish the okrugs and to divide their functions between the two remaining levels, the republic and the raion.[45]

There are indications that Ukrainian nationalists did not favor elimination of the okrugs,[46] although it is not clear precisely why. In certain respects the okrug level was like the guberniia level, interposing itself between the localities and the republic and hence weakening Ukrainian authority. This point was made by a number of leaders who praised the abolition of the okrugs, emphasizing the new importance of republic direction of the raions and suggesting that republic responsibility was now to be increased.[47] On the other hand, there are no indications that the okrugs had ever developed the close ties with Moscow enjoyed by the guberniias, nor does it appear that the okrugs had come to be used, as had the guberniias, as transmission links between the Union and the localities, by-passing the republic. On the contrary, the okrugs were apparently closely subordinated to republic agencies, and there were suggestions that their interference with administrative work was largely an interference with Union rather than republic direction.[48] Nationalist leaders were perhaps fearful that the abolition of the okrugs would strengthen direct Union influence over the raions and hence over local affairs in the Ukraine.

In any event the liquidation of the okrugs and the formation of a two-tiered administrative system was only a temporary measure. Perhaps Union leaders had intended it to be so from the beginning. If not, the collectivization difficulties experienced by the Ukraine in 1931 and 1932 convinced them that a new directive level of administration was required. The raions, it was charged, had shown themselves unable to accomplish alone the important political and economic tasks assigned them, including especially the task of grain collection. The Ukrainian republic, for its part, had been unable to give adequate guidance to the cities and to Soviet construction there.[49] Consequently, it was decided early in 1932 to form an intermediate stage between the republic and the raions. The new level was to be not the old okrug, with its forty or more units relatively unresponsive to central direction, but an oblast level comprising, initially, only five units—Kiev, Kharkov, Vinnitsa, Dnepropetrovsk, and Odessa.[50] The new structure therefore bore a close resemblance to the old guberniia system. Although the oblasts were created by the Ukrainian government and had no initial ties with Moscow as had the guberniias, their large size and small numbers made it possible for them to develop as competitors of the Ukraine and to establish direct contacts with the Union. Apparently it was intended that the oblasts would grow in the future as powerful centers of administrative and Party work, providing the Union a more suitable base than the republics for directing economic life.

THE NATIONAL QUESTION

The disagreements between Ukrainian and Russian Bolsheviks over centralization of economic and administrative life were not basically national disagreements, although the national question inevitably played a role. The disagreements arose primarily out of the natural tendency of local and regional officials to resist expansion of central authority and to support the widest and most independent scope for local programs. It seems likely the disagreements would have appeared even if the Ukraine had been inhabited exclusively by Russians with little consciousness of regional distinctiveness. On occasion, as in the case of Volobuev, regional interests came to be identified with Ukrainian national interests, and the two oppositions to Russian centralism reinforced one another. Undoubtedly the Ukrainian separatist movement was stimulated by the unfair, discriminatory practices many Ukrainians felt were being applied to their republic. Yet to the nationalist Bolsheviks regionalism posed many problems. It tended to blur the distinctly national struggle, since regionalism was not directly related to any Ukrainian-Russian national differences. Of greater consequence, it tended to set off the Ukraine against the Union as a whole in a way which struck very basically at the effort of the nationalist Bolsheviks to build the Ukraine as a distinct but nevertheless inseparable part of the Soviet Union. It is noteworthy that Skrypnik, as one of the most resolute nationalist Bolsheviks, refused on a number of occasions to support demands for greater development of the Ukraine. Ukrainians, he insisted, were obliged to recognize the broader interests of the Union as a whole and were best advised to work out their peculiar forms of expression within a general, overall Union framework.[51] From the viewpoint of the nationalist Bolsheviks, it was the distinctly nationalist effort prompted by Skrypnik which outweighed in importance the unsuccessful campaign for regional concessions.

The Debate

The years after 1925, as we have seen, were years in which the strong resolve of Russian Bolsheviks to emphasize the national question and the rights of the national minorities diminished gradually under the superior requirements of Soviet planning and the heavy centralizing pressures from Party leaders who could not avoid identifying Soviet success with Russian success. That the lessening of resolve had reached the highest Bolshevik leaders was indicated by Stalin's severe letter of 1926 on "Shums'kyism." That it had penetrated widely into the Bolshevik leadership corps in the Soviet Union was indicated by the general support Larin won in his campaign against Ukrainization. That it had been accepted readily by the majority of Party members in the Ukraine as elsewhere was attested by numerous complaints of Ukrainian and central leaders and by the slow progress of Ukrainization work within the Party ranks. By 1927 there was no question that the initial enthusiasm which had launched the localization program in the USSR was gone.

As the reconstruction plans for Soviet industry and agriculture unfolded after 1927, attacks on the nationalities policy continued to grow. Increasing numbers of Party members and spokesmen, particularly in the republics, began to adopt the position that the concessions to the nationalities which had been appropriate in the tolerant atmosphere of the New Economic Policy could no longer be admitted under the rigorous conditions of the Five-Year Plan. As early as the Fifteenth Party Congress (December, 1927) workers in the republics were accused of hindering Soviet industrial development by their insistence that each republic be developed separately as a self-sufficient economic unit.[52] Subsequently, the attacks became broader and deeper until they began to include

criticisms of many of the basic national principles adopted by the
Party in 1923. In articles published in *Bol'shevik* in 1928 emphasis
was placed on the necessity of subordinating national rights to
socialist demands. Local nationalism was described as a growing
danger which had become more troublesome than Russian chauvinism and could no longer be explained away as a simple reaction
to Tsarist oppression.[53] Even within the All-Union Central Committee it was urged that, in view of the new socialist centralization in the USSR, the national question was no longer of importance and that, consequently, the Party should place emphasis
on the building of a single socialist culture rather than numerous
local national cultures.[54] The slogan, "the right of nations to
self-determination," was attacked on the grounds that it had lost
its pre-revolutionary importance and had become a counter revolutionary motto threatening the unity of the Soviet Union.[55]
Altogether, the attacks amounted to a serious campaign against
Soviet national policy. Although they were never expressed officially or by the highest Party leaders, they were sufficient to
reopen consideration of the problem. Throughout 1928 and 1929
this reconsideration became an important aspect of Party work in
the Ukraine.

The first question pressing seriously on Ukrainian leaders was
the question of the status of the Russian population in the Ukraine
and, specifically, the question of Ukrainization of the urban areas.
The problem was remarkably complex, not only because it brought
the conflict between ethnic Russians and ethnic Ukrainians to a
concise focus, but because it became a central part of the question
of control of the rapidly growing proletariat of the Ukraine. Because
of the significance of the problem it is not surprising that both
Ukrainian and Russian leaders approached the matter gingerly.

For Ukrainian Bolsheviks the problem presented three difficulties.
The first arose from the lack of a settled policy among central
leaders and, specifically, from the lack of a clear statement by
Stalin, who at one point spoke in favor of the ultimate transformation of the cities into Ukrainian centers and at another
point criticiz ed efforts to accelerate the process by forcing the
urban proletariat to abandon its predominantly Russian character.

Perhaps Stalin was hoping through such an equivocal stand to avoid alienating either those Ukrainians who placed great faith in the Ukrainization program or those Russians in the cities who feared their position might be challenged. In any case, he provided no answer to the problem beyond a general statement that the important question was the question of timing and that what might ultimately be accomplished through a slow and gradual process should not now be forced.

The problem also offered difficulties because of the disagreement it prompted within the CP(b)U. This disagreement arose out of the old schism which had plagued the Party for so long—the schism between the pro-Russian groups in the eastern industrial and urban centers of the Ukraine and the more distinctly Ukrainian elements in the rural districts. From the time of the Revolution conflicts had resulted from the schism, and there had been shifts from one side to the other with first the pro-Russian faction and then the Ukrainian faction gaining the ascendancy. There is no clear evidence indicating which group was larger within the CP(b)U in 1928, but it seems likely that Party membership was predominantly pro-Russian and anti-nationalist. At least until 1925 Russians comprised the largest bloc of Party members and, in combination with Russified members of other ethnic groups, they remained dominant throughout 1934.[56] The many complaints in the Ukrainian press of the failures of Party members to support Ukrainization attest to the importance of anti-Ukrainian feeling.[57] Countering this hostility was the favorable attitude of Party leaders. Influential posts in the CP(b)U were held by strong advocates of Ukrainization such as Skrypnik and Butsenko, and by more modest advocates such as Petrovs'kyi, Chubar', and Liubchenko. The principal leaders of the Party—Kaganovich, Kosior, Medvedev, and Postyshev—were without national enthusiasm themselves, but they also supported Ukrainization in accordance with central policy. Their willingness to urge pro-Russian Party members to accept Ukrainization of the cities helped to balance the opposition which otherwise dominated the Party.

The most critical factor in Soviet indecision on Ukrainization of the cities, however, was the extraordinary impact the policy promised to exert on the whole political atmosphere in the Ukraine. The problem was a simple one. In the pre-revolutionary period and during the early years of Soviet power Bolshevik authority had been constructed almost exclusively on the support of workers in the cities—workers who were overwhelmingly Russian by ethnic origin or by choice. To a greater extent than in any other region of the Soviet Union the native population, living primarily in the rural areas, had rejected the Bolsheviks. Before 1927 Soviet leaders had tried to remedy the situation by encouraging ethnic Ukrainians, particularly farmers and intellectuals, to support the Party, but they had enjoyed only modest success.[58] They had continued, therefore, to rely on the cities. With the advent of the industrialization and collectivization programs, however, the composition of the cities had begun to change, as Ukrainian peasants—now surplus in the countryside because of the mechanization of agriculture— migrated to industrial centers. There was, at the same time, a steady flow of Russian technicians into the cities, but the influx of Ukrainians was larger. Gradually the ethnic balance of the proletariat shifted until by 1930 a clear majority of the Ukraine's workers were ethnic Ukrainians.[59] As a result, Soviet leadership was forced to consider the disturbing possibility that its principal supporting group in the Ukraine—the urban proletariat—as it became predominantly Ukrainian rather than Russian, would move toward a more distinctly nationalist and anti-Russian position. It was this disquieting vision which underlay much of the argument over the national question carried on after 1928.

The first response to the situation was made by the old Russian core of the Party, joined now by the many technicians and plant managers but recently come from Russia. Irritated by the inconveniences resulting from the increasingly strict requirement that only the Ukrainian language be used in public intercourse,[60] the group urged that the dominant position of Russians in the Ukraine's industrial and urban centers be openly accepted. Limitations on the scope of the Ukrainization program as applied to the cities should be adopted, and the new Ukrainian migrants to the cities should be Russified, thereby maintaining the primacy of Russian institutions. The Ukrainization program was objectionable because it failed to safeguard the rights of the Russian minority and because it stimulated the growth of a local nationalism hostile to the principles of Soviet society. The program needed to be re-examined and a whole new statement prepared on Bolshevik national aims and purposes.

The national policy this group supported was outlined in articles published in *Bol'shevik* and in *Bil'shovyk Ukrainy* and at sessions of the Kiev organization of Cultural Active Workers and within the Ukrainian Institute of Marxism-Leninism at Kharkov.[61] The group's basic premise was that conditions in the Soviet Union had changed materially since 1923, when Bolshevik national policy had last been clearly elaborated, and that the new conditions required a new approach. First, it was suggested that, as a result of the abandonment of the New Economic Policy and the inauguration of the Five-Year Plan, the left deviation in Soviet political life had been replaced by the right deviation as the principal threat to Soviet authority. In regard to the national question, this meant that local nationalism—which, it was argued, was identified with the right deviation—had now become a greater menace than great-state nationalism or Russian chauvinism. Hence Party emphasis should be shifted toward a more resolute battle with nationalists and a greater acceptance of Russian elements.

Secondly, it was urged that local nationalism, which at one time had developed primarily as a reaction to Russian persecution, had now become identified with the peasant question, specifically with the interests of the kulaks, and hence had become an independent movement with its own economic driving force. As a result, the problem of local nationalism could no longer be solved solely by attacking Russian chauvinism. Instead a resolute, direct campaign was required. Moreover, the close ties which had developed between peasants and nationalists meant that in the future, as the battle for collectivization expanded and rural antagonisms increased, Ukrainian national sentiment would also grow and become more sharply hostile. Kulaks would embrace nationalist slogans in their effort to fight Soviet farm policy, and

Ukrainian nationalists in turn would appeal to the aggrieved farmers for support. Hence the broad and crucial question of the success of Bolshevik policy in the countryside would be answered in part by Soviet willingness to take a firm stand against Ukrainian nationalism.

Finally, it was urged that Bolshevik internationalism, as expounded by Lenin and endorsed by the Party, was incompatible with the Soviet localization policy, particularly its requirement that each local group in the Soviet Union be strengthened an developed as a distinct nationality.[62] Leninism, it was declared, required the abolition of states and national divisions and the amalgamation of all into a single whole with a single language and a single culture. Although it was reasonable that such a policy could not be achieved at once, it was important that a beginning be made and that local nationalisms be discouraged and local languages drawn closer together. The Party's localization policy, it was claimed, moved in the opposite direction, interfering with Bolshevik internationalism. As a result, it endangered the success of the revolutionary world movement.

Although these views were appealing to the Russian minority in the Ukraine, they were opposed by the principal leaders of the CP(b)U. Among Party leaders at the time were many of the same men who had spoken so strongly for Ukrainization in 1926,[63] and there are no indications that they had altered their views. Kaganovich, who as First Secretary of the CP(b)U had consistently affirmed Stalin's national policy in the Ukraine, was recalled to Moscow in July, 1928,[64] but his successor, S. V. Kosior, continued to support localization work. The most outspoken and forceful of the Party leaders was Nikolai Skrypnik who, following the ousting of Shums'kyi from his government and Party posts, had become not only the principal defender of the Ukrainization program, but also the chief architect of Bolshevik national and cultural policy in the Ukraine. Skrypnik was now a full member of the Central Committtee of the All-Union Communist Party[65] as well as a member of the Ukrainian Politburo and head of the critical Ukrainian Commissariat of Education. Although other Party leaders played larger roles in general Party affairs, attaining membership in the Union Politburo which Skrypnik did not, his voice was apparently decisive in questions of education, culture, and national policy. It seems likely that Party resolutions on these questions adopted in the years from 1927 to 1932 were reflections of Skrypnik's views if not actually drafts of his making.

The first high-level retort to the anti-nationalists came from Kosior who noted in October, 1928, that the Ukrainization program needed to be speeded up.[66] Subsequently, the problem was examined again and again by both Skrypnik and Kosior.[67] At the end of 1929 the Central Committee of the CP(b)U adopted two resolutions purporting to express the Party's approach to the national question under the new conditions of "socialist reconstruction."[68]

The new conditions of the Five-Year Plan, it was observed, had not eliminated the national question as a key element in Bolshevik policy. On the contrary, the importance of the problem had increased. Skrypnik declared:

There was a time when cultural work was considered third in line and third in importance after the military and economic fronts; there was a separate cultural front. Now cultural work has received its due recognition and appears as an inseparable part of our general work of socialist reconstruction.[69]

The task of national-cultural construction, Skrypnik continued, had become a vital feature of socialist building under the industrialization and collectivization programs. In fact, national-cultural construction had become one of the prerequisites for socialist building, since the new programs could succeed only with the widest support from all the peoples of the Soviet Union, and since such support could be guaranteed only if the localization program was emphasized. As an example, Skrypnik referred to the problem of technical cadres.[70] In the Ukraine, he noted, both the collectivization and industrialization programs were suffering from a shortage of technicians. But new technicians were not being trained in sufficient numbers because many technical schools presented work only in Russian and were therefore closed to the mass of the local population. The problem obviously could be solved only if

the schools were shifted to Ukrainian. Thus was illustrated, Skrypnik suggested, Lenin's dictum that without a satisfactory solution
of the cultural question, socialist construction was impossible.[71]

In the matter of Ukrainization of the cities, Party leaders also
expressed a sense of urgency. The problem was difficult, they
agreed, because it involved the question of control of the Ukraine's
urban areas. But it could be solved only if the Party understood
the importance of the new influx of Ukrainian peasants into industrial centers and the tremendous growth in the Ukrainian
element in the cities. It was foolish to suggest, as did the opposition, that these Ukrainians could be Russified as in the past
and drawn as Russians to the Soviet program. Such efforts would
serve only to increase nationalist feeling and to set Ukrainians
against the Bolsheviks. Instead, it was necessary to transform
the cities into Ukrainian centers in order that they might receive
the new Ukrainian migrants with their own language and draw
them to the Bolshevik fold in terms they were able to understand.
The program of Ukrainization of the cities was interpreted, therefore, not as a program for strengthening Ukrainian influence in
opposition to Russians and Bolsheviks, but as the only program
under which Soviet leaders could ensure mass support from urban
Ukrainians and the growing Ukrainian proletariat.

Complicating the problem was the fact that the cities of the
Ukraine were traditionally Russian and included many Russians
and Russified Ukrainians who were considerably inconvenienced
by the change to the Ukrainian language and culture. As minorities in the Ukraine, these groups could demand the same concessions and national guarantees that Ukrainians demanded for
themselves as a minority in the Soviet Union. Ukrainian leaders produced optimistic figures indicating that a majority of the urban
dwellers were Ukrainian, but the figures were to a degree mislead-
ing, for many Ukrainians considered themselves Russian in all but
name.[72] As a practical matter Russian institutions seemed generally more acceptable in the cities than Ukrainian institutions. As
a result, efforts by Ukrainian leaders to force urban Russians to
learn and use the Ukrainian language were opposed by Russians
as a form of national oppression of an ethnic minority. The ar-

gument was especially trenchant being directed against Ukrainians who had insisted so vociferously and for so long on their own cultural rights and, specifically, on the rights of the Ukrainian minorities in other Soviet republics. Ukrainian leaders therefore found themselves in the position of being forced to abandon either their arguments for Ukrainization of the cities or their defense of Ukrainian rights in other parts of the Soviet Union. The dilemma was a difficult one and was the chief cause for the slowness of Ukrainian leaders in developing an acceptable policy.

By 1929 Skrynik had begun to suggest an approach to the dilemma based on a policy of "voluntary Ukrainization."[73] The policy was to apply both to Russians and to Russified Ukrainians, but in different ways according to their different situations. For the first group the policy called for a clear recognition of the group's special status and for guarantees that its language and culture would be not only tolerated but encouraged and developed. Nevertheless, the group was not expected to remain exclusively Russian, for it was anticipated that its members would voluntarily learn Ukrainian once they had come to recognize its importance as the language of the majority of the workers. There was also the expectation that ultimately the Russians would become completely Ukrainized as they grew convinced of the advantages of the official state language and of Ukrainian customs and traditions.

For the second group—the Russified Ukrainians—the policy was to be less flexible and lenient although also voluntary. To begin, Skrypnik declared, it was necessary to recognize that Russified Ukrainians were not Russians, as sometimes claimed, but were a distinct element, Ukrainian by background, Russian by association, and both Ukrainian and Russian by language. They were an unfortunate survival of the colonization policy of the Russian Tsars—a hybrid group speaking neither pure Russian nor pure Ukrainian, but a combination language including elements of both. In addition, Skrypnik suggested, it was necessary to recognize that Russified Ukrainians had strong natural sympathies for the Ukraine, that they considered themselves Ukrainians despite their ignorance of the Ukrainian language, and that they had great interest in

Ukrainian culture and Ukrainian literature. Consequently, the Party should accept them as Ukrainians and should determine as its policy to encourage them, without compulsion but in a positive way, to return to their original nationality and to relearn their Ukrainian language.

Skrypnik's views on Ukrainization of the cities were never endorsed completely by the Party. Nevertheless, it seems clear that the general approach he favored was acceptable to most leaders. The national question was still interpreted as requiring a resolute struggle against Russian chauvinism and a deliberate effort to foster Ukrainian institutions in the Ukraine's urban as well as rural districts. In effect, Ukrainian Bolsheviks were endorsing once again the liberal national policies adopted in 1923. Yet Party leaders did not intend that the limitations they had set on localization work be forgotten, nor did they mean that activity outside the bounds would be tolerated. After 1929 the Party's limitations were expressed again in many fields including literature and language policy and were most dramatically expressed late in 1929 when a nationalist organization—the Union for the Liberation of the Ukraine (*Spilka vyzvolennia Ukrainy*)—was "uncovered" and accused of treasonous work.

The Lesson

According to official accounts,[74] the Union for the Liberation of the Ukraine was a counterrevolutionary organization established in 1926 as a successor to a subversive Kiev group, the Brotherhood of Ukrainian Statehood (*Bratstvo ukrains'koi derzhavnosty*). The members of the Union, it was charged, were drawn from the intelligentsia, from the wealthy peasantry, and from bourgeois elements in the cities. Its head was Serhii Iefremov, former secretary of the Historical Division of the All-Ukrainian Academy of Sciences, said to be the Union's principal center. The Union was accused of acting under the direct influence of anti-Soviet *emigrés* including former leaders such as Petliura, Mazepa, Livits'kyi, and others. The Union was charged also with working, on the one hand, toward the destruction of Soviet power in the Ukraine with the help of foreign states and, on the other hand, toward the restoration of capitalism in the form of an independent "Ukrainian National Republic."[75] Specifically, the Union was accused of conducting anti-Soviet progaganda among youth through a subsidiary organization the Union of Ukrainian Youth (*Spilka ukrains'-koi molodi*),[76] of organizing individual and mass terrorist measures,[77] of developing the Ukrainian Autocephalous Church as a counterrevolutionary organization,[78] and of entering into Ukrainian cultural work in an effort to corrupt Soviet cultural programs.[79] In March, 1930, forty-five members of the Union were brought to trial and, after a long and widely-publicized hearing, were convicted and all but nine sentenced to varying prison terms.[80]

Although there is no conclusive evidence, the Soviet charges against the Union seem questionable, and it has been suggested that the organization itself existed only in the minds of Soviet leaders. From the wide publicity attending the trial and the light sentences given the accused it seems clear Soviet leaders viewed the trial as serving certain indirect purposes. As one of several trials conducted throughout the Soviet Union in 1930 and 1931, it was clearly meant by Stalin to strike at oppositionists—particularly "Rightists"—and to affirm collectivization and industrialization. On the national question the trial indictment and confessions of the defendants became a broad Party pronouncement and a warning that Ukrainization was not to be construed as a license for opposition. In a sense the trial was a restatement of Stalin's declaration that distinct national cultures would be tolerated only as long as they were unquestionably socialist in content: Ukrainian nationalists were not to use Ukrainization as a shield for developing contacts with *emigré* nationalists or for attacking Soviet industrialization and collectivization programs; Ukrainian cultural autonomy was to be interpreted in a more limited way than before, and areas such as philology, literature, science, and history—areas in which considerable freedom had been granted in the past—were to be more carefully controlled. The trial was therefore closely related to the discussions of Ukrainian literature, history, and language which had recently assumed such importance.

Further, the trial indictment emphasized that the accused had worked especially within organizations such as the Ukrainian Autocephalous Church[81] and the All-Ukrainian Academy of Sciences.[82] The defendants were charged, for example, with having seized control of the Ukrainian Academy's Institute of Ukrainian Scientific Terminology and of the Academy's Scientific-Pedagogical Society. Whether or not the charges were accurate, they served a distinct purpose, for they discredited the Academy and the Church and provided a pretext for later attacks on these bodies. Moreover, the attacks could easily be broadened to include Ukrainian nationalists against whom there was no evidence of direct anti-Soviet work, but who were suspected because of their nationalist views and could be discredited because of their assocation with these nationalist centers. Since the trial also introduced for the first time the question of treason, the stage was set for a new approach to nationalist expressions. Henceforth, the most fervent nationalists were not simply to be corrected for their deviationism, but were to be identified with organizations of uncertain loyalty and hence represented as enemies of the state.

The lessons of the trial were subsequently confirmed by proceedings against a second nationalist group, the Center for Counterrevolutionary Work in the Rural Economy of the Ukraine. The group was "uncovered" and brought to trial only shortly after the Union for the Liberation of the Ukraine.[83] Twenty-nine members of the Center were named as defendants, including M. Reznikov, a member of the CP(b)U and of the collegium of the Ukrainian Commissariat of Agriculture. The Center was accused of opposing the Soviet collectivization program and of engaging in acts of sabotage against efforts to increase agricultural production and procurement. Above all, the Center was charged with endeavoring to maintain a capitalist economy in the countryside through the preservation of private farms and kulak estates. Again, as in the case of the Union for the Liberation of the Ukraine, the trial was given wide publicity, again apparently with the aim of warning Ukrainians that concerted opposition to established Soviet policies would not be tolerated.

The reaction of Ukrainian leaders to these trials, with their suggestion that nationalist expressions and oppositions to central authority were to be fought in the most serious way, is not clearly known. Republic officials had little responsibility for the trials which were prepared and managed by the State Political Administration (GPU), although heard by Ukrainian courts. In statements following the trials, CP(b)U leaders hailed them as major battles in the war against foreign intervention, Ukrainian bourgeois nationalism, and the counterrevolution. Kosior praised the trials for helping to stamp out Ukrainian nationalism and for exposing the oppositionist work of the old Ukrainian intelligentsia.[84] Liubchenko emphasized that the trials unveiled the vicious plots of Poland and the Ukrainian emigration.[85] Skrypnik noted that the trials emphasized the dangers of all efforts to set the Ukrainian culture off against the Russian.[86] Undoubtedly Ukrainian leaders accepted and endorsed the general lesson of the trials, that Ukrainians, regardless of their cultural and national demands, were obligated to avoid scrupulously all expressions hostile to socialism and Soviet policies. On this point the trials said no more than Skrypnik and others had declared earlier in opposing Shums'kyi and Khvyl'ovyi. On the other hand, Ukrainian leaders were undoubtedly disturbed by the suggestion that Ukrainian national expressions were to be more critically regarded in the future and also by the possibility that the trials would be used as a pretext for new attacks on Ukrainization by pro-Russian members of the CP(b)U. Kosior indicated apprehension on this score when he noted in his report to the Eleventh Congress of the CP(b)U (June, 1930) that the trials actually went far toward liquidating the problem of Ukrainian nationalism and that all attempts to use the trials to revise the Party's national policy should be sternly resisted.[87]

The Decision

In June, 1930, the national question was discussed at the Sixteenth Congress of the All-Union Communist Party. The Sixteenth Congress was the first to be called in nearly three years—the longest interval between congresses since the Revolution. More significantly, it was the first congress to meet following the shift from the New Economic Policy to socialist planning and hence the first opportunity for the Party as a whole to hear its leaders' evalution of the new programs.

In regard to the national question the Sixteenth Congress was of special significance. No comprehensive Party discussion on the subject had been held for over seven years —since the Twelfth Congress in 1923—and events in the interim had suggested that Party leaders had moved away from their initial liberal position. Attacks on the Party's national policy had steadily increased particularly from those anxious to limit the authority and independence of the republics. The attacks had been made in connection with the drive for socialism and had included strong declarations that the Party's national policy had become outmoded under the new conditions of Soviet life with their requirements for greater centralization in so many areas. The uncovering of the Union for the Liberation of the Ukraine with its lesson of Soviet unwillingness to tolerate opposition suggested a firmer approach toward the nationalities. All these developments indicated a turning by the Party away from Ukrainization. Undoubtedly many Party members expected the Sixteenth Congress to express such a turning in a more formal way.

In the principal address to the Congress, however, Stalin insisted that the national problem remained basically unchanged in the eyes of Party leaders.[88] The principal danger to the Party, he declared, was now as before the danger of Great-Russian chauvinism, especially the chauvinism of those who were urging that with the transition to socialism in the economic field the time had come for the Party to turn to internationalism in the national-cultural field, to abandon its support of the minority national cultures, and to press for the formation of a single socialist state with a common language and culture. Such suggestions, Stalin declared, showed a basic misunderstanding of true Bolshevik internationalism. It was necessary to make a careful distinction between a socialist state encircled by capitalist countries—the situation in which the USSR found itself—and a universal socialist state established on a world scale. For the former there was no possibility of the merging of separate nationalities into one. On the contrary, the equality of nations demanded by Leninism led inevitably to a flowering of each national culture. To argue otherwise, Stalin said, was to endanger the growing solidarity of the socialist nations and to fall into the "clutches of reactionary Great Russian chauvinists." Even in the second case, Stalin continued, when a world socialist state had been established, separate national cultures would disappear only slowly and gradually and, above all, only voluntarily as each national unit came to see the advantages of a common culture. Thus, he argued, the Party should continue to support the flowering of national cultures for the time so that ultimately, with the establishment of a world socialist state, the conditions would be prepared for the merging of all into one.

Specifically, Stalin reasserted a number of precepts adopted earlier by the Party: the minority nationalities, such as the Belorussian and the Ukrainian, were not to be Russified but were to be "regenerated and developed as independent nations"; national differences in language, culture, and way of life were not to be ignored; there was to be no further talk about the liquidation of the republics; the Party's policy of localizing the schools, the administrative apparatus, the press, etc., was not to be undermined. Stalin qualified these precepts by insisting as he had done previously that a firm battle be waged also against local nationalism and that the development of the nationalities did not mean that their cultures would be other than socialist. Furthermore, he presented the precepts in a negative way, emphasizing the pitfalls to be avoided rather than the tasks to be accomplished as he had done in 1923. Nevertheless, the burden of his argument was plain. The Party's position on the national question had not changed. The revisionists who had recently become so outspoken were not to be followed. Emphasis was to continue to be placed on the development and growth of the separate nationalities, with their individual cultures and national forms.

Why Stalin chose the Sixteenth Congress to re-emphasize a liberal national policy is not clear. In the eyes of many Party leaders his comments must have seemed untimely in view of the de-

mands for greater centralization and uniformity then dominating
Party attention. In 1923, when Stalin had insisted so strongly
on localization, he had defended his position above all by emphasizing the urgent need of the Bolsheviks to stimulate local
support in the border republics: the localization policy was a reflection of Bolshevik insecurity and of Stalin's uncertainty about
his own leadership. By 1930, however, the Party was firmly
established. As a result, there had been a shift away from localization and toward greater centralization not only of economic
and political life, but also of cultural affairs. Stalin's restatement
in 1930 of the rights of the nationalities, and especially his defense of those rights, not in terms of their immediate, practical
significance for the Bolsheviks, but on a more general, theoretic
level suggested a major break with the trend of recent years.

Stalin's own explanation for his stand was an orthodox Marxist
one. The inauguration of socialist programs in 1928, he declared,
had led to a sharpening of the class struggle in the USSR and to
an intensification of national friction and a growth in the deviation toward Great-Russian chauvinism. His purpose in speaking
now was to expose this deviation and to answer it.[89]

More probably, however, Stalin was influenced by immediate
practical considerations, above all, once again, the question of
support. Apparently Stalin, in his recent personal struggle with
the Right Opposition, had relied, as before 1925, on the support
of the Ukrainian Party organization. There is no evidence that
Stalin's chief rival, Bukharin, had made any serious organizational
effort to challenge Stalin's control over the Ukraine, nor any
indication that either nationalist or Russian leaders of the CP(b)U
—with the exception perhaps of Skrypnik—would have supported
Bukharin despite his call for a more flexible collectivization policy.
Stalin's stand at the Sixteenth Congress represented both a recognition of the Ukraine's loyalty and a bid for continued support
as Stalin sought to strengthen his yet not unshakeable position.

Moreover Stalin may have been influenced by the arguments
Skrypnik had marshalled in his defense of Ukrainian cultural autonomy. With the advent of collectivization and industrialization, the
peasants in the Soviet Union had become key factors in the success

of the Bolshevik program. On the one hand, peasants were being drawn to the cities where they swelled the ranks of the urban proletariat—the group on which Soviet leaders relied for support. On the other hand, the peasants remaining in the countryside were being confronted with collectivization, and it seemed reasonable to assume that the program would be facilitated if the peasants could be led to cooperate. In both areas the Bolsheviks felt the importance of building closer and more friendly links between the Party and the peasants. In November, 1929, the Party Central committee had stressed the problem in a broad resolution calling on the CP(b)U "to strengthen its work in the organization of the proletarian masses of the coutryside and in the raising of its cultural level," and to move closer to the countryside by improving and expanding rural Party work.[90] These changes could be accomplished in the Ukraine, however, only through the Ukrainian language, for the peasants were overwhelmingly non-Russian. Consequently the national question had become once again a vital one, calling for Party recognition of the rights of the minorities and for renewed attention to the growth ot local institutions. Stalin's report to the Sixteenth Party Congress was apparently both a theoretical justification of Soviet policy and a repetition of his warning of 1923 that unless the Bolsheviks adopted national demands as their own they could not win the support of the USSR's minorities, and hence could not accomplish Bolshevik programs.

THE DEMAND FOR UNIFORMITY

Although the sessions of the Sixteenth Congress were permeated with an atmosphere of confidence, even jubilation, over the successes of the Five-Year Plan, the Congress clearly marked the end of the first, easy phase of the socialist drive and the beginning of a difficult and unstable period for the Bolsheviks. Hints of the impending troubles had appeared before the convening of the Congress in the turmoil which had accompanied collectivization in many districts and in the uncertain production of agricultural commodities, especially livestock.[91] In the years after the Congress and continuing until 1934 the difficulties increased steadily as opposition to collectivization mounted, and farm production, hindered by unfavorable climatic conditions and peasant resistance, fell to levels far below those of pre-revolutionary Russia.[92] The situation in many rural areas became critical, rivaling the disorganized conditions of the Revolution itself. As a result, the period from 1930 to 1934 presented problems of a most troublesome kind.

In the Ukraine, as in other parts of the Soviet Union, there were few indications in the first months after the Congress of the great upheavals to come. Kosior, in his address to the Eleventh Congress of the CP(b)U (June, 1930), spoke optimistically of the progress of collectivization and industrialization and of the prospects for increased farm production.[93] On the national question Ukrainian leaders heralded Stalin's denunciation of Great-Russian chauvinism and his reaffirmation of the rights of the minorities.[94] The stimulus given by the Congress to the nationalist wing of the CP(b)U was indicated by numerous articles in the Ukrainian press urging renewed emphasis on Ukrainization and a resolute battle with Great-Russian chauvinism.[95] Skrypnik, for whom the Congress was a vindication, assumed a more prominent role in Ukrainian cultural affairs, speaking frequently and authoritatively on questions of education, Leninism, literature, history, and the national problem. For the moment, open attacks on the Ukrainization policy ceased.

It gradually became apparent, however, that the nationalist victory was less complete than it had seemed at first. Although Stalin had recalled Party members to the basic tenets of Soviet national policy, he had done little, except by emphasis, to resolve the old practical difficulties which had arisen as these tenets had been applied. His defense of the formula "socialist in content, national in form" had assured continuation of localization programs in the republics. But the difficult conflicts in the Ukraine had risen not over the formula itself, but over disagreements on its application. The disagreements were two-fold: there was contention over the application of Ukrainian national forms to the non-Ukrainian minorities, particularly Russians; there was disagreement over the question of what aspects of cultural work were matters of form, and hence to be developed along national lines, and what aspects were matters of substance to be guided along socialist lines. The first argument had centered on the sensitive problem of Ukrainization of the cities; the second had developed chiefly over questions of literature and history, as Ukrainians had tried to create distinctly Ukrainian forms without violating socialist requirements—a task which had grown more difficult as socialism had come to be defined in a more restrictive, yet comprehensive way. To these two most difficult questions Stalin's report to the Sixteenth Congress had provided no answers. Although the tenor of his address encouraged the nationalists, it was not long before opposition voices were raised once again.

The immediate issue prompting opposition arose over the work being done in two Ukrainian institutions: the Ukrainian Institute of Marxism-Leninism and the Ukrainian Academy of Sciences, particularly its historical division. Historians in these institutions had been given responsibility for preparing studies emphasizing aspects of Ukrainian history but also developing Marxist themes. Their task was not unlike that assigned Ukrainian writers who had been instructed to build a literature, nationalist in form but socialist in content. As has been noted, Ukrainian writers had largely failed in their work in the eyes of Party leaders, and their failure had led to the broad attack of 1926 on Ukrainian literature and the Ukrainian writer Khvyl'ovyi. Although Ukrainian historians had avoided the most obvious pitfalls into which Ukrainian writers had fallen, their work, too, had come under mounting Party criticism until in 1929 a major campaign against them was inaugurated.

The first subject for attack was Matvii Iavors'kyi, a Ukrainian historian who had prepared the standard history of the Ukraine used throughout Ukrainian schools.[96] Iavors'kyi was a member of the CP(b)U, who in the past had himself criticized non-Communist historians such as Hrushevs'kyi for their nationalist perversions.[97] In 1929, however, as Soviet leaders began to demand greater orthodoxy in cultural affairs, Iavors'kyi also became a target for criticism. At sessions of the Ukrainian Institute of Marxism-Leninism he was accused of exaggerating the role played by Ukrainian bourgeois and kulak classes in the 1917 revolutions, of idealizing the non-Bolshevik Ukrainian socialist parties, and of minimizing the general importance of the proletariat in the Ukraine.[98] Iavors'kyi at first defended his work—which was also upheld by certain Party leaders—but he was forced finally to confess his errors and was removed from his posts in the Institute and the Academy of Sciences.

Subsequently, in the aftermath of the Sixteenth Party Congress, the importance of the attack on Iavors'kyi was minimized. But by 1931 new oppositions to nationalist historians appeared. The immediate target now was the venerable dean of Ukrainian historians, Mykhailo Hrushevs'kyi, leader of the Central Rada in the early months of the Revolution and foremost scholar in the Ukraine. Following the Revolution Hrushevs'kyi had voluntarily exiled himself from the Ukraine, but in 1924 he had returned, refusing to join with the Bolsheviks but agreeing to continue his historical work. Appointed head of the historical division of the Ukrainian Academy of Sciences, he had founded a technical journal, *Ukraina*, and had stimulated publication of many archival studies. In general, he had discreetly avoided topics with political implications and had thereby escaped severe Party attack if not occasional criticism.[99] Early in 1931, however, the official journal of the CP(b)U, *Bil'shovyk Ukrainy*, published an article denouncing his work.[100] He was accused of expressing bourgeois-nationalist conceptions and of showing himself hostile to Ukrainian-Russian friendship. More significantly, he was attacked for his neutrality, the article insisting that in the great task of socialist construction no truly proletarian historian could ignore important political events such as, for example, the uncovering of the Union for the Liberation of the Ukraine. The article was only a prelude to more serious charges, and shortly Hrushevs'kyi was accused of belonging to a nebulous subversive organization, the Ukrainian National Center. He was ousted as chief of the historical division, removed from the Academy of Sciences and, finally, deported from the Ukraine.[101]

The attacks on Hrushevs'kyi and Iavors'kyi were only the more obvious signs of a steadily increasing opposition to all expressions of Ukrainian localism. Throughout 1931 and 1932 Ukrainian writers, scholars, and artists were harried and their societies placed under steadily growing restrictions. On March 15, 1931, the Central Committee of the CP(b)U adopted a resolution informing historians that their work would be considered inadequate in the future if it did not emphasize problems of socialist construction, the class struggle, and the Soviet cultural revolution.[102] In June the powerful Ukrainian Institute of Marxism-Leninism was broken into a federation—the All-Ukrainian Association of Marxist-Leninist Institutes—and ordered to shift in its future work to the task of mass propaganda and the training of scientific cadres.[103] In September schools throughout the Soviet Union were directed to increase the scope of political training and to exercise greater care in selecting only reliable non-bourgeois teachers.[104] In April, 1932, all separate literary organizations in the Soviet Union were, in effect, abolished and a single Union of Soviet Writers established.[105] In July the All-Ukrainian Academy of Sciences was ordered to reorganize itself in order to emphasize scientific and technical work and studies on proletarian themes.[106] In area after area Soviet leaders made plain that they intended to increase control over cultural activities, to establish more comprehensive and limiting requirements for cultural work, and to insist more firmly and inflexibly on absolute acceptance of official standards.

The new demands seemed to violate the spirit of Stalin's report to the Sixteenth Congress, but the violation was more apparent than real. Although Stalin had emphasized the rights of the nationalities, suggesting even that they be expanded, it became clear in the following years that it was not his intention either to relax pressure for the achievement of socialist programs or to allow national demands to interfere with Soviet policy. On the contrary, his purpose in defending nationality rights was to prevent the growth of opposition among minority groups by removing one of their most important grievances—the discriminatory practices applied against minority languages, minority customs, and the minority peoples in general. His defense of the minorities was basically a defense of their language rights and of their right to participate equally with Russians and without prejudice in the building of a Soviet society. To the extent that attacks on the nationalities after 1930 reflected Russian prejudice, they were contrary to the decisions of the Sixteenth Congress. But to a considerable degree the attacks represented, not Russian chauvinism, but two new elements which Stalin and the Party had come to accept as basic for Soviet national policy.

The first element was the conviction that a neutral attitude toward the Soviet program was impossible and that all aspects of Soviet life, without exception, needed to be marshalled behind the broad socialist programs being undertaken. Such a conviction had been implied in 1926 in Stalin's observation in his letter on Shums'kyism that culture could not be divorced from politics. After 1930 this suggestion had become more firmly accepted and more widely applied. The argument was more than a negative insistence that there be no anti-Bolshevik implications in cultural work. It was the positive requirement that all cultural as well as political work be organized so as to contribute to the building of a Soviet society. As the principle was applied, the areas of unregulated activity in the republics were reduced so far that little opportunity for original work remained. Themes for history, literature, art, and science were prescribed in terms so rigid that the republics could do little more than translate them into local languages or emphasize their significance for the local situation. Even in these matters there was increasing interference, for Soviet leaders began to regard the principle of the unity of the republics as a fundamental Soviet precept and hence to view efforts to emphasize the distinctiveness of local languages and local institutions as divisive and counterrevolutionary. Ukrainian philologists were attacked for endeavoring to substitute for Russian words, long accepted in the Ukrainian language, Ukrainian words from Eastern Galicia or from the Ukrainian countryside.[107] Ukrainian historians who emphasized the glories of the ancient Ukraine were denounced for displaying "harmful manifestations of bourgeois chauvinism."[108] All such efforts were counterrevolutionary, it was declared, because they tended to set the Ukraine off against the Soviet Union and to weaken the brotherhood of the Ukrainian and Russian peoples. Thus, matters which had been considered "form" in an earlier period and only of local concern were now examined for their most subtle political implications and brought under central direction.

The second element prompting central opposition to Ukrainian nationalism was the growing apprehension of Soviet leaders that Ukrainian nationalists—Communists and non-Communists alike—were failing to ensure the political orthodoxy of national institutions, forms, and programs. There was overwhelming evidence to the contrary: in area after area Ukrainian nationalists had condoned deviations from Soviet policy. That this was especially true after 1930 was a reflection of the growing strictures of Soviet rule and of the new requirements handed down in every field of public life. Undoubtedly, many Ukrainian nationalist deviations resulted only from well-intentioned efforts to preserve a measure of independence from central control or to moderate a particularly distasteful Soviet requirement. But there were also other deviations prompted by a real opposition to the Bolsheviks and by an ill-defined hope for the destruction of the Soviet Union and the establishment of an independent or autonomous Ukraine. As a result, central leaders began to view the nationalists as potential traitors who could not be drawn to support Soviet rule and who would serve in the future only as centers of disaffection. The pressure to adopt stern measures against these people and to drive them out of all responsible positions mounted steadily in 1931 and 1932.

The Farm Problem and the New Party Discipline

Compounding the Soviet distrust of Ukrainian nationalists was the issue of collectivization and especially the difficulties engendered by the emergence of resistance to collectivization in the Ukrainian countryside. This resistance had begun to assume major proportions in 1930, when many peasants had refused to join the collective farms or, when forced into them, had preferred to destroy their livestock rather than transfer it to communal herds. In 1931 and 1932 the resistance became wider as peasants continued to shun the collectives and to withhold grain deliveries to the state at its low fixed prices. Kolkhozes as well as private farms became centers of opposition, and the problem was magnified at every point by the unfavorable climatic conditions of these years and the resulting poor harvests. During the grain collection periods in 1931 and 1932 conditions similar to those of the civil war appeared in some districts, as peasants refused to deliver their grain, fought against grain-collection officials, and broke into storage depots to seize the produce officials had confiscated. The situation became so grave that Soviet leaders feared they would be forced to abandon the farm program or that food supplies for the cities would be so reduced that anti-Bolshevik uprisings would result.

It is not clear to what extent Ukrainian nationalists in the cities were connected with the turbulence in the countryside, or to what extent dissident peasants looked toward national independence as an answer to their plight. Peasant opposition in some districts developed nationalist aspects, as Russians from the cities were sent to the farms to assume the onerous tasks of grain collection and kolkhoz supervision; their arrival among the Ukrainian farmers undoubtedly revived the traditional peasant distrust of alien urban influences. Soviet leaders insisted in strong terms that subversive nationalists were largely responsible for peasant unrest. Both Kosior and Postyshev in addresses to the Seventeenth Congress of the All-Union Communist Party (January, 1934) declared that nationalists had "played an exceptionally important role in creating and extending the breakdown in [the Ukraine's] rural economy."[109] They referred to "typical" kolkhozes in which five out of seven leadership posts were held by subversive nationalists;[110] they accused high Party leaders with nationalist sympathies of sabotaging grain collection and aiding hostile kulaks.[111] These attacks were undoubtedly exaggerated, for Party leaders were seeking scapegoats to be blamed for the failure of the farm program. Yet it seems likely that connections between nationalists and dissident peasants did exist and that Soviet leaders were fearful the bonds between the two groups might grow, providing the basis for a powerful nationalist-peasant rebellion.[112]

In the early months of 1932 the first measures against nationalists and peasants were adopted. In part the new campaign was a propaganda campaign, and the Ukrainian press was filled daily with resolutions of Party and government organs demanding more enthusiastic efforts in farm production and produce collection. In part the campaign was political and included changes in Party and government structure and shifts in Party and government leadership.

The first corrective steps were directed at the local level. In decisions adopted in February and May, 1932, the Central Committee of the CP(b)U denounced Party units in the countryside for their failure to build mass enthusiasm for the farm program.[113] Special attention was given to raions where farm work had been particularly weak. In several instances Party officials were removed from their posts, expelled from the Party, and brought to trial.[114] In July the Central Control Commission of the CP(b)U —the body charged with verifying Party decisions—ordered its local branches to increase control over Party work in the raions and to wage a stronger battle against deviations and distortions.[115]

At the republic level central leaders began to interfere more directly in Ukrainian affairs. As the farm campaign proceeded in the spring of 1932, it became clear that the difficulties which had interfered so seriously with agricultural production in 1931 had not been overcome. To Party leaders in Moscow it appeared that the CP(b)U was much to blame for the shortcomings. In an effort to impress Party members with the urgency of the situation, a special Ukrainian Party Conference was convened in July, 1932.[116] Molotov and Kaganovich, sent to the Conference as representatives from Moscow, gave impassioned speeches demanding greatest attention to the Ukraine's rural areas and a resolute struggle against weak and oppositionist work wherever found.[117] The two leaders were sharply critical of the CP(b)U: of its leaders, its Central Committee, and especially its local organizations in the countryside. Many speakers to the Conference, Kaganovich noted, had been too concerned with justifying their failures and not enough concerned with the tasks that stood before them.

These tasks are great. We must not underestimate their complexity. The reports to the Conference by raion leaders have not reflected the magnitude of the serious tasks that stand before us. You must now energetically organize the harvest so that it will not fail, particularly in the sugarbeet districts. You must prepare and develop your work in order to achieve the plan for grain collection completely. . . . You must now prepare yourselves for the fall sowing campaign. You must in the villages and in the raions raise the spirits of certain active workers who today have been demobilized among you.[118]

If the Party did not fasten resolutely upon these tasks, Kaganovich concluded, the agricultural campaign would not be won.

Nevertheless, despite the Party Conference and the pressure of central leaders, the farm situation did not improve but continued to worsen in the following months. As the fall harvest season opened, it became apparent that crops were small and, as the harvest progressed, the quantity of produce collected and turned over to the state fell far short of assigned quotas. In early October Soviet officials concluded that only the most far-reaching measures could assure the collection of foodstuffs adequate for the cities.

On October 12 two central leaders—M. M. Khataevich and I. A. Akulov—were sent from Moscow to the Ukraine. They were appointed to the Central Committee of the CP(b)U and to its Politburo and Orgburo; Khataevich was also named Second Secretary of the Party, and Akulov was chosen head of the Party organization in the Donets oblast.[119] The appointments apparently did not indicate any specific dissatisfaction with other leaders of the CP(b)U, who were kept in their posts,[120] but suggested rather that central officials believed new and more inflexible leaders were needed. Both Akulov and Khataevich had previously worked briefly in the Ukraine, but neither was Ukrainian by nationality or identified particularly with the Ukraine as a distinct area.[121] Akulov had held the highest posts in verification agencies in the Soviet Union, including that of First Deputy Chief of the Unified State Political Administration (OGPU). Khataevich had been active in organization work in the Party and had headed a number of regional Party organizations. As Second Secretary of the CP(b)U, he quickly·replaced Kosior as Party leader. Almost immediately he ordered a complete purge of five raion Party organizations[122] and, in a series of addresses to regional and republic Party groups, called on Party members and officials to increase their role in the most aggressive way in the task of achieving the Party's farm goals.

In December, 1932, two further steps were taken. The first was a resolution calling for a wide purge of the ranks of the Party to include the temporary suspending of new member enrollment, the careful verification of old members and candidates, and the expulsion of members whose work was shown to have been unsatisfactory.[123] The second step—a resolution adopted by the CP(b)U Central Committee on December 14—was a broad criticism of the Party's failure to overcome its difficulties and a stern injunction for the Party to seize the initiative in guiding both political and economic work.[124]

By the end of 1932 reports on farm work were suggesting that the situation was far worse than it had appeared in October. Official statistics indicated that total grain collections were nearly 26 percent below assigned quotas, while in the month of December less than 35 percent of planned amounts were collected.[125] Serious as were these deficiencies, they were overshadowed by the graver danger that Soviet officials in the Ukraine might lose control of districts in which peasant resistance was particularly strong. In great numbers the farmers were deserting the collectives they had been forced to join[126] and, on the verge of starvation, were refusing to deliver their grain. The story of the harsh measures taken to treat with this resistance has been graphically told by many observers and need not be repeated here.[127] Yet the measures were not succeeding, and it was becoming increasingly clear that local officials in many cases were not in sympathy with the farm program or at least with the ruthless way in which it was being carried out. Ukrainian leaders found themselves in the difficult position of attempting to enforce an unpopular policy through subordinates who were oftentimes unreliable.

At the highest level in the Soviet Union the decision was taken early in 1933 to strike at these difficulties through a thorough reorganization of the whole structure of Party relationships in the rural areas. In January Stalin explained this reorganization to a joint plenum of the Central Committee and Central Control Commission of the All-Union Communist Party. He began by emphasizing the many weaknesses in farm work throughout the Soviet Union and especially the failures of Party members and leaders "to understand the new situation" in the countryside and to give effective guidance to the new collectives.[128] In many districts and regions, he noted, the Party had set itself apart from the collective farms, allowing them to be taken over by counterrevolutionaries, Ukrainian nationalists, and pseudo-Communists. As a result, many collectives had failed in their policital work of destroying kulak elements and strengthening Soviet power in the rural areas. Unfortunately, Stalin warned, it was the Party itself which was responsible for these shortcomings:

It is not in the village that we must seek for the real failures in grain collection, but among ourselves, within our own ranks, for *we* stand at the helm, *we* control the resources of the state, *we* are responsible for leading the kolkhozes, and *we* are obliged to assume full responsibility for work in the countryside.[129]

If the defects were to be remedied, Stalin concluded, as indeed they must, it could only be on the basis of the strengthening of Party leadership.

In response to Stalin's plea, the plenum adopted as the vehicle for the reinforcement of Party work a system of Political Departments to be established in each Machine-Tractor Station and in each state farm.[130] The Departments were to be formed as teams of three or four tested Party workers to be recruited chiefly in the cities and sent out to the rural areas. There they were to verify the work of the state farm or collective, correcting deficiencies and ensuring the reliability of farm leaders. Each Department was to take charge of Party and Komsomol work in its district and was authorized to supersede local Party workers, establishing itself as an autonomous unit reporting directly to central officials. Thus, it was hoped, the indifferent or hostile attitude of local workers would be countered by the enthusiasm of dedicated urban cadres.

For the Ukraine the decisions of the plenum were considered insufficient by themselves. As in 1925, central leaders had become convinced that the highest leadership in the CP(b)U was inadequate. At a special meeting of the Central Committee of the All-Union Communist Party on January 24, a resolution on the shortcomings of the CP(b)U was adopted:[131] "The Central Committee accepts as an established fact that the Party organizations of the Ukraine have not succeeded in accomplishing the Party tasks charged to them in the areas of organization of grain storage and completion of the plan for grain collection." Three of the Ukraine's seven oblasts—Odessa, Dnepropetrovsk, and Kharkov— were singled out as particularly blameworthy, and their Party leaders were removed and new ones appointed. For the Ukraine as a whole, three members of the Politburo and Secretariat were removed, and Pavel P. Postyshev, a secretary of the All-Union Communist Party and one of Stalin's closest associates, was named Second Secretary with the broadest authority to reorganize the Party and to purge it of undesirable elements.[132] The resolution was remarkable, since, in a break with previous practice, the changes were made directly by the All-Union Communist Party rather than through the regular machinery of the CP(b)U as required by the Party rules. They represented therefore the most obvious example of central interference in Ukrainian Party affairs since the dissolution of the Sapronov opposition.

In April similar changes were made in the Donbass. A central resolution criticized Party shortcomings, and a "brigade" of workers headed by Molotov and Kaganovich was sent from Moscow to enforce corrective measures.[133]

The decisions forming Political Departments and shifting Ukrainian Party leadership were crucial for the CP(b)U. Throughout 1933 mass transfers of Party personnel took place, as workers from outside the Ukraine whose loyalty was unquestioned were injected into the Party and city workers were transferred to the countryside. By October, 1933, 3,000 were sent into the Political Departments, 1,340 to high posts in rural Party units, and nearly 10,000 to the collective farms.[134] Of this number, perhaps a third or more came not from the Ukraine but from urban centers in Russia, principally Moscow and Leningrad.[135] The new workers were little acquainted with the problems of the countryside and were unsympathetic to the peasant's individualist values and Ukrainian national sentiment. It is not surprising that their assumption of leadership in Party and government bodies in the rural districts produced a major transformation in the character of the CP(b)U.

In two further decisions central leaders sought to oust from the Party all suspected of too little enthusiasm for Party programs. In February a new chief of the State Political Administration (GPU) was sent to the Ukraine to strengthen the work of the secret police in ferreting out "counterrevolutionary wreckers."[136] Almost immediately a subversive organization operating in the agricultural commissariat was uncovered, and seventy of its members were brought to trial on charges of destroying state farm property and interfering with farm work.[137] Subsequently, other groups and individuals were similarly charged and removed from their posts and deported or imprisoned. In April the All-Union Central Committee ordered a complete purge of the Party to include the reregistration of Party members and "the removal from the Party ranks of untrustworthy and unstable . . . elements."[138] More comprehensive than any previous Party purges, the verification resulted in the expulsion of nearly 20 percent of the Ukraine's Party members[139] and in the replacement of nearly 50 percent of local Party leaders.[140]

Although no quantitative measurement of the impact of the changes of 1933 is possible, there is no question that the CP(b)U was remarkably changed: Party members who had viewed with misgivings the Soviet farm program were gone; a core of new leaders, oriented toward Moscow and convinced of the necessity of Bolshevik discipline, was established at all levels; the right of central officials to direct Party affairs in the Ukraine—long recognized in the Party rules—was broadened as Party leaders assumed the right to act directly in the Ukraine. The attitudes of the mass of ordinary Party members were similarly changed. The procedure of the purge, with its requirement that each member's record be examined and instances of disagreement with Party policy exposed and used as a basis for expulsion, placed a premium on orthodoxy and demonstrated that the chief qualification for Party membership in the future was to be a willingness to accept decisions from above. Members could no longer lightly disregard Party edicts or modify them even where changes seemed in the Party's best interests. As a result, the CP(b)U became, to a remarkable degree, an instrument for enforcing central policy in the Ukraine rather than a deliberative body participating in the formation of policy and interpreting Ukrainian peculiarities to central leaders.

The National Question and the New Party Discipline

The changes accomplished in 1932 and 1933 were prompted largely by the farm problem and by the problem of Party and government elements considered responsible for failures in collectivization and agricultural production. Yet the changes inevitably became broader in scope, encompassing other aspects of public life including cultural matters and above all the still perplexing problem of Ukrainian nationalism. It has been suggested that the radical measures adopted in 1932 and 1933 were the result of a deliberate decision on the part of Stalin and other central leaders to destroy every basis for anti-Soviet opposition in the Ukraine. There is no evidence that so direct a resolve was ever made. But there is much to suggest that the pressures and tensions of the collectivization and industrialization programs led central leaders to regard expressions of independence in cultural matters as attacks on the Party itself. And the rebirth of German militarism prompted Soviet leaders mindful of the earlier German sponsorship of Ukrainian nationalism to regard all nationalist manifestations as indications of subversive activity. It was therefore not unreasonable for Party leaders to conclude that for Soviet security as well as the success of Soviet programs Ukrainian nationalists had to be restricted or destroyed.

Apparently at a very early point, anti-nationalist criticisms began to center on the Ukrainian Commissariat of Education and on the person of its chief, Nikolai Skrypnik. Skrypnik had often been attacked in the past for his advocacy of decentralization and Ukrainian cultural rights, but his position of leadership in the Party and government had never been seriously challenged. At the end of 1931, however, severe criticisms of his work began to appear. At the December Plenum of the CP(b)U he was attacked for his deviations on the national question and for his erroneous interpretations of Party history.[141] In March, 1932, his mistakes were discussed by the Politburo of the CP(b)U, and he was asked to recognize his errors. He did not do so, however, and the matter apparently was dropped.[142]

In September, 1932, a campaign was inaugurated against Skrypnik's stronghold the Ukrainian Commissariat of Education. To a degree the campaign was part of an All-Union drive to reform the school system of the whole Soviet Union in order to emphasize the training of technicians and scientists and the preparation of politically reliable cadres for industry and agriculture.[143] At the same time, the campaign developed also as a direct attack on the particular mistakes of the Ukrainian Commissariat. In a September decision of the Ukrainian government the Commissariat was censored for its inability to prepare capable and reliable cadres of teachers and for its failure to provide methodical direction of the work of the schools.[144] In February, 1933, the Commissariat was criticized for preparing improper textbooks for the schools, for adopting incorrect positions on a number of theoretic questions, and for permitting incorrect statements to appear in the Commissariat's official journal.[145] On February 28, 1933, the first direct step against Skrypnik was taken by relieving him of his post as Commissar of Education and assigning him to the less sensitive position of chief of the Ukrainian State Planning Commission.[146]

Meanwhile, all aspects of the national question were being discussed by Ukrainian leaders at meetings of the Politburo and Central Committee of the CP(b)U. The arrival of Postyshev in the Ukraine in January, 1933, had considerably strengthened pro-Russian elements in the CP(b)U and correspondingly weakened Skrypnik's position. In February the Central Committee was again asked to demand from Skrypnik a recognition of his nationalist deviations,[147] and the matter was now apparently serious. Records of Party deliberations in the crucial months from February to May, 1933, are not available, and it is not clear what support Skrypnik was able to muster. The only leaders who might have been expected to defend him were Petrovs'kyi and Chubar', and it is unlikely that either was willing to take a stand in the face of the strong mandate Postyshev had brought with him to the Ukraine. In any case the Central Committee and its Politburo were dominated by pro-centralist elements.[148] By March or April the decision was taken to attack the national question in the harshest way. Skrypnik was perhaps the only leader who refused to accept the decision.

The first open signs of the attack on Ukrainian nationalists came on May 1, 1933, with the publication of three addresses on Soviet national policy by Party leaders.[149] The tenor of the addresses was basically the same. In the past the Soviet Ukraine had made great strides in national-cultural construction; but, as a result of infiltration by Petliurist elements, bourgeois nationalists, and foreign agents, important mistakes had recently appeared, demanding most serious attention from the Party. In the field of history bourgeois nationalists such as Hrushevs'kyi and Iavors'-kyi had filled their work with anti-Soviet themes, including the theory of the classless Ukrainan state and the theory of national-Bolshevism. In the field of education the Ukrainization program had been carried too far and had led to discrimination against Russian schools, a refusal to prepare teachers for the non-Ukrainian minorities, and a campaign to force Russian children to give up their native language in favor of Ukrainian. In the field of language nationalists had worked to separate the Ukrainian and Russian languages through the adoption of foreign words and expressions and the deliberate fostering of a western orientation for Ukrainian.

There now stands before us the task of resolutely correcting our mistakes. We must decisively rebuff both Ukrainian and Great-Russian chauvinists, we must explain and interpret the sharp battle that we are now conducting and must conduct in the future against nationalism, above all against Ukrainian bourgeois nationalism which has recently been strengthened as a revision of the national policy of the Party. We must strengthen the battle for the preparation of Bolshevik Ukrainian cadres.[150]

In June, 1933, the long-developing attack on Skrypnik was brought before the Party. At a plenary session of the Central Committee (June 8-11, 1933) Skrypnik was asked to recognize his mistakes and to withdraw publicly from his nationalist deviations. In a report to the plenum he refused to do so. He denied carrying on anti-Bolshevik work or deviating from the Party's national policy; he attributed criticisms of his work to disagreements over questions of national form such as the Ukrainian alphabet and language; he refused to admit that important mistakes had been made under his aegis in the fields of literature, education, and culture.[151]

In a sharp rebuke, Postyshev denounced Skrypnik for the completely unsatisfactory tenor of his adress. There was no longer any question, he declared, that all the aspects of Ukrainian life that had come under Skrypnik's control—above all the educational system of the Ukraine—had become filled with "hostile, counterrevolutionary, nationalist elements." Moreover, it was plain that no battle against these elements had been carried out and that, on the contrary, they had received strong and authoritative support from certain "obviously blind and deaf 'Communists.'" Such grievous mistakes could not be passed off lightly, he declared, by referring to them as disagreements over the Ukrainian alphabet. The fact was that Ukrainian nationalists had taken control of the Ukrainization program, that enemies of the Soviet Union such as Badan, Iavors'kyi, and Erstniuk had maliciously perverted cultural work, and that Skrypnik had tolerated, if not directly fostered, their activities. For these mistakes, Postyshev concluded, Skrypnik could not avoid his measure of responsibility.[152]

Despite Postyshev's denunciation, the Central Committee took no action against Skrypnik. Perhaps Soviet officials were reluctant to move directly against the individual so long identified as the spokesman for the Soviet's minorities and the chief witness to the moderation of Soviet nationality policy. But in the following weeks new criticisms of his work were expressed in addresses and resolutions: on June 14 Postyshev condemned him again in the strongest terms before Party workers in Kharkov;[153] at a meeting of writers and teachers at the end of June, Party leaders denounced him for allowing Ukrainian bourgeois nationalists to distort the Ukrainian language;[154] on July 5 Panas Liubchenko, one of the secretaries of the CP(b)U, devoted an entire address to Skrypnik's nationalist failings—his overevaluation of the national question, his idealisation of the bourgeois Central Rada, his support for bourgeois nationalist theories on the Ukraine.[155] At the same time, great pressure was brought to bear informally on Skrypnik to force him to reverse his stand. Whatever else the campaign may have accomplished, it apparently convinced him in a forceful way that there was nothing he could do to preserve his position in the Party. On July 7, before further steps against him could be taken, he committed suicide.[156]

In the light of Skrypnik's martyrdom, it is not surprising that some Western observers and Ukrainian nationalists have glorified his opposition into a type of western liberal protest against the strictures of Soviet rule. More accurately it represented perhaps a simple struggle for political dominance, if not in the entire Soviet Union, at least in the Ukraine. Yet the attacks on Skrypnik grew sharply after his death, emphasizing the differences which had separated him from central Party leaders. At the basis of these differences lay a fundamentally antagonistic approach to the problem of conformity. Skrypnik on his part, although always affirming the tenets of Marxism-Leninism, had never adjusted easily to authority or the stern demands of Party discipline. Throughout his Party career he had shown a greater willingness than other Ukrainian Bolsheviks to speak out against central leaders and against Soviet policies he disliked. His oppositionist views had focused on three aspects of Party doctrine on which he had developed an approach unacceptable to central officials. Involved were Party pronouncements on the questions of internationalism, constitutionalism, and localism.

On the question of internationalism Skrypnik had adopted the position expressed by Lenin that the class struggle was an international struggle and that national sentiments and national antagonisms served only to hinder the march of the proletarian revolution. Marxism applied equally to national groups everywhere, and neither Russians nor Ukrainians could declare themselves its exclusive or even principal prophets. On this basis, Skrypnik had consistently opposed Russian chauvinism and particularly the dominant position of Russians in the Ukraine and the efforts of central leaders to remake the Ukraine in the Russian image. At the same time, he had also opposed Ukrainian chauvinism, especially at those points where it seemed to threaten the solidarity of the Soviet republics and the Bolshevik principles which for him were primary. At times he had defended Ukrainian interests in an exclusive way, enabling his critics to label him a bourgeois-nationalist. In general, however, his defense of Ukrainian national interests seemed to have reflected less a desire to glorify the Ukraine in opposition to other states—an objective he had denounced when found in Bolsheviks such as Shums'kyi and Khvyl'ovyi—than his eagerness to preserve the Ukrainian pattern against Russian encroachment.

Skrypnik's constitutionalism had been expressed especially during the years from 1924 to 1931 when he had served as one of the leaders of the Soviet Union's parliament—its Central Executive Committee. More than other officials he had been mindful of constitutional requirements. "Our Constitution," he had declared, "is not merely a formal document, is not merely something that we can change lightly, but is the foundation of our life, the formulation of those aspirations out of which have been forged, by the workers and peasants, the Soviet republics."[157] His defense of the constitution may have been based primarily on the consideration that the constitution could be used by the republics as a defense against central encroachments. More broadly, however, Skrypnik had exhibited a general confidence in constitutional forms which had run counter to the prevailing tendency among Soviet leaders to ignore legal requirements where they interfered with the achievement of Bolshevik objectives.[158]

In the matter of localism Skrypnik had disagreed basically with central leaders in his attachment for regionalism and his admiration for decentralization and local autonomy.[159] In 1927, in an address to the USSR Central Executive Committee, he had summarized his position as follows:

Organizing the fraternal Soviet Union, we categorically and decisively rejected the old, centuries-long development of states with classes, traditions of human inequality, the practice of setting one people off against another. . . . We guarantee each separate people its free development. And no one now suggests that his people, his separate culture should dominate on the territory of the Soviet Union. We value and recognize the importance of the Russian culture, the culture of the Russian workers and peasants, we know that in its language are written great literary works, that in its language are written also the works of our great leader and the leader of the world revolution, comrade Lenin. Because of this we hold a high and important regard for the Russian culture and the Russian language, but apart from this, not one conscious worker or peasant tries to suggest that the Russian language, the Russian culture should dominate on the territory of our Union. The Russian people have their territory, as a part of the whole territory of our Union, they have their culture as a part of the general cultural activity of our Soviet Union, but on other territories where the majority of the population consists of Bashkirs, Ukrainians, Georgians, Karelians, where Russians form a national minority, there must be guaranteed the full independence of each separate people. This independence was established by the October Revolution and has been achieved in the course of the past ten year period. . . .

Comrades, speakers in their reports have spoken on the question of the differences between the work of separate Soviet republics and their commissariats of education. They have, for example, spoken on the question of the differences in the system of our vocational-labor education in the Ukraine and in Russia, etc. There are other questions also not now presented, such as, for example, the differences between the Ukrainian and Russian film organizations. We need not fear the existence of such differences—they are inevitable when each separate people proceeds to carry out its work. But in general, the joint discussion of these differences here, before the workers of the whole Soviet Union, from the tribune of the Central Executive Committee, the joint discussion of all these questions smooths away misunderstandings and emphasizes the fact that the path of Union interest is not the path of the decree, or of the command, or of the edict from above—such a path is not to be tolerated in the area of culture—but is the path of the joint elimination of all misunderstandings, of the recognition of the general needs of our Union, and of the delineation of the general path of development.[160]

For Skrypnik, therefore, it was not the task of the Union to organize cultural institutions in the republics or to hand down orders on cultural activities. Among the highest goals of Soviet society was the free development of each separate people, and such development could be assured only if cultural programs were locally administered. If differences arose from such local programs, as indeed they would, the differences were not to be feared.[161] The essential point was the recognition of the widely varying conditions in each national area and the importance of developing each national group within its own particular framework.

It was on this last point that Skrypnik had come into direct conflict with central leaders. In 1930 Stalin, before the Sixteenth Party Congress, had specifically condemned those who tried "not to see what draws together and unites the working masses of the nations of the USSR and to see only what can separate them from one another."[162] Subsequently, increasing stress had been placed on the importance of emphasizing cohesive elements in Soviet life and of minimizing divisive elements. By 1933 this insistence on uniformity had come to be applied far more widely than to the economic fields which had originally called it into being. And, as it had been extended to cultural fields, it had come to oppose directly Skrypnik's insistence that "the path of Union interest [in the area of culture] is not the path of the decree, or of the command, or of the edict from above." For central leaders it seemed necessary to regulate cultural as well as political and economic activities and to draw all into conformity with Soviet policies. Skrypnik's unwillingness to accept such direction had left him with no role to play among the Party elite.

Following Skrypnik's death the Party's campaign against Ukrainian nationalism and Ukrainian cultural activities was accelerated. On July 9, at a mass meeting in Kharkov called to denounce Skrypnik's suicide, three secretaries of the CP(b)U—Popov, Kosior, and Postyshev—reviewed the history of nationalist work in the Ukraine and denounced the many perversions of Party policy.[163] In the following weeks similar meetings were held in the principal cities of the Ukraine, and numerous resolutions attacking Skrypnik and the nationalist deviations were adopted.[164] At the same time, direct steps were taken to remove the last of the nationalists from their posts in the Party, government agencies, and public organizations: on July 17 the Institute for the Study of Philosophy was attacked and many of its members expelled;[165] on August 9 and December 15 the All-Ukrainian Academy of Agricultural Science and the Shevchenko Institute were purged;[166] on January 12, 1934, the All-Ukrainian Academy of Sciences and the Institute of Red Professors were reorganized.[167] Throughout the period innumerable teachers, professors, and members of professional and scholarly societies were removed from their jobs and, in many cases, accused of subversive work and imprisoned or deported.

During these months of reorganization and purification it became clear that a re-evaluation of Soviet national and cultural policies was in progress within the CP(b)U. Although no comprehensive program was adopted, the new approach to national problems was suggested in a number of addresses in the second half of 1933 and in reports to the congresses of the Ukrainian and All-Union Communist Parties in January, 1934.[168] The suggestions were related specifically to the unsettled conditions then prevailing in the Ukraine, but they reflected a fundamental change in the attitudes of Soviet leaders and, hence, were to provide a new framework for Soviet nationality programs.

First, Ukrainian leaders noted that the Party had failed in the past to maintain sufficient vigilance in combatting Ukrainian nationalism and that foreign elements hostile to the Soviet Union had come to control the nationalist movement and were using it to strike at Soviet power. As a result, Ukrainian nationalism had become a more serious danger to the Soviets than Great-Russian chauvinism. At the November Plenum of the Central Committee of the CP(b)U the Party expressed the situation as follows:

As in the past, Great-Russian chauvinism is the chief danger confronting the Soviet Union as a whole and the All-Union Communist Party as a whole. But this in no way alters the fact that in certain republics of the USSR, especially in the Ukraine, the chief danger at the present moment is local Ukrainian nationalism which is now joined with imperialist interventionists.[169]

The new formula did not mean, according to Kosior, that the struggle with Great-Russian chauvinism could be abandoned. On the contrary, the Party needed to exercise care to ensure that Great-Russian chauvinists did not take advantage of the situation to attack Ukrainian institutions. Nevertheless, it was now incumbent on the Party to concern itself chiefly with Ukrainian nationalist deviations and to work above all to "rouse the broad masses of toilers of the Ukraine to the fight against Ukrainian nationalism" and to the fight against interventionists masquerading behind nationalist slogans.[170]

Secondly, Ukrainian leaders insisted that there be complete allegiance to the principle of the solidarity and unity of the Soviet republics. In the past a measure of tolerance had been shown toward those emphasizing the distinctive attributes of each nationality, and Bolshevik leaders as well as others had urged the development of separate cultures in the republics. Now the interests of the Union were clearly to be paramount in all fields. The principle was expressed by the November Plenum as follows:

> Those who try in the least degree to weaken or to break the ties between the Ukraine and the Soviet Union, who sow discord among the toilers of the Soviet Republics, are working in the cause of the enemy, in the cause of Ukrainian and Russian counterrevolution, and are surrendering the Ukrainian people to be gobbled up by the Polish and German landlords and capitalists.

> To offer determined resistance to all attempts to break or to relax the ties between the Ukraine and the Soviet Union, to strengthen these ties, to educate the masses of the Ukrainian people in the spirit of internationalism, and to strengthen the militant revolutionary unity of the masses of the toilers of all the Soviet Republics against international imperialism and internal nationalist and every other counterrevolution—such are the most important tasks of the Party in the Ukraine.[171]

Thirdly, Party officials suggested an approach to the Ukrainization program which was so weakened that it signalled virtually an end to the program. On one hand, Soviet leaders announced that the basic objectives of the Ukrainization program had been largely achieved and that Ukrainians were now free to develop their own culture in their own language and were able to participate equally with Russians in the political life of the Ukraine. Emphasis on Ukrainization work was, therefore, no longer necessary.[172] On the other hand, Party leaders denounced aspects of the Ukrainization program as it had been administered in the past, declaring that the program had been carried out mechanically, without regard for local conditions, and that nationalists had dominated the program and endeavored to use it both to oppress the minorities in the Ukraine and to weaken Ukrainian ties with the Soviet Union.[173] Kosior insisted that attacks on the Ukrainization program were no more to be tolerated than in the past, but he also insisted that the Party would no longer countenance the program of "forcible Ukrainization" advocated by Skrypnik and others. Ukrainian Bolshevik cadres, he observed, were needed now as before, but emphasis in the future must be on the recruitment of "tried and tested persons who are educated in the Bolshevik spirit" rather than on the recruitment of ethnic Ukrainians of uncertain political reliability.[174]

Finally, Ukrainian officials demanded a sterner approach to problems of Ukrainian cultural development. In the future, they insisted, the guiding principle in cultural programs was to be not the importance of developing local national forms but the necessity of extending the spirit of "proletarian internationalism" and specifically the spirit of fraternal union among the peoples of the Soviet Union. In the field of history it was necessary to destroy once and for all nationalist glorification of the pre-revolutionary, anti-Bolshevik Ukrainian political parties as well as nationalist theories which attempted to set the Ukraine off against the other Soviet republics and which urged that the Ukraine had developed in an unorthodox Marxism fashion.[175] In the field of literature and art the Party was to strengthen "the cultural link between Ukrainian Soviet literature and art and the literature and art of the other nations of the Soviet Union" and to eliminate once and for all "the nationalist lines pursued with the assistance of Skrypnik to separate Ukrainian culture from the proletarian culture of the Russian working class."[176] In the field of languages the nationalist effort to separate Ukrainian from Russian by shifting its alphabet away from Cyrillic and by adopting "archaic" words used in the countryside was to be defeated.[177] This cultural struggle, it was suggested, was in some respects the most important, for it was in this area that the nationalists had been most active and it was here that they had achieved greatest successes in opposing Soviet power.

The extent to which the new policies of Ukrainian leaders reflected the sentiments of Party menbers generally in the Ukraine cannot be determined. There were large elements within the Party which had always disapproved of the concessions to the nationalities and now rejoiced at the Party's more stringent approach to national problems. In any case the situation within the Party was not what it had been the year before: opposition elements were gone, and Party members who remained were unwilling to speak against official policies. As a result, the new positions were heard and applauded, and pledges of support were everywhere given. At the Seventeenth Party congress (January, 1934) Khataevich, speaking for the CP(b)U, declared that the Party could now regard the Ukraine with tranquility because "under the heroic leadership of Stalin and the Central Committee of the All-Union Communist Party," the great problems which had appeared in the preceding years had been completely liquidated.[178]

The march of events in the Ukraine in the period from 1927 to 1934 so affected the political climate of the republic and so transformed its political, economic, and cultural institutions that it would be difficult to overestimate their impact on Ukrainian life. The Party was altered in membership and leadership; the government was sternly subordinated to central authority; direction of the cultural and economic life of the country was transferred into the hands of leaders in Moscow or their appointed representatives in the Ukraine. Possibilities for developing programs independently of central projects or for imparting a distinct Ukrainian coloration to All-Union activities were reduced sharply except in relatively minor areas in technical and scientific fields. The growth of Ukrainian institutions which had proceeded at so rapid a pace in earlier years was halted, and in many cases the process was reversed.

Yet, despite these great changes, the basic principles on which Soviet national policy had been founded remained generally the same. That this was so was a tribute to the remarkable flexibility of those principles—a flexibility which had enabled Soviet leaders from the beginning to adapt to various circumstances in their effort to build a proletarian dictatorship. At the opening session of the Seventeenth Party Congress (January, 1934) Stalin declared again his confidence in those principles. As always, he announced, Bolsheviks were required to fight resolutely against nationalist deviations, whether the deviations were toward Great-Russian chauvinism or local nationalism. The mistakes of Skrypnik and the dislocations in the Ukraine, he suggested, did not weaken Bolshevik principles, but indicated merely that survivals of Ukrainian nationalism were more tenacious than had been recognized. Hence, Ukrainian nationalism had become a greater danger than Russian chauvinism and had come to require a more resolute battle. However, he concluded, as in all aspects of the national problem, "the question of the principal danger in the area of the national question is decided not by empty, formal arguments, but by a Marxian analysis of the situation at a given moment and by a study of those mistakes which have been made in this area."[179]

The most notable feature of Stalin's report was his failure to discuss those aspects of the Bolshevik national policy which in the past had given heart to the leaders of the minorities and provided limitations on Russian centralists. There was no mention, as there had been before, of the viciousness of Great-Russian chauvinism, of the importance of developing support among the national minorities, of the inevitably slow process by which the cultures of the separate republics would in the distant future be amalgamated. And the failure to mention these points was not a careless omission but a reflection of a considerable shift in Soviet attitudes as well as a sensible recognition that the points were not at the moment pertinent to the building of the proletarian dictatorship. In the matter of Great-Russian chauvinism there was no question that Soviet leaders had ceased viewing the problem as a serious one. Rather, they had come to identify Soviet interests with Russian interests so completely that they could see few contradictions between them.[180] Soviet dependence on Russian aid in pressing collectivization in the nationality areas—particularly in the Ukraine —had strengthened this identification. Similarly, Bolshevik reliance—and specifically Stalin's personal reliance—on support from the minorities had diminished as the strength and authority of the Russian Bolshevik organization under Stalin's leadership had become established. At the same time, the opposition of Ukrainian peasants to the Soviet farm program had taught central authorities that concessions to the minorities in cultural and national matters did not necessarily assure their support in economic and other questions and that the minorities could in fact be controlled, without the lure of broad national concessions, by stern and repressive measures. Taken together, these factors prompted Soviet leaders to abandon their support for the national minorities and the preservation of separate cultures, and to emphasize elements of unity and loyalty wich they felt would now advance Soviet programs more effectively.

V. THE NEW LOYALTY AND NATIONAL RIGHTS, 1934-1944

The grievous and crucial events which had convulsed the Ukraine in the years before 1934 had been so penetrating and all-encompassing in their scope that they had constituted a second revolution, scarcely less significant than the upheavals of 1917. From the viewpoint of the Bolsheviks the revolution had been successful, for it had brought the CP(b)U under closer central control, had weakened or destroyed nationalist elements, and had established the collectivization and industrialization programs as key elements in Ukrainian Soviet life. The death of Skrypnik—the leading protagonist in the Ukraine of the nationalist position—and the political liquidation of those suspected of endorsing his views had removed the chief elements opposing Russian and centralist influences. The great debate over the national question which had waxed so strong, calling forth severe statements from central leaders and much disagreement at both Union and republic levels, was finally concluded. Nevertheless, the revolution had been a costly one and had left within both Party and government organizations a legacy of confusion and national bitterness which threatened to interfere with future Soviet programs in the Ukraine. The period immediately following the revolution—from early 1934 to the end of 1936—was therefore designated a reconstruction period, and Ukrainian Bolsheviks were ordered to rebuild their Party organizations and to endeavor once again to win the loyalty and support of the Ukrainian people.

THE RECONSTRUCTION PERIOD

Responsibility for the reconstruction work was assigned to Postyshev—Second Secretary of the CP(b)U—and to the new Party

Politburo chosen in January, 1934.[1] Surprisingly, the new Politburo included almost the same leaders elected in 1930, despite
the changes made generally throughout the Party in the intervening
years. Only three of the Politburo's seventeen members and candidates were newly appointed since 1930, and only seven of its
old members had been dropped.[2] It has been suggested these were
years in which Stalin prepared cautiously for his coming frightful
attack on the Party, relying for the moment on the support of
the Ukrainian organization: Skrypnik's liquidation removed the
only high Ukrainian leader identified with the nationalist opposition, while others of the Ukrainian Politburo were considered
personally loyal, at least eight of them having been chosen directly
in Moscow and dispatched to the Ukraine.[3] There was every reason
to expect that Ukrainian leadership would develop the reconstruction program in closest ties with the center and without the divisions which had earlier plagued it.

The first of the reconstruction programs was a full-scale campaign aimed at rebuilding the CP(b)U following the losses the
Party had suffered from the exchange of members and local
leaders forced upon it in 1933. The exchange had weakened the
Party by loosening its organization structure and widening the
gap separating the Party from the mass of Ukrainian peasants.[4]
The most serious dislocations had occurred at the local level, particularly in the rural areas. Here the many Bolsheviks sent from
the cities to press the collectivization program had come to interfere seriously with regular Party work. A number of the organizers had gone to the farms reluctantly, and their hostile attitude toward rural life, aggravated by their ignorance of farm
problems, had led them to antagonize the peasants. In many
cases the new organizers had seized control of Party organizations
from local leaders, destroying Party responsibility and weakening
Party structure. Particularly blameworthy had been the Political
Departments which had become competitors of the regular raion
Party groups, replacing them, in some cases, as Party centers. As
a result, local Party units throughout the Ukraine's countryside
had been disrupted and demoralized, their organizational ties with

higher Party bodies broken, and the Party as a whole alienated from the mass of local Ukrainian workers.

Early in 1934 Party leaders instituted a rebuilding campaign at the local level. Initially the campaign was directed at the work of regular Party organs, and orders were issued for these bodies to increase agitation-organization work among the non-Party masses, to place greater emphasis on the training of new Party members and the recruitment of Party workers from among the local population, and to insist more strongly on firm discipline in farm and factory work.[5] But gradually it became clear that the Political Departments were a major obstacle to reform. The obvious solution was the liquidation of the Departments, but they had consistently shown themselves more reliable and steadfast than the regular Party groups. Late in 1934 the Bolsheviks conceived a method of using the Departments to fortify the local Party organs by incorporating their members into the regular Party structure instead of returning them to the cities. Accordingly, the Departments were abolished, and in the following months their workers were [transferred to government and Party organizations in the local areas.[6] By March, 1935, when the reform was completed, lower Party units in the Ukraine were more strongly dominated by non-Ukrainian elements than they had been following the changes of 1933.

A more important reconstruction program was a program directed at rebuilding the Ukraine's economic and cultural life under the new conditions established by collectivization, the completion of the first Five-Year Plan, and the Party's altered approach to the national question. This phase of reconstruction was to proceed under the broad slogan, "Transform the Ukraine into a flowering, progressive Soviet Republic,"[7] and was to emphasize chiefly the expansion of Ukrainian industrial and farm production.[8] It was also to include attention to the task of rebuilding the Ukraine's cultural institutions and emphasis on the clarification of Bolshevik attitudes toward national minorities in the light of recent Bolshevik attacks on Ukrainian nationalists. In the matter of economic reconstruction there was little controversy within the Party: all were agreed that the collectivization and industrialization programs were to be pressed and that the production of farm and industrial commodities was to be expanded as rapidly as possible. In the matter of the national question, however, the situation was not as clear. The recent campaign against Ukrainian nationalists had left national institutions under a suspicion of disloyalty, and many Party members—opposed to all forms of concessions to the nationalities—were interpreting the campaign as an invitation to attack the entire Bolshevik national program. To Party leaders it seemed necessary to restate Bolshevik cultural and national aims and to modify certain of the harsh conclusions suggested by the Party pronouncements of 1933.

Neither central nor Ukrainian leaders meant to withdraw from their previous attacks on Ukrainian nationalists. With consistency and unanimity they declared that the old expressions of Ukrainian nationalism as evidenced in the works of Shums'kyi, Khvyl'-ovyi, Hrushevs'kyi, Skrypnik, and others could not be tolerated in any form. The nationalists were denounced, as they had been before, for plotting with foreign agents against the Soviet state, for encouraging kulaks and other Bolshevik enemies, for fighting against the construction of a Soviet culture in the Ukraine, and for advocating a form of nationalism which inevitably resulted in opposition between the Ukraine and the other Soviet republics.[9] In the future such expressions were not to be allowed, it was announced, and Party workers and sympathizers as well as all those in influential posts were to recognize that it was their duty to be socialists and Unionists above all and only secondarily, and within an approved framework, Ukrainians and localists.

Moreover, both central and Ukrainian leaders insisted there be no modification of the requirement that the question of cultural development revolve around the primary task of building a Soviet culture rather than the secondary task of preserving a national culture. In the field of literature Ukrainian Bolsheviks took a strong stand, demanding that writers abandon their interest in a uniquely Ukrainian socialist literature and concern themselves rather with disseminating Soviet themes. At the First All-Ukrainian Congress of Soviet Writers (June, 1934) both Kosior and Postyshev emphasized the point. Postyshev insisted that "literature always has had tremendous educational and propaganda importance" and that Soviet writing could not be mere fantasy but should be "an integral part of the building of our socialist society."

Our literary work is not an abstract puff of wind, but is a sword in the battle for the building of socialism.

Our writer is not simply a talented artist with a rich imagination, but a fighter armed with the theory of Marx-Lenin-Stalin. . . .

[It is the task of the lyricist, the dramatist, the writer] to describe a new people, a people which is creating a new life, to depict simply, forcefully, with great artistry this new life, this new people, to describe the motive force and leadership of this life—the All-Union Communist Party, to describe the contradictions, the baseness and meanness, the rottenness and criminal nature of the old life.[10]

Kosior declared even more strongly that "the destruction of the nationalists in the Ukraine and of nationalist elements in the CP(b)U has purged the atmosphere also on the literary front." As a result, he announced, it was now possible to move ahead to great new literary tasks—to the tasks of depicting the remarkable achievements won in the past under Soviet rule, of aiding the Party in its great work for the socialist transformation of the people, of strengthening the ties between Russian and Ukrainian writers and between Russian and Ukrainian literature, and of continuing to expose those fighting against Soviet programs.[11] Both Kosior and Postyshev suggested that Ukrainian literary and cultural activities were to be completely dedicated to the defense of the Soviet regime and to the liquidation of divisive influences whether of nationalist or anti-Soviet origins. The ambiguity of previous statements on cultural policy which had seemed to encourage Ukrainians and other minorities to develop independent national-cultural expressions was thereby laid to rest.

On the other hand, Ukrainian Bolsheviks continued to insist that Soviet national policy was not to be reversed and that the Bolsheviks were determined, specifically, to maintain a Ukrainization program. In speeches to Party workers in Kiev on October 17, 1934, and February 22, 1935, Postyshev noted that attacks on Ukrainization work had become a serious matter for the Party.[12] Certain members of the CP(b)U, he declared, who had never accepted the Ukrainization program, were suggesting that the recent

Bolshevik assault on Ukrainian nationalists had signalled the end of Ukrainization work. And these members were being joined by "remnants" of the Ukrainian nationalists who argued that the Bolsheviks were seeking to destroy Ukrainian culture. Of course Postyshev declared, both groups were wrong. The Ukrainization program of the past with its anti-Soviet, nationalist overtones and its predominantly anti-Bolshevik leadership was no longer to be tolerated. But Bolsheviks were obligated now as before to support and develop a *Bolshevik* Ukrainization program, and to this task the Party needed to pay "primary attention."

Precisely what was meant by the term "Bolshevik Ukrainization" was never explained by Ukrainian leaders. Apparently it was to be distinguished from the nationalist Ukrainization of Shums'kyi and Skrypnik by the requirement that it be directed toward Soviet rather than nationalist goals. Yet in two respects the new program seemed remarkably like the old. First, it called, as had the old, for special emphasis on the training of Ukrainian cadres. That such emphasis still was needed in the Ukraine was indicated by the shortage of technicians, Party and government staffs, and skilled factory workers—a shortage which had become especially serious after 1933 as the demand for trained personnel had increased under the industrialization programs and the expansion of Party and government work, and as the number of experienced workers had been reduced by the Ukraine's purges. If additional levies on the already inadequate supply of technicians and administrators inside Russia were not to be made, it was clearly necessary to recruit new leaders and skilled workers from the mass of Ukrainian peasants. Moreover, Soviet leaders continued to view the problem of cadres as one aspect of the larger problem of mass support and hoped by raising Ukrainians to positions of leadership to increase also Ukrainian acceptance of Soviet rule. In March, 1935, Postyshev emphasized the special importance of this problem, urging Party leaders to stress the building of new cadres from among the Ukrainian peasants and intelligentsia and their recruitment to Soviet and Party work.[13]

Secondly, the new program called for emphasis on the language and cultural aspects of Ukrainization. As Postyshev ob-

served, Ukrainization work after 1933 had disintegrated as many
Ukrainian institutions—especially Party organizations at the republic and oblast levels—had begun to lapse in their use of
the Ukrainian language and had ceased to emphasize the development of Ukrainian cultural institutions.[14] These shortcomings were
serious: they interfered with the preparation of cadres; they supported nationalists in their argument that Soviet rule aimed at
the destruction of Ukrainian culture; they separated the Party from
the masses of the Ukrainian people, preventing effective Marxist
leadership. The weakening of Ukrainization work, Postyshev insisted, served only to strengthen Soviet enemies and to interfere
with Soviet construction.[15] Party members and leaders were obligated to re-emphasize study of Ukrainian history, economics,
and culture. "If we do not do this," Postyshev concluded, "we
shall make a great mistake in the matter of Marxist-Leninist development of members of the Party and Komsomol."[16]

On the basis of these declarations a modest effort was made
from 1934 to 1937 to revitalize the Ukrainization program. In
June, 1934, as a concession to nationalist sentiment, the capital of the Ukraine was shifted from Kharkov to Kiev. Although
the move was justified for a variety of reasons,[17] Bolshevik leaders
apparently approved the shift because of their growing confidence that Ukrainians in the west as well as in the east would
support the Soviet regime and because of their expectation that
Kiev, as the traditional Ukrainian capital, would better serve
as a focal point for Ukrainian Soviet political life. Together
with the shift, emphasis was placed on the widened use of the
Ukrainian language and on an increase in the number of ethnic
Ukrainians serving in important government and Party posts.
Soon Soviet leaders were able to report that the number of
Ukrainians in high positions was nearly double the number
serving at the beginning of 1934:[18] at many levels Ukrainians occupied 50 percent or more of the highest posts, and in training
programs and the schools the percentages were larger. In the field
of publications it was reported in 1935 that 75 percent of the journals of the Ukraine and 90 percent of its newspapers were being
printed in Ukrainian. Thus, although ethnic Ukrainians continued

to hold less than their share of responsible jobs and continued to find opposition to the use of the Ukrainian language, the margin of bias steadily diminished.

Apart from the increase in Ukrainan cadres and use of the Ukrainian language, however, the Ukrainization program was in no way comparable with the program as visualized before 1933. Ukrainian leaders continued to press in a limited way for the development of Ukrainian literature and culture and for a more serious study of the history of the Ukraine, of its Communist Party, and of its economic growth,[19] but negligible progress was made. In part, the failure reflected the lack of enthusiasm for the program within the CP(b)U. But, as before, the failure reflected more basically the incompatibility between Soviet demands for unity and conformity and Soviet sponsorship of local development. The task of reconciling Soviet requirements with Ukrainian themes had become a virtually impossible one. Few writers, historians, or economists were there who could adequately incorporate required Soviet dogma into each aspect of Ukrainian studies. And for those who were successful there was the growing possibility that, because they had chosen to discuss Ukrainian themes, they would be charged with contributing to divisiveness and disunity in the Soviet Union. As part of a campaign for building mass support Soviet leaders were willing to press for broader use of the Ukrainian language and the incorporation of larger numbers of Ukrainians into Soviet and Party work. Other aspects of the Ukrainization program, however, were not to be developed.

LOYALTY AND THE PURGES

More critical than the Ukrainization shifts were changes affecting the pattern of Ukrainian-central political relationships. The basis for these changes had been laid in 1933 when central leaders had interfered directly in Ukrainian political affairs, selecting the highest Ukrainian officials and assigning Party workers from other parts of the Soviet Union to leadership work in Ukrainian districts. As a result, Ukrainian politics had become tied so directly to All-Union politics that in the future few aspects of political life in the Ukraine were to develop independently of accompanying events in the Soviet Union as a whole. Thus the political situation—as also the cultural situation—became very different from that prevailing before 1933, when the CP(b)U had accepted Ukrainian nationalists as members, when regional considerations had exercised a powerful influence on republic leaders, and when key political issues had been resolved by local officials acting somewhat independently of central leaders. These elements had always been tempered by Moscow's supervision of Party affairs: on occasion, as in the matter of the Sapronov opposition and particularly following the appointment of Kaganovich as Political Secretary of the CP(b)U, central authorities had acted directly in the Ukraine. Moreover, both local and central leaders had been governed in their approach to Ukrainian problems by political events in the Soviet Union, and the whole Soviet national policy had been colored by Bolshevik eagerness to win local support. Nonetheless, before 1933 the CP(b)U had emerged as something more than a regional subdivision of the All-Union Communist Party. After 1934 the differences between the two parties were to grow smaller, and the relationship between political events in the Ukraine and the Soviet Union was to become an intimate one.

The most striking indication of the intimacy came in the broad sweep of events associated with the Party purges of 1934 to 1938. During this period the whole body of the All-Union Communist Party was subjected to examination and review, and on a scale which dwarfed previous purges all suspected of opposition to Stalin or lack of enthusiasm for Stalinist policies were expelled from the Party and imprisoned, exiled, or executed. The story of the purges is only dimly known and covers too broad a field to be included here in detail. Yet the implications of the purges for political life in the Ukraine were so sweeping that a brief summary of their main outline is required.

The purges were set in motion by the assassination on December 1, 1934, of Sergei Kirov, Leningrad Party boss and principal figure in the Party hierarchy apart from Stalin himself. Almost at once the assassination was declared to be but one aspect of a broad counterrevolutionary conspiracy directed against the whole Soviet leadership,[20] and both Zinoviev and Kamenev as well as a host of lesser Party figures were implicated and shortly imprisoned or executed. Subsequently, Soviet secret police embarked on an intensive investigation aimed at uncovering all anti-Bolshevik elements within the Soviet Union. At the same time, the Party inaugurated a program of reregistering its members, the purpose of which was to verify individually the reliability and orthodoxy of its ranks.[21] Under the two programs a steadily growing circle of Party and non-Party people were arrested and placed under the most serious charges of treason and disloyalty. In August, 1936, January, 1937, and March, 1938, the most well-known of the accused—Zinoviev, Kamenev, Radek, Piatakov, Rykov, Bukharin, and others—were tried publicly and, following their startling confessions, all were convicted.[22] Of greater importance a program of secret purges was inaugurated which struck far more widely than the trials and in a less spectacular but more effective way removed from the Party and from leadership posts large numbers of potential, actual, or imagined oppositionists.

There are no indications that the purge as carried out in the Ukraine differed in any substantial way in its early stages from the purge in other parts of the Soviet Union. On the death of Kirov thirty-seven Ukrainians were charged with participating in the assassination,[23] but their involvement did not mean that the CP(b)U lay under a darker shadow than other regional Party organizations. In the subsequent investigations which continued throughout 1935 and the first half of 1936 no particular emphasis was placed on the Ukraine or on subversive groups there. At the first of the public trials in August, 1936, a number of Ukrainians were "exposed" as Trotskyites, but none were primary figures and the national question played no role.[24]

In the matter of reregistration of Party members, on the other hand, leaders of the CP(b)U suggested that the Ukraine presented certain unusual problems. In an address of January, 1936,[25] Postyshev declared that the verification program had "especial importance" for the CP(b)U because counterrevolutionaries in the Ukraine—including Trotskyites and kulaks—had always concealed their subversive aims by hiding behind nationalist slogans and had gained special strength through the support given them by foreign interventionists in central and eastern Europe. Furthermore, he noted, the Communist Party in the Ukraine had been hindered in its growth more than other regional Party organizations by the many national Communists admitted to its ranks, while in the recent period the whole political situation in the Ukraine had deteriorated considerably because of the upheavals of the collectivization years. It was not surprising, Postyshev implied, that the problem of verifying the reliability of Party members was more critical in the Ukraine and was a task requiring the most serious and sustained attention from Party organizations and workers.

Nevertheless, the full impact of the purge did not strike the Ukraine until after the first of the public purge trials in August, 1936, when Party leadership throughout the Soviet Union began to fall under what was apparently a carefully-prepared program of eliminating the slightest vestige of anti-Stalinist opposition. Only fragmentary information is available, but it seems likely from what is known that, following the trial, Postyshev, together perhaps with others such as Ordzhonikidze, began to quarrel with Stalin over the question of the purge and perhaps as well over Stalin's authoritarianism. By now the purge had reached incredible proportions. One after another, the old Bolsheviks who, on any occasion, had opposed Stalin were charged with the most serious crimes, and even the least deviations in speech and attitudes became sufficient to place a cloud of suspicion over Party workers regardless of position or influence. Included among the dogmas all Party members were required to uphold was the sanctity of the purge itself, and all were expected not only to affirm it but to carry it along by exposing deviations wherever found. It seems likely that it was this dogma which Postyshev refused to accept and which provided the basis for his quarrel with Stalin.

In any case, early in January, 1937, the stage was set for a broad attack on the highest leadership of the CP(b)U. The immediate pretext was the Kiev Party organization, which, it was charged, had been divided and torn in the preceding months by disagreement over the purge and over the activities of a number of its members and leaders accused of Trotskyite leanings. According to official accounts[26] the principal agitator in the Kiev organization had been a Party member by the name of Nikolaenko who "for an entire year [had] signaled about the bad conditions in the Party organization in Kiev, [and had] exposed the exclusive, narrow-minded Philistine approach to the workers, the suppression of self-criticism, and the predominance of Trotskyite wreckers."[27] These criticisms had not been accepted by the Kiev organization or by the CP(b)U, and Nikolaenko had been expelled from the Party. At this point, however, Russian leaders had intervened and, after investigating, had discovered, according to Stalin, that the criticisms were accurate and that the Kiev organization was indeed dominated by Trotskyites and was guilty of ignoring Bolshevik principles of self-criticism and Party democracy. As a result, the All-Union Central Committee in mid-January adopted a strong resolution on Party work in the Ukraine, criticizing local and regional organizations in Kiev and other oblasts and apparently demanding the removal of Postyshev as secretary of the Kiev oblast Party organization.[28] On January 16 the Kiev Party committee met with Kaganovich as a representative of the Russian Politburo and, in accordance with the central decision, removed Postyshev from his Kiev post, replacing him with a Party worker only recently sent to the Ukraine, S. O. Kudriavtsev.[29]

Perhaps the Kiev incident was meant as a warning to Postyshev rather than a preliminary step in his liquidation. If so, he apparently chose to ignore it. In any case it must have been clear to him his position was weakening, but he continued to oppose broadening of the purge. How strong a position he took is not known although it has been suggested in a speculative way that he participated in the formation of an opposition group of high Party leaders determined to halt further purge excesses.[30] In any case, it is known that at the February-March (1937) Plenum of the All-Union Central Committee he expressed serious reservations about the correctness of the purge, commenting that he did not think it possible that so many Party members who during the harsh years of industrialization and collectivization had fought so steadfastly for the Party had now shifted into the camp of the enemy.

I personally do not believe that in 1924 an honest party member who had trod the long road of unrelenting fight against enemies for the party and for socialism, would now be in the camp of the enemies. I do not believe it. . . . I can't imagine how it would be possible to travel with the party during the difficult years and then, in 1934, join the Trotskyites. It is an odd thing.[31]

By 1937, however, the purge had become too well established and too strongly identified with Stalinist rule to be modified by Postyshev or other leaders. Statements such as Postyshev's succeeded only in arousing Stalin's ire and placing those who made them under suspicion of disloyalty.[32] Almost at once Stalin, supported probably by a majority of the Politburo, ordered Postyshev's transfer from the Ukraine; on March 17 the Ukrainian Central Committee dutifully approved the transfer and relieved Postyshev of his post as Second Secretary.[33]

Simultaneously, the whole scope of the purge became deeper and wider in accordance with decisions taken by the All-Union Central Committee at its February-March Plenum. On the one hand, the purge was pressed by the secret police, who, on a larger scale than before, imprisoned, executed, and sent into exile uncounted Party and non-Party people. On the other hand, the purge was carried forward within the Party, first, by renewed expulsions of Party members and, secondly, through a program of electing new leaders at every level of Party organization.[34] Ostensibly the latter program was established to prepare for the Thirteenth Congress of the CP(b)U to be held in May, 1937. But its chief purpose seems to have been to remove from positions of leadership those suspected of supporting Postyshev or other Party figures accused of disloyalty. The sweep of Party officials was a broad one : at the oblast level nearly two-thirds of the Party leaders were replaced, and in the local and raion organizations nearly one-third.[35] The purge did not reach the top level of the CP(b)U, and the Party leadership chosen by the Thirteenth Congress remained almost unchanged.[36] At lower levels the shift of Party leaders exceeded in its scope even the extensive purges of 1933.

In the second half of 1937 the purge gradually extended upward to higher Party leaders. In July and August, 1937, the secret police arrested I. S. Shelekhes, member of the Ukrainian Politburo, and A. A. Khvylia, member of the Central Committee of the CP(b)U. On August 30 Panas Liubchenko, Ukrainian Prime Minister and Politburo member, committed suicide in anticipation of his arrest.[37] In the closing months of 1937 M. M. Khataevich, Second Secretary of the CP(b)U, disappeared from the Ukraine as did V. P. Zatons'kyi, member of the Politburo and Commissar of Education. In January, 1938, the Party's highest official, its First Secretary S. V. Kosior, was recalled to Moscow.[38]

Again, as in January, 1933, Russian Bolsheviks were apparently convinced that the most forceful measures were required to draw Party organizations in the Ukraine under firm control. The 1937 purge had not established the reliability of the CP(b)U, and it seemed necessary to reorganize the Party from top to bottom. At a plenary session of the All-Union Central Committee in January, 1938, Soviet leaders criticized the manner in which the purge had been conducted and called upon Party organizations to ferret out and remove all responsible for careless or malicious work and to re-examine the records of Party members earlier expelled.[39] To carry out the work in the Ukraine, the Central Committee appointed the secretary of the Moscow Party organization, Nikita S. Khrushchev, to the post of First Secretary of the CP(b)U.[40] Accompanying Khrushchev to the Ukraine was M. O. Burmistenko, official in the central apparatus of the All-Union Communist Party, who was chosen Second Secretary of the CP(b)U and given responsibility for handling problems of leadership cadres.

The arrival of Khrushchev and Burmistenko in the Ukraine signaled the beginning of a more thorough and uncompromising reorganization of the CP(b)U and Ukrainian government than had been attempted previously. In contrast to the 1937 purge, the reorganization affected relatively few changes at the lower levels, where only 22 percent of the Party leadership was replaced.[41] But at higher levels the reorganization was carried out in a thorough fashion, and most Party and government leaders were ousted and their places taken by "verified" Bolsheviks. In the months from February to June each of the first secretaries of the twelve oblast organizations of the CP(b)U was replaced as were most second secretaries.[42] During May and June the entire Ukrainian government under its Prime Minister, D. S. Korotchenko, was revised and new officials chosen to head government commissariats.[43] At the Fourteenth Congress of the CP(b)U (June, 1938) a whole new leadership body for the Party was chosen: the Party Central Committee elected by the Congress included among its eighty-seven members and candidates only three members chosen in the preceding years;[44] the Politburo, Orgburo, and Secretariat subsequently appointed by the Central Committee comprised thirteen members and candidates, not one of which had served previously.[45] Gone were the old Party stalwarts, such as Petrovs'kyi and Zatons'kyi, who had guided Ukrainian affairs from the beginning of the Revolution. For the first time in the Ukraine the continuity of political leadership was completely broken, and the whole Party and government structure at all levels was brought under the control of new leaders sent from Moscow—leaders foreign to the Ukraine and to its traditions and political life. The principal basis for a unique development of Party life and institutions in the Ukraine was destroyed, and the complete subordination of the CP(b)U to central leadership established.

Unlike the purges of 1933, when officials and Party leaders had been removed because of their opposition to Soviet farm and national policies, the purges of 1934-1938 followed no consistent pattern, but struck widely, almost illogically throughout the Ukraine. Implicated were convinced Communists as well as "counterrevolutionaries," Russian sympathizers as well as Ukrainian nationalists, and ultimately the whole Party leadership regardless of individual attitudes or loyalties. In the absence of detailed and reliable reports or of official records of the purges, no precise estimate of their significance can be made, but a number of broad conclusions can be suggested.

First, it seems unlikely that the national question played any important role in the purges. Russian and Ukrainian leaders, when speaking about the purges, referred frequently to "bourgeois nationalists," classifying them with "Trotskyite wreckers" and "foreign agents" as the chief enemies of the proletariat and, hence, the principal targets of the purges.[46] But apart from such general statements little attention was given the problem of Ukrainian nationalism, and specific charges of nationalist activity were brought against only a few leaders: Liubchenko, Zatons'kyi, Khvylia, and Poraiko.[47] The only serious effort openly disclosed to link the purges with nationalist activities was made in the case of G. F. Grin'ko who testified at his trial in March, 1938, that since the early twenties he had worked against Soviet power for Ukrainian independence and that since 1934 he had plotted with foreign agents to separate the Ukraine from the Soviet Union.[48] Less substantial charges were brought against Khvylia and Liubchenko, who were accused informally by the Soviet press of supporting Ukrainian nationalists in the Ukrainian Academy of Sciences and of endeavoring to enlarge the differences separating the Ukrainian and Russian languages.[49] None of the attacks were given prominence, and it seems unlikely that they represented the most important accusations brought against these men. In any case, only a small number of the Ukrainian officials who were purged were identified as nationalists, and there is no evidence that others, such as Postyshev, Kosior, Khataevich, and Kudriavtsev, harbored nationalist sympathies or supported nationalist programs more strongly than was acceptable.[50]

Similarly there is no evidence that Trotskyites exercised special influence over Ukrainian leaders or that any important number of those purged in the Ukraine were Trotsky's ideological followers. Traditionally the CP(b)U had included a solid core of oppositionists which had exercised considerable influence; but by 1934 the oppositionists had been almost completely eliminated. In 1937 and 1938 official accusations against Trotskyites were as unsubstantial and unconvincing as the accusations against nationalists. The only specific accusations publicly disclosed were those against "Trotskyite wreckers" in the Kiev organization,[51] and the situation there was never discussed in any complete way. The concrete charges which were published were probably only ancillary charges.[52] Undoubtedly there were Ukrainian Party leaders who disagreed

with aspects of Soviet policy, and their disagreements may have
ripened into general ideological oppositions; in at least one address
Postyshev urged Soviet internationalism in a way which might
have been construed as opposition to the Soviet policy of "socialism
in one country."[53] It seems unlikely, however, that such views
were held by any significant fraction of those who fell subject to
the purges.

The most obvious unifying factor in the purges was the element
of loyalty to Stalin. When charges other than disloyalty were
made, they served a valuable purpose by providing a pretext for
removing suspected officials and by serving as a warning to others
not to engage in activities opposed by Soviet leaders. But loyalty
was the chief concern. Apparently in the fall of 1937 Stalin became
especially anxious about the CP(b)U. Perhaps he was alarmed
that the CP(b)U, as a powerful regional organization, might develop
as an opposition center; or perhaps he was disturbed over the
support Postyshev had received from other Ukrainians in his quarrel
with Stalin. According to Yugoslav and *emigré* sources,[54] he was
sufficiently disturbed to dispatch to the Ukraine a delegation of
Russian leaders including Molotov, Khrushchev, and Ezhov to
investigate the situation and to remove Kosior, Petrovs'kyi, and
Liubchenko from leadership. But, in a remarkable action, both
the Central Committee and Politburo of the CP(b)U refused to
accept central demands. Stalin's determination to wipe out the
whole Ukrainian leadership stemmed, it is suggested, from that
refusal. Perhaps the structural arrangement of the Communist
Party in the Soviet Union was such as to encourage leaders of the
Party's regional organizations—especially the CP(b)U—to develop
regional sympathies and to express them as a group against the
center. Whether or not this was the case, Stalin apparently feared
it to be so. By removing the Ukraine's highest and middle Party
leaders as well as Union officials identified with the Ukraine,[55] he
hoped to build a new regional organization directed by leaders
whose identification with the Ukraine and with previous Ukrainian
officials was small and whose personal loyalty to Stalin was beyond
question.[56] The purges were political not ideological, and the
Ukrainians who fell before them were ousted because they were

identified with anti-Stalinism or, in the later stages of the purge, because they were identified with a regional Party organization which, as an organization, had fallen under suspicion.

THE END OF UKRAINIZATION

The purges of 1937 and 1938 produced no direct shifts in Soviet national policy. But the distrust accompanying them spread to other areas of public life, prompting Russian leaders to view with suspicion each manifestation of disunity and localism and to affirm more strongly than before the principles of Soviet unity and Soviet solidarity. As the purges widened, Party leaders began to emphasize the centralizing aspects of Soviet national policy and, contrary to the relatively liberal principles only recently reaffirmed by Postyshev and others, to press for new restrictions on national institutions in the republics.

The new atmosphere was suggested in November, 1936, when Stalin gave before the Extraordinary Eighth Congress of Soviets his defense of the USSR draft constitution then being presented for ratification.[57] It was necessary, he declared, for the Soviet people to recognize the vastness of the transformations undergone by the USSR in the years since its founding. At the time of the Union's formation, he noted, there had been great divisions among the peoples of the USSR.

This was a period when relations between peoples were not yet duly repaired, when survivals of the mistrust of Great Russians were not yet removed, when centrifugal forces everywhere still continued to operate. It was necessary under these conditions to repair the brotherly solidarity of our peoples on the basis of economic, political, and military joint aid, bringing our people into a single, multi-national state.

By 1936, he continued, this work had been largely completed, and it was now possible to report that:

The characteristics of the peoples of the USSR have been changed at their very roots, . . . the spirit of mutual distrust among them has disappeared, . . . the spirit of cooperative friendship has developed, and . . . in such a manner there has been constructed the present brotherly cooperation of peoples in a system of a single union state.

As a result we have now fully completed and tested the experiment of a multi-national socialist state, the stability of which could be the envy of any national state in any part of the world.

In the future, he declared, it would be possible for the USSR to emphasize in its national policy the solidarity, unity, and cooperative friendship of all Soviet peoples.

At the same time, Stalin joined his call for closer union with a restatement of Soviet acceptance of the principle of national and racial equality. Differences between nations and races, he observed, such as skin color or language, cultural level, or stage of political development could not serve as a basis for justifying national inequality. "All nations and races regardless of their past or present development and apart from their strength or weakness must enjoy in general the same rights in all spheres of economic, social, governmental, and cultural life." Only on such a principle, he declared, could Soviet internationalism be founded; only through such a principle could the unity of the Soviet peoples—so important for Communist success—be assured. Stalin made it clear, however, that the principle of equality was not now to be considered as important as it had been at various times in earlier years. Since an adequate basis for solidarity had been laid throughout the Soviet Union and mutual distrust largely destroyed, emphasis was to placed on unity above all, and principles of equality were to give way wherever they promised to lead to disunity.

Stalin's rather cautious blending of the principles of unity and equality suggested the emergence of a troublesome dilemma. As long as Soviet leaders had emphasized a union of equal peoples, none to be preferred or set above another, Soviet minority policy had been easily justified—and distinguished from Tsarist policy—as at least a non-discriminatory one: restrictive measures against the minorities were meant only to eliminate anti-Soviet attitudes or prevent the growth of anti-Russian sentiment. Now in the mid-thirties Stalin was to embark on a clearly discriminatory program, glorifying Russia and Russian ways. Such a program could not easily be defended to the minorities. It seems likely that emphasis on principles of unity and equality was meant to introduce the new program in the most favorable way.

In the following three years Stalin's views were elaborated upon by Ukrainian and Russian officials. In 1937 and 1938 articles in the Soviet press emphasized the theme of the friendship of the Soviet peoples.[58] At Party meetings leaders expressed again and again Stalin's demand for the closest union of Soviet republics against foreign intervention. At the Fourth Conference of the Kiev oblast Party organization (June, 1938) Khrushchev attacked those working to separate the Ukraine from Russia and adopted a strong centralist position, declaring: "The Ukrainian workers and peasants are united with the Russian workers and peasants by a single thought, by a single will; and that will is the Stalinist will."[59] At the Fourteenth Congress of the CP(b)U (June, 1938)[60] and again at the Eighteenth Congress of the All-Union Communist Party (May, 1939) Ukrainians repeated these views, demanding the solidarity of the Ukraine and of the CP(b)U "around the Stalinist Central Committee and around its beloved leader—our great Stalin."[61]

In practice, the emphasis on unity was expressed politically through measures aimed at consolidating government functions and eliminating republic multiformities. In the 1936 constitution the central government was given enlarged powers: it was authorized to form administrative-territorial units within each republic and to administer banks and industrial, agricultural, and trading enterprises of national importance; Union organs were given greater responsibility over equivalent organs in the republics; the structure of the republic governments was defined more precisely, and republic powers were more carefully limited.[62] These constitutional provisions were supplemented in 1938 by new laws on citizenship and court structure—laws similar to those proposed in 1924 but rejected as being excessively centralist following the objections of Skrypnik and other republic leaders.[63] Also in 1938 a new military system was adopted, abolishing the old territorial units with their contingents of local reserves, and establishing a cadre system in which all military personnel were drawn into full-time service and assigned regardless of nationality to units which were considered Russian and were to be stationed at any point throughout the USSR.[64] Subsequently, the few exclusively national, non-Russian units which had been formed, including apparently one Ukrainian division, were merged with regular units.

Soviet leaders also re-examined the question of language policy and the question of the role to be given Russian institutions in the republics. As has been noted, in the mid-twenties central officials had urged the fostering of local languages and institutions, encouraging republic leaders to draw Russians toward republic ways. In 1927 and 1933 restrictions on the program had been adopted, and after 1934 it had no longer been pressed with enthusiasm. At the first All-Union Congress of Soviet Writers, for example, Gorkii had suggested that: "Soviet proletarian literature in the Russian language is already ceasing to be the exclusive literature of Russian-speaking people and people of Russian origin, and is gradually acquiring an international character even in its form."[65] But the language program had not been abandoned and had continued to receive support from leaders such as Postyshev and others. By 1937, however, the pressure against independent, separate languages and the downgrading of Russian institutions had grown and, in the aftermath of the purges, the programs were brought under strong criticism.

Signs of the change first appeared in 1937 in glorifications of the Russian language and of Russian institutions. In a typical article published in April, 1937, the Soviet writer M. Tulepov declared:

> The Russian language is studied by the toilers of the whole world. In his time Marx paid tribute to the mighty Russian language, studying it and utilizing in his work primary sources in the Russian language. . . .
>
> In our situation the Russian language is the language of the international community of peoples of the USSR. Knowledge of the Russian language enables the peoples of the USSR to acquire the highest of cultural values. It follows therefore that only deliberately arrogant bourgeois nationalists can object to the natural tendency of the toiling Turkmen, Ukrainians, Belorussians, Kazakhs, Kirghiz and others to learn to perfection the Russian language.[66]

Similar praises were sounded of Russian writers and artists and of the Russian people as a whole, who were extolled for their revolutionary successes and clothed with a mystical cloak of Marx-

ian superiority over other peoples in the Soviet Union and throughout the world.

> The Russian people are a great people. They have advanced the
> movement of all mankind toward the triumph of democracy and
> socialism. Under the leadership of their working class, the most ad-
> vanced in the world, the Russian people have been the first in
> history to be liberated from capitalist oppression and exploitation.
> The Russian working class has helped to liberate from national,
> political and economic oppression the whole numerous family of
> peoples inhabiting former Tsarist Russia. The Russian people have
> aided all the Soviet peoples in brotherly solidarity to build a so-
> cialist life.[67]

Specifically, emphasis was placed on Russian cultural achievements which were glorified as superior to the achievements of
other countries and nationalities. To Russia's great writers—Lo-
monosov, Pushkin, Gogol, and Tolstoy—were attributed the closest
ties with revolutionary movements, and all were acclaimed for
their contributions to socialism. At the same time, efforts were
made to identify the outstanding cultural figures in the non-
Russian republics with their Russian counterparts and with Soviet
thought and the traditional Russian heritage. The best example
of these efforts in the Ukraine involved the pre-eminent Ukrainian
writer Taras Shevchenko, a peasant from the Kiev area who had
gained prominence in the middle of the nineteenth century through
his stirring attacks on social and national inequities. Shevchenko
had come to be hailed by Bolshevik leaders almost from the beginning of the Revolution because of his opposition to the Russian
nobility and to the powerful and oppressing landowners of the
Ukraine. However, he had also come to be glorified by Ukrainian
nationalists because of his identification of oppression in the Ukraine
with Russian rule and because of the general nationalist spirit of
his writings. As a result, Soviet leaders had found it difficult to
adopt a clear stand on his work. In 1934 N. N. Popov, one of the
secretaries of the CP(b)U, indirectly criticized Shevchenko by
declaring that, although he was a great revolutionary poet, it was
also necessary to recognize that he "was a bourgeois democrat,
a product of his era," and that he "was not and could not have
been a Marxist-Communist."[68] Unfortunately, Popov continued,

Shevchenko's nationalist views had been fastened upon by a group of Communists who had emphasized them, neglecting the more important revolutionary aspects of his writings. Shevchenko had come to be depicted as upholding national rather than class liberation and as supporting the wider development of the Ukraine rather than the wider development of its toiling masses. Such interpretations of Shevchenko were not accurate, Popov declared, and it was necessary for the Party to fight against them and to adopt instead a "proper Marxist evaluation" of his works, minimizing nationalist interpretations whenever they were presented.

Popov's call for a modified approach to Shevchenko's writings suggested that nationalist figures of the past were to be drawn to a fuller measure of support for Soviet rule. Whatever policies these figures had advocated which were opposed by the Bolsheviks were to be interpreted away, and the nationalists themselves were to be identified as completely as possible with Russian and Soviet traditions and with Bolshevik authority. In the case of Shevchenko an article appearing in *Visti* in February, 1937, outlined the approach Bolsheviks were expected to take.[69] Comparing Shevchenko with the Russian Pushkin, the article praised the works of both and insisted that the two had never exhibited differences over the national question but as "great representatives of two brother cultures" had fought for the same fundamental ideas: freedom from reaction and despotism, destruction of Tsarism and church oppression, liberation of the peasants and workers. Pushkin and other Russian writers, it was suggested, had played an important role in the development of Shevchenko's works and of the works of virtually all important Ukrainian writers. Their influence had been decisive in the growth of Ukrainian culture itself. Hence Shevchenko did not represent—as Ukrainian nationalists insisted— an anti-Russian figure opposing Russian culture and institutions but a great genius in the tradition of Ukrainian and Russian artistic development who had drawn on the common heritage, extending it in the fight against social oppression. By interpreting the revolutionary movement to the Ukrainian people in the Ukrainian language he had become a socialist hero above all and only secondarily a nationalist hero.[70]

In practice, glorification of the Russian language and of Russian institutions led to a more restrictive language policy in the Ukraine. The restrictions took two forms. First, the requirement handed down in 1933 that the Ukrainian language be brought steadily closer to the Russian in alphabet, vocabulary, and grammar[71] was restated and given new emphasis. In articles appearing in October and December, 1937, an intimate union of the two languages was demanded. A recently prepared Ukrainian-Russian dictionary was denounced on the grounds that it had fallen under the control of nationalists and fascists who had ignored the Ukrainian language of the cities with its many Russian elements, and had emphasized bizarre Ukrainian terms borrowed from Poland and the western rural areas.[72] Ukrainians were ordered to prepare a new dictionary emphasizing language similarities.[73]

Secondly, the Bolshevik principle of the supremacy of local languages in the republics—the principle on which the whole Ukrainization policy had been based—was denounced and a campaign inaugurated to press the use of the Russian language. In no other area of national policy did Bolshevik leaders reverse themselves so completely. Russians living in the Ukraine were no longer to be castigated for failing to study Ukrainian, nor were officials to be criticized for refusing to accept it as an official tongue. On the contrary, pressure was once again to be brought against Ukrainians to adopt Russian as an alternate if not a primary tongue. In the months after 1937 one after another of the old language programs of the Ukrainization period were abandoned. On January 1, 1938, the two big Ukrainian-language newspapers *Visti* and *Komunist* were supplemented by a Russian paper *Sovetskaia Ukraina*:[74] subsequently it became customary practice for the republic to publish one Ukrainian and one Russian-language newspaper.[75] In April, 1938, a new law was adopted on the matter of Russian language instruction in the schools.[76] Under the previous act (July, 1927),[77] study of both Ukrainian and Russian had been made compulsory throughout the school system; but apparently many institutions—particularly in the rural areas—had ignored Russian completely or taught it only in a desultory way.[78] The situation had become intolerable not only because Soviet leaders had grown more sympathetic toward Russian institutions but because the new military system with its lumping together of citizens from all the republics into common Russian units required at least a minimum facility in the Russian language. The new law provided for a rigid system of language training designed to ensure that all Ukrainians, including those completing no more than four years of schooling, would be able to converse fluently in simple Russian and to read and write the language in an elementary way. No similar emphasis was given the teaching of Ukrainian in non-Ukrainian schools. The old Ukrainization policy of transforming the predominantly Russian cities into Ukrainian centers was apparently to be abandoned in favor of a policy aimed at extending Russian influences into the predominantly Ukrainian countryside.

At the Fourteenth Congress of the CP(b)U (June, 1938) Khrushchev summarized the new situation on the language front as follows:

Comrades, now all the people study the Russian language because the Russian workers ... helped to forward the flag of revolution. The Russian workers have set an example to the workers and peasants of the whole world as a call to battle, as a call to avenge themselves on their enemies, and as a call to win their freedom.

Comrades, Bolsheviks have studied the German language so that they might read in the original the theories of Marx. The theories of Marx and Engels have been developed further by the theories of Lenin and Stalin in the Russian language. Hence, comrades, the people of all areas are studying and will study the Russian language in order to study Leninism and Stalinism and to be taught to destroy their enemies. . . .

The bourgeois nationalists, the Polish and German spies, as they made their way into certain sections of the cultural front, understood remarkably well the force and influence of the Russian language, of the Russian culture, the influence of the teachings of Lenin and Stalin on the minds of the Ukrainian people. Because of this they drove the Russian language from the schools. But the Ukrainian people, who in the course of many centuries have battled against their enemies alongside the Russian workers and peasants, are completely dedicated to the general aspirations of the workers' class of the Soviet world. They are tied by vital bonds to the Great-Russian people and will fight together with them under the banner of Lenin and Stalin for the complete victory of Communism.[79]

LOYALTY AND WORLD WAR II

Although the purges of 1937-1938 and the accompanying Russification drive were prompted chiefly by internal political considerations, they were prompted also by the concern Soviet leaders felt over the growing challenge to the USSR represented by Nazi Germany. That the two motivations proceeded hand in hand was suggested by the many references in official statements and the Soviet press to German and Polish espionage agents and to the alleged close connections between bourgeois nationalists and Trotskyites, on the one hand, and hostile foreign powers, on the other. It seems doubtful that such connections did in fact exist or that Stalin personally was convinced of what was so convenient a weapon with which to strike against the opposition. In a period of external instability, however, the national virtues of unity, patriotism, and loyalty grew steadily in importance and seemed also to require greater emphasis on Russian institutions and an unquestioned acceptance of Stalin's leadership.

In the case of the Ukraine the problem was particularly acute because the republic occupied a vulnerable spot on the Soviet Union's frontier and because German leaders had traditionally shown special interest in the republic. On many occasions high Nazis had emphasized the importance of the Ukraine for the Third Reich,[80] and the German government had openly cultivated anti-Bolshevik *emigré* Ukrainian nationalists for possible future use in their homeland.[81] Soviet leaders were mindful of this German interest and of the German occupation of the Ukraine in World War I and were prompted to emphasize loyalty more strongly in the Ukraine than in the other Soviet republics. For a brief period after June, 1938, the purge of Ukrainian Party workers continued, although on a much smaller scale than in the previous year.[82] But more troublesome to central leaders was the question of the loyalty of the mass of the Ukrainian people. In the years preceding World War II, major emphasis was placed on the building of popular opposition to Germany and Poland and on the strengthening of general Ukrainian support for central rule.

The task was not an easy one. As in the mid-twenties and early thirties the problem was that of building a kind of mass support which, to be effective, could not be based on coercion but only on a broad identification by Ukrainians with Soviet rule. Moreover, the problem was tied with Soviet foreign policies, particularly Soviet efforts to prevent German expansion and avoid involvement in World War II. And setting a limit to Soviet efforts was Stalin's unwillingness to grant even modest concessions of an economic or national character to the USSR's minorities. It is not surprising that no clear policy for building support was adopted and that campaigns of a differing sort were pursued at different times.

The first campaign was instituted in 1938 and continued until the signing of the German-Soviet Non-Aggression Treaty in August, 1939. Two themes were emphasized: 1) the viciousness and depravity of the German and Polish governments which, it was claimed, were interested in the Ukraine solely as a colony to be exploited in the interests of German Fascists and Polish nobles; 2) the brutal and enslaving conditions to be found in the western Ukraine under Polish rule as contrasted with the liberating and stimulating conditions in the Soviet Ukraine. At the Second Session of the USSR Supreme Soviet (August, 1938) the Ukrainian writer and Party leader O. E. Korniichuk expressed these themes as follows:

> The millions of Ukrainian peasants of the western Ukraine are being denied the right to equality of language. The Ukrainian schools are being destroyed and closed. There is not a single gymnasium or one higher school teaching in the Ukrainian language in the western Ukraine.
> What has the Polish republic given to the millions of Ukrainians in the western Ukraine? It has given them poverty, hunger, arbitrary justice, and the degrading name of *khlopa* [blockheads].
> And this Fascist, Polish nobility together with German Fascism dreams even today of harnessing a yoke on the necks of the free citizens of the Ukrainian SSR. They dream of transforming them into *khlopa*. But the Soviet Ukrainian people are calm because their sons and daughters are citizens of the great, invincible Soviet Union. . . . Over the golden seas of grain, over tender, green-velvet sugar beets, over the strong workers of the Dnieper, which drives

great turbines, over the kolkhozes, the great factories and mines of the Ukraine ring the clear songs of the free Ukrainian people.[83]

At the same time, Soviet leaders began to insist again, as they had in 1934, that Party organizations be drawn more closely to the Ukrainian masses and that the base of the CP(b)U, which had grown so narrow under the purges and the restrictions on enrollment of new Party members, be broadened.[84] In January, 1938, with the arrival in the Ukraine of Khrushchev and Burmistenko, a campaign to increase Party membership was instituted. The campaign was to be, not a mass enrollment program, but a selective expansion directed particularly at elements such as kolkhoz workers and inhabitants of small towns which, in the past, had been farthest removed in sympathy and contact from the Party.[85] After two years of the campaign, in May, 1940, Khrushchev was able to report that the campaign had been at least a quantitative success and that over 235,000 members and candidates had been added to the Party, increasing its size by nearly 85 percent.[86]

With the signing of the German-Soviet Treaty in August, 1939, and Soviet occupation of the Polish districts of the Ukraine (September, 1939) and the Rumanian provinces of Bessarabia and Northern Bukovina (June, 1940), propaganda themes in the Ukraine were shifted. A scrupulous neutrality toward Germany was adopted, and attacks on German interest in the Ukraine were halted. Emphasis was placed on themes such as the friendship of the Soviet republics for one another and the glorious achievements of the USSR under the fatherhood of central leaders.[87]

Of greater interest were the policies applied to the newly acquired areas. At the moment of Soviet occupation these districts presented a confused picture. The Ukrainian population was in general dissatisfied with Polish and, to a lesser extent, Rumanian rule but could not agree on a positive solution to its difficulties. In the early years after World War I—during the Ukrainization period in the Soviet Ukraine—the accommodating policy of the Bolsheviks had appealed to many, and the Communist Party of the Western Ukraine had developed into a large and powerful organization. Subsequently, following the restrictive measures adopted after

1927, many had turned away from the Soviet Union and begun to look to Germany or even to the Polish government for assistance, joining with groups that had been strongly anti-Soviet from the beginning. When Soviet armies moved into the western Ukraine, they therefore found a divided population including elements which were bitterly hostile, others which were warmly sympathetic —remnants of the Communist parties in Poland—and the largest groups which were skeptical but hopeful.

Whatever opportunities these divisions offered Soviet rulers were, however, largely ignored. Soviet leaders apparently decided to incorporate the new areas as quickly and fully as possible into the regular fabric of the UkSSR and to make no allowance for local peculiarities. As the provinces were added to the Ukraine, only a few local inhabitants were given even nominally important jobs,[88] and overwhelming them were thousands of administrators, teachers, journalists, etc., sent from the Soviet Union to assume direction of every aspect of public life.[89] Within two months the areas were formally incorporated into the UkSSR,[90] and Party and government leaders for each oblast were named by the CP(b)U and sent to their posts.[91]

Yet the areas were not to be easily absorbed. In the formerly Polish territories the predominantly rural character of the population, the strength of the Greek Catholic Church, the existence of a powerful nationalist sentiment providing support for organized, conspiratorial parties, all served to limit local acceptance of Soviet rule.[92] Moreover, as the process of Sovietization was pressed, including collectivization of agriculture and nationalization of industry and trade, wide-spread dissatisfaction was aroused.

The Soviet response to these difficulties seemed uncertain. On the one hand officials made plain that anti-Soviet sentiment would not be tolerated, and the most prominent Ukrainian nationalists were removed from their work and, in some cases, imprisoned or executed.[93] But on the other hand Ukrainian institutions were fostered and the use of the Ukrainian language encouraged, and a great Ukrainian National Congress was called (October, 1939) to stimulate support for the occupation: apparently no large-scale effort was made to eliminate dissident elements. Perhaps it was the Soviet hope that a measure of flexibility and acceptance of Ukrainian forms would facilitate the transition to socialism. But in the short period of Soviet control the program was unsuccessful. As one authority has observed,[94] the Bolsheviks succeeded only in antagonizing the local population without acting with sufficient strength to destroy the possibility of future nationalist revivals. Hence, it was in these western districts that anti-Soviet sentiment smoldered most threateningly, erupting after the German attack on the Soviet Union to provide the most serious challenge to Soviet rule.

The German invasion of the USSR shifted the problem of Ukrainian loyalty to a different plane. The speedy occupation of the western parts of the Soviet Union by the German Army forced the Ukrainian government to flee from its capital to the eastern city of Ufa, lying near the Ural Mountains. The Ukrainian people were now shut off from Soviet control, and the way was opened for nationalists to express their feelings more directly, although under the new controls of the German occupation. The story of nationalist attempts to win autonomy or independence is outside the purview of this study and has been dealt with in other works.[95] But brief mention must be made of the Soviet reaction to the occupation and of Soviet efforts to retain Ukrainian loyalty.

Two avenues of activity were open to the Soviet government. The first was the development of partisan and underground operations in occupied territory behind the German lines. Apparently these operations were to be directed at the destruction of military targets but were also to bear to the people of the occupied territories witness to the vitality of Soviet power. The presence of partisan bands would help to discourage collaboration with the Germans, and, where it did not, the partisans would serve as arms of the Soviet state, punishing those suspected of disloyalty without waiting for reoccupation by Soviet forces. The partisan movement would maintain a measure of the coercive aspects of Soviet rule as a guarantee of loyalty even in the absence of direct, legitimate Soviet authority.

Plans for partisan warfare had been drawn up before the German attack, but they had not been widely circulated[96] and in the confusion of the rapid German advance were put into effect only at scattered places. Apparently the intention had been to form a complete network of underground Party organizations operating throughout the Ukraine at both the oblast and raion levels. In the districts along the Dnieper River and to the east—districts furthest from the German advance where time was available—such organizations were formed in a partial way. But despite intensive Soviet efforts[97] the units quickly disintegrated under the pressure of German military forces. In other parts of the Ukraine the lack of preparation and the harsh countermeasures adopted by the Germans forced Soviet leaders virtually to abandon the program.

In its place, efforts were concentrated on building individual partisan detachments wherever conditions were suitable. The efforts were most successful in the areas along the Ukraine's northern border and, near the end of the war, in the western districts: in these sections marshlands, broken terrain, and forest vegetation provided natural cover favorable for clandestine operations. Best conditions were in the north where partisan groups such as the famous Kovpak band[98] came to dominate large parts of the Sumy, Chernigov, Kiev, Zhitomir, Rovno, and Volynia oblasts. Led by dedicated Communists and maintaining limited ties with Ukrainian officials behind Soviet lines, the partisans succeeded in winning or forcing support by segments of the local population. In the west the partisans were further from the Soviet center and found themselves competing with Ukrainian nationalist bands which refused to join them: only as the Soviet army approached did they become effective forces. Elsewhere the partisan effort was largely unsuccessful. The open steppe terrain, which characterizes nearly 80 percent of the Ukraine, provided no suitable refuge areas, and the German occupation noted only sporadic, isolated partisan incidents. In the cities and industrial centers underground Party groups existed but provided no challenge to German control. For most Ukrainians the sense of a "Soviet presence" Russian leaders had hoped the partisans would bring was too cloudy to be influential.

In a second effort to ensure Ukrainian loyalty, Soviet leaders expanded their pleas to the Ukrainian people, urging them to resist the German invasion and to work for the restoration of Soviet rule. The Soviet press was filled with assurances of the ultimate triumph of the Soviet armies, praise for the cooperative friendship of the Soviet peoples, and revelations of the harsh conditions of the German occupation.[99] On several occasions great meetings of Ukrainian leaders were called at Ufa, Saratov, and Moscow. The meetings adopted resolutions praising Soviet life and its rulers and calling the Ukrainian people to a new struggle against the occupation.

Let the enemy perish. Let him know that the Ukraine will not kneel before him. Liberated Ukrainians, offspring of the Slavic warriors who have battled for their native land—Daniel Galitskii and Sagaidachnii, Bogdan Khmel'nitskii and Bogun, Taras Shevchenko and Ivan Franko, Bozhenko and Mikola Shchors—will never be German slaves. In the free land of the Soviet peoples the Ukraine has grown and flowered. With our brothers—the Russians, Belorussians, Georgians—we have earned our freedom, and together with our brothers we will fight for our happiness and freedom. In the free land of the Soviet peoples the Ukraine again in the future will grow and develop.[100]

Thus Soviet leaders identified themselves with Ukrainian aspirations by appealing to the great figures of the Ukraine's past.

Other modest efforts to accomodate Ukrainian nationalist feelings were made throughout the war. The Soviet press gave brief space to Ukrainian themes by printing plays, poems, and writings of a nationalist character;[101] references were made to the Ukraine's historic tradition of struggle against Polish and German imperialism; songs were composed praising the Ukraine as the birthplace of a noble people; studies in Ukrainian archaeology and history— largely ignored since 1931—were revived in a limited way.[102] In October, 1943, a military award was created—the Order of Bohdan Khmel'nits'kyi—designed to honor Ukrainian partisans by identifying them with the classical Ukrainian hero of the seventeenth century.[103]

The importance of these measures as appeals to Ukrainian sentiment should not be underestimated, but as a practical matter they represented only the most modest concessions to nationalist demands. In the light of earlier Soviet practice it was surprising they were as limited as they were. In previous crisis periods—during the Stalinist drive for Party control from 1923 to 1927 and during the collectivization years from 1930 to 1933—central leaders had emphasized local rights and local programs, bidding for support by accepting national aims in a modest way. In the more serious crisis provoked by the German armies, however, nationalist demands were almost forgotten. There were no calls for an expanded use of the Ukrainian language, no orders to Party leaders for an enlargement of Ukrainian cadres serving in high posts, no resolutions that the Ukraine's Russified cities should be brought closer to Ukrainian ways. On the contrary, the war years saw an increase in glorification of the Russian people and their achievements[104] and a steadily growing emphasis on the unity, brotherhood, and friendship of the Soviet peoples.[105]

In part, the difference in approach may be explained by a difference in the nature of the crisis. In earlier periods Soviet difficulties were internal difficulties: it was support inside the USSR that was wanted. With the German occupation the problem of nationalism became an external one involving a foreign power mindful of the possibilities of exploiting Ukrainian dissidence. Were Soviet leaders to give broad support to nationalist aims, an impetus might be given the separatist movement, encouraging Ukrainians to cooperate with the Germans who, as a practical matter, could offer them more than could the Russians. Fortunately for Soviet leaders, the Germans made no serious bid for nationalist support. But in any case, the war years required emphasis on centralism, unity, and solidarity rather than localism, ethnic peculiarities, and diversity.

More broadly, the unwillingness of Soviet leaders to reaffirm Ukrainian national aims may be explained as a reflection of Stalin's altered approach to the national question. As has been noted earlier, by 1933, or more surely by the end of 1936, Stalin had become convinced, first, that concessions to Ukrainian national sentiment would no longer serve to strengthen Ukrainian support for Soviet rule and, secondly, that coercive measures—previously frowned upon as tending to alienate the national minorities—might now be used effectively against nationalists as well as oppositionists. Thus the two conditions prompting a flexible national policy were held no longer to apply. It may be, as Khrushchev has suggested,[106] that during the course of the war Stalin grew so personally hostile to Ukrainians that he was no longer willing to consider concessions regardless of their immediate practical value. In any case the Bolsheviks now identified Soviet rule with Russian rule and the national minorities with divisive and oppositionist tendencies. As the Germans occupied large parts of the non-Russian lands, Soviet leaders came to view the Russians as the bulwark of Soviet defence and hence the group to which appeals should be addressed. Under these circumstances, there was no enthusiasm for nationality concessions.

VI. THE CULMINATION OF NATIONAL RESTRICTIONS, 1944-1953

Shortly before the end of 1943 Soviet southern armies recaptured Kiev from the Germans and in the following months continued their westward sweep, clearing all the Ukraine including the formerly Polish and Rumanian territories by October, 1944. The successes of the Red Army enabled Ukrainian leaders to re-establish themselves in Kiev and to turn again to the practical tasks of building the Ukraine along accepted Soviet lines and drawing it into closer association with other parts of the Soviet Union. It seems clear that central officials were determined to carry forward the Stalinist policy of uniformity and central control. The postwar years developed as a period of mounting restrictions in all areas of Ukrainian life, leading to a greater insistence on republic conformity than in any previous period.

THE PERIOD OF PERSUASION (1944-1946)

Yet despite the attitude of central leaders few restrictive measures were adopted in the early months but, on the contrary, a moderate policy was pursued. Perhaps the chief explanation was the situation in the Ukraine, so altered from that prevailing before the German occupation: the Ukraine's industrial plant—its factories and mines, power plants and mills—was now greatly weakened and its farm equipment largely destroyed;[1] elements of the Ukrainian people, as Soviet leaders pointed out, were infected with anti-Soviet ideas as a result of their separation from "truthful Soviet information" and their exposure to "lying Fascist propaganda";[2] the war itself continued—though now outside the Soviet Union— requiring the same loyalty and support that had been demanded before the German invasion. Thus Soviet leaders were confronted with the task of rebuilding the Ukraine's economy, of rewinning the allegiance of those whose sympathies had strayed or removing those whose allegiance could not be rewon, and of completing these difficult tasks under the urgencies of the war when production and support were critical problems and Soviet attention was necessarily directed elsewhere. Coercive measures could not easily be applied and could not be expected to guarantee the elimination of opposition. On this basis central officials adopted a policy best described as one of persuasion and re-education.

The policy was implemented along three lines. First, there was inaugurated in the fall of 1944 a campaign to expand propaganda and agitation work in the Ukraine and to direct it along interpretive channels which would build local enthusiasm for Soviet programs. The campaign was to convince Ukrainians of the advantages of Soviet rule as opposed to German exploitation and was to draw them closer to the spirit and practice of Bolshevik society. Special attention was given the Ukraine's western districts where Soviet rule had been established only shortly and where programs such as collectivization and nationalization had not yet been completed. In November, 1944, the Central Committee of the All-Union Communist Party adopted a decision recognizing the unsatisfactory state of affairs in the western districts and calling on Party workers to improve mass-agitation work.[3] The workers were to strengthen supervision of the press, to expand oral agitation in the rural areas, to pay closer attention to mass organizations, and to increase the number of agitators and their level of education and training. To supervise these programs the head of the Party's Administration for Propaganda and Agitation, G. F. Aleksandrov, was sent from Moscow to the Ukraine, and one of his adherents K. Z. Lytvyn was appointed chief of the Propaganda and Agitation Administration of the CP(b)U.

The themes of the campaign indicated the emphasis to be placed on the development of voluntary cooperation. Party workers were to explain government and Party measures so that all Ukrainians might understand their importance for the growth of the Ukraine and its people: peasants were to be shown how Soviet farm policy would restore the land seized by the Germans; city dwellers were to be convinced of the more plentiful life to be expected under Soviet rule; all were to be acquainted with the cultural improvements the Soviet Union guaranteed its citizens and the national rights it assured its republics.[4] With regard to anti-Soviet elements in the Ukraine the campaign was to point out the viciousness of "German-Ukrainian nationalists," showing how they had become enemies of the people, how they had served loyally as tools of the "German ravagers," how they had "butchered" Soviet partisans and "terrorized" the Ukrainian population, how they hoped "to transform our free people into submissive slaves" of foreign imperialism.[5] In the matter of Soviet unity propagandists were to build a strong feeling of identification between the Ukraine, on the one hand, and Russia and the Soviet Union as a whole, on the other: Ukrainians were to be told of the greatness of Russia and its people, of the role played by Russians in liberating the Ukraine from the German armies, of the importance of the unity of all the Soviet peoples for both victory in war and reconstruction in peace.[6]

The second line followed by Soviet leaders was that of granting modest concessions to demands for greater republic autonomy and authority. In February, 1944, the USSR Supreme Soviet agreed to the transformation of the commissariats of defense and foreign affairs from All-Union commissariats operating solely under the authority of the central government into Union-republic commissariats with responsibilities divided between the republics and the Union.[7] As discussed by Molotov, the change was of revolutionary importance.

This proposal is not concerned with the ordinary transformation of two commissariats. The proposal is concerned above all with the establishment of new responsible tasks for Union republics. . . .

The purpose of the suggested transformation is perfectly clear. The transformation signifies a great increase in the activity of the Union republics which have become more important as a result of their political, economic and cultural growth, in other words—as a result of their national development. We cannot help but see in this a new important step in the practical working-out of the national question in our multi-national Soviet state; we cannot help but see new victories for our Lenin-Stalin national policy.[8]

In the area of defense the new program called for the formation
in the republics of separate military units which were to form constituent parts of the Red Army but were nevertheless to be directed immediately by the republic commissariats of defense.[9] In
the area of foreign affairs the republics were expected to establish
separate diplomatic representations with foreign states and to negotiate treaties and agreements independently of the USSR in
fields of special republic importance. According to the Ukraine's
president, M. S. Hrechukha, the change was for the Ukraine a
reflection of its "growing political and cultural importance" as well
as a recognition of its increased "cultural and economic requirements which cannot be satisfied in full measure by the All-Union
government outside its frontiers and which demand the establishment of direct relations between the Soviet Ukraine and foreign
states."[10] Although Molotov made plain that Union interests in
both the foreign and military fields would remain paramount, the
changes promised a considerable increase in the activity and prestige of the republics.

For the Ukraine and Belorussia a further remarkable concession
came twelve months later when Stalin and Molotov pressed successfully at the Yalta Conference for United Nations membership
for the two republics. It seems clear that Stalin was interested
chiefly in enlarging the Soviet Union's role in the United Nations.
But the justifications he gave for his request suggested also an
interest in building republic support. As reported by Roosevelt,
Stalin declared that "his position in the Ukraine was difficult and
insecure," that "a vote for the Ukraine was essential . . . for
Soviet unity."[11] The two western republics had suffered greatly
from the war, Stalin noted, and a vote in the General Assembly
would serve as a gesture, would hearten them and "help to build
them up."[12]

A third conciliatory line followed by Soviet leaders was that
of appealing in a limited way to Ukrainian national sentiment.
As articles discussing cultural matters appeared in the Soviet press,
a shift toward national rather than Soviet themes emerged. In
March, 1945, the pre-Soviet Ukrainian composer N. V. Lysenko
was heralded in an article celebrating the one-hundred-and-third

anniversary of his birth. The article commented briefly in standard form on Lysenko's importance as a revolutionary figure but in addition placed special emphasis on his contributions to the "Ukrainian national liberation movement." Lysenko was guided by the beacon of national culture, the article declared, and his work "took the form of a protest against national oppression on the part of the [Tsarist] government, for he aroused in the masses of the Ukrainian people a sense of national consciousness and a faith in their strength."[13] Thus Lysenko was to be described as a truly great national composer to be compared with the Czech Dvořak, the Norwegian Grieg, and the Russian Glinka. Other articles of a similar character were published in the following months.[14] Ukrainian folklore—legends, stories, and proverbs—and Ukrainian folksongs of the pre-revolutionary period were praised for their aesthetic achievements and for the inspiration they had provided to both Ukrainian and non-Ukrainian composers and writers. The Ukrainian theater, opera, and ballet were criticized, not for Soviet failings, but because they had sponsored and produced so few Ukrainian works. Compositions with national titles and themes, such as Shtoharenko's symphony-cantata "My Ukraine," were upheld as examples to be emulated by others.

It seems doubtful that Soviet leaders accepted these appeals as deliberately as they had accepted the other conciliatory programs. Apparently the articles reflected the attitudes of some cultural and educational leaders in the Ukraine who in the mild cultural and ideological climate of the closing years of the war were allowed to express their views. Soviet insistence on the unity of the republics remained the major theme, and there were no indications that local nationalisms were to be stimulated as during the Ukrainization period. In Party resolutions and reports there was a notable silence on the whole question of nationality policy. And providing a jarring note to Ukrainian nationalists were two indications that centralizing and unifying pressures remained strong.

The first was a revival of the Russian nationalism which had been accepted in a limited way in 1926 and then in full measure in 1937. The new chauvinist upsurge was a direct consequence of the war and its patriotic animations; but its acceptance by central officials indicated the extent to which the Party identified itself with Russian interests. The identification was expressed by Stalin in May, 1945, at a meeting of Red Army officers called to celebrate the German surrender.

Comrades, permit me to propose still one last toast.

I would like to propose a toast to the health of our Soviet people and above all of the Russian people.

I drink above all to the health of the Russian people because it is the most outstanding nation of all the nations included in the Soviet Union.

I propose a toast to the health of the Russian people because it has merited in this war public recognition as the guiding force of the Soviet Union among all the peoples of our country.

I propose a toast to the health of the Russian people not only because it is the guiding people, but also because it possesses a clear mind, a staunch character and patience.

Our government made not a few mistakes and there were moments in 1941-42 when our situation was desperate, when our army had retreated, had abandoned our own villages and towns of the Ukraine, Belorussia, Moldavia, Leningrad oblast, the Baltic area, the Karelo-Finnish republic, had abandoned them because there was no other possibility. Another people might have said to its government: you have not fulfilled our expectations, away with you, we shall establish another government which will conclude peace with Germany and bring us rest. But the Russian people did not do so, because it believed in the correctness of the policy of its government, and it sacrificed itself in order to ensure the destruction of Germany. And this faith of the Russian people in its Soviet government became the decisive force which guaranteed our historic victory over the enemy of mankind—over Fascism.

Thanks to it, the Russian people, for its faith !

Hail the Russian people ![15]

The significance of Stalin's remarks was underscored by the disciplinary measures taken only shortly before against minority nationalities accused of collaborating with the Germans. In the period from 1943 to 1944 six ethnic groups had been declared disloyal and removed from their homes and dispersed to Asiatic parts of the USSR.[16] To Soviet leaders and a large segment of the Soviet people Stalin's characterization of the Russian people as the most steadfast in the USSR seemed an accurate one. Thus a new basis was established for Soviet support of Russia and Russian institutions.[17]

For the Ukraine the problem of loyalty was a very real one. Cut off from Soviet control during the war, the Ukraine had witnessed a resurgence of anti-Soviet nationalism despite the general indifference or hostility of German leaders. How broadly and deeply opposition to Soviet rule had developed cannot be determined, but central leaders themselves considered it a major problem: according to Khrushchev—speaking perhaps with some exaggeration—Stalin viewed the Ukrainians as one of the minorities disloyal to the Soviet Union and was prevented from deporting them after the war "only because there were too many of them and there was no place to which to deport them."[18] It is known that in certain Ukrainian districts—chiefly in the formerly Polish territories—nationalists had supported the occupation or at least had refused to cooperate with Soviet forces in fighting against it.[19] In any case, in the years immediately following the war many nationalists in the Ukraine's western districts—some armed with German weapons—refused to accept Soviet rule, establishing themselves in remote regions where they opposed state authority both openly and indirectly.[20] It was their challenge which most seriously disturbed central leaders, prompting them to take an inflexible stand against the nationalist movement. The nationalists were denounced for their treasonous associations with the Germans and for their counter revolutionary program which, it was claimed, was directed not toward national independence but toward bourgeois enslavement. Compromise with these elements was impossible,[21] it was announced, and loyal Ukrainians were asked to pledge themselves to their complete annihilation.[22]

Thus the Soviet policy of concessions and persuasion was never more than partially accepted. Opposing it were powerful pressures strengthened by the war: Russian chauvinism, an exaggerated insistence on absolute loyalty, and the weight of mighty central institutions. Yet it was clear that stern and inflexible measures could only with difficulty be adopted. Direct anti-Soviet activity such as the work of nationalist partisans in the western Ukraine was classified with German military activity and opposed as effectively as the Red Army was able to bring forces to bear. For the country as a whole, however, no such measures were possible, and Soviet officials accepted modest expressions of national sentiment in the hope that Ukrainians of varying shades of opinion would be encouraged to support restoration of Soviet rule.

THE PERIOD OF RESTRICTIONS (1946-1953)

The relatively permissive attitude of Soviet leaders began to harden at the end of 1945 after the Japanese surrender. The ending of the war freed Soviet leaders of their overwhelming occupation with military and foreign problems, enabling them to turn more seriously to questions of internal policy. The prospect of internal opposition was less frightening than it had been during the war, and military units were available to enforce state authority. The generally unsatisfactory state of affairs in the Ukraine suggested that the moderate appeals of the previous months had not succeeded and that sterner measures were required. Finally, there was Stalin's general tendency to place reliance on coercive rather than persuasive measures coupled with the broad drive for ideological conformity in cultural life mounted by Andrei Zhdanov in 1946 throughout the Soviet Union.

Reconstruction of the CP(b) U

Foremost among the sterner measures was that of rebuilding and fortifying the CP(b)U. At higher Party levels the problem was not serious since most leaders had been returned to the Ukraine following the war and continued to hold Stalin's confidence: at the republic level, eight of the Party's fifteen top leaders, including the first and third secretaries and all but two of the Politburo members, continued to hold their posts;[23] at the regional level, sixteen of twenty-four oblast chiefs were returned to the Ukraine.[24] All were acclaimed as wartime heroes and praised for their participation in partisan or army affairs.[25] Khrushchev was particularly favored through his membership in the All-Union Politburo[26] and through his appointment as Chairman of the Ukrainian Council of People's Commissars.[27] Two major figures added to republic leadership were D. Z. Manuil'skii, Commissar of Foreign Affairs,[28] and V. P. Herasymenko, commander of the

Kiev Military District and Commissar of Defense.[29] With these exceptions the continuity of leadership was remarkable considering the dislocations of the war.

At lower levels in the Party the problem was more difficult. Although little information is available for the immediate post war years, it is clear that the war and the German occupation had left lower Party groups in a disorganized state. During the war little emphasis had been placed on intra-Party work,[30] and in the occupied parts of the Soviet Union Party organizations had been uprooted, their members and leaders entering the Red Army, evacuating ahead of the German advance, or remaining to work in partisan bands or to be liquidated by the Germans. Particularly harshly affected had been primary Party groups in the rural areas. In many instances leaders and members had failed to return at the close of the war: in certain districts whole Party groups had failed to survive, and in others there remained only a small nucleus of pre-war workers. Thus the unfavorable conditions of the post-collectivization years of 1934 to 1936 were duplicated, and Party leaders were forced to turn seriously to reconstruction work among local organizations.

In 1944 the Party began expanding its leadership cadres to fill the gap at the lower levels. As in earlier crisis periods, heavy reliance was placed on cadres imported from other parts of the Soviet Union: in April, 1944, nearly 3,000 such workers were drawn to local organizations in the Ukraine.[31] Other leadership cadres were formed by promoting to directing work Ukrainian Party members who had had no previous experience. In the Stalino oblast, for example, it was reported in the fall of 1944 that nearly 85 percent of the secretaries of primary Party organizations were new to their posts.[32] Many of the cadres, apparently, were considered qualified solely by virtue of their military service during the war.

Yet this mass injection of Party leaders at the local level was not successful. As early as December, 1944, criticisms of the reorganization began to appear. In an article in *Pravda Ukrainy* H. Babak, leader in the Organization-Instruction Administration of the Central Committee of the CP(b)U, attacked Party workers in the Ukraine's western districts for their failures in intra-Party organization work and mass agitation and propaganda work.[33] Babak noted, for example, that in the Stanislav oblast only 171 primary Party organizations had been established since the war and that many of these were weak and operating at an unsatisfactory level: in some groups meetings were held infrequently or not at all; leaders were young and inexperienced; insufficient emphasis was placed on training Party members and building a socialist spirit. With such unsatisfactory conditions, he declared, it was impossible for Party groups to organize and develop the masses "for the fulfillment of measures of the Party and the Soviet state." It was necessary, he concluded, to devote special attention to the strengthening of the organization and structure of the raion and primary Party groups, particularly in the rural areas.

Subsequently, republic and oblast leaders made strong efforts to improve the quality of local leaders. In 1945 and 1946 a purge was carried out which resulted in the replacement of nearly half the Ukraine's Party and government officials, including 38 percent of the raion Party secretaries, 64 percent of the heads of the raion soviets, and two-thirds of the directors of the machine-tractor stations. In one oblast—the Sumy oblast—91 percent of the raion leaders were ousted, while in one machine-tractor station four different directors were appointed and replaced in less than two years.[34]

These shifts not only failed to improve Party and government work but, on the contrary, increased instability and led to the appointment to leadership posts of people who were poorly trained and inadequately tested.[35] As noted by Khrushchev, the whole matter of the "preparation, selection, and assignment of leadership cadres [had] been carried out in an unsatisfactory manner in the Central Committee and oblast committees of the CP(b)U." The broad problem of leadership in the Ukraine needed to be restudied and remedial measures adopted.

In 1946 the problem was considered by the Central Committee of the CP(b)U and was discussed again and again in journals and newspapers in the Ukraine and Moscow.[36] The tenor of the discussions was everywhere the same: the raion and primary Party organizations had not grasped the importance of intra-Party work; they had not built up their organizational structures to the level required for effective political leadership; they had failed to promote to leadership posts the best people in each organization; they had not drawn each Party member into active political work.[31] In many instances, it was reported, group leaders had been chosen on the basis of favoritism rather than political and administrative capabilities. Party meetings had degenerated into formal sessions with no active discussion of real political and economic problems. Workers in various sections of the Party groups had fallen into bureaucratic habits emphasizing form rather than substance. Little concern was being shown for the accomplishment of Party and government decisions, for verifying the work of Party members, for drawing new cadres of local people into the Party. Intra-Party training programs were being ignored, little attention was being given the teaching of Marxist-Leninist theory or the guidance of non-Party groups such as the Komsomol. The list of criticisms was long and comprehensive, and led to the general conclusion that Party work in the Ukraine had fallen to its lowest level since the revolutionary years.

At every point discussions of intra-Party work were joined with discussions of the status of farm work and farm production. The Party's interest in the condition of its primary organizations—especially in the rural areas—was not an abstract organizational interest but a deep concern that the Ukraine was failing to reconstruct its economy or to re-establish farm production at pre-war levels. The weaknesses of the Ukraine's rural economy had become obvious in 1945 when the republic had produced in agricultural commodities less than in 1940 and far less than the modest requirements of central planners.[38] In 1946 it appeared that the increases demanded for the new year were not to be achieved and that perhaps even the low levels of 1945 were not to be met.[39]

At the same time two less critical but important problems were pressing on Ukrainian leaders. The first was the continued activity of nationalist partisan bands in the forested and mountainous sections of the western Ukraine. Apparently Soviet forces were unable throughout 1946 to eradicate the bands.[40] And to Ukrainian leaders the problem seemed closely linked with the weaknesses of Party groups in the western Ukraine and with the inadequacies of Party work. Similarly, Ukrainian leaders were confronted in mid-1946 with the demand from Moscow that they inaugurate a new campaign against nationalist deviations in all aspects of Ukrainian life, particularly in fields such as literature and history.[41] Again it seemed clear that the work could be carried through successfully only if Party organizations were strengthened.

In July there was a modest reorganization of republic leadership. At the Twelfth Plenum of the Central Committee of the CP(b)U, Korotchenko was promoted to the long-vacant post of Second Secretary of the Party and K. Z. Lytvyn was named Third Secretary; I. D. Nazarenko was chosen Secretary for Propaganda, and A. A. Epishev, Secretary for Cadres.[42] Subsequently, Ukrainian leaders were ordered to report to the All-Union Central Committee on measures taken to strengthen lower Party groups.[43] When their report was given (August, 1946) it was greeted with a barrage of criticism. Ukrainian work had been generally unsatisfactory, it was declared, particularly the programs for training and utilizing leaders, which had been inadequately conceived and poorly executed. The Ukrainians were ordered to re-examine their cadres policies and to adopt corrective measures. In mid-August a plenary session of the Central Committee of the CP(b)U discussed these criticisms and in a comprehensive resolution admitted the Party's shortcomings. Instances of the poor selection and assignment of local leaders were presented, and groups responsible for cadres work were criticized. Party leaders at the republic level were charged with ignoring their basic task of checking and confirming appointments of leaders to posts in government, Party, and economic organizations, and hence of allowing a separation between the Party and other groups which weakened Party control and led to serious distortions of Party policy. The discussion of these matters ranged far beyond the limited problem of cadres and suggested the need for a comprehensive reorganization of Party methods and Party work.

In the following months no reports were made public on the progress of reorganization work, but apparently central leaders grew convinced that the corrective measures were not succeeding. In any case, it became obvious as the year 1946 drew to a close that the farm situation in the Ukraine was unsatisfactory and that farm production would rise little above the levels of 1945. Central officials began, apparently for the first time, to question seriously the effectiveness of the Ukraine's highest leaders. Throughout November and December it appears that Khrushchev was frequently in Moscow for discussions—discussions which it seems likely were unsatisfactory to Union leaders. In February, 1947, a plenary session of the All-Union Central Committee was called to adopt remedial measures for the Soviet Union's farms and to fortify the leadership of the CP(b)U. On the farm question a lengthy resolution was adopted calling for rigorous changes in farm organization and farm work throughout the USSR.[44] On the question of Ukrainian leadership it was decided to free two of the Union's highest officials—L. M. Kaganovich and N. S. Patolichev—from their duties and to dispatch them to the Ukraine to take charge of Party affairs.[45]

The assignment to the Ukraine of Kaganovich and Patolichev did not indicate any broad dissatisfaction with Ukrainian leaders. Although Khrushchev was replaced as First Secretary of the CP(b)U, he remained head of the Ukraine's Council of Ministers, member of the Ukrainian Politburo and Orgburo, and member of the Union Politburo. The office of Second Secretary of the CP(b)U was abolished, but the Second Secretary, Korotchenko, retained his other posts and was appointed to the newly created position of Secretary for Agriculture and Procurement.[46] No other significant changes in Party or government leadership were made at the republic level.

In the following months it appeared also unlikely that fundamental changes were to be made at the middle level of the CP(b)U or that there were to be introduced shifts in farm policy or in the Party's approach to the national question. From March to September a campaign aimed at increasing farm production was carried out, but as far as is known it was not distinguished from earlier campaigns.[47] In July and August a special effort was made to correct weaknesses in primary Party organizations, but the number of leaders replaced did not compare with the number shifted in the previous two years. At the oblast level two Party secretaries were removed, but only one was accused directly of inadequate leadership.[48] Apparently whatever improvements were achieved in the Ukraine in 1947 resulted from a general recovery from wartime disruptions rather than from any particular changes introduced by Kaganovich and Patolichev.[49]

In any case, by the end of 1947 the difficulties which had prompted direct interference by central leaders in Ukrainian affairs disappeared: the production and collection of farm products rose above planned schedules;[50] Party organizations were stabilized to the satisfaction of Ukrainian and central leaders; nationalist expressions in cultural fields were largely eliminated; the number of nationalist partisans was considerably reduced. In December, 1947, Kaganovich was recalled to Moscow, Khrushchev was restored as First Secretary of the CP(b)U, and the Party was in general returned to its pre-1947 conditions.[51]

There were left, however, several legacies of the Kaganovich period. As Kaganovich left the Ukraine, Korotchenko was dropped as Party Secretary for Agriculture and Procurement; although he was retained on the Ukrainian Politburo and reappointed head of the Ukrainian Council of Ministers, he was no longer to play a prominent role in Party affairs. His place was taken by a Russian leader from the Donbass, L. G. Mel'nikov. Mel'nikov had earlier been promoted by Kaganovich from oblast to republic work and had been named director of the Administration for the Verification of Party Organs,[52] a newly created but powerful Party office which had been given chief responsibility for reorganizing Party groups at all levels in the Ukraine.[53] As Second Secretary, Mel'nikov was to continue to play a prominent role in organizing and staffing lower Party groups. The Party First Secretary, N. S. Khrushchev, seemingly emerged from the Kaganovich period with his authority and prestige undiminished. His temporary demotion had not weakened his influence in Party matters but, on the contrary, had enabled him to strengthen his position among leaders in Moscow; apparently he also won the renewed confidence of Kaganovich.

Thus, although he returned to Party work in the Ukraine, his voice in 'the counsels of central leaders remained strong.

New Restrictions in Cultural and National Policies

Accompanying the Soviet drive to reorganize Party groups in the Ukraine was a drive to establish new standards as guides for cultural and scientific work and to define in a more careful way the Bolshevik attitude toward national-cultural expressions. The drive was inaugurated in mid-1946 and was continued with strong force through 1947 and with less emphasis throughout the last years of Stalin's life. It can be regarded as the final development in Stalin's conception of the national-cultural question as applied to Soviet groupings, multi-national or international in form. The drive as carried out in the Ukraine was not unique but was part of a general campaign aimed at drawing cultural and scientific work throughout the USSR to closer support of Soviet rule.

The policy was first outlined on August 14, 1946, in a resolution of the All-Union Central Committee entitled "On the Journals *Zvezda* and *Leningrad*."[54] The specific purpose of the resolution was to correct weaknesses and distortions Soviet leaders charged had crept into the two journals, but the resolution made clear that the changes were to be adopted by all engaged in literary work. Subsequent Central Committee decisions extended the requirements beyond the field of literature to other cultural and scientific areas including drama, music, philosophy, history,[55] and later, biology and philology. Consequently, the policy came to be accepted as establishing general standards for work in all cultural and scientific fields.

Simply stated, the policy established the requirement that work in cultural and scientific fields be considered an integral part of the campaign for building a Soviet society. Neither scientific nor cultural activities were to be considered "apolitical" but rather as "powerful instruments of the Soviet state in the task of developing the Soviet peoples."[56] Artists, scientists, and educators were obligated not only to avoid anti-Soviet themes but also to avoid "un-ideological, apolitical, art for art's sake" themes. Their works were to reflect the positive values of Soviet society and were to be judged not solely or even primarily on their artistic merits, but on the effectiveness with which they aided the state to develop Soviet citizens.

The specific emphasis to be given scientific and cultural programs was incorporated in the key phrase "socialist realism," a nebulous expression meant to encompass Soviet life, not as it could most accurately be portrayed at the moment, nor as it could be expected to develop in the future, but rather as Soviet leaders conceived it most ideally to be under the particular conditions of the time. In the field of literature and drama the matter was simplest. Writers were to follow two basic rules: 1) they were to treat themes of Soviet importance such as collectivization, the "Great Fatherland War," the friendship and unity of Soviet peoples; and 2) they were to develop these themes in such a way that readers might see, amid the difficulties confronting the Soviet people and the natural hesitancies to which they were subject, the responses and attitudes ultimately expected of all.[57] In the areas of painting and music artists and composers were to emphasize, in their search for realism, the beautiful directness of Soviet life, eschewing modern forms with their distortions and ugliness and depicting the harmony and grace of the world Soviet society was constructing.[58] In history and philosophy scholars were to show the evolution in thought and in history of the dialectic and of the Marxist-Leninist ideal, interpreting events and ideas as they contributed to or interfered with the forward march of socialist themes and combatting the introduction of bourgeois, anti-Leninist elements from the West. These requirements in their general outlines had been stated before,[59] but the precise way in which they were set forth and the broader application they were given suggested that the Soviet conception of cultural matters was to be more carefully drawn and that there was to be less toleration of even minor deviations.

The resolution made no mention of the problem of national-cultural construction and, initially, no effort was made to include it. Nevertheless, the demand that cultural expressions be directed along Soviet lines applied equally or even especially to national expressions, and the republics began to re-examine their national-cultural work and to establish new standards.

In the Ukraine the matter was first discussed even before the Central Committee's August decision. In a June address K. Z. Lytvyn, Propaganda Secretary of the CP(b)U, suggested to Party propagandists that artistic and ideological work had fallen to unsatisfactory levels and that serious weaknesses had appeared, particularly in the Ukraine's western districts.[60] Literary works, theatrical productions, films, and historical studies were being inadequately prepared and were not emphasizing sufficiently the positive aspects of Soviet building. In the field of history it was necessary to oppose anti-Leninist conceptions more firmly and to combat specifically the harmful bourgeois-nationalist deviations of Hrushevs'kyi and his school. In the field of literature Ukrainian writers were obligated "to create a type of works in which would be engraved forever the strength, power, and greatness of [the Ukrainian] people, its services before the peoples of the world. . . . The task of literature is to raise Soviet man through the medium of the artistic word to the full and speedy fulfillment of the Stalin plans for the construction of communism in one country."

Lytvyn did not take a severe stand in his address and avoided attacking specific writers or their works, presenting only a general restatement of the national principles adopted in 1933 and 1934. Almost at once, however, the campaign assumed a stronger tone. In June and July stern criticisms appeared of two recently published works which had been accepted earlier but were now denounced for ideological weaknesses and bourgeois-nationalist deviations. The first was an *Outline of the History of Ukrainian Literature* published in 1945 by the Institute of Languages and Literature of the Ukrainian Academy of Sciences as a textbook for secondary school courses in Ukrainian literature. The *Outline*, it was charged, had failed to give "a correct Marxist analysis of the development of Ukrainian literature" and was especially to be censored because it had introduced, in a number of important questions, "major theoretic mistakes of a bourgeois-nationalist character."[61] The *Outline* had mistakenly treated the national question "as a separate independent question apart from its ties with the general question of the power of capital and the proletarian revolution. Thus was hidden the fact that the national question is a part of the general question of the proletarian revolution, of the dictatorship of the proletariat." Specifically, the *Outline* had erred in its discussion of Ukrainian literature in the pre-revolutionary period. In this period literature should have been discussed as one aspect of the battle between the forces of "revolutionary-democracy" and the forces of "landlord liberalism and bourgeois nationalism." Emphasis should have been placed on the battle of advanced Ukrainian writers together with the Great-Russian people against Tsarist oppression and for social and national liberation. The closeness of the brother literatures of the Ukrainian and Russian people should have been stressed. The *Outline*, however, had adopted another point of view, interpreting the liberation movement in the Ukraine separately from the liberation movement in Russia and describing it as a national rather than a social liberation movement. Writers such as Shevchenko and Vovchok had been separated from their Russian brothers and identified with west European liberalism, with humanism and nationalism, with the peasantry rather than the workers. The revolutionary importance of Ukrainian literature had been ignored and its anti-revolutionary aspects, exaggerated.

The second work condemned as nationalist and deviationist was the first volume of a massive *History of the Ukraine* being prepared by the Institute of History of the Ukrainian Academy of Sciences. The volume had been published in 1943 and had been initially well-received. In the sterner climate of the post-war years, however, many shortcomings and nationalist deviations were uncovered.[62] The work had been conceived, it was charged, in the spirit of Hrushevs'kyi, ignoring the Party precept that "all historic events must be regarded from the point of view of the class struggle" and interpreting the Ukraine's past so as to emphasize its national peculiarities and to minimize the importance of its common heritage with other Slavic peoples. The work had adopted the pro-German theory of the Norman origins of Russia, had agreed with Hrushevs'kyi that the Ukrainian people had been separate and distinct from the Russians and Belorussians since the fourth century, had exaggerated the importance of western as opposed to Russian influences in the Ukraine's history, and had virtually ignored the development of class forces and the class struggle in early Ukrainian history. As a result, the work not only had failed to expose the weaknesses of nationalist Ukrainian histories but had supported the nationalists in their efforts to separate the Ukraine from Russia and to restore capitalist, counter-revolutionary rule.

In the following months criticisms of Ukrainian cultural and scientific work steadily increased. The Ukrainian theater was denounced for failing to present dramas based on Soviet themes.[63] Ukrainian newspapers and journals were attacked by both central and Ukrainian leaders for paying too little attention to questions of Soviet ideology, for failing to attack nationalist and bourgeois deviations, and for printing works of a bourgeois-nationalist spirit.[64] Ukrainian writers, historians, and university professors were accused of disseminating anti-Soviet, nationalist ideas.[65] The Ukrainian opera, it was charged, had failed to perform a single work by a contemporary Soviet composer presenting a view of contemporary Soviet life.[66] Ukrainian composers were denounced for failing to prepare music drawn from contemporary themes.[67] The Institutes of Economics, Art, and Ethnography and Language of the Ukrainian Academy of Sciences were attacked for their inadequate work in opposing "bourgeois-nationalist conceptions and reactionary theories" in Ukrainian social sciences.[68] Every aspect of cultural activity in the Ukraine was criticized, and cultural workers in all fields were ordered to re-examine their work in the light of the new Soviet requirements.

Restrictions were also adopted in Ukrainian government work, most notably in the two recently created Ministries of Foreign Affairs and Military Affairs. Molotov's promise of 1944 that the Ministries would be developed as powerful arms of the Ukrainian government and would be given major responsibilities in the military and international fields was not substantiated in a practical way. The Ministry of Military Affairs, headed initially by V. P. Herasymenko, was never organized, and when Herasymenko was removed from the Ukraine no successor was appointed.[69] Greater attention was given the Ministry of Foreign Affairs, which was actually organized as an operating ministry, but the only important function the Ministry assumed was that of handling Ukrainian participation in United Nations affairs. The promised right of exchanging diplomatic missions with other states was never granted.[70]

Undoubtedly many Ukrainians, particularly writers, artists, and scholars, disagreed with the new cultural and governmental restrictions. Unlike the period before 1934, however, when wide disapproval of similar restrictions had been expressed, no Ukrainian leaders arose to organize and stimulate opposition, and there were no open dissents to compare with those of Skrypnyk and others. There were two indications, however, of opposition. The first was the record of attacks by Party leaders on individual Ukrainian cultural workers. The list of those rebuked was long and included writers and scholars such as V. Cherednychenko, Iu. Ianovs'kyi, E. Kyryliuk, S. Kryzhanivs'kyi, A. Kundzich, A. Malyshko, T. Masenko, S. Maslov, T. Mihal', P. Panch, I. Pil'huk, O. Rzhenets'kyi, I. Senchenko, L. Smilians'kyi, M. Vozniak, and a host of others. In some instances—notably in the cases of Vozniak and Kyryliuk— there were repeated attacks, indicating that the accused refused to accept Party criticisms and to reform their work.[71] The editorial board of the Ukrainian journal *Vitchyzna* was removed for its failure to correct its mistakes,[72] and the journal's principal editor, Iu. Ianovs'kyi, was denounced for refusing to recognize his errors "honestly and in a straightforward way" and for refusing, even after criticism, to incorporate into his work the "true spirit of the Leninist-Stalinist principle."[73]

The second hint of opposition involved Soviet attacks on a group of Ukrainian writers accused of advancing the theory of "the right to make mistakes" (*pravo na oshibku*). The leaders of this group were two members of the presidium of the Ukrainian Union of Soviet Writers, P. Panch and Ia. Horods'kyi.[74] The views of these writers are not clearly known, but it appears that they took the position that Ukrainian authors should be allowed to introduce into their works characters, including the protagonists, who did not always live and act according to Soviet conceptions. Panch and Horods'kyi defended their position mainly on literary grounds, urging that perfect characters were stereotyped and unreal and that effective writing could be done only if variations were introduced. But their theory could easily be expanded beyond the narrow question of literary standards. Apparently there were other writers who suggested that in general no ideological framework of a rigid character should be handed down and that, in any case, the right of cultural workers to make ideological mistakes should be accepted.

Soviet leaders refused absolutely to accept such modifications. It was not a small matter, they declared, but a basic confusion of the true purpose of literature in a Soviet state. All cultural work, they insisted, was to serve the real interests of the Soviet people. Consequently, the right to make mistakes in ideological questions could not be viewed simply as an abstract right but as a practical invitation for deviations from Soviet ideology. It was a right to oppose the building of a Soviet state, a right to freedom from criticism. The demand for such a right was not unlike that presented twenty years earlier by Khyvl'ovyi and his associates, who had insisted that Ukrainians be allowed to turn to non-Soviet and non-Russian sources. The acceptance of such a right would mean in practice the introduction into Ukrainian cultural work of anti-Soviet themes and oppositionist practices and the weakening of criticisms at a time when critical work was especially needed if the deviations which had crept into Ukrainian cultural life were to be eliminated.

From the many and detailed discussions of cultural and national questions in the Ukraine and from the answers of Party leaders to the mild oppositions of a few Ukrainians, several principles emerged as the basic requirements of Soviet national-cultural policy. At the root of Soviet policy was the conviction that national and cultural activities could not be guided by any absolute standard or measure, but only pragmatically by the requirements of the socialist state. In cultural matters, such as literature, the relativist nature of Soviet policy was suggested by Nazarenko as follows:

Literary people and writers are required to guide themselves by *whatever* constitutes the basis of the Soviet regime, of the policy of the Soviet state. The strength of Soviet literature, the most advanced literature in the world, is to be found in the fact that it is a literature in which *there are not and cannot be any other interests* except the interests of the people, the interests of the state.[75]

For Soviet journals the Central Committee of the CP(b)U declared: "Every Soviet journal, whether it be scientific, literary, or any other, must be first of all a politically purposeful organ of the battle for a Communist society, for the development of the wide masses of the Soviet people in the spirit of the ideology of Bolshevism."[76]

Where the national question was involved it too was not an independent question separate from the Soviet question, but a secondary element to be evaluated as only one part of the Soviet question. The early comments of Lenin and Stalin on the subordination of the national question were restated and reemphasized: "The basic essence of the Bolshevik approach to the national question may be found in the fact that Bolsheviks always have regarded the national question in its inseparable relationship with revolutionary perspectives."[77] The essential element was the complete subordination of cultural and national questions to political demands, and the subordination was to be more than a negative avoidance of expressions hostile to the state and was to include also the positive demand that national-cultural work contribute directly to the construction of socialism.

In the republics it was the subordination of the national question rather than the cultural question which was particularly emphasized. Although Ukrainians were expected, as Soviet leaders declared on numerous occasions, to measure their cultural work by the same standards of "socialist realism" being enforced throughout the Soviet Union,[78] they were to pay greater attention to national problems which were more serious because of the Ukraine's long national tradition and the recent German occupation.[79] In the matter of the relationship of the cultural and national questions, the guiding principle was to be Lenin's conception of the presence within each nation of two opposite cultures: one, democratic and socialist, rising out of the working and exploited classes; the other, bourgeois, dominating, and exploiting. In the development of an international proletarian culture the bourgeois elements of each specific national culture were to be eliminated, but the democratic, socialist elements were to be fostered and incorporated, ultimately, into the whole.[80] During the early years of Soviet rule—under Lenin and for a time under Stalin—republic leaders had been allowed considerable freedom in deciding which elements were socialist and which were bourgeois. By 1946, however, central leaders had begun to define a number of general principles to be applied as yardsticks to the national culture of each minority region.[81]

For the Ukraine the first of these general guides was the requirement that, in depicting Ukrainian institutions and forms, emphasis be placed on Soviet rather than pre-Soviet or non-Soviet elements. In the field of literature, it was observed, certain authors had come to write exclusively about traditional Ukrainian life, describing peasant ways and pre-Soviet customs with a nostalgia that led some to believe that the old life was better than the new.[82] The duty of the Ukrainian writer was to show instead the superiority of the features of Soviet man. Authors were to describe and glorify the Leninist conception of the world, the strength, power, and greatness of the Soviet people,[83] the flowering of mankind which was taking place as Soviet plans were being fulfilled. They were to stress the achievements of the maturing Ukrainian proletariat as opposed to the backwardness of the traditional Ukrainian peasant.[84] In the field of history theories and interpretations of a non-Soviet character were to give way to Soviet and Marxist views. Emphasis was to be placed on the chronicling of "progressive" social-political movements in the Ukraine; on the study of the formation of the Ukrainian worker's class, the general revolutionary movement in the Ukraine, and the culminating November Revolution and Ukrainian civil war; on the recording of the progress of socialist construction in the Ukraine and the importance of the Bolshevik Party and its leader, Stalin, as the guiding forces in the new Soviet life.[85] By emphasizing Soviet rather than non-Soviet elements, cultural workers would help the broad masses of Ukrainians to understand the goals of Soviet life and to accept them as superior to provincial nationalist and peasant goals.

The second requirement involved the matter of patriotism and national identification. As has been noted, Soviet participation

in World War II had led to a strengthening of Russian nationalism
and a glorification of the USSR as a national unit. The process
by which Soviet leaders had increasingly identified themselves
with the Soviet Union had thereby been accelerated, and by the
end of the war the Soviet Union had come to be regarded as the
"fatherland" in a sense little different from that so carefully fostered
in Nazi Germany. In the period after World War II Soviet leaders
had openly accepted this conception of the state, charging cultural
workers in the republics with advancing Soviet nationalism among
the non-Russian nationalities. The fatherland of the Ukrainian
people was not the Ukraine or even the Ukrainian Soviet Socialist
Republic but the USSR, and writers and historians, through their
works, were to stimulate Ukrainian identification with the Soviet
Union as a whole.[86] They were to emphasize themes such as the
Stalinist friendship of all the peoples of the Soviet Union and the
wartime and post-war achievements of the USSR. They were to
avoid work tending to set off the Ukraine as distinct from the
other republics. They were to avoid depicting Ukrainian culture
as developing in opposition to or even separately from the cultures
of other Soviet areas such as Russia and Belorussia. They were to
oppose nationalist views such as Hrushevs'kyi's thesis that the
Ukraine had developed historically along different lines from other
parts of the Soviet Union.[87] Although they were to be allowed to
use the Ukrainian language and to discuss the Ukraine's national
and cultural development, they were to do so in ways which would
emphasize the "progressive" aspects of Ukrainian life and contribute
to the solidarity and unity of all the Soviet republics.[88]

   In the same way, central officials insisted that emphasis be placed
on the building of a close union between Ukrainians, on the one
hand, and Russia and the Russian people, on the other. In the
field of history scholars were to study topics such as the history
of the unification of the Ukraine with Russia, the unifying traditions of the Russian and Ukrainian peoples, the solidarity of
Russian-Ukrainian relationships in the Soviet period.[89] In the field
of literature writers were to show the closeness of Russian and
Ukrainian literary development and the importance of Russian
influence on Ukrainian culture.[90] The Russian language was to be

accepted as equal with Ukrainian, and its use by Ukrainian writers was not to be censored.[91]

Liberal Expressions on "Cosmopolitanism" and Linguistics

The tightening of restrictions on the development of national cultures did not signify total Soviet acceptance of either central control or complete uniformity. There remained a measure of flexibility, and by the end of 1947 Soviet leaders were again speaking favorably of national diversity and provincial loyalties. In August, 1947, the Ukrainian writer O. Korniichuk declared:

One of the peculiarities of Soviet culture is its multiplicity of national forms with a single Socialist content. In literature this multiplicity is expressed as a multiplicity of artistic methods, the rich beauty of one's own language, above all the many-centuried history of each national culture, of all that is progressive in this national culture.[92]

In the following April Stalin took a similar position, declaring before a Finnish delegation his support for national peculiarities and forms.

The Soviet people know that each nation—all equally—whether great or small, has its particular peculiarities, its specific culture which belongs only to it and which no other nation can claim. These peculiarities are the endowments which each nation brings to the general treasure-house of world culture and adds to it and enriches it.[93]

Subsequently, other Ukrainian leaders attempted to soften attacks on national cultures. At the Sixteenth Congress of the CP(b)U (January, 1949) Manuil'skii insisted that, while the dangers of nationalism should not be minimized, it was also necessary for the Party to expose the many workers in its ranks who were guilty of "cosmopolitanism," a deviation which Manuil'skii defined as a tendency to view all national peculiarities in a negative way, regarding them as nationalist remnants and nationalist perversions and hence to be opposed. Such people, he declared, fail to see the great and positive achievements of Ukrainian culture during the thirty years of Soviet power and, under slogans such as "the unity of the interests of all mankind" and "the indivisibility of the culture of all mankind," seek "to cut according to one pattern the culture

of each people, of the whole population of the USSR, ignoring the
richness of the multi-national contributions of each culture, Soviet
in its content."[94]   Such a position, Manuil'skii announced, is not
the Soviet one. The Soviet position proceeds "from the fact of
the existence in our Soviet state of nations and nationalities, from
the recognition of their full equality, from the principle of recip-
rocal help and the friendship of peoples. We proceed from the
fact of the national variety of our Soviet culture, a variety which
produces the diversity and richness of its forms."

In March, 1949, a similar view was presented by the Ukrainian
Minister of Education, Pavlo Tychyna, at the Twelfth plenary
session of the Directorate of the Union of Writers of the Ukraine:

Comrade Stalin teaches that the development of a culture, national
in form, socialist in content, is the firm principle of our socialist
society. Proletarian internationalism is built not on the basis of
the impoverishment and depreciation of national culture, but on
the contrary, it is developed where national culture flowers and
grows stronger. Internationalism demands appreciation for other
peoples, but there cannot be any internationalist who does not
love his own people. We love our country, we love the free Ukrainian people and are full of pride because it is moving arm in arm with
the great Russian people, with all the peoples of the Soviet Union
to its single aim—to the building of a Communist society.[95]

In the following year the liberalizing trend was given further
emphasis by a discussion, conducted in the early summer months,
of the question of language in a socialist state. The discussion
was held, it was officially declared, "to overcome the stagnation
in the development of Soviet linguistics and to give a correct direction to the further development of scientific work in this field."[96]
In the course of the discussion a number of articles by Soviet language experts were published,[97] and a series of questions on the
matter was answered by Stalin himself.[98] The discussion was general, dealing with technical and theoretical questions on the origin
of language and the course of its development under capitalist
and socialist systems. Nevertheless, it suggested several principles of language development bearing on the problem of national cultures in the republics.

According to Stalin, it was necessary to correct interpretations of two aspects of language development which in the past had been confused. The first was the formula propounded by N. Y. Marr that language was a superstructure which arose out of the economic base of a given society and, hence, like institutions of politics, law, property, etc., took differing forms under differing societies—socialist, capitalist, or feudal. Such a formula could not be accepted, Stalin declared. Language was not a superstructure to be transformed with each shift in society, but was a common tool which, like Russia's railroad system or industrial plant, could be used alike by Tsarists or Soviets, although for different ends. Although languages changed slightly from period to period, they remained basically the same, serving society as a whole no matter what its foundation or its form.

Similarly, Stalin attacked Marr's thesis that languages were products of a given class and that national languages common to all people of a society, independently of class, were impossible. In a brief resumé of the development of languages, Stalin urged that languages had grown historically as means of communication for all members and all classes of society and that, although each class had striven to turn the national language to its own purposes, developing a dialect of its own or adopting a foreign tongue, the fundamentally national and classless character of language remained unchanged. Whatever modifications a class succeeded in introducing did not prevent a language from remaining a common national attribute, serving bourgeois and proletarian classes alike. Indeed, Stalin concluded, it could not be otherwise, for were a language to become solely the property of one segment of society it would lose its value as a means of intercourse between all the people and would inevitably degenerate and ultimately disappear.[99]

For the national question, Stalin's remarks were significant because of their clear suggestion that language was to continue to be regarded as a matter of form rather than substance and that national languages distinct from Russian were to continue to be accepted as media for cultural work. It was important, Stalin noted, to recognize the difference between culture and language and to understand "that culture changes in content with every new period in the development of society, whereas language remains basically the same throughout a number of periods, equally serving both the new culture and the old."[100] As a matter of form and as an element constant and stable despite social and political shifts, language was "apolitical" and, as distinguished from culture, could not be classified as socialist or capitalist, as Soviet or counter-revolutionary. Consequently, no language could be branded in Marxian terms as superior to any other, and attempts by philologists or cultural workers to transform the minority tongues into Russian or to replace them by Russian were not to be accepted.

The importance of these two liberalizing influences in Soviet cultural policy—the insistence that national peculiarities were not to be abolished and that national languages were not to be transformed—should not be exaggerated. In the aftermath of the severely controlling and centralizing demands placed on cultural work in 1946 and 1947 the statements were a powerful reassurance to national workers in the republics. But they did not affect substantially any of the basic tenets of Soviet cultural policy and, on the contrary, included elements which tended to limit further Soviet concessions to the nationalities.

The first limitation involved the matter of the relative importance of local nationalism as opposed to Great-Russian chauvinism. As has been noted previously, one of the earliest principles of Bolshevik national policy was the principle that both types of nationalism were dangerous but that, because of the long history of Russian domination, the chief danger was Russian nationalism. Throughout the twenties the principle had remained basically unchanged, but emphasis had shifted gradually until by the early thirties Soviet leaders had begun to insist that, although the two dangers remained theoretically equal, local nationalism had become in fact the major problem because it was the problem which had been largely ignored. Subsequently, attention was concentrated almost exclusively on local nationalism and, as Bolshevik leaders identified themselves more closely with Russia and Russian institutions, only the most casual and infrequent references to the dangers of Russian chauvinism were made. Following World

War II all mention of the Russian danger disappeared. When Ukrainian leaders began to suggest again after 1949 that local nationalism was not the only danger, they referred not to Great-Russian chauvinism, as in the past, but to the vague menace of "cosmopolitanism." The specter of Great-Russian chauvinism was dead and, in the future, excessive attacks on nationality rights were to be opposed not as survivals of Russian prejudice, but as expressions of a form of anti-Soviet, pseudo-internationalism.

The second restriction was suggested by Stalin in his discussion of the language question and was related to his conception of the future development of national languages into a single international tongue. In earlier periods Stalin had declared resolutely that there was no possibility that the various languages of the USSR would be absorbed into Russian.[101] On the contrary, he had declared that all would remain distinct and separate and that only after a considerable period of proletarian world rule would they begin to fuse into a common form which would be neither Russian nor German, but a completely new international tongue. In 1950 Stalin spoke less clearly, referring somewhat obliquely to the possibility that other languages might merge with Russian. In general, he declared, the mixing of languages historically had resulted not in the development of a new third tongue, but in the victory of one language over the other and in the disappearance of the vanquished. This had been the case, he noted, with the Russian language "with which the languages of a number of other peoples mixed in the course of historical development, and which always merged the victor."[102] That this would not necessarily happen again under Soviet conditions he implied by declaring that oppositions between languages were a result of competitions between cultures and that under Soviet power, where cultural competitions ceased, language oppositions also would disappear.[103] He refused, however, to repeat in any form his strong declaration of 1930 that national languages would flower and develop separately under Soviet rule. He did not suggest that the national languages would be absorbed into Russian in the near future, and there were subsequent denunciations of philologists who tried to insert Russian words directly into other languages.[104] But Stalin indicated that the flowering and development of national languages was not to take place independently of Russian and that the trend of previous years of drawing the minority tongues closer to Russian was, in general, not to be reversed.[105]

The Drive for Party Responsibility and National Conformity

The restrictive policies which in the period from 1946 to 1950 had been applied chiefly to cultural and national questions were broadened after 1950 to apply to political and governmental questions as well. Throughout the USSR there was inaugurated a campaign to tighten Party and Soviet controls at all levels. In the Ukraine the campaign was directed primarily at the western, newly acquired districts, where the situation was a particularly unsatisfactory one from the viewpoint of the Bolsheviks. Soviet efforts to incorporate these districts into the Ukraine after World War II had not been wholly successful. In the immediate post-war years efforts had been directed at subduing the nationalist partisan bands which dominated remote areas and at destroying the most inflexible anti-Soviet elements including institutions such as the Greek Catholic Church. In 1948 and 1949 a second program had been inaugurated in the form of a collectivization drive. Both programs had been emergency programs pressed not by regular Party and Soviet organs, but by security forces and special Party groups sent out from the Ukraine's cities and eastern districts. By mid-1950 both programs had been fundamentally completed with 93 percent of the farms collectivized[106] and most of the partisan bands destroyed or driven underground to passive measures of resistance. Some of the security forces and special Party groups assigned to the area were withdrawn, the authority of local leaders was enlarged, and the area assumed a more normal aspect in the Ukraine as a whole.

Yet this normalization meant only that the most direct and harsh measures of Sovietization were completed, not that the difficult problems of agricultural production and local acceptance of Soviet rule were solved. On the contrary, it became clear in 1949 and 1950 that the repressive aspects of the collectivization and anti-partisan programs had aggravated popular attitudes. As early as May, 1949, the Central Committee of the CP(b)U called on Party workers in the western Ukraine, and particularly in the Lvov oblast, to give more serious attention to the problem of ideological-political development of the masses.[107] Soon central leaders also began to express concern, and in mid-1950 the All-Union Central Committee ordered Party officials in the Lvov oblast to report directly to Moscow on their work.[108] Apparently their report was unsatisfactory. Oblast leaders were sharply criticized for their failures, especially among the intelligentsia, and were ordered to introduce basic changes in their work. Nevertheless, the situation did not improve but was subjected to many critical discussions in the following months.[109]

Underlying the attacks on Party activity in the western districts was a growing conviction that nationalist sentiments were contributing to the difficulties of building mass support. The problem was magnified because the opposition of nationalists and individualist-minded peasants was no longer an open opposition to be combatted by direct measures such as forced collectivization, deportation, etc., but was indirect and was expressed by a lack of enthusiasm for kolkhoz work and by a general indifference toward Party programs of all kinds. Thus, for example, although almost all farmers had been incorporated into collectives, the new farms were small and weak and were operating at unacceptably low levels.[110] Little effective stimulus was provided by the Party because it was so poorly organized. In one raion—the Brody raion near Lvov—the Party counted no more than 300 members and, of the total, only twenty-five worked in kolkhozes, the others remaining clustered in towns and villages.[111] In the cities the situation was also poor: nearly one-third of the industrial plants were not meeting quotas,[112] and among the intelligentsia there was little support for Soviet rule.[113] At the same time, there were enough expressions of national sentiment to convince central officials that Ukrainian nationalism was a significant element contributing to Party failures.

On July 2, 1951, a second campaign against Ukrainian nationalism was inaugurated by a *Pravda* article "Against Ideological Perversions in Literature."[114] The article was prompted by the publication in the literary magazine *Zvezda* of a series of Ukrainian poems including one by Volodymyr Sosiura entitled "Love the Ukraine."[115] Sosiura's poem had been initially published in 1944 in the latter part of the war, when it had been interpreted as a patriotic call for Ukrainian opposition to the Germans. According to *Pravda*, its re-publication in 1951 was a grave error, not only because conditions were far different than during the war, but because in the intervening years conceptions of Soviet patriotism had been more carefully defined and the obligations of Soviet writers more expressly stated. The essence of Soviet patriotism, *Pravda* declared, was the harmonious combining of "the national traditions of peoples with the general, vital interests of all the workers of the Soviet Union." But Sosiura had failed not only to mention the Soviet Union as a whole or the friendship of all its peoples, but had even neglected to contrast the old Ukraine with the new. Consequently, in ignoring the great advances of Soviet life, he had described a timeless Ukraine which was as well nationalist and counter-revolutionary as internationalist and Soviet.

Beyond its attack on Sosiura, *Pravda* criticized generally the whole cultural field in the Ukraine: other poets and writers had written in Sosiura's style; musical works with nationalist elements, such as the opera *Bohdan Khmel'nits'kyi*, had been accepted and produced; critics and the Ukrainian press had failed to censor these works and had even praised them as written in the spirit of "friendship of peoples" and "internationalism." In the future cultural workers dealing with national subjects were to underscore the mutual inter-relationship of the "friendly family of Soviet republics" and to emphasize the differences between pre-Soviet life under oppressive and exploiting conditions and the flowering of each national society under socialist rule. It was the task of Ukrainians to stress the fact that "in the brotherly family of peoples of the Soviet Union under the guidance of the Bolshevik Party, the Ukrainian nation has achieved outstanding successes in the building of Communism." Underlying all was the injunction that Soviet culture could have no other interests than "the interests of the people and state."

Almost at once those criticized by *Pravda*—Sosiura, Korniichuk, and Ryl's'kyi—admitted their mistakes and pledged themselves to correct their works.[116] But in the next months the campaign assumed greater proportions. Other writers and composers were singled out for attack, and the *Pravda* injunctions were discussed again and again at Party meetings, at meetings of writers and musicans, and in the press.[117]

Moreover, the campaign was broadened to include attacks on the Ukraine's Party organization. Since the end of 1949 the Party had undergone a number of changes both at the republic and oblast levels. In December, 1949, the First Secretary of the CP(b)U, N. S. Khrushchev, had been called to Moscow to Party work there, and his place had been taken by L. G. Mel'nikov, promoted from Second Secretary. O. I. Kyrychenko, a Ukrainian raised apparently at Khrushchev's behest from secretary of the Odessa oblast, was given membership in the Politburo and Orgburo and named Second Secretary.[118] In April, 1950, a second of Khrushchev's protegés, the Ukrainian Minister of Agriculture V. V. Matskevich, was also added to the Politburo. At the oblast level even greater changes were made. In the period from December, 1949, to June, 1951, fourteen of the Ukraine's twenty-five oblast leaders were shifted.[119] These many changes led not only to a disorganization of Party leadership, but also indicated the considerable concern with which central officials viewed Party work in the Ukraine.

The first general criticisms of the CP(b)U came in the same *Pravda* article attacking nationalist deviations in cultural matters.[120] The Central Committee of the CP(b)U, the article declared, was "insufficiently concerned with ideological questions." It had failed to criticize cultural work adequately, had allowed mistakes to go unchallenged, and had ignored the important task of developing the ideological level of the Ukraine's intelligentsia. Hence the Central Committee was at least partly responsible for "the serious weaknesses and mistakes in ideological-development work in the Ukraine."

The *Pravda* criticisms inaugurated a period of intense reconstruction within the CP(b)U. In July, 1951, the Party's Central Committee adopted a decision accepting its share of the blame for weaknesses and mistakes in ideological work and calling for changes in cultural organizations such as the Ukraine's Union of Soviet Writers.[121] Apparently the Central Committee had concluded that there were two principal weaknesses in Party work: first, that local leaders were either inadequately trained or were indifferent to their responsibilities; secondly, that the Party had failed to keep itself informed of the work of cultural organizations and hence had not provided proper leadership. Party groups in the Lvov oblast were singled out for attack.[122] Although the city of Lvov boasted some of the largest and strongest cultural organizations in the Ukraine, it was charged, Party officials had given them little attention, contenting themselves with attending occasional meetings, and failing to supervise practical work. As a result, writers, musicians, and artists had produced anti-Bolshevik works which Party leaders had been unable to citicize because they knew nothing about them.

In September, 1951, leaders of nine of the Ukraine's oblasts were replaced,[123] and a campaign was inaugurated to inject new leadership also at the raion level. Under the guidance of K. F Moskalets, head of the Party's Division of Party, Trade Union, and Komsomol Organizations, special brigades for the verification of the work of the raions (brigadi po proverke raboti raionov) were established. By May, 1952, it was reported officially that as many as a third of the raion leaders of the various oblasts had been shifted.[124] As in the past, principal attention was given to the western parts of the Ukraine, particularly to the Lvov oblast. Early in 1952 Kyrychenko took a special investigating commission to the area, and in April the commission removed the Secretary of the Lvov city committee, Kostenko, together with a number of lower Party workers for allowing anti-Soviet and nationalist elements to infiltrate key posts. In April, 1952, the First Secretary of the Lvov oblast, V. D. Chuchukalo, was ousted[125] and his place taken by S. T. Serdiuk, a secretary of the CP(b)U and long-standing head of the Kiev oblast.[126] Yet the situation remained unsatisfactory. At a plenary session of the Ukrainian Central Committe (May, 1952) Kyrychenko noted that, despite the many changes, the Party could not yet rely on its leadership cadres and that even at the highest levels of the Party many examples of poor work were to be found.[127] He criticized the head of the Party's Division of Propaganda and Agitation, Pashko, for failing to maintain more critical supervision over the work of local propaganda sections, and he rebuked the Party's Third Secretary, I. D. Nazarenko, for ignoring Pashko's mistakes. He censored the government Committee for Art Affairs for its lax attitude toward deviations in cultural affairs, particularly toward bourgeois-nationalist perversions. He attacked a number of Party leaders including Moskalets, N. K. Belogurov, and Chervonenko for serious shortcomings in their work.

In the fall of 1952 there was a third great exchange of oblast Party leaders, affecting nine oblasts including five in the western Ukraine.[128] The shifts were made in preparation for the Seventeenth Congress of the CP(b)U (September, 1952) and the Nineteenth Congress of the All-Union Communist Party (October, 1952). But the shifts continued the trend of previous years of transferring to Party work in the west leaders drawn from Party posts in the east.

Despite the many changes, Party officials continued to suggest throughout the months preceding Stalin's death that Party units were functioning in an unsatisfactory way, that cultural organizations were tolerating improper work, and that Ukrainian bourgeois nationalism remained a powerful and dangerous influence. At the Seventeenth Congress of the CP(b)U the Party's leader, Mel'nikov, noted that ideological work, despite its advances, was weak and unsatisfactory. He criticized, specifically, the Ukrainian Academy of Sciences, including its Presidium, its Division of Social Sciences, and its Institute of Literature. He denounced the Party once again for failing to uncover and correct all the serious ideological perversions in the works of writers and cultural workers. He spoke in the strongest way against nationalist influences.

The Ukrainian bourgeois nationalists have always been malicious enemies of the Ukrainian people. All their hostile activity has been directed against what is most dear for the workers—the Leninist-Stalinist friendship and brotherhood of the Soviet peoples, against the Russian culture and its highest achievement, Leninism. The viperous attack of the ideology of Ukrainian bourgeois nationalism is directed against the vital principles of the Soviet regime—the policy of the Communist Party, to which the Ukrainian people are obligated for the flowering of the economy and culture of their republic, for the realization of the dream of reunification of all the Ukrainian lands into a single Ukrainian Soviet state.

Always and everywhere the Ukrainian bourgeois nationalists have pursued the aim of separating the Ukrainian people from their brother Russian people and turning them over to colonial bondage to foreign imperialists. The Ukrainian bourgeois nationalists have always betrayed the Ukrainian people, have always been spies, diversionists, agents of imperialist espionage. Now they have been purchased by new masters—the American-English imperialists.

Bourgeois nationalism is the most vital and politically dangerous survival of capitalism in the minds of our people. We must unmask any manifestation of Ukrainian bourgeois nationalism wherever it may be expressed.[129]

It is difficult to assess the whole significance of the strong anti-nationalist drive and the many shifts in Party leadership which occurred in the last years before Stalin's death. It seems likely that certain of the major changes in the Party, such as the appointment of Matskevich to the Politburo and his subsequent removal and the ousting of Manuil'skii from high leadership, were moves reflecting political developments in the Soviet Union as a whole rather than exclusively local developments. Perhaps they were prompted by the campaign it has been suggested Stalin waged during the period to ensure the personal loyalty of Party officials everywhere to himself.[130] Or perhaps the changes resulted from rivalries between factions competing within the Party at the Union level. The same influences may have produced also Party shifts at lower levels in the Ukraine and may have served to intensify the anti-nationalist campaign.

Yet it seems clear that the changes were a result chiefly of the determination of central leaders to establish and enforce the most rigid standards for cultural and Party work in the Ukraine. In Party matters their determination arose out of their concern over the many shortcomings they saw in the western Ukraine—opposition to Sovietization, the slow development of collective farms, the activity of nationalist anti-Soviet partisans. In cultural affairs the new standards reflected Stalin's conviction that development of the USSR's ethnic minorities had to be subordinated not only to the demands of socialist and proletarian programs but also to the requirements for building solidarity within the Union and for inculcating respect and admiration for things Russian. The restrictiveness of these policies suggested the distance Soviet leaders had traveled since 1922 and Lenin's call for the full independence of the republics in all matters but military and foreign affairs. The strong and sustained ideological campaign and the many shifts of local Party leaders from the cities to the rural areas and from the eastern to the western Ukraine were the obvious alternatives to a policy of concessions which to Stalin and others was no longer conceivable.

V.II. THE NEW LEADERSHIP, 1953-1957

With Stalin's death in March, 1953, political relationships in the Soviet Union shifted abruptly. Foremost in the minds of Party leaders was the urgency of safeguarding the Party's commanding role during the immediate transition period when opposition elements might be tempted to challenge Party leadership. It seemed of chief importance to present a unified front, and in the first weeks after Stalin's death statements by Party officials and articles in the press emphasized the necessity of preserving Bolshevik unity and suggested the solidarity of Party, government, and military leaders. Yet there was also the difficult problem of the sucession; and, although all for the moment declared "collective leadership" the answer, it is clear that from the beginning a sharp though concealed struggle for position and support assumed major importance.[1]

THE TRANSITION

So powerful were these issues that for a time they dominated other political problems in the USSR, bending official policies and prompting unusual shifts in Party and government personnel. And again, as during the purges of the late 1930s, political events in the Ukraine and other Soviet republics became largely reflections of central conflicts and programs. As central officials moderated harsh Stalinist policies in order to stimulate popular support, so they relaxed controls and restrictions in the republics; and as they vied with one another for authority, so they competed at the republic level where regional Party groups promised to play a role in determining the succession.

Both elements were soon obvious in the Ukraine. In April, 1953—little more than a month after Stalin's death—Beria, in a clear effort to strengthen his position in the Ukraine's Ministry of Internal Affairs, ousted its head, T. A. Strokach, appointing to the post one of his own adherents, P. Ia. Meshik.[2] Apparently Beria acted also in the Western Ukraine—where the influence of the security police had always been especially strong—assigning a new head, Menshtein, to the Lvov apparatus. In the following month it was announced that the Ukraine's old President and Party leader, H. I. Petrovs'kyi, purged by Stalin from Ukrainian leadership in 1938, was officially restored to Party favor and awarded the Order of the Red Banner of Labor[3]—a rehabilitation which was apparently intended, first, to reassure the Soviet people that their new government meant to divorce itself from the most arbitrary of Stalin's repressive policies and, second, to suggest a more sympathetic attitude toward the republics and nationalities. Then in June a spectacular change in policy and leadership was announced. At a plenary session of the Ukrainian Central Committee, the Party's First Secretary, L. G. Mel'nikov, was sternly censored for failing to provide correct leadership in the Ukraine's western districts and for distorting the Leninist-Stalinist policy of national friendship by adopting measures aimed at Russifying the western districts.[4] Specifically, he was accused of sanctioning the "vicious practice" of appointing to high posts in the western Ukraine Party leaders drawn from the eastern oblasts and of allowing a gradual shift from the Ukrainian to the Russian language in the higher schools. He had failed to provide satisfactory leadership, the plenum declared, and had permitted "gross errors in the matter of the selection of cadres and the carrying out of the Party's national policy." He had made "major mistakes" in the task of strengthening the kolkhozes of the western Ukraine and in leading the work of economic and cultural construction. Accordingly, the plenum removed him as First Secretary and member of the Bureau of the Central Committee and promoted to his post the Party's Second Secretary, O. I. Kyrychenko.[5]

Accompanying the leadership changes were shifts in the Party's approach to the national question. The criticisms of Mel'nikov had centered on his violations of the Party's national policy. In the weeks following his removal these violations were discussed and efforts made to correct them. Principal attention was given the western Ukraine where the national problem was most serious and where the Party had experienced greatest difficulties in its Sovietization program.[6] Similar changes were applied also, however, to the eastern Ukraine.

The first change involved the old question of leadership cadres. From the time the western areas had been incorporated into the Ukraine, Party officials had followed the practice of transferring tested workers from the eastern Ukraine to leadership work in the west. In view of the general unreliability of western Ukrainians and the shortage of qualified local leaders the practice had been a reasonable one, but it had provoked antagonism between the Party and the local population. Accordingly, the practice was now to be stopped. The Party's chief task, it was announced, was the training and development of the local intelligentsia and their recruitment into leadership work in all fields.[7] Specialists were to be prepared to work among their own people in their own language and were to be given wider opportunity to express Soviet themes in ways which had special meaning in their own localities.[8] If this were not done, the Party would not regain the contact it had lost with the masses and would be unable to raise the political vigilance of the Ukrainian people "in the battle against internal and foreign enemies of the Soviet people, and against the agents of imperialist states—the Ukrainian bourgeois nationalists."[9]

The second change involved the matter of language. Again it applied chiefly to the western districts. The important element, the new policy suggested, was that emphasized many years before during the Ukrainization period, namely that the Ukrainian language was a valuable, even indispensable tool for the Communist development of the masses. As long as the majority of the local people preferred to speak in Ukrainian, their ideological, cultural, and political growth could be assured only through that tongue. Yet in the western districts the Party had permitted a steady decrease in the use of Ukrainian, particularly in the higher teaching institutions which had been shifted gradually to Russian. Even in the east the problem had grown serious as Party leaders had gone to such absurd lengths as, for example, to translate Ukrainian lectures prepared by the Party's Propaganda and Agitation Administration into Russian even though Ukrainian was known by all.[10] These misguided efforts had interfered with the Party's program of building leadership cadres from the local population and had weakened ties between the Party and the masses. Hence, they too were to be reversed.

The circumstances surrounding these shifts and the motives prompting Mel'nikov's removal are not completely clear. Undoubtedly a major role was played by Beria, who earlier had forced even greater changes in the Georgian republic[11] where he had also accused Party and government officials of distortions of the Party's national policy.[12] Apparently he was pursuing two objectives. First, he sought to strengthen his hand in the republics by removing from leadership supporters of his principal rivals in Moscow: in the Ukraine Mel'nikov was considered perhaps to be most closely identified with Kaganovich and hence an obstacle to Beria. Second, he sought to establish himself as the champion of the Soviet Union's minorities, thereby enlisting their support in his leadership drive. By attacking Mel'nikov as the personification of Russifying and centralizing policies, he hoped to appeal to those in the Ukraine who, because of national feelings or regional loyalties, were dissatisfied with Stalinist rule. Thus he expected, perhaps, to follow the policy Stalin had adopted so successfully in the mid-twenties when he had posed as the chief opponent of Great-Russian chauvinism, winning almost by default the support of nationalist-minded Bolsheviks.

Yet in the Ukraine Beria's role was not as complete or decisive as in Georgia. The purge in the Ukraine was a modest one, and the overwhelming majority of Party and government leaders remained in their posts and hence presumably loyal to Khrushchev, under whom they had most closely worked.[13] Similarly, Mel'nikov's removal profited Beria but little, since the new Ukrainian Party chief, Kyrychenko, also retained his principal allegiance to Khrushchev. Moreover, it seems clear that the policy of concessions to the national republics was not supported solely by Beria—although he may have pressed it most strongly—but was accepted jointly by the "collective leadership" and above all by Khrushchev, as part of a general policy of relaxing controls. Perhaps it was Beria's critical mistake—one to be made later also by other high officials—to underestimate Khrushchev's position and to center his initial attack on Malenkov and Kaganovich.

In any case, in less than two weeks Beria was himself removed from his Party posts and accused of the most serious crimes against the state. Among these was the charge that he had sought "by various cunning means to undermine the friendship of the peoples of the USSR," endeavoring to sow friction among them and "to activate bourgeois-nationalist elements in the Union republics."[14] Yet it is noteworthy that the specific changes in national policy he had instituted in the Ukraine were not mentioned in the charges and that no subsequent steps were taken to reverse either his call for greater use of the Ukrainian language or his demand that west Ukrainan leaders be drawn from the local intelligentsia. On the contrary, there were suggestions that these policies were to be continued, at least in part, in the future.[15]

In terms of the political struggle, however, Beria's dismissal was of considerable importance for the Ukraine. He alone of central leaders had been willing to challenge Khrushchev's authority in the republic Khrushchev had controlled for so long. Hence he alone had served seriously after Stalin's death to block a clear recognition of Khrushchev's pre-eminence in the Ukraine. His failure and removal, together with Mel'nikov's dismissal, enabled Khrushchev to re-establish his firm personal authority. As a result, the transition period between the old leadership and the new—a period which was to continue many months in the Soviet Union as a whole—was in the Ukraine very brief.

THE NEW PARTNERSHIP

The new situation in the Ukraine was indicated immediately after Beria's dismissal. Mel'nikov was not restored as Party secretary, but the dismissed Minister of Internal Affairs, Strokach—long identified with Khrushchev—was reappointed to his post.[16] Khrushchev, already claiming the allegiance of most Ukrainian Party leaders, was apparently determined to bring the whole Party

organization under his control. In August, 1953, the post of Second
Secretary of the Communist Party of the Ukraine—vacant since
Kyrychenko's promotion to Party headship— was filled by the
Party leader from the Kharkov oblast, N. V. Podgornyi.[17] In the
late fall of 1953, following Khrushchev's elevation to the post
of First Secretary of the Communist Party of the Soviet Union,[18]
a number of changes at lower levels of the Ukrainian Party were
made. Khrushchev's long-standing friend, A. I. Struev, was promoted out of the Ukraine from the Stalino oblast to the job of Party
Secretary in the Molotov oblast; he was replaced by a Ukrainian,
I. P. Kazanets'. Three oblast secretaries, two of whom had been
promoted by Mel'nikov—O. P. Kondratenko, I. H. Horobets', and
M. H. Rohynets'—were dropped from their posts and replaced by
men apparently identified with Khrushchev—V. H. Komiakhov,
I. D. Kompanets', and V. S. Markov.[19] Corresponding changes
were made in governmental posts.[20] Neither the Party nor the
government changes indicated major shifts in the Ukraine. But
they represented, it seems clear, direct intervention by Khrushchev
aimed at establishing the Communist Party of the Ukraine as a
personally loyal group, completely unified under his immediate
leadership.

At the same time, as Khrushchev's influence in the Soviet Union
mounted, a variety of benefits and privileges were granted the
Ukraine and its Party leaders. In February, 1954, the republic
was enlarged by the addition of the Crimean oblast, detached from
the RSFSR.[21] The shift was made, it was announced, because of
the Crimea's juxtaposition to the Ukraine and because of the natural
communications and economic ties between the two areas.[22] But
emphasis was placed also on the transfer as an example of the remarkable national policy of the Soviet Union—the only country
"where the ideology of the friendship of peoples is victorious,
and where all the foundations for the enslavement of one people
by another have been destroyed."[23]

A more important expression of Khrushchev's influence was
a major campaign, pressed in the last months of 1953 and throughout 1954, emphasizing the brotherly friendship of the Russian and
Ukrainian peoples. The year 1954 was the tercentenary of the

signing of the Treaty of Pereiaslav—the treaty which, according to Soviet history, had joined the Ukraine with Russia—and the entire year was set aside as a period of celebration. The basic theme of the campaign was not new, since the Bolsheviks had steadily urged the abolition of hostilities between national groups. As the campaign advanced, however, two aspects distinguished it from earlier campaigns.

First, relatively little emphasis was placed on the element which had dominated previous drives for Soviet friendship—the subordination of the minority nationalities to the Great-Russian. In its place considerable attention was paid to the past achievements of the Ukraine, its traditions, and its contributions to the Soviet Union. For example, Bohdan Khmel'nits'kyi, the Ukrainian leader who had negotiated the Treaty of Pereiaslav and who had earlier been denounced by the Bolsheviks as a "traitor and violent enemy of the rebelling Ukrainian peasantry,"[24] was now glorified as a great statesman who had recognized the necessity of tying the Ukraine inseparably with Russia:[25] a Ukrainian city and oblast and a street in Moscow were named in his honor.[26] Ukrainian writers and cultural workers such as Shevchenko, Franko, Kotsiubins'kyi, and others were praised for their great role in "the development of the self-consciousness of the Ukrainian working masses."[27] Their achievements were identified with socialism in the Ukraine and with the brotherly aid of the Russian people, but a modest balance was preserved which, in campaigns in the later years of Stalinist rule, had been missing.

Second, the campaign introduced for the first time in the Soviet period the element of partnership as a major aspect of Russian-Ukrainian relations. The partnership was not presented as a completely equal one, for the Russian people were described again, as they had been earlier, as the principal "bearer of the great revolutionary ideas of freedom and progress."[28] However, the Ukrainians were now given the role of associates with the Russians in the building of a Soviet world and to a considerable degree were set apart from the other ethnic minorities in the Soviet Union and identified as co-leaders in the USSR. In a stronger way than in previous years the two peoples were depicted as forming only slightly distinct branches of the same basic Slavic family and were described as working together in a spirit of cooperation and solidarity in the building of a Soviet society. In a proclamation sent to the government and Party leadership of the Ukraine at the height of the tercentennial celebrations USSR leaders declared:

The Ukrainian people first after the Russian people stepped forth on the glorious path of socialism. Hand in hand, shoulder to shoulder, the workers of Russia and the Ukraine battled for the victory of the Great October socialist revolution, struggled on the fronts of the civil war, built a socialist society, and defended the freedom and independence of our Native Land in the Great Fatherland war.[26]

The two people, it was implied, were the pre-eminent nationalities in the Soviet Union and hence bore responsibility together for the guidance and leadership of the Communist world.

How far Soviet leaders intended the partnership theme to be carried is not clear. It was undoubtedly given greater importance in the press and in public meetings than it realistically merited. The whole foundation of the tercentenary celebrations was the closeness and solidarity of Russians and Ukrainians, and this foundation led naturally to emphasis on the similarities of the two peoples. In addition, the theme was important as an argument in the continuing drive to win Ukrainian support for Soviet rule: for Ukrainians the partnership theme carried the implicit message that, as an equally responsible and privileged people with the Russians, they were expected to associate themselves as closely with Soviet programs as did the Russians and were to provide as dedicated support. The partnership theme was desirable as a motivational slogan as long as it stopped short of the point of alienating other national groups in the Soviet Union.

Nevertheless, the partnership theme represented also a modification of the Stalinist view of the role of the national minorities in the USSR. Stalin, traditionally, despite his ethnic background, had viewed the minorities with distrust, regarding them as separatist in character and disruptive and divisive in the Soviet Union. His distrust had been aggravated by his accompanying suspicion of the Soviet Union's regional centers outside Moscow—a suspicion which had prompted him to view Kiev, for example, as not only a center for anti-Russian Ukrainian nationalism, but also a possible locus for Russian anti-Stalinist opposition. The two elements had created a considerable hostility in his mind to the republics, leading him to identify the Soviet regime and his personal rule almost exclusively with Russians.

As Khrushchev became the predominant influence in the Soviet Union, a more sympathetic view of the minorities was taken. Unlike Stalin, Khrushchev had long been associated closely with the Ukraine. For nearly twelve years he had served as Party boss of the republic and in that time had built up a powerful regional Party organization. After Stalin's death Khrushchev turned to that organization not only for its direct support in his bid for the succession but also as a source of loyal adherents to be assigned to leadership posts in other parts of the Soviet Union: in addition to Struev, whose transfer to work outside the Ukraine has been mentioned, the list included Brezhnev and Kyrychenko, who were promoted to the Presidium of the Central Committee of the Communist Party of the Soviet Union; Markov, Kirilenko, Serdiuk, Stakhurskii, Iakovlev, and Rudakov who were transferred to regional Party work outside the Ukraine; Matskevich, Dudorov, Serov, Korniets', and Rudenko who were given high government posts in Moscow.[30] As a source of considerable political support, the Ukraine was naturally viewed by Khrushchev with a more sympathetic eye than it had been regarded by Stalin before him.

In addition, Khrushchev apparently came to recognize in the Ukraine what Stalin earlier had been unable to see, the existence of a large group of Ukrainian Bolsheviks who were closely identified with the USSR and its Soviet regime. Complete figures on the ethnic composition of the Communist Party of the Ukraine and of the Ukrainian government are not available, but the few statistics which have been released suggest that in the period after World War II there was a considerable increase in the number of ethnic Ukrainians working in Party and government organs. From 1940 to 1956 the percentage of Party members who were Ukrainians increased from 63.1 percent to 74.2 percent,[31] while the percentage of leading Party workers who were Ukrainian jumped from 40.0 percent to 67.8 percent.[32] In the government the numbers of Ukrainians were greater: in 1956 nearly 76 percent of the deputies to the Ukrainian Supreme Soviet were Ukrainian, while in all soviets, the figure was over 84 percent.[33] Since Ukrainians in this period comprised approximately 76 percent of the total population,[34] their under-representation in the government and Party, so marked in previous years, was largely eliminated. The change was not accidental but indicated that larger numbers of Ukrainians were being drawn into Party and government work and were being accepted, as they had not been before, as reliable and loyal workers. In contrast to the situation in the 1930s, when Stalin had viewed Ukrainian leaders such as Petrovs'kyi, Chubar', Skrypnik, and Liubchenko as potential or actual disloyal nationalists, Khrushchev regarded the Communist Party of the Ukraine and its Ukrainian leaders as, basically, as reliable a group as Party organizations in the principal Russian centers.

Khrushchev's confidence in Ukrainian Party leaders was apparently justified on two counts. First, although the leaders were frequently Ukrainian in name and background, in most cases they had spent much time in the cities of the eastern Ukraine where they had been exposed to strong Russian influences. Together with other Russified Ukrainians, they had been taught the Russian language, sent to Russian schools, and infused with attitudes which were more strongly Russian than Ukrainian. As a result, they were as far removed from the Ukrainians of the countryside as Communists sent from Russia, or as the earliest Ukrainian Bolsheviks such as Zatons'kyi, who had shown themselves more centralist and anti-nationalist than many Russian leaders.

Secondly, it seems likely that Ukrainian leaders understood and accepted the requirement that, as republic leaders, they were not to challenge the unity and inviolability of the Soviet Union. Ukrainians were acceptable as leaders only to the extent that they identified themselves with the interests of the Union as a whole and devoted themselves to the task of ensuring the reliability and loyalty of the Ukraine. If successful, Khrushchev's policy suggested, they might be eligible for the highest leadership posts in the Soviet Union without the hostile discrimination of the Stalin era. With this understanding, they came to view nationalists and anti-Soviet separatists as major problems in the Ukraine, not only because they threatened the Soviet regime with which the leaders were identified, but also because they challenged the understanding on which ethnic Ukrainians were permitted to hold high posts. Consequently, Ukrainian Communists opposed the nationalists more strongly and with greater venom than did central leaders. In January, 1954, the Party's Second Secretary, N. Podgornyi, warned against efforts by foreign imperialists— "relying on Ukrainian nationalists"—to break down and destroy the close union of the Ukrainian and Russian peoples.[35] In March, First Secretary Kyrychenko declared before the Seventeenth Party Congress that the Party organizations of the western Ukraine must increase their vigilance in the battle against the remnants of Ukrainian nationalists, "who must not be allowed to infiltrate our kolkhozes, enterprises, or schools, there to carry on their hostile work."[36] In May, he attacked the nationalists more savagely, striking especially at *emigrés* who had fled the Ukraine and sought shelter in "American rubbish heaps" where, "tied by chains of dollars to their masters, . . . they whine about a 'free Ukraine.'"[37] These statements were intended perhaps to emphasize to Ukrainians that Soviet opposition to separatist, anti-Soviet nationalism was as implacable under the new regime as under the old and to demonstrate to central officials that Ukrainian leaders could govern the Ukraine in as loyal a spirit as Russians.

The basic objective of the policy of accepting ethnic Ukrainians as republic leaders was that of divorcing the element of Ukrainian nationality from the anti-Soviet separatist aspects with which it had been identified by Stalin. Ukrainians were or could be loyal Bolsheviks, Khrushchev was convinced, as well as faithful adherents of the Soviet Union's Russian regime. This theme was emphasized in the program of the tercentenary celebrations. In discussing the history of Ukrainian-Russian relations, for example, the program adopted those positions which emphasized the closeness and solidarity of the two peoples and rejected positions suggesting their differences and separateness: the original Kiev state was Russian, not distinctly Ukrainian; the Treaty of Pereiaslav established a complete state union of Russia and the Ukraine rather than a loose alliance; anti-Russian rebellions of Ukrainian groups were Polish-inspired attacks directed basically against the Ukrainian people.[38] The conclusion was clear that the true core of the Ukrainian people had always been united with the Russians and was now cooperating in the building of a Communist society. On the basis of such a core, Khrushchev believed, it was possible to promote ethnic Ukrainians to leadership posts, thereby justifying Soviet national policy in a way Stalin had been unable to do and shifting the battle against nationalist separatists from Russians to Ukrainians.

THE NEW PROGRAM

The emphasis on the partnership of the Ukrainian and Russian peoples was accompanied by other modifications of Stalinist policy toward the nationalities. Like the drive for Soviet "legality" and the call for greater production of consumer goods, the more liberal policy was part of the de-Stalinization campaign and was meant to show the moderation of the new regime and the differences which separated it from the old. But in addition the changes indicated a lessening in the pro-Russian, centralist conceptions of Stalin and a return to a more sympathetic attitude toward the nationalities and the federalist principle.

The first aspect of the program was its deliberate emphasis on Leninist national theory as opposed to "Stalinism." The long period in which Stalin had served as spokesman on the national question—antedating the Revolution—was passed over, and Party leaders and theorists alike began to refer primarily to Leninist writings. The titles of newspaper and journal articles published in the period indicated the shift: "The Great Strength of the Ideas of Lenin on the Friendship of Peoples"; "Leninism, the Highest Achievement of Russian and World Culture"; "The Great Role of V. I. Lenin in the Organization of the Union of Soviet Republics"; "Leninist National Policy and Its Realization in the Ukraine"; "Leninist Principles on the National Policy and Its Realization in the Ukraine"; "Leninist Principles on the National Policy of

the Communist Party of the Soviet Union." In 1956 Lenin's role
as the originator of Soviet national policy was emphasized in two
publications. The first was a re-examination of his views on the
national problem entitled *V. I. Lenin on the National and National-
Colonial Question*.[39] The second was the publication for the first
time inside the Soviet Union of Lenin's letter of December, 1922,
attacking Bolsheviks for Great-Russian chauvinism and demanding a flexible approach toward nationality problems.[40] It was
necessary, *Pravda* declared, that the whole history of the formation
of the USSR be re-examined, since in the past the role played by
Lenin had been neglected and Stalin's influence exaggerated and
distorted.[41] It was necessary to describe frankly Stalin's efforts
to establish a Russian Federated Republic rather than a Union of
Soviet Socialist Republics and to explain Lenin's role in opposing
these efforts. The implication of these statements was clear: it was
necessary for the Party to correct the errors introduced by Stalin in the national question as in others and to return to the true
principles expressed by Lenin.[42]

Two Leninist principles were specially emphasized. The first was
the principle of the international character of the revolutionary
socialist movement. Proletarianism, it was suggested, was not
the property of the Russian people alone, either in its origins or
in its consequences, but was a product of the cultural achievements
of all mankind regardless of nationality.

Leninism proceeds from the fact that every people is capable of the
independent development of culture, that any nation, great or small,
makes its own special contribution to the development of world
culture.[43]

Within each nationality was to be found a progressive and revolutionary culture which, when separated from the exploiting nationalist culture with which it was joined, was capable of contributing to the world socialist movement. In the past Bolsheviks
had drawn heavily from the works of men of various nationalities,
including Darwin, Voltaire, Newton, and Pushkin. So it was necessary in the current period for the Soviet Union to pay close
heed to the cultural and scientific work of other non-Russian nationalities and to absorb their "progressive" elements.[44]

The second element was Lenin's insistence on the need of accommodating national feelings and emphasizing national equality
and freedom in order to remove the grounds for national mistrust.[45]
As opposed to Stalin, it was observed, Lenin had consistently urged
the principle of voluntarism in matters relating to the nationalities.
A union of peoples, he had insisted, whether a European federation
or a joining of backward areas with industrial nations, was not
to be forced, but was to be based on voluntary agreement, and
such agreement could be obtained only on the basis of friendly
feelings. Hence, it was necessary for Russian Bolsheviks to adopt
the most accommodating attitude toward minority groups. Specifically, it was noted, Lenin had ordered Bolsheviks in the Ukraine
to observe "very strictly the equality of the Ukrainian language
and culture, to consider it mandatory for all officials to study the
Ukrainian language, etc., etc."[46] The Leninist stand was far different from that adopted by Stalin. Shortly after the Revolution,
it was recalled, Lenin had accused Stalin of conducting a "truly
nationalistic Great-Russian campaign,"[47] and in recent years,
Khrushchev observed, Stalin had prompted through his arbitrary
deportations of whole national groups "rude violations of the
basic Leninist principles of the national policy of the Soviet state."[48]

The significance of the many references to Leninism lay not
only in the suggestion that the new regime intended to break
with Stalinist policies and return to the "original" foundations
of Bolshevism, but also in the suggestion that it was the liberal
aspects of Leninism which were to be emphasized. There were
some exceptions to the rule: there were references to unifying and
centralist statements by Lenin; his opposition to local nationalism
and to divisive influences was noted as well as his undeviating
insistence on the solidarity of the proletariat and the eventual
amalgamation of all peoples into a single world society.[49] But the
principles repeated most often were those directing the Party
along flexible, moderate lines. At the Twentieth Party Congress
(February, 1956) it was the rights of the nationalities rather than
the requirements of the Union that were underlined:

In its national policy the Party has proceeded and is proceeding
along the Leninist position that socialism not only does not destroy

national differences and peculiarities but, on the contrary, guarantees
the widest development and flowering of the economy and culture
of all nations and peoples. The Party must henceforth, in the most
attentive way, take into account these peculiarities in all its practical
work.[50]

The implication for Party workers and leaders in the republics
was that, without discarding Bolshevik insistence on the subordination of the national question to proletarian demands, greater
attention was to be given to the rights and authorities of the localities and to the separate development of the nationalities.

Nationality Rights

The problem of Russification   Specifically, the new approach
was expressed in two programs. The first was in the area of nationality rights. As noted earlier, under Beria's direction there had
been issued in June, 1953, a call for greater emphasis in the Ukraine
on the use of the local language and on the appointment of local
workers to leadership posts. Although the call was minimized
after the ousting of Beria, it was not dropped. Evidence of continued interest was shown by the reporting in 1953 and 1954 of
figures on the ethnic composition of schools, accompanied by
statements praising Leninist national policy because it "fully
guaranteed . . . the possibility of teaching the children of workers
in their own language."[51] The Ukrainian Minister of Culture, K.
Z. Lytvyn, noted with favor the steady growth in the number of
specialists, teachers, and technicians trained from the local population in the western Ukraine and assigned to work there.[52]
The statements were modest but noteworthy because they represented the first efforts since the Ukrainization period to emphasize greater Ukrainian participation in the educational and
leadership life of the republic.

Of greater significance was an article published at the end of
1956 in *Pravda Ukrainy*.[53] The article continued the trend of
previous years by praising the steady growth in the national rights
of the Ukrainian people and the improvement in the numbers of
Ukrainians serving as Party and government leaders.[54] But the
article's chief revelations came in its description of the status of
the Ukrainian language in the republic's schools. Two sets of

figures were given. The first compared the number of *schools* employing each of the languages used in the republic. The figures were as follows:[55]

	Number	Percent
Ukrainian schools	24,977	83.1
Russian schools	4,008	13.3
Other schools	251	.8
Mixed schools	125	.4
Total	30,063	100.0

The second set of figures compared the number of *students* enrolled in each category of language schools:

	Number	Percent
Students enrolled in Ukrainian schools	3,814,869	69.1
Students enrolled in Russian schools	1,369,145	24.8
Students enrolled in other schools	44,517	.8
Students enrolled in mixed schools	55,092	1.0
Total	5,524,754	100.0

The two sets of figures were significant not only for the picture they painted of the language situation in the Ukraine's schools but more broadly for the conclusions they suggested on the problem of Ukrainization versus Russification.

First, the figures showed a remarkable decrease in the number of schools teaching in other than Ukrainian and Russian, suggesting that the old policy of the Ukrainization period of encouraging even small minorities to retain their linguistic identity had been abandoned. A similar conclusion had been suggested earlier by Party membership figures which had indicated a sharp drop in Party representation from the Ukraine's small minority groups.[56] The figures on school enrollment confirmed that the minorities were being deliberately removed from the Ukraine or assimilated into Ukrainian or Russian language groups. Apparently the practice of the 1920s of transferring Jews to Yiddish schools, for example, or of establishing separate Bulgarian, Belorussian, or Polish schools was no longer being followed. It seems likely also that the practice of establishing separate raions and soviets for local minorities had been abandoned as well as the use of other than Russian and Ukrainian in the courts and government offices. The suggestion was strong that in the future the Ukraine was to become a bi-lingual republic.

Second, the figures indicated that, despite the Ukrainization work of the twenties and the opposite Russifying pressures of the late 1930s and 1940s, the old division of the Ukraine into an urban area which was distinctly Russian and a rural area which was distinctly Ukrainian remained basically unchanged. That this striking dichotomy had not been affected by Soviet rule was indicated by the difference reported in the number of pupils enrolled in Ukrainian as opposed to Russian language schools. In the former the average enrollment was 152.7; in the latter it was 341.6. Russian schools were more than twice as large as Ukrainian. The difference can best be explained as a result of the difference in the type of school represented by each language group: Russian schools apparently remained predominantly city and town schools and hence had large enrollments; Ukrainian schools apparently remained equally concentrated in the villages and rural areas and hence enrolled few students. The figures were a strong indication that the Ukraine's countryside remained linguistically Ukrainian while the urban areas remained linguistically Russian.

That the linguistic structure of the Ukraine had not changed can be explained as follows. In the period after the Revolution a great effort had been made, in keeping with Leninist policy, to transform schools in predominantly Ukrainian areas to the Ukrainian language. The campaign had been pressed most strongly in the period from 1923 to 1925 and, since Ukrainians were predominantly a rural population, it is not surprising that the campaign was most successful in the rural areas and hence in the lower-level schools, which were virtually the only educational institutions outside the cities. Thus, by 1925, 71 percent of the primary and incomplete secondary schools had been shifted to Ukrainian.[57] In the higher schools and in the lower urban schools the problem had been more complex: enrollment was almost exclusively Russian; available textbooks were Russian; there were difficulties in the practical task of conversion and strong opposition pressures from teachers and Russian leaders. As a result, conversion had proceeded slowly, and the controversy it engendered had played a major role in the Ukrainization disputes of the years after 1925. Apparently there were some gradual successes, but the successes had led in turn to greater opposition, and by the early thirties the program had been dropped as a working program. Subsequently, most of the gains had been lost as the schools were re-established as Russian institutions. It was the extension of this Russifying program to the higher schools of the western Ukraine—where there were few Russians and, hence, little justification for the program—which had served as the excuse for Beria's intervention in the Ukraine following Stalin's death.

In contrast to the cities, a comparison of the 1925 and 1956 figures on school enrollment indicates that in the rural areas Russification pressures had not led to any significant decrease in the use of Ukrainian in the schools. On the contrary there is the clear suggestion that a moderately consistent policy was followed of establishing only Ukrainian language schools. In the thirty-one-year period between 1925 and 1956 the percentage of Ukrainian schools—urban and rural combined—increased from 71 percent of the lower schools to 83 percent of all schools. Since the post-revolutionary program of converting schools to Ukrainian had been carried basically as far as it was to go by 1925, the increase in Ukrainian schools can be explained only on the assumption that the large majority of schools created after 1925 were Ukrainian. The assumption seems reasonable since the Bolshevik program of expanding educational facilities gave emphasis, in the early years, to the rural areas where few schools existed. That the program had achieved impressive results is indicated by a comparison of the 1926 census figures with the 1956 school enrollment figure: in 1926, 86 percent of the rural population spoke Ukrainian; in 1956 almost the same percentage of the rural schools were teaching in Ukrainian. The figures suggest that Stalin and his successors alike agreed that, whatever the language program for the cities, the Ukrainian character of the countryside was to be maintained.

Third, the figures on the percentage of students enrolled in Ukrainian language schools, when compared with the number of Ukrainians in the population as a whole, provide a measure of the extent to which Ukrainians had been Russified under Soviet rule prior to 1956. In 1956 the population of the Ukraine was apparently approximately 76 percent Ukrainian. Since only 69 percent of the students were enrolled in Ukrainian language schools apparently nearly 10 percent of Ukrainian families were sending their children to Russian language schools. The figure can be assumed to represent the number of Russified Ukrainians.[58] Inasmuch as few Russian schools were to be found in the countryside, apart from exclusively Russian districts, such families were undoubtedly concentrated in urban areas.

From the foregoing it seems reasonable to conclude that although Soviet language policy may have been successful at one time in prompting Russians and Jews to learn Ukrainian and at another time in prompting Ukrainians to learn Russian, it had not altered basically the natural pattern of language use either in the cities or in the rural areas. In the early period, during the twenties, language policy had been identified with Ukrainization, and non-Ukrainians had been forced or induced to study the local language, and government and Party agencies, the press, and the schools had been shifted in a modest way to Ukrainian. The program had achieved no real success, however, in converting the republic's urban population to Ukrainian as its primary tongue. It was this failure which had aroused first Shums'kyi's and then Skrypnik's ire, prompting them to demand a more severe language program which would set as its goal the ultimate transformation of the Ukraine into an exclusively Ukrainian republic. The decision of central leaders to avoid pressing in an active way for such a transformation had meant that the cities were to remain predominantly Russian centers.

In the later period—in the 1930s and 1940s—the situation had been reversed as Soviet leaders had begun to stress Russian as the common tongue for the Soviet Union as a whole. The teaching of Russian had been made compulsory in the schools, and the old emphasis on expanding the use of Ukrainian in Party and government work had been dropped. The program had resulted in a considerable increase in the number of Ukrainians moderately fluent in Russian. But, as with the Ukrainization program of the twenties, little success had been achieved in converting the Ukraine's rural population to Russian as its primary tongue. It seems doubtful that central leaders had meant to require such a conversion, although the Russification measures adopted by Stalin for the western Ukraine following World War II suggested that such a program was in the offing. In any case, following Stalin's death, his successors had repudiated these measures, indicating their intention to preserve Ukrainian language use in those areas where Ukrainian was the generally accepted tongue.

Under these conditions it is not surprising that there was a steady increase in the number of Russian-speaking Ukrainians. Inasmuch as Russian was the common tongue for the USSR and the accepted language for Union organizations and agencies, there was a considerable premium on its use particularly by those seeking high posts in the Party, the government, industry, or even the professions and the arts. Moreover, once the decision had been made in the late twenties or early thirties that the Ukraine's cities would not be forcibly transformed from Russian to Ukrainian centers, the premium placed on Russian language use had grown larger. As the industrialization and urbanization programs had proceeded under the Soviet five-year plans, Ukrainian peasants had been drawn to the cities where they had been received, not by the Ukrainian culture Skrypnik had hoped to establish, but by the Russian culture which had historically predominated. Regardless of official state policies, these Ukrainians had been confronted with informal economic and social pressures—pressures similar to those experienced by minority groups in any society—which had led them, if not in the first generation then in the second, to accept Russian as their primary tongue. In the countryside, where such pressures did not exist, there had been no corresponding shift. The critical official decision had been the rejection of Skrypnik's plea for Ukrainization of the cities. Once made, Russification had proceeded naturally as a product of sociological pressures and as a consequence of the advantage enjoyed by Russian as the USSR's common tongue. The extent of Russification was more a measure of the Ukraine's urbanization

trend and of the growing mobility of the USSR's population than
of influence exerted by official Russifying policies.

The problem of national culture   The death of Stalin led also
to a greater measure of flexibility in the area of national culture
—an area which, as one aspect of the general problem of cultural
freedom in the Soviet Union, became the subject of much discussion after 1953. The problem was first seriously raised by cultural workers in articles appearing at the end of 1953 and early
in 1954.[59] The articles were concerned with various cultural fields,
but their arguments were basically the same. In the past, it was
declared, the stern requirements of Soviet cultural policy had
tended to stifle creativeness in artistic work. Insistence on sharp
Party supervision of cultural activity together with exaggerated
emphasis on the use of proper themes had shackled composers
and writers to the point that originality had been lost. Thus, although many works had been produced which were "externally
proper," their content was shallow and their "artistic significance
almost zero." Many were monotonous and stereotyped, either because they excluded human factors from their portrayal of Soviet
society, or because they emphasized only the good, glossing over
real evils and difficulties and adopting "bourgeois artificiality."
The solution to these problems, the critics asserted, was to be
found in a greater acceptance by the Party of the independence
of the cultural worker and of the importance of encouraging novel,
original work. As Shostakovich declared: "It seems to me that
the Union should not 'guard' our composers from a search for
the new, from following independent untrod paths of art. We
should fear not daring, creative originality, but 'safe' superficial-
ity, dullness, and stereotyped work."[60] *Pravda* expressed similar
views: "May the new, the bold, and the expressive in our art be
born constantly in artistic experiments. Art cannot stand still:
it demands inspiration and a cool mind but a burning heart."[61]

The criticisms were widely published but were not endorsed by
Party leaders. Despite careful efforts by the critics to avoid direct attacks on "socialist realism," there was the unmistakable suggestion that the concept, as narrowly defined by over-zealous Party bureaucrats, was responsible for the impoverished state of So-

viet culture. Such a suggestion was perhaps unavoidable, since "socialist realism" demanded a subjective interpretation of society,
with cultural workers presenting carefully prescribed pictures of
Soviet life; there was little room for artists who insisted on originality, sincerity, and inventiveness. Party officials were aware of
the contradiction and recognized they could not accept the criticisms without abandoning substantially their insistence on Party
guidance of literature and art in the interests of Soviet society.
Hence, in the following months the criticisms were denounced,
and an effort was made to restate Soviet principles in such a way
as to emphasize the importance of "socialist realism" yet admit
a greater measure of flexibility and individuality.

The chief statements appeared in a series of articles in *Pravda*
and the Party journal *Kommunist* in May and June, 1954.[62] The
articles made plain that no opposition to the basic concept of
"socialist realism" would be accepted. The Party's 1946 and 1948
decisions on cultural matters were declared to be as valid in 1954
as in earlier years and were praised for striking a sharp blow against
"apolitical, passive, formalistic tendencies in the works of a number of writers and cultural workers." Literature and art were
declared again to have no interests "except those of the people,
the interests of the socialist motherland"; it was their purpose to
serve as a "principal means for the Communist development of
the workers," and to achieve this purpose they were "to present
a truthful, historically accurate portrayal of life in its revolutionary development." The articles emphasized again the obligation of
writers and artists to affirm through their works the method of
"socialist realism."

Yet the "socialist realism" of 1954 was not the same as the
"socialist realism" of 1948. Even in those articles restating the principle most firmly it was conceded that "socialist realism" was not to
exclude the sincerity and originality cultural workers demanded.

The experience of Soviet writers has clearly demonstrated that socialist realism does not level literary individuality but, on the contrary, fosters its utmost development and affords unlimited opportunity for individuality in constructing the artistic picture by the
most abundant and varied means of portrayal in all types and gen-
res.[63]

Apparently Soviet leaders expected that writers and artists would so immerse themselves in revolutionary theory, Marxist-Leninist esthetics, and active public service that their most sincere and original works would reflect the socialist world and its achievements. In August, 1957, Khrushchev declared:

> If struggle for the ideals of Communism and for his people's happiness is the artist's goal in life and if he lives by the people's interest, thoughts, and aspirations, then no matter what theme he chooses or what phenomena of life he depicts his works will accord with the interests of the people, Party, and state.[64]

There was no question that cultural work could be justified only as it served "the interests of the people, Party, and state"; there was no question that the Party was to hold fast to its authority to direct cultural work, guiding it along acceptable paths. But there was to be less dogmatism, greater effort to avoid stereotypes, and broader critical discussion of cultural works from the viewpoint of artistic merit as well as socialist acceptability. Khrushchev summarized the new cultural program as a moderate path avoiding the pitfalls of liberalism, on the one hand, and of dogmatism, on the other.

> The main line of development is that literature and the arts must always be inseparably linked with the people's life, must truthfully portray the wealth and variety of our socialist reality, and vividly and convincingly show the Soviet people's great work of transformation, the nobility of their aims and aspirations, and their lofty moral qualities. The highest social purpose of literature and the arts is to arouse the people to a struggle for new victories in the building of Communism . . . .
>
> It is impossible to deny, of course, that mistakes were made in the last years of J. V. Stalin's life, under the conditions of the cult of the individual. . . .
>
> It goes without saying that we are against this kind of an approach to the appraisal of works of literature.
>
> The Party has resolutely condemned the errors that were committed in all spheres of life, including ideological work, during the cult of the individual, and it is consistently rectifying them. However, at the same time the Party vigorously opposes those who try to make use of these past errors to resist the guidance of literature and the arts by the Party and the state.[65]

On the specific problem of national cultures the same modest changes in Stalinist policies were indicated. The changes were suggested in many relatively minor ways. Khrushchev denounced Stalin, for example, for considering the Ukrainian writer Maxim Ryl's'kyi a bourgeois nationalist merely because Ryl's'kyi had glorified the Soviet Ukraine "with deep patriotic feeling" and without praising Stalin.[66] The Soviet journal *Voprosy istorii* called for a more objective evaluation of the North Caucasian nationalist, Shamil', who had been accused in the past of being an imperialist agent rather than a progressive nationalist, fighting against Tsarist oppression.[67] There were occasional references to the problem of Great-Russian chauvinism and to the dangers of forcing the Russian language and culture on the minority nationalities.[68] There was praise of the growing number of literary works from all countries being translated into Ukrainian and of the publication in many languages of works by Ukrainian authors.[69]

But more important than these fragmentary suggestions were statements pointing to a major modification of Stalin's venerable slogan that separate cultures should develop "national in form, socialist in content." In the past the slogan had implied a uniformity in the *content* of national cultures inasmuch as socialism was presumably single and universal. With the growing dogmatism of the Stalin regime, the diversity promised in the phrase "national in form" had also become negligible as the phrase had come to be applied almost exclusively to the area of language. By the time of Stalin's death it was the prevailing conception that national cultural expressions should be identical with one another albeit translated into separate tongues.

The first challenge to this conception was a plea that the whole problem of national forms be re-examined and a concrete statement elaborated, defining the specific elements included in the phrase and the manner in which they were to be applied. In the past, it was suggested, there had been a strong tendency to speak only in a general way about differences in national forms; there had been little effort to describe the differences specifically, and in practice emphasis had been given only to the single aspect of national languages.[70] Yet there were other national differences

which needed to be reflected in the cultural work of the minorities
if their development was to be stimulated: differences in geographic
environnemt and historical background; unique forms of economic
growth; peculiarities of psychological make-up, folk customs, etc.[71]
Efforts to suppress such differences, one writer implied, were akin
to the de-nationalizing theories of "nihilism" and "cosmopolitanism."[72]

The second challenge to the Stalinist conception was broader
and more inclusive though less precise. It was rooted in the relatively flexible attitude the new leaders took to the phrase "socialist in content." The phrase had never required necessarily a
centralist or rigidly unifying interpretation and, when initially proclaimed by Stalin, had been presented as a reassurance to the
nationalities. In succeeding years, however, it had been applied
in an increasingly stern manner until it had come to mean that
there was but one single form of true socialism, one single true
path toward the Communist goal, and that cultural activities among
the nationalities would be acceptable only as they promoted the
single socialist dogma.

The new leaders took a more lenient stand. At the Twentieth
Party Congress (February, 1956) Khrushchev quoted Lenin as follows:

All nations will arrive at socialism—this is inevitable—but not all
will do so in exactly the same way. Each will contribute something
of its own in one or another form of democracy, one or another
variety of the dictatorship of the proletariat, one or another rate
at which socialist transformations will be effected in the various
aspects of social life. There is nothing more primitive from the
viewpoint of theory or more ridiculous from that of practice than
to paint *this* aspect of the future in a monotonous gray "in the name
of historical materialism." The result would be nothing more than
Suzdal daubing.[73]

In July, 1957, Khrushchev restated these views:

Each country of the socialist camp has its own peculiarities,
its distinctive customs, based on its historic, economic, and cultural differences, its national traditions.

In each country, in each Communist and worker's party there
is a unique approach to this or that particular question, to the solution of this or that problem. Each party carries on its own work,

proceeding out of the concrete conditions in its country and the level of economic and cultural development.[74]

Khrushchev had in mind chiefly the satellite countries outside the USSR, but other spokesmen applied the lesson as well to the minorities within the USSR. Referring also to Lenin, they stressed his insistence that each national culture had its progressive elements which, when combined with the progressive elements of other cultures, would form a new international socialist society. The suggestion was strong that there was no single perfect socialist culture to be handed down dogmatically to all nationalities, but rather a progressive development of everything that was "advanced and democratic" within the separate cultures.[75] A Ukrainian writer affirmed that "the development of all the national cultures of the peoples of the USSR is a necessary condition for their merging, in the process of which they mutually enrich one another."[76]

At the same time, there was a restatement also of Soviet policy toward national sentiments. In the past, particularly in the years after World War II, Stalin had demanded that patriotism be identified solely with the USSR and that local patriotisms—the national feelings of a Ukrainian for the Ukrainian republic or of an Armenian for Armenia—be not only subordinated to Union loyalty but essentially eliminated. Khrushchev took a somewhat different stand before the Twentieth Party Congress (February, 1956).[77] He noted that in the period after World War I, Lenin had defended Russian patriotism, declaring that a feeling of national pride toward one's motherland and national language was not at all incompatible with proletarian internationalism.[78] The same view, Krushchev indicated, should be adopted toward non-Russian national groups both inside and outside the Soviet Union.

Absolute clarity on this question is important not only for carrying out national policy correctly, in Leninist fashion, inside the country, but also in order to build the right mutual relations with the working people of other countries, including those of the socialist camp. Unfortunately, there are some comrades who believe that love of one's motherland contradicts international solidarity of the working people and socialist internationalism. Such an interpretation insults the national sentiments of people and certainly does not contribute toward strengthening cooperation among the working people of all countries....

The organic combination of socialist patriotism and international-ism is the ideological basis for strengthening fraternal ties among the socialist nations. Our Party has always been and will always be guided by this in its national policy.

The many suggestions that the new leadership intended to pur-sue a more flexible national policy were striking and should not be underestimated. Yet they did not represent a reversal of the basic principles traditionally upheld. Throughout the period from 1953 to 1957 appeals for flexibility and moderation were accompa-nied by renewed declarations that socialist demands were superior to national ones. Apparently central leaders, having opened the door to modifications of Stalinist strictures, felt impelled to strike out against the many suggestions for more basic changes prompted by the freer atmosphere. Many examples can be given. In 1954 an official review of the first volume of a new *History of the Ukrainian SSR* praised the work for exactly those elements of historical in-terpretation required earlier by Stalin.[79] At the Third Congress of the Union of Soviet Writers of the Ukraine (October, 1954) the addresses insisted that "literature must serve as one of the levers of socialism" and that it would fulfill its task only as it battled against "each manifestation of bourgeois ideology and above all the ideology of Ukrainian bourgeois nationalism."[80] In the matter of language and culture there were declarations that, despite the new flexibility, the Russian tongue and literature were still to be recognized as the most advanced, respected, and influential.[81] Lenin was quoted to the effect that the assimiliation of Ukrain-ians into Russian culture as a result of the pre-revolutionary Russification of Ukrainian cities was "unconditionally progressive," since it broke down the national exclusiveness of Russians and Ukrainians.[82] Above all, there were the firm requirements that state unity be preserved, state interests placed above all others, and Party leadership accepted without question.[83] Apparently the new program was to be distinguished from the old by its moder-ation and flexibility, its emphasis on voluntarism and cooperation, its sympathetic attention to the nationalities and their distinctive interests. But it did not represent a reversal of the old nor a les-sening of resolve to carry forward the unifying programs the Bolsheviks had always sponsored. Khrushchev summarized the program as follows:

While strengthening the training of the masses in proletarian internationalism, we have done and will continue to do everything in order that the economy of the Union republics may grow and develop and that their culture, national in form and socialist in content, may flourish even more. At the same time, we must firmly repulse all manifestations of bourgeois ideology, including nationalism; we must safeguard the purity of our Communist ideology, tirelessly pursue still greater unity of the peoples of the USSR, and further strengthen their great friendship.[84]

The New Federalism

The second of the broad programs inaugurated after Stalin's death was a program of decentralization aimed at expanding the authority and activity of the republics and localities. The program was directed against the excessive centralization Khrushchev and other leaders agreed had developed in previous years. The centralization was blamed variously on Stalin, on the stern requirements of the period of World War II, and on the cult of the individual.[85] It had spread, it was charged, to the government, to administrative bodies, to the Party, to economic and cultural organizations.

The first hint of decentralization came in an article appearing in December, 1953, in the Party journal *Kommunist*.[86] The article was a discussion of the principle of democratic centralism as it applied to Party life. In traditional fashion the article emphasized the importance of centralist leadership as the sole method by which the unity of action and discipline required in a Soviet state could be achieved. Party decisions, even at the lowest level, it was noted, were essentially political decisions which, inasmuch as they involved the interests of the masses, could not be made independently but required central direction. Nevertheless, the article continued, central direction was not to be confused with bureaucracy and standardization. As Lenin had noted, the purpose of democratic centralism was to create "the possibility of full and unfettered development not only for specifically local features, but also of local initiative, of a diversity of ways, methods, and means of moving toward the common goal." Conditions in the Ukraine were not the same as in Kazakhstan or other republics; if a mechanistic, stultifying approach were to be avoided, it was necessary that local leaders be given the authority and encouraged to exercise the initiative required to allow for republic peculiarities.

In 1954 the Central Comittee of the Communist Party of the Soviet Union discussed the problem at its February Plenum. Khrushchev, in his report to the Committee, emphasized the difficulties created by excessive centralization in planning work.[87] Not only did centralization prevent local workers from making use of their special knowledge about local conditions, it discouraged them from developing creative initiative and weakened their interest in improving production. As a first step toward a solution of the problem, Khrushchev called for the downgrading of a number of Union ministries to Union-republic ministries. Initially, his proposal was applied only to industrial ministries such as Ferrous Metallurgy, Coal Industry, Oil Industry, etc., but, subsequently, it was expanded to include the Ministry of Higher Education and a number of Union-republic ministries which were transformed into exclusively republic bodies.[88] The result of these changes was to enlarge the authority of the republics to administer programs under central direction and to establish and carry out programs of their own.

In March, 1955, the Party Central Committee ordered a major change also in the procedure for planning agricultural work.[89] In the past, the Central Committee noted, the USSR State Planning Committee, the Ministry of Agriculture, and the Ministry of Procurements had operated in an excessively centralizing manner, establishing detailed indexes setting forth the specific items and amounts to be produced in each collective farm. This procedure had led to many mistakes, such as in the southern Ukraine, for example, where central planners had insisted on the sowing of spring wheat although local officials, more familiar with the situation, had urged the planting of winter wheat. To eliminate such errors, a decentralized planning procedure was to be followed in the future. Central planners were to submit only general requirements to the republics where the requirements were to be broken down and transmitted to the oblasts, then to the raions, and finally to the collective farms where specific detailed projects were to be prepared. These plans were then to be directed upward along the same line of the pyramid until ultimately they were to be presented for approval by central planners. The change in procedure was significant not only because it permitted local farmers to prepare their own production schedules—albeit under direction from above—but because it enabled republic, oblast, and raion leaders to play a more influential role in the whole agricultural planning process.

At the Twentieth Party Congress (February, 1956) Khrushchev justified these changes and urged that they be carried further:

Before, when there were few specialists locally, when cadres in a number of republics were weak, and when there were not so many industrial enterprises either, the management of nearly all enterprises was exercised through Union ministries. Now the situation has changed: along with industry, the peoples of all the Union republics have developed; national cadres have been forged, and the general cultural level of all the peoples of the USSR has risen sharply. Under these new conditions, the old methods of managing the economy require substantial revision. While leaving the Union ministries in charge of general direction, of setting plan goals and of checking on their fulfillment, of supplying equipment and financing capital investments, it is necessary at the same time to enlarge considerably the powers of the republic ministries.[90]

More careful attention needed to be given to the economic requirements of the republics, to changes in their economic and cultural life, and to prospects for their development. Moreover, "petty tutelage" of the republics was not to be allowed, and the republics were to be encouraged to decide for themselves specific questions on the development of particular segments of their economy. "This will further strengthen the sovereignty of each republic and the mutual trust among republics; it will help each of them to develop the utmost initiative in the use of local resources."[91]

The call of the Twentieth Congress was clear, and in the succeeding months the decentralizing process moved rapidly ahead. As industrial ministries were transferred to the republics, a growing number of industrial enterprises were placed under republic control. By February, 1957, Ukrainian leaders were able to report that 1,696 such enterprises were being managed directly by republic officials.[92] From 1953 to 1956 the percentage of total industrial output in the Ukraine accounted for by locally directed plants increased from 36 percent to 79 percent. Accompanying these changes in industrial management was a sharp growth in the Ukraine's republic budget: in 1953 the budget totalled eighteen billion rubles; in 1957 it amounted to nearly forty-four billion rubles. "All this," the Ukrainian Premier Kal'chenko noted, "attests to the strengthening and enlarging of the leadership role of the republics in budget and industrial matters."[83]

Yet Khrushchev did not consider the changes adequate, and in March, 1957, he presented a further revolutionary proposal.[84] In order to decentralize the management of industrial enterprises, he recommended the establishment of regional economic councils (*sovnarkhoz*) to be given direct control of plants and factories within each of ninety-two areas. In most republics one council was to be formed; in the Ukraine there were to be eleven; in the Russian republic, sixty-eight. Union planning organs were to retain general authority to set plans and ensure their fulfillment, but individual plants were to be responsible directly to their regional economic councils, and the councils in turn were to report to the republic councils of ministers. The authority of the Union Council of Ministers was to be exercised only indirectly through the republics and through its authority over the various Union planning organs.

On May 31, 1957, the Ukrainian Supreme Soviet instituted the new system in the Ukraine.[95] Eleven councils were formed and given control over the industrial enterprises in their districts, the number varying from seventy-seven in the Zaporozh'e district to five hundred and thirteen in the Stalino district. At the same time, eleven ministries and administrations which had been supervising industrial enterprises were abolished. No mention was made of a republic coordinating body to supervise the work of the eleven councils, but apparently the Ukrainian Gosplan and Council of Ministers were to perform this function.

At the same time, there were suggestions that similar reorganizations might in the future be accomplished in other fields.

In an address in Leningrad on May 22, 1957, Khrushchev declared:

We are now reorganizing the administration of industry.... Furthermore, we must reorganize the trade unions. Many unnecessary persons are also in that administration. Apparently, we should also
re-examine the structure of the Party and Soviet organs in the
raions, oblasts, and republics, as well as re-examine the structure
of the Central Committee of the Communist Party of the Soviet Union
and release a considerable number of persons. But, comrades, we
cannot turn our attention to everything at once. Let us first do
one thing—let us first remodel the administration of industry and
construction.[96]

Moreover, in other areas practical changes strengthening the
republics were made. On February 12, 1957, the USSR Supreme
Soviet agreed to enlarge the constitutional authority of the republics: they were to be allowed to establish their own internal administrative boundaries, to adopt legislation on court structure
and court procedures as well as basic codes on criminal and civil
law, to assume direction of transportation and communications
facilities of republic though not of Union importance.[97] Subsequently, Khrushchev announced that the Russian republic and its
Party and government organizations were being divorced from the
central institutions of the Soviet Union with which they had been
so closely identified in the past: in the period following the Twentieth Congress, Khrushchev noted, a Russian Republic Bureau had
been established within the Central Committee of the Soviet Union
to handle Party affairs in the RSFSR; in addition, the Russian
Council of Ministers was being given powers which would place
the RSFSR more closely on a par with the other Soviet republics.[98] Significantly, these measures were all steps which Skrypnik
and other Ukrainian leaders had earlier demanded as necessary
if the rights of the republics were to be safeguarded from Union
encroachment and if the Union was to be distinguished from the
Russian republic.[99]

The extent to which these modifications in the Soviet Union's
federal system were to be carried was not immediately made
clear: a number of the proposed changes were not at once put into
effect, and in other cases little information was provided on the
practical workings of the programs. Nevertheless, several conclu-

sions can be suggested. First, it appears, as emphasized by Khrushchev, that the changes were designed in part to enhance the importance of the republics and thereby to suggest a strengthening
of the role of the separate nationalities in the Soviet Union. In
his report to the USSR Supreme Soviet on the program of regional
control of industrial enterprises, Khrushchev said:

Along with their immense economic importance, the planned measures are also of prime political importance because they signify a
new, long step forward in implementing Lenin's national policy,
prepared by the entire course of socialist construction. The broad
rights given the republics in economic construction will help still
more to stimulate the initiative and creative activity of the masses,
to unfold the material and spiritual forces of all nations and peoples
of the Soviet Union, and to strengthen still further friendship among
peoples of our country.[100]

Later he commented:

All the peoples of our Soviet Union are making their great contribution to the building of Communism. The invincible strength of
our Soviet system lies in the indestructible fraternal friendship of
all the peoples of our multinational land of Soviets.[101]

It was not accidental, of course, that Khrushchev's political fortunes
had in the past been closely tied with the Soviet Union's territorial
organizations rather than its center. By enlarging the authority
of the regions he laid claim to the support of those who, if not
directly tied to him as in the case of the Ukraine, were prepared to
view him as their most sympathetic advocate. His political success
was a testimonial to the effectiveness of this appeal. Perhaps his
stress on regionalism was motivated more by these political considerations than by considerations of efficiency and creativity.

Second, the changes seemed designed to establish the republics more firmly as major links in the Soviet Union's administrative system—links which were to be given increased authority to
handle problems of strictly local importance and to supervise the
administration within the republics of Union programs submitted
from Moscow. Unlike the American federal system with its distinct separation of state and national functions, emphasis was to
be on the republics as regional arms of the central government.
The expansion of republic powers and duties was adopted because

it promised to correct weaknesses in the old system arising from the tendency of central administrators to bypass intermediate administrative levels. As *Pravda* observed:

A correct relationship between over-all state and national interests is to be achieved through a skillful, scientific combination of centralization in administration of the national economy and local initiative, with the republics being given complete freedom to solve local problems on the basis of the USSR constitution.

The Party and government have established that in the practical guidance of the economy there have been deviations from these principles in a number of matters. In particular, planning agencies have tried to plan from the center a detailed list of products to be produced by a republic for its own needs. There have been certain deficiencies in drafting the budgets of national republics. The Party and government have explained that such petty supervision of Union and autonomous republics leads to infringement of the rights of these republics and to decreased responsibility of local officials.[102]

Finally, it seems unlikely that the changes signified any weakening of the ultimate responsibility and authority of central bodies for Party and government work. The confidence Bolshevik leaders had traditionally expressed in the effectiveness of centralized planning and direction was not to be lost. Khrushchev restated it to the Twentieth Party Congress as follows:

It must always be remembered that a most important condition for the development of our country and of each Soviet republic is unity of the efforts of all the peoples of the USSR, a certain centralization of our national economy, combined with the broad initiative and independent activity of the republics. Planning is the great advantage of the socialist economic system. We are not renouncing this advantage and never will.[103]

Union interests were primary, and efforts at "making national traits absolute, setting them off against over-all state interests" were declared "harmful and inadmissible."[104] As Khrushchev became identified increasingly with central Party and government machines, it would be expected his enthusiasm for the federalist principle would diminish. In any case his call was for less detailed and direct interference from Moscow, not for a narrower scope of central decisions or their less rigorous local enforcement.

VIII. CONCLUSION

In a general way the Ukraine has appeared in three characters to Soviet leaders, each character posing its own problems and prompting separate ideological and political programs. As a distinct ethnic region differing in language, traditions, and culture from central Russia, the Ukraine, with other minority areas, has forced the development of a nationality theory and significant modifications of political practices. As a distinct physical and political region, possessing a certain economic and territorial unity apart from its nationality character, the Ukraine has confronted Soviet leaders with a type of regional exclusiveness and ethnocentrism. And as a collection of districts in the Soviet Union, the Ukraine has most fondly been viewed by Russian officials as but one part of a single, uniform Russia with a system of politics integrated into the All-Russian system. Because the three characters have so differed from one another, it is not surprising that Soviet policies in the Ukraine have not always been consistent.

The most distinctive feature of the Ukraine has been its nationality character, and in the press and in official statements and studies the nationality question has been given much attention. But the most common theme of these discussions has been the relative unimportance of the nationality question and its subordination to the class question and the building of a Soviet state. Nationality questions are assumed to have no basic revolutionary importance and hence no permanent place in Bolshevik dogma. National feelings and hostilities result from economic rivalries and class pressures, existing only because they have been artificially stimulated by imperialist governments, anxious to win domestic support for imperialist ventures, or because they have developed among exploited peoples as a reaction to oppression. In neither case is nationalism more than a noxious by-product of the competitive struggle characterizing the capitalist era. On occasion the class struggle may take the form of a national struggle, which then appears as a liberating movement. But its role remains only secondary. The dialectic as a mechanism for the progressive evolution of society applies only to class relationships; competitive processes between separate nationality groups are not of themselves progressive. Efforts to emphasize—"to exaggerate"—nationality differences only serve to blur the class struggle and must therefore be resisted.

Yet so easy and negative a theoretic answer has never been sufficient for Soviet leaders. Almost from the beginning they were confronted with the difficulty that, if nationality characteristics were only neutral—neither progressive nor essentially hostile—then no national group could claim superiority over any other, Russians no more than Ukrainians. Bolsheviks could not support the Russification of the Tsarist days, for to do so would be to emphasize the national question above the proletarian. They were to work for a truly international culture, identified with no single nationality but drawn from the "progressive" elements of all. What was required was a broad acceptance of different national forms and even the stimulation of separate cultures in order that they might reach full fruition, then to be drawn together. In this rather narrow cultural sense, the Bolsheviks were not to oppose nationalisms but were to support them as part of the process of building a proletarian world society.

Moreover, in a very practical political sense, the Bolsheviks viewed the nationalities in the period before the Revolution as "progressive." As sources of disaffection toward the Tsarist government, which discriminated against them, the nationalities were potential allies in the revolutionary struggle. The national and proletarian movements followed the same path, and Bolsheviks, by supporting the one, could advance the cause of the other.

Whatever importance these considerations had in the early days began to diminish as Soviet rule was established. Allies against the Tsarist government no longer were needed. And gradually acceptance of the neutrality of nationality institutions was aban-

doned as Russia and Russian ways came to be preferred. Russian superiority was defended initially on the grounds that Russia
was more advanced than the minority nationalities in Marxist
terms, having a better developed industrial plant, a sizable proletariat, and a stronger consciousness of the class struggle.
Ukrainians and others were to look to Russia as the model to be
followed, as their regions emerged from their lower stage as peas-
ant-feudal societies. Later, Russian institutions were more broadly glorified as the institutions of the first successful proletarian
revolution in the world. Russian was the language of Lenin and
Stalin, and the revolutionary movement was best expressed through
Russian art and literature, music and drama. Later still, in the
1930s and 1940s, emphasis was placed on Russia as the bulwark
of the Revolution against outside attack. No other people had
so stalwartly defended Soviet society, while the minority groups
had seemed sometimes unenthusiastic or even in opposition.
Throughout the period of Soviet rule the Russian language and
Russian institutions had come to be accepted, in a practical way,
as powerful aids to the building of national unity. None of these
changes meant the abandonment of Soviet internationalist theory,
and the rights of the minority peoples continued to be stressed.
But each change strengthened the position of those emphasizing
Soviet-Russian unity and the unimportance of the national question against those emphasizing national equality and the flowering
of separate cultures.

More basic than these considerations has been the overriding
problem of support, especially troublesome because of Soviet inability to decide clearly whether to view the nationalities as friendly or hostile, or whether to adopt a policy of concessions or repression. Again and again Soviet leaders have appeared uncertain,
suspicious that national hostilities ran deeper than Marxist theory allowed, threatening Soviet unity and Soviet rule, but also
optimistic that with proper programs minority groups might be
led voluntarily to give support. On the one hand, the nationalities were not class enemies and had been co-revolutionaries in
their opposition to Tsarist Russification. On the other hand, the
nationalist movements as separatist movements seemed incompat-

ible with preservation of the Russian empire and challenging to Leninist principles of centralism and hierarchical organization. As each expression of nationalism appeared, it required a decision, first, whether it was threatening or might be directed to provide support and, second, whether it should be suppressed or tolerated with the expectation it would disappear.

It is this pragmatic, relativist attitude which has chiefly characterized the Soviet approach to the nationalities. Where policy differences have appeared, they have resulted from different estimates of the relationship of the national question to revolutionary, class questions, to the question of support and political success. In the early years, before the Revolution and until 1923, Lenin's stress on the importance of winning the minorities to Bolshevism prevailed, and a broad program of concessions was adopted, leading ultimately to the suggestion that the border regions be given complete self-government except in matters of defense, and foreign affairs. After 1923 Lenin's place was taken by Stalin who rejected suggestions for broadening the authority of the border regions and showed little concern over the problem of winning the minorities to Bolshevism. However in his personal struggle with Party oppositionists he appealed widely for support from nationalist elements, endorsing a localization program for the republics in cultural and leadership matters which went far beyond Lenin's programs. Again in 1929 and 1930, as collectivization was pressed, support from the minority peoples seemed necessary, and the localization policy was re-emphasized.

But in the early 1930s major shifts occurred. The early assumption that the minorities were essentially neutral in the class struggle and might be won to Bolshevism was dropped, as Stalin became convinced they were divisive and opposed to collectivization, hence, anti-proletarian and anti-revolutionary. Nationality concessions as a means of winning support seemed less important, as Stalin's hold on the Party and government was strengthened and greater reliance placed on Russian elements. There were convincing indications that the policy of concessions had failed to ensure the loyalty of the minorities, perhaps even stimulating local nationalism and anti-centralism. Finally, the growing stability of Stalin's position gave him confidence that harsh, repressive measures would succeed where conciliatory ones had not. In 1934 the last of the compromising policies was dropped and replaced by a stern program of centralization and conformity.

The basic questions on which Lenin and Stalin disagreed were these: 1) How essential for the success of the Soviet program was local support from the non-Russian nationalities? 2) How effectively could support be stimulated by nationality concessions and the elimination of nationality inequities? 3) How extensively and in what areas could local variants in the determination and execution of socialist policies be permitted without challenging central authority and interfering with basic programs? Lenin's answers, particularly in the period from 1919 until his death, were generous, stressing the necessity of local support, the effectiveness of concessions to the nationalities, and the flexibility of Soviet programs. Stalin, in his time, was more restrictive, demanding uniformity and unity and showing little concern for winning voluntary rather than coerced acceptance of Soviet rule.

With Stalin's death and the liberalization which followed, new emphasis was given the national question. The element of mass support was crucial as it had been for Stalin in the early years of his rule, and the new leaders were more willing to accept Lenin's optimistic faith that support could be won by a policy of concessions. As a practical matter, Khrushchev relied heavily on the Ukrainian Party organization, in return giving it and the Ukraine as a whole a larger role in Soviet life.

Of greater interest were indications that the internationalism of the early Soviet period, with its toleration, even stimulation of national differences, was to be revived. Suggestive was the considerable attention given Lenin's thesis that within each nationality were found two cultures—one progressive and one counter-revolutionary—and that the first was to be accepted despite its national peculiarities. The proletarian pattern established in the Soviet Union under Russian leadership, Khrushchev intimated, was not necessarily the only pattern nor the most suitable one for other socialist societies or a world society. Presumably the areas of freedom allowed the nationalities in their separate development should be widened.

In practice, the new emphasis was confined within narrow limits. It was applied to cultural rather than political matters and only to "progressive" aspects of culture. When cultural workers sought to broaden the suggestion to a recognition of their right to "creative independence" from Party supervision, they were denounced for striking at Lenin's primary conviction that the Party was the guiding, controlling body for all of Soviet life. But the emphasis was a reassurance to the nationalities that the general liberalization of the period was to apply also to them and that certain of the Russifying measures of the past were to be modified in cultural areas. More basically, it turned Soviet leaders away from Stalin's increasingly dogmatic position to the earlier flexibility of the post-revolutionary years and to a shifting but more nearly even balance between voluntarism and compulsion, concessions and repression.

Because of their approach to the nationality question, Soviet leaders have been chiefly occupied in the Ukraine with concerns little different from those in other parts of the Soviet Union. Problems of Party membership and leadership cadres, of mass education and guidance, of Party and government organization and direction have dominated in the Ukraine as elsewhere, eclipsing the nationality question despite the attention it has received. In some areas the two concerns have been inseparable. In the development of cadres, for example, a decision to press promotion of city workers automatically favors Russians, promotion of peasants favors Ukrainians. However such problems have increasingly been decided on the basis of other factors, and this is perhaps the best indication that in the minds of Soviet leaders the nationality question has been growing less important.

From the beginning, greatest stress has been placed on building control through leadership cadres, For Lenin in the pre-revolutionary period it was difficult to conceive of any pattern of political life but a centralized one with a highly structured Party organization directed by a small elite. Infallible in its Marxist

dogma, the elite was to guide society in a comprehensive and exclusive way along the socialist path. What was needed was an
iron discipline and control from above, a bureaucratic machine
that would differ from the Tsarist only in the character of its
leadership.

Bolshevik weakness and the speedy disintegration of the Russian empire after the Revolution prevented Lenin from building
so centralist a system. For a period, with the chaos of the Civil
War, he seemed uncertain how to proceed, but then moved gradually in the direction of his basic conviction that the Bolsheviks,
however they might compromise on lesser points—federalism, acceptance of Borotbists, nationality concessions—could not lose control of the commanding leadership posts. Initially this was largely a matter of personalities, and in a haphazard way Lenin
dispatched officials in whom he had confidence to the Ukraine to
direct the army, the government, and the Party. At one point,
in the case of the Sapronov Opposition, he seemed to view the
Ukraine as a lesser region to which oppositionists could be com-
fortably exiled, but the effort failed, he momentarily lost control
of the Ukraine and as a result came to accept it as a major center,
second in importance only to Moscow and Leningrad.

The policy of appointing top leaders directly to the Ukraine
was successful in holding the area for the Bolsheviks, but it provided a kind of artificial leadership and served to widen the gap
between local, potentially supporting groups and military and political centers of power. In some instances, local leaders, both
Ukrainians and Russians, were given Party and government posts
but not the highest ones, and the gap remained. Gradually the
role of the Party in the Ukraine began to grow, in part because
the ending of the Civil War lessened military influence, but above
all because recognition of the Ukraine's independence provided
for separate governmental machinery—an undesirable separation
from the point of view of the Bolsheviks—while the Party in the
Ukraine remained, at Lenin's insistence, only one subordinate
part of the All-Union Party and hence a more easily manipulated
and dominated body. The Party grew, but as it did so it developed not into the single, tightly-knit, monolithic organization Len-

in so often had praised, but into an ill-defined collection of regional
groups dominated by various factions and pulled together less by
their own Ukrainian Party machine than by the ties Lenin at
the center managed to maintain with each of them. The pattern of politics remained until Lenin's death largely a personal one.

The most important shift for the whole of the Soviet period
came in the early years of Stalin's rule. Dominating Party organization as he did, it was natural for Stalin to emphasize organizational questions, particularly in districts such as the eastern Ukraine where Party leaders were unsympathetic or hostile.
In a sense, he reversed Lenin's practice of appointing lieutenants
directly to high posts, relying instead on Party machinery to produce, with appropriate stimulation, suitable leaders of its own.
In the Ukraine he was encouraged to do so by his early success
in forming an alliance with local Ukrainian leaders against the
anti-nationalist and anti-Stalinist Party machines in the east. Initially he accepted the decentralized character of the Party in
the Ukraine, suspecting perhaps that any All-Ukrainian leadership
would be dominated by the opposition. Stress he placed instead
on the building within each Party group of loyal, Stalinist elements. Later, after 1925, he began to strengthen the central
Ukrainian organization, gradually extending its authority over
lower Party groups. At the same time, he returned to Lenin's
practice of appointing directly the highest government and Party
leaders. Thus, by the late 1920s, central control—increasingly Stalinist control—was assured both by central domination of Party
machinery in general at every level and by the informal hold central leaders kept over the Party and government officials they had
chosen.

The pattern thus established has remained the principal characteristic of central domination of Ukrainian political life. With
the tensions of collectivization and industrialization, Party organization was further tightened, especially in the countryside, and
leaders directly injected not only at the republic level but also at
oblast and city levels and even below. As Stalin grew increasingly
suspicious of the machine he had created, he began to defend his
control by more and more frequent changes of Party leadership

until it became difficult for local Party workers to rise to highest positions without periods of tutelage and supervision in Party work ouside the Ukraine or under Stalin's closest associates. Demoralizing as such a policy may have been within the Party ranks, it prevented. the rebirth of those attitudes of independence and self-sufficiency which had characterized elements of the Ukrainian Party organization in its earliest years.

The biggest shift in the post-Stalin era was in the renewed confidence expressed by central leaders in the Party machine itself at every level and in its ability to manufacture its own leadership with less intervention from the center. Present were the same elements which had prompted Stalin in his early years to stress organizational questions: lack of a single, clearly accepted authority in Moscow; an inevitable downward movement of decision-making as officials at the top competed for control; the obvious value of the Party machine as an element in the intra-Party struggle. In addition there was now Khrushchev's personal confidence in the Ukrainian Party organization—in contrast to Stalin's distrust of the early 1920s—and his general dislike of the arbitrary authority Stalin had exercised over regional leaders: it is possible that Khrushchev's victory of 1957 was essentially a victory of the regional organizations over the center. As Khrushchev drew Party workers out of the Ukraine to higher posts at the center, there developed a more natural circulation in which officials at the oblast and republic levels—including even Podgornyi at the top,were pulled up from below within their own organizations. The importance of the change should not be overstressed. It seems unlikely the pattern will be preserved, as Khrushchev loses his close ties with the Ukrainian Party. Moreover, central leaders may increasingly use their power to approve regional officials as a device to select them, though they may not intervene as obviously as did Stalin in dispatching workers directly from the center or in arbitrarily removing them. Given Soviet acceptance of the necessity of centralized leadership, a greater measure of freedom for the Ukrainian Party organization could only be considered an invitation to a kind of threatening regional autonomy.

Outside the Party, the Bolsheviks agreed at an early period that the Ukraine's regional character should be recognized through some form of special status. Initially accepted as nominally independent, the Ukraine was later absorbed as one part of the Soviet Union's federal system—a system the Bolsheviks adopted not because they favored it but as an accommodation to regional loyalites and as one of the "transitional forms on the road to complete unity."

When Lenin recommended in 1922 that the system be a sharply decentralized one, he was concerned chiefly with support. That his recommendation was not adopted was a sign of Stalin's growing authority and less flexible attitude toward questions of centralism and regionalism. Willing to grant the most liberal concessions to the nationalities in matters of national and cultural form, Stalin refused to grant more than the barest minimum of concessions in matters of policy and control. In the years which followed, as Union authority was expanded despite the protests of nationalist leaders and of Russians in the Ukraine who favored regional autonomy, Stalin displayed a centralizing spirit which penetrated the whole state apparatus. The only effective limit came to be the practical one set by administrative and supervisory inadequacy.

Under Khruschhev there were indications centralist pressures were to be lessened. In matters such as legal codes, court structure, budgetary rights, supervision of industrial and agriculture production, Khrushchev took steps to strengthen the position of the republics or indicated such steps should be studied. To a considerable degree the administration accepted the arguments of Ukrainian Bolsheviks such as Skrypnik, Petrovs'kyi, and Chubar' who had opposed the centralist trend in the 1920s and early 1930s. Very broadly, Khrushchev agreed that relationships between the republics and the Union should be re-examined over a long period and the functions of the localities expanded wherever feasible.

Although this flexible position was pleasing to regional leaders, it created the thorny problem of setting new boundaries between Union and local responsibility. The problem was similar to that faced earlier by Lenin in his pre-revolutionary efforts to reconcile the centralism of an integrated hierarchical organization with the democratic traditions he openly supported. For Lenin the solution lay in the distinction to be made between the two functions of policy determination and program administration. For the first, Lenin suggested, flexibility was needed, including free deliberation at all levels and an acceptance of opposition and disagreement; the decision-making process was to be democratic and, in a sense, decentralized. For program administration Lenin called for a disciplined approach, including an absolute acceptance of central authority: decisions at one level were to be rigorously executed at the next, and criticisms were to be allowed only on technical points and were to be discussed and conflicts resolved at higher levels. In this principle of "democratic centralism" Lenin hoped for a balance between democracy and organization, consensus and authority, localism and centralism.

Yet in practice the solution was inadequate. Lenin had approved democratic procedures for decision making on the assumption that the purposes of Bolshevik society were commonly understood and that specific policies would develop naturally in a direct and logical, simple and obvious way. But the experience of the Bolsheviks did not bear him out, either because basic Bolshevik purposes were not as simply accepted by all as Lenin had hoped or because his distinction between program administration and policy determination assumed too easily that the functions were unrelated and could be compartmentalized. In practice it proved difficult to prevent them from blurring together. As a result, the Bolsheviks abandoned the distinctions and the democratic procedures, establishing instead centralized, authoritarian control over both programs and policies.

Khruschchev's call for a return to decentralization was therefore a call for a new acceptance of Lenin's separation of programs and policies. Khrushchev's purpose, however—apart from its political one—was not that of accommodating democratic and authoritarian principles but the practical aim of increasing bureaucratic efficiency by localizing administrative work. Hence he reversed Lenin in his approach, retaining central, authoritarian control over policy determination and extending republic autonomy in questions of program administration and local interest. Critical political questions and matters of Union concern would continue to be decided centrally, and the concession to the republics was chiefly one of size and functions, permitting an increase in routine administrative activity with an accompanying increase in prestige and local leadership. To the extent that program administration inevitably influenced policies, the change meant somewhat more, offering the republics the opportunity of a broader and more general participation in government affairs.

The liberalization of the post-Stalin era seems likely to pose troublesome questions for Soviet leaders. One of the traditional objectives of Soviet policy has been to prevent the formation of regional groupings which might develop as competitive or oppositionist centers. Stalin, with his arbitrary and ruthless domination of the Party, his tendency to centralize governmental functions in Moscow, and his opposition to nationalist expressions, succeeded in establishing conditions unfavorable to such groupings. The more liberal atmosphere following Stalin's death may also have initially discouraged them by removing some of their more obvious grievances. But the new conditions opened the door too for the development of a more tightly knit regional Party organization, a more powerful republic governmental machine, and a renewed interest in distinct Ukrainian features—all developments which had proved so troublesome in the 1920s. Because the relaxation has been modest, the possibilities have been limited, but it seems likely the concessions will generate pressures for further liberalization. Undoubtedly such pressures will become increasingly distasteful to Khrushchev as he builds his own personal central organization. Perhaps the Party with its present machinery can accommodate these pressures without major change. If not, a critical point may be reached at which Khrushchev will be faced with the difficult alternative of returning to harsher, Stalinist policies or of accepting a form of Party factionalism and administrative regionalism which would seem hardly compatible with traditional principles of unity and centralism.

NOTES

INTRODUCTION

1. Harold Laski, *A Grammar of Politics* (New Haven, 1929), p. 44.
2. Charles E. Merriam, *Systematic Politics* (Chicago, 1945), p. 39.
See also Kenneth D. Benne, *A Conception of Authority* (New York,
1945).
3. Robert M. MacIver, *The Web of Government* (New York, 1948),
p. 78.
4. Alfred G. Meyer, *Leninism* (Cambridge, 1957), p. 21.

I. THE BOLSHEVIK APPROACH TO NATIONALISM AND THE UKRAINE

1. Iosef V. Stalin, *Sochineniia*; 13 vols. (Moscow, 1946-1951), I,
42. (Hereafter referred to as *Stalin.*)
2. J. V. Stalin, *Marxism and the National and Colonial Question*
(New York, 1935), p. 25. At other times both Lenin and Stalin
urged that the national question was subordinate to the "proletarian
question." V. I. Lenin, *Sochineniia*; 4th ed. (Moscow, 1941-1951),
XX, 406. (Hereafter referred to as *Lenin*; except where otherwise
noted, references are to the 4th edition.) Apparently both men
viewed the national and agrarian questions as problems requiring
solutions before the dictatorship of the proletariat could be established; of the two questions, the agrarian was considered more important and more difficult. See below, pp. 23-24.
3. Stalin, *Marxism and the National Question*, pp. 192-93. See
also his later statement that "the right to self-determination cannot
and must not serve as an obstacle to the realization of the right
of the working class to its own dictatorship." *Stalin*, V, 265.
4. *Lenin*, XXII, 326. Earlier, Lenin had noted that "the bour-
geosie always places its national demands in the forefront. It urges
them unconditionally. But for the proletariat [these demands] are
subordinated to the class struggle." *Ibid.*, XX, 382. See also XXII,
137-38, 139, 330; XXVII, 342; XXVIII, 186.
5. Stalin, *Marxism and the National Question*, p. 75. See also
Lenin, XX, 376-80, 383. For an opposite view expressed later by

Trotsky and for Trotsky's evaluation of Stalin's position see Leon Trotsky, *The History of the Russian Revolution* (New York, 1932), III, 55-58.

6. Stalin, *Marxism and the National Question*, p. 14. Lenin suggested that nationalism was always an outgrowth of the development of capitalism and should be stimulated only as it benefited the proletariat: "the working class should least of all make a fetish of the national question, since the development of capitalism does not necessarily awaken *all* nations to an independent life. But to brush aside the mass national movements once they have started and to refuse to support what is progressive in them means, in effect, to encourage *nationalistic* prejudices." *Lenin*, XX, 407. See also XX, 1-12, 406. It is important that nowhere in pre-revolutionary Bolshevik writing is there the suggestion that diversity of national cultures, customs, and institutions is useful or desirable.

7. *Stalin*, I, 36. See also *Lenin*, XX, 381-82, 413; XXIV, 51-52.

8. Stalin, *Marxism and the National Question*, p. 17.

9. *Ibid.*

10. Vsesoiuznaia Kommunisticheskaia Partiia (bol'shevikov), *Vsesoiuznaia Kommunisticheskaia Partiia (bol'shevikov) v rezoliutsiiakh i resheniiakh s"ezdov, konferentsii i plenumov TsK, 1898-1935*; 5th ed. (Moscow, 1935), I, 20-24. (Hereafter referred to as *VKP(b) v rezol.*)

11. *Ibid.*, I, 22.

12. It is noteworthy that Stalin, in his article discussing the national demands of the Second Congress, "Kak ponimaet sotsial-demokratiia natsional'nyi vopros?" [How does Social-Democracy Understand the National Question?] *Stalin*, I, 32-55, refused to analyze the problem. He brushed it aside with the assertion that the solution would depend on the particular conditions under which the problem arose.

13. *Marxism and the National Question*, pp. 3-61. There seems to be little question that the views expressed by Stalin were developed in part by Lenin, though there were areas of disagreement. See Richard Pipes, *The Formation of the Soviet Union* (Cambridge, 1954), pp. 37-41; Alfred D. Low, *Lenin on the Question of Nationality* (New York, 1958), pp. 10-11.

14. Stalin, *Marxism and the National Question*, pp. 18-19.

15. *Ibid.*, p. 19.

16. *Ibid.*, pp. 18-19. The italics are mine. See also *Lenin*, XX, 381-82.

17. Stalin, *Marxism and the National Question*, p. 53. Lenin agreed that the proletariat, while "recognizing equality of rights and an equal right to a national state above all, treasures and urges a union of the proletariat of all nations, evaluating each national

demand, each national separation from the viewpoint of the class struggle of the workers." *Lenin*, XX, 383. See also *Lenin*, XX, 404-5, 423; XXII, 135-36. Cf. the fifth paragraph of the resolution on the national question adopted by the Summer Conference (1913) of the Central Committee of the Russian Social Democratic Workers' Party. *Lenin*, XIX, 386.

18. Stalin, *Marxism and the National Question*, p. 20.
19. *Ibid.*, p. 21.
20. *VKP(b) v rezol.*, I, 216.
21. Stalin, *Marxism and the National Question*, p. 64.
22. Vsesoiuznaia Kommunisticheskaia Partiia (bol'shevikov), *Protokoly VIII s"ezda RSDRP(b)* (Moscow [1934]), pp. 48-49. (Reports of Party Congresses and Conferences are hereafter referred to by number alone, as follows: *VIII s"ezd RSDRP(b)*.) Piatakov and Bukharin had attacked the absolute right to self-determination as early as November, 1915. At that time they had sent Bukharin's thesis, "The Slogan of the Right of Nations to Self-Determination," to the Party Central Committee. The thesis concluded as follows: "We do not under any circumstances support the government of the Great Power that suppresses the rebellion or the outburst of indignation of an oppressed nation; but, at the same time, we ourselves do not mobilise the proletarian forces under the slogan 'right of nations to self-determination.' In such a case, our task is to mobilise the forces of the proletariat of both nations (jointly with others) under the slogan, 'civil class war for socialism,' and conduct propaganda against the mobilisation of forces under the slogan, 'right of nations to self-determination.'" V. I. Lenin, *Selected Works* (New York, 1935-1939), V, 379-80. Piatakov stoutly defended these views at the Seventh Conference of the Party in April, 1917. *VKP(b) v rezol.*, I, 230-45. At the Eighth Party Congress he went so far as to declare that even the proletariat of a national group does not have the right of self-determination. "There is now taking place a battle for the establishment of the dictatorship of the proletariat in the Ukraine, and you know perfectly well that the fate of the Ukraine is of great interest not only to the working masses of that country, but also to the working masses of Russia, Latvia, Belorussia and other Soviet republics... Can we declare that the form of existence of the proletarian-peasant Ukraine can be determined solely and absolutely by the working masses of the Ukraine? Of course not!" *VIII s"ezd RSDRP(b)*, p. 82. Both Lenin and Stalin attacked the Left Wing Communists at the Seventh Party Conference (April, 1917) and at the All-Russian Military Conference in June, 1917. C. E. Rabinovich, *Vserossiiskaia voennaia konferentsiia bol'shevikov 1917 goda* (Moscow, 1931), pp. 35-38; *VKP(b) v rezol.*, I, 246-55. It was not, however, until the Eighth

Congress in March and April, 1919, that the issue was clearly joined.

23. *VII s"ezd RSDRP(b)*, p. 49.

24. Earlier (before 1919), both Lenin and Stalin had expressed themselves uncertainly on the question. In 1903 and again in 1914 Lenin had urged that the Bosheviks were primarily concerned with "self-determination not of peoples and nations, but of the proletariat within each nation." *Lenin*, VI, 294, 412; XX, 398. Similarly, Stalin had urged in January, 1918, "the necessity of interpreting the principle of self-determination as a right to self-determination not of the bourgeoisie, but of the working masses of a given nation." *Stalin*, IV, 31-32, 8-9. Only three weeks earlier, however, he had emphasized the importance of applying the principle to the *bourgeoisie* of Finland. *Ibid.*, pp. 22-24. After 1919 the question was resolved in favor of the broader interpretation.

25. *VII s"ezd RSDRP(b)*, pp. 54-55.

26. *Ibid.*, esp. pp. 92-100. See also X. J. Eudin, "Soviet National Minority Policies, 1918-1921," *The Slavonic and East European Review*, XXI (November, 1943), 31-55.

27. Stalin, *Marxism and the National Question*, pp. 56-57.

28. *Lenin*, XXIV, 265, 268. See also XXVI, 41.

29. Rabinovich, *Voennaia konferentsiia*, p. 36. The Conference also denounced the "oppressive" tactics of the Provisional Government. "The Provisional Government on the one hand recognizes the right of nations to self-determination, but on the other hand, prevents the Ukrainians from putting this right into practice." *VKP(b) v rezol*, I, 251.

30. Rabinovich, *Voennaia konferentsiia*, pp. 37-38. See also *Stalin*, III, 221-25.

31. Rabinovich, *Voennaia konferentsiia*, p. 38.

32. *VKP(b) v rezol.*, I, 251.

33. For a study of the growth of Ukrainian nationalism during and immediately after World War I, see John S. Reshetar, *The Ukrainian Revolution, 1917-1920* (Princeton, 1952).

34. See especially Rabinovich, *Voennaia konferentsiia*, pp. 35-38.

II. BOLSHEVIKS AND THE REVOLUTION, 1917-1920

1. "Deklaratsiia prav narodov Rossii" (November 15, 1917), *Istoriia sovetskoi konstitutsii v dekretakh i postanovleniiakh sovetskogo pravitel'stva 1917-1936* (Moscow, 1936), pp. 31-32.

2. *VIII s"ezd RSDRP(b)*, pp. 80-83. Stalin later criticized these views as follows: "They threatened us, finally, with the disintegration of Russia, with its breaking apart into numerous independent states, and they hinted thereby that the right of nations to self-

determination proclaimed by the Council of People's Commissars was a 'fatal mistake.' But I must declare categorically that we would not be democrats (I say nothing of socialism!), if we did not recognize for the peoples of Russia the right of free self-determination." *Stalin*, IV, 3.

3. "The task of the [proletarian] parties in their national policy must be two-fold: the recognition of the right to self-determination for nations, . . . and the closest inseparable alliance in the class struggle of the proletariat of all the nations in a given state." *Lenin*, XX, 404. See also p. 423. For later statements see XXI, 373-74, 377; XXII, 135-37; XXIV, 264-65.

4. *Ibid.*, XX, 423.

5. *Ibid.*, XXI, 377; XXII, 135-36; XXIV, 51-52.

6. See especially his statements on the question of Polish and Finnish independence, *ibid.*, XXIV, 264-68, and Stalin's explanation for the grant of independence given to Finland, *Stalin*, IV, 3-4, 22-24. See also *VII s"ezd RSDRP(b)*, pp. 54-55.

7. In a statement of October 9-10, 1917, Lenin insisted on the granting of independence to Finland, the Ukraine, Armenia, and the Turkish areas immediately on the assumption of power by the Bolsheviks. *Lenin*, XXVI, 40-42. He at once made plain, however, that he expected these areas to rejoin Russia voluntarily once their independence had been recognized. *Ibid.*, XXVI, 40-42, 74-75. See also Stalin's easy assurances given at the end of November, 1917, that the minority groups would not want to withdraw. *Stalin*, IV, 3-4.

8. Pipes, *Formation of the Soviet Union*, pp. 114-240.

9. Evgeniia Bosh, *God bor'by* (Moscow, 1925), pp. 1-2; Dmitrii Lebed', *Sovetskaia Ukraina; natsional'nyi vopros za piat' let* (Moscow, 1924), pp. 3-4.

10. Bosh, *God bor'by*, p. 11. See also M. Ravich-Cherkasskii, *Istoriia kommunisticheskoi partii (b-ov) Ukrainy* (Kharkov, 1923), p. 3; Kurshchyn, V. M. *Gosudarstvennoe sotrudnichestvo mezhdu Ukrainskoi SSR i RSFSR v 1917-1922 gg.* (Moscow, 1957), pp. 8-11.

11. The most powerful agrarian parties were the socialist revolutionary parties. The elections to the Constituent Assembly held in December, 1917, indicated that 77 percent of the voters in the Ukraine supported these parties and only 10 percent, the Bolsheviks. *Lenin*, XXX, 230-33; Oliver Henry Radkey, *The Election to the Russian Constituent Assembly of 1917* (Cambridge, 1950), pp. 29-31, 78-80. The Bolsheviks were most strongly supported in the eastern provinces of Chernigov (28 percent), Ekaterinoslav (18 percent), and Kharkov (12 percent). The southeastern part of the Donbass has been excluded from the figures. If it were included, the total Bolshevik vote would be somewhat higher.

12. See below, pp. 29-33.

13. Figures are taken from the 1926 census. The criterion of nationality based on language has been used. Tsentral'noe statisticheskoe upravlenie SSSR, otdel perepisi, *Vsesoiuznaia perepis' naseleniia 1926 goda* (Moscow, 1927), XI, 8-30. Sixty-one percent of all urban population in the Donbass region of the Ukraine was Russian according to the 1923 census. Tsentral'noe statisticheskoe upravlenie, otdel demografii, *Trudy*, Vol. XX: *Itogi vsesoiuznoi gorodskoi perepisi 1923 g.* (Moscow, 1924), Part IV, pp. 40-51. See also Ravich-Cherkasskii, *Istoriia KP(b)U*, p. 4.

14. The combination of anti-Russian and anti-urban sentiments which motivated many Ukrainians in opposition to the Bolsheviks was expressed by a Ukrainian writer: "The city rules the village and the city is 'alien.' The city draws to itself almost all the wealth and gives the village almost nothing in return. The city extracts taxes which never return to the Ukrainian village. In the city one must pay bribes to be freed from scorn and red tape. In the city are warm fires, schools, theaters and music, plays. The city is expensively dressed, as for a holiday; it eats and drinks well; many people promenade. In the village there is nothing besides hard work, impenetrable darkness, and misery. The city is aristocratic, it is alien. It is not ours, not Ukrainian." Peter Skorevetanskii, *Revoliutsiia na Ukraine* (Saratov, 1919), pp. 7-8, quoted in H. R. Weinstein, "Land Hunger in the Ukraine, 1905-1917," *Journal of Economic History*, II (May, 1942), 25. See also Trotsky, *Russian Revolution*, III, 44-46; Iwan Majstrenko, *Borot'bism, a Chapter in the History of Ukrainian Nationalism* (New York, 1954), pp. 7-10.

15. The Russian Provisional Government on August 17, 1917, had recognized the differences in the Ukraine by including within the purview of the Central Rada only the five northwestern provinces — Kiev, Volynia, Podolia, Poltava, and Chernigov. Pipes, *Formation of the Soviet Union*, p. 64. At that time, the Bolsheviks had denounced the Provisional Government for pursuing an imperialist policy. M. Suprunenko, *Velika zhovtneva sotsialistychna revoliutsiia na Ukraini* (Kiev, 1948), p. 37. Subsequently, however, they adopted the same position. See below, pp. 32-33.

16. "Recognizing that authority in the whole state, as in each individual territory, should be placed in the hands of the whole of revolutionary democracy; and regarding as impermissible the transfer of all authority exclusively into the hands of the soviet of workers' and soldiers' deputies which is but a segment of organized revolutionary democracy, the Ukrainian Central Rada hereby expresses its disapproval of the Petrograd uprising." Quoted in Reshetar, *Ukrainian Revolution*, p. 83.

17. In July, 1917, three of the fourteen cabinet posts in the Ukrainian General Secretariat were offered to the Bolsheviks; in November two Bolshevik representatives were admitted to the Revolutionary Committee of the Central Rada. *Ibid.*, pp. 68, 82. See also Pipes, *Formation of the Soviet Union*, pp. 67-73, 114-16.

18. *Izvestiia*, No. 235, December 8, 1917.

19. *Stalin*, IV, 8-9. At meetings on December 9 and 12, 1917, the Supreme Council of National Economy adopted resolutions calling for a normalization of trade with the Ukraine and specifically for the purchase of 17 million rubles of coal. Kurshchyn, *Gosudarstvennoe sotrudnichestvo*, p. 16.

20. Pipes, *Formation of the Soviet Union*, p. 120.

21. *Izvestiia*, No. 235, December 8, 1917.

22. *Istoriia sovetskoi konstitutsii*, p. 45. An English translation is available in Arnold D. Margolin, *From a Political Diary* (New York, 1946), p. 184. The complete note together with the reply of the Central Rada is printed in Bosh, *God bor'by*, pp. 81-84. See also James Bunyan and H. H. Fisher, *The Bolshevik Revolution* (Palo Alto, 1934), pp. 439-40.

23. Bosh, *God bor'by*, p. 82.

24. E. Bosh, one of the leaders of the Ukrainian Bolsheviks, attested to the effective manner in which the Central Rada used the ultimatum as a propaganda weapon. "The propaganda of the Central Rada, pretending that the Council of People's Commissars did not wish to recognize for the Ukrainian people the right to self-determination and therefore, so to speak, had forced war on the Ukraine, had as its consequence in the early period not only the development of a distrustful attitude on the part of the masses to all who supported the Council of People's Commissars — mainly, the Bolsheviks — but also it pushed many into the decision to support the Central Rada as the instrument of national power, even though it was not fully so. A number of workers and military organizations, not having representatives in the Central Rada, began to elect their delegates and to adopt resolutions giving full support to the Rada." Bosh, *God bor'by*, p. 110.

25. *Stalin*, IV, 8-9. See also pp. 15-21, 33-35.

26. A. V. Likholat, *Razgrom natsionalisticheskoi kontrrevoliutsii na Ukraine (1917-1922 gg.)* (Moscow, 1954), p. 34. The four men had been born in the Ukraine and had previously (before the February Revolution) been active in Party work there. However, all had worked in other areas of the Soviet Union and abroad and were considered loyal supporters of the Petrograd Bolsheviks. See also Suprunenko, *Velika zhovtneva sotsialistychna revoliutsiia*, pp. 13-47.

27. Bosh, *God bor'by*, p. 10.

28. Until July, 1917, united Bolshevik-Menshevik Social Democratic organizations remained in existence in parts of the Donbass. These were dissolved, and separate Bolshevik organizations established. See N. N. Popov, *Outline History of the Communist Party of the Soviet Union* (Moscow, 1934), I, 384, 394 (hereafter referred to as *History of the CPSU*); Suprunenko, *Velika zhovtneva sotsialistychna revoliutsiia*, p. 47.

29. Likholat, *Razgrom natsionalisticheskoi kontrrevoliutsii*, pp. 46-47. The commander of the troops was the Russian Bolshevik V. A. Antonov-Ovseenko.

30. Bosh, *God bor'by*, p. 11.

31. *Ibid.*, pp. 38-40.

32. The Bolshevik groups at Shostka and Konotop were the most active in the western Ukraine. *Ibid.*, p. 23.

33. In Volynia there was not a single local Party organization in June, 1917 and only "very weak" groups by November. *Ibid.*, pp. 22, 24. In Podolia the only active Party group was in Vinnitsa. *Ibid.*, pp. 23, 33.

34. In the Kherson province the largest Bolshevik groups were in Odessa, Nikolaev, and Elizavetgrad (Kirovograd). In all three cities the Bolsheviks had initially formed joint organizations with the Borotbists, and in Odessa the latter group was in control. In Nikolaev the Bolsheviks split with the Borotbists before the November Revolution, but remained somewhat apart from the Ukrainian Party organizations. The Elizavetgrad Bolsheviks did not separate from the Borotbists, but maintained closer ties with other Ukrainian Bolshevik groups. In the Poltava province the Bolsheviks and Borotbists were also united. Their joint organizations began to work with other Bolshevik groups in the Ukraine only after the November Revolution. *Ibid.*, pp. 24-26.

35. *Ibid.*, pp. 20-36. At the first Party regional conference in April, 1917, only four of the eight Ukrainian provinces were represented (Kiev, Chernigov, Volynia, and Podolia). Subsequent conferences were broader, with delegates from the Kherson and Poltava provinces and representatives from the Donets-Krivoi Rog Regional Party organization in the east.

36. At the Fourth and Fifth Party Conferences of the Southwestern Region held at the end of September and the middle of December representatives from the Donets-Krivoi Rog Region were present as observers. At the Fifth Party Conference it was decided to merge the Southwestern and Donets-Krivoi Rog regions into a single Regional Party Committee. The decision was not approved by the Donets-Krivoi Rog representative, however, nor confirmed by the eastern organization. *Ibid.*, p. 36.

37. N. R. Donii, "Obrazovanie Kommunisticheskoi partii Ukrainy" [Formation of the Communist Party of the Ukraine], *Voprosy istorii KPSS*, II, No. 3 (1958), 33-49.

38. B. P. Bortsov, N. N. Lipovchenko, and Ia. E. Pashko, "K osveshcheniiu voprosa ob obrazovanii KP(b) Ukrainy i ee taktiki v 1918 godu" [Toward the Clarification of the Question of the Formation of the CP(b) of the Ukraine and its Tactics in 1918], *Voprosy istorii KPSS*, IV, No. 3 (1960), 65-89.

39. Kurshchyn, *Gosudarstvennoe sotrudnichestvo*, pp. 11, 22. See also Donii, *Voprosy istorii KPSS*, II, No. 3, 33-49.

40. Pipes, *Formation of the Soviet Union*, p. 128. See also Lenin's telegram of February 3, 1918 (*ibid.*), and Stalin's mild statement to Ukrainian Bolsheviks on November 30, 1917. I. V. Stalin, *Statti i promovy pro Ukrainu* (Kiev, 1936), pp. 15-16. Also Kurshchyn, *Gosudarstvennoe sotrudnichestvo*, pp. 11, 22.

41. The period was characterized by N. Skrypnik as a period of decentralism. Party leaders later denied this and defined it as a period of growth. Lebed', *Sovetskaia Ukraina*, pp. 14-15.

42. At the time of the November Revolution Bolsheviks controlled the Shostka and Konotop soviets and "exercised great influence" in the soviets in Vinnitsa and Chernigov. Bosh, *God bor'by*, pp. 23-26. In the eastern Ukraine most of the soviets in the industrial centers of the Donbass were under Bolshevik control (Popov, *History of the CPSU*, I, 394), although a regional conference of soviets of the eastern Ukraine held in mid-October found the Bolsheviks still in a minority. Trotsky, *Russian Revolution*, p. 44.

43. The Bolsheviks controlled the Kiev Soviet of Workers' Deputies for a short period in the middle of September. At other times they were generally defeated by more moderate groups. The Soviet of Soldiers' Deputies was considered before the Revolution as an organ of the Russian Provisional Government. Bosh, *God bor'by*, pp. 55-60. In Kharkov the Bolsheviks were more successful, but they did not take control of the Soviet until December 25, 1917. *Ibid.*, pp. 88-92.

44. On November 17, in a meeting of the Kiev Soviet which included Mensheviks, Socialist Revolutionaries, and other groups as well as the Bolsheviks, a resolution favoring a speedy meeting of a Congress of Soviets was approved while a proposal that the Kiev groups withdraw immediately from participation in the Central Rada was rejected. *Ibid.*, pp. 58-59. Also, pp. 26, 48-50, and Appendix II.

45. In a note of November 30, 1917, Stalin, in the name of the Russian government, urged the Ukrainians to call a Congress of Soviets: "We all think that you — citizens of Kiev, Odessa, Kharkov, Katerinoslav and others should immediately declare yourselves for

the calling of such a Congress." *Statti*, pp. 15-16. See also N. N. Popov, *Oktiabr' na Ukraine* (Kiev, 1934), p. 58.

46. On December 7 the Kiev and Kharkov Soviets adopted resolutions approving the convocation of the Congress. At the urging of the Kiev Soviet the Odessa and Kremenchug Soviets adopted similar resolutions. Subsequently, the Kiev group sent invitations for the Congress to other soviets in the Ukraine. Suprunenko, *Velika zhovtneva sotsialistychna revoliutsiia*, pp. 83-84.

47. Bosh, *God bor'by*, p. 88.

48. *Izvestiia*, No. 254. December 30, 1917.

49. Pipes, *Formation of the Soviet Union*, p. 123.

50. Gustav Gratz and Richard Schuller, *The Economic Policy of Austria-Hungary During the War in Its External Relations* (New Haven, 1928), pp. 103-13.

51. Apparently the immediate cause of Trotsky's interruption of negotiations at Brest-Litovsk was his refusal to accept German recognition of the Central Rada as the government of an independent Ukrainian state. *Ibid.*, pp. 106-107, 112-13. See also John W. Wheeler-Bennett, *The Forgotten Peace, Brest Litovsk* (New York, 1939), pp. 219, 225-26.

52. U.S. Department of State, *Papers Relating to the Foreign Relations of the United States, 1918, Russia* (Washington D. C., 1931), I, 443.

53. *Stalin*, IV, 43. See also pp. 45-48.

54. *Lenin*, XXVII, 90. See also p. 296.

55. U.S. Department of State, *Papers Relating to the Foreign Relations of the United States, 1918, Russia*, II, 685.

56. *Stalin*, IV, 82-84. The Russians were anxious also to obtain coal and grain supplies, but it quickly became apparent that no supplies were available. An armistice was signed on June 21, but no agreement could be reached on the demarcation of the Russian-Ukrainian frontier. Subsequent negotiations were sporadic and uninspired, and were used by the Russians chiefly to carry on agitation in the Ukraine.

57. Bosh, *God bor'by*, pp. 90-92, 99-107. Bosh notes that the Kharkov Bolsheviks refused to assist in finding lodging or office space for the Kiev Bolsheviks, that they opposed the publication of the Kiev newspaper and refused to provide it with information, that there was argument over the name to be given the new Soviet government and over the question of the number of posts to be held by eastern as opposed to western Ukrainians.

58. *Ibid.*, p. 103.

59. Isaak Mints and E. Gorodetskii (eds.), *Dokumenty o razgrome germanskikh okkupantov na Ukraine v 1918 godu* (Moscow, 1942), p. 227; Bosh, *God bor'by*, pp. 107, 137. Bosh asserts that the establish-

ment of the republic was contrary to the wishes of Russian Party leaders, but there are other indications that Russian Bolsheviks approved the measure hoping it would prevent the German Army from occupying the Donbass. See Ravich-Cherkasskii, *Istoriia KP(b) U*, pp. 50-51; below, n. 61. Two other republics — Crimea and Odessa — were also established on Ukrainian territory but only nominally.

60. Bortsov, *Voprosy istorii KPSS*, IV, No. 3, 65-89.

61. V. A. Antonov-Ovseenko, *Zapiski o grazhdanskoi voine* (Moscow, 1924-1933), II, 23-24. Bosh emphasizes that the decision was taken only by the Ukrainian Soviet Republic and in the absence of representatives from the Donets-Krivoi Rog Republic. Bosh, *God bor'by*, p. 174. It is noteworthy that the meeting was held only two days after Bosh, Lebedev, and Piatakov — leaders of the western Bolsheviks — returned to the Ukraine from Petrograd. See also *ibid.*, Appendix 20.

62. The government of the Donets-Krivoi Rog Soviet Republic continued functioning separately unt.l the end of April when the eastern parts of the Ukraine were occupied by German forces. Mints and Gorodetskii, *Dokumenty*, p. 53. Indicative of the uncertain and cloudy state of affairs in the Ukraine in March and April was the selection of Artem to serve as Commissar of Trade and Industry for the Ukrainian Republic while he was also serving as Chairman of the Sovnarkom of the Donets-Krivoi Rog Republic. Bosh, *God bor'by*, pp. 137, 175-76.

63. See the "Resolution on State Structure" adopted by the Second All-Ukrainian Congress of Soviets, March 18, 1918 (Bosh, *God bor'by*, Appendix 20), and the "Declaration of the Ukrainian Central Executive Committee of Delegates from Soviet Organizations of the Ukraine to the IV Extraordinary All-Russian Congress of Soviets," March 16, 1918 (*Istoriia sovetskoi konstitutsii*, pp. 59-61).

64. Bortsov, *Voprosy istorii KPSS*, IV, No. 3, 65-89.

65. Bosh, *God bor'by*, pp. 218-23. There were no representatives from the Kharkov or Donets-Krivoi Rog regions at the Taganrog Conference. The resolution represented only the views of the western leaders and chiefly those from Kiev. Ravich-Cherkasskii, *Istoriia KP(b) U*, pp. 52, 56.

66. See Skrypnik's statement to the Eleventh Congress of the Russian Communist Party, *XI s″ezd RKP(b)*, pp. 78-79. A recent Soviet source suggests the decision was neither accepted nor rejected. N. R. Donii, *Voprosy istorii KPSS*, II, No. 3, 33-49.

67. Ravich-Cherkasskii, *Istoriia KP(b) U*, p. 55.

68. The name, Communist Party (Bolshevik) of the Ukraine (*Kommunisticheskaia Partiia [bol'shevikov] Ukrainy*), was adopted by the Conference to distinguish the Party from a non-Bolshevik

group, the Ukrainian Communist Party. The name is hereafter abbreviated as CP(b)U.

69. Of the 969 delegates to the Congress, 421 were Bolsheviks, 414 were Russian and Ukrainian Socialist Revolutionaries, 40 were Ukrainian Social Democrats, and the remainder were from scattered Parties or were without affiliation. Bosh, *God bor'by*, p. 177.

70. Maiorov notes that in May, 1918, there were no ties between the Kiev Bolsheviks and Moscow. At the end of May he and several other Bolsheviks came to Kiev and informed Party workers of developments within the Ukrainian *emigré* government. M. Maiorov, *Iz istorii revoliutsionnoi bor'by na Ukraine* (Kiev, 1922), pp. 82-83.

71. Kurshchyn, *Gosudarstvennoe sotrudnichestvo*, p. 34.

72. Kommunisticheskaia Partiia (bol'shevikov) Ukrainy, *Pervyi s''ezd Kommunisticheskoi Partii (b) Ukrainy* (Kharkov, 1923), p. 1; Ravich-Cherkasskii, *Istoriia KP(b) U*, pp. 69-82.

73. See the resolution, "Concerning the Party." The Ukrainian Party was to be autonomous where local questions were involved and was to supervise and control all Party organizations in the Ukraine including those established by Russian Bolsheviks. The resolution was adopted by 33 affirmative votes with 5 negative votes and 16 abstentions. See *Visti vseukrains'koho tsentral'noho vykonavchoho komitetu*, July 4, 1928.

74. Bortsov, *Voprosy istorii KPSS*, IV, No. 3, 65-89.

75. Nikolai N. Popov, *Narys istorii komunistychnoi partii (bil'shovykiv) Ukrainy*; 3rd ed. (Kharkov, 1928), pp. 171-72. See also Komunistychna Partiia (bil'shovykiv) Ukrainy, Tsentral'nyi Komitet, Otdel propagandy i agitatsii, *Borot'ba za radians'ku Ukrainu* (Kharkov, n.d.), pp. 25-48.

76. Maiorov, *Iz istorii*, pp. 91-92. Maiorov attributes the decision directly to Lenin. Apparently Lenin, despite his generally greater sympathy for national movements, failed in the period from mid-1918 to mid-1919 to understand the importance of Ukrainian nationalism. In March, 1919, he agreed with Piatakov that Ukrainian nationalism was less important than the nationalisms of other regions inasmuch as the Ukraine had been separated from Russia under unusual and artificial circumstances. *Lenin*, XXIX, 171-72.

77. *VKP(b) v rezol.*, I, 313. The italics are mine. The Party Rules adopted in 1919 as well as the 1922 revision were silent on the point — perhaps because the rules applied only to the Russian Communist Party. *Ibid.*, I, 326-31, 464-70.

78. On November 8, 1918, Lenin stated that "never have we been as near to an international proletarian revolution, as now." *Lenin*, XXVIII, 142. See also many other statements made in October and November. *Ibid.*, pp. 82-83, 94-97, 102-3, 109, 130-31, 144-45, 159.

79. Pipes, *Formation of the Soviet Union*, pp. 137-38. The principal negotiator for the Russian Bolsheviks was D. Manuil'skii, and for the Ukrainians, Vynnychenko. The agreement was consistent with Lenin's view that the Ukraine was a rural society which required a period of development and socialist education before a proletarian revolution could be accomplished.

80. *Stalin*, IV, 171-73, 163-66. See also Popov, *Narys istorii KP(b) U*, pp. 182-83.

81. Pipes, *Formation of the Soviet Union*, pp. 140-41.

82. See especially the reports of Khmel'nits'kyi and Sverdlov, *Visti*, March 5, 1919.

83. *Istoriia sovetskoi konstitutsii*, pp. 88-89.

84. The original constitution is printed in A. Malitskii (ed.), *Sobranie sovetskikh konstitutsii i konstitutsionnykh aktov* (Kharkov, 1928). An English translation including all amendments adopted to 1927 is available in W. R. Batsell, *Soviet Rule in Russia* (New York, 1929), pp. 388-401.

85. See the resolution adopted by the Eighth Conference of the Russian Communist Party (December, 1919), *VKP(b) v rezol.*, I, 322, 324-25.

86. *Istoriia sovetskoi konstitutsii*, p. 89. See also the manifesto of January 28, 1919, *ibid.*, pp. 103-5.

87. *L' Ukraine Sovietiste, Quatre Années de Guerre et de Blocus* (Berlin, 1922), p. 10.

88. Malitskii, *Sobranie*, Article I, Section 4.

89. Russia, Poland, Czechoslovakia, and Germany.

90. See especially the interesting series of notes between Rakovskii and Chicherin, the Russian Commissar of Foreign Affairs, dealing with the Polish question. *L' Ukraine Sovietiste*, pp. 145-55. The Ukraine here formally requested Russia, as a neutral third party, to mediate the Polish-Ukrainian dispute.

91. *Ibid.*, pp. 17-18. Of the thirty-two treaties or agreements to which the Soviet Ukraine was a party in the period from 1919 to 1924 (excluding those signed between the Soviet Ukraine and Soviet Russia), fifteen were negotiated and signed by representatives of the Russian government acting on behalf of the Ukraine, fourteen were negotiated at Moscow by representatives of Soviet Russia but were also signed by Ukrainian representatives, three were negotiated and signed by Ukrainian representatives alone, See Leonard Shapiro (ed.), *Soviet Treaty Series* (Washington, D. C., 1950), I, 22-222. For an official recognition of the influence exerted by Russia during this period see Andrei Y. Vyshinsky, *The Law of the Soviet State* (New York, 1948), pp. 261-62.

92. "Ob ob"edinenii voennykh sil sovetskikh respublik" (On Unification of the Military Forces of the Soviet Republics) (May 18, 1919), *Istoriia sovetskoi konstitutsii*, p. 122.

93. "Ob ob"edinenii sovetskikh respublik: Rosii, Ukrainy, Latvii Litvy, Belorussii dlia bor'by s mirovym imperializmom" [On Unification of the Soviet Republics: Russia, the Ukraine, Latvia, Lithuania, Belorussia for the Battle with World Imperialism] (June 1, 1919), Malitskii, *Sobranie*, pp. 206-7. The arrangement was not actually ratified by the Russians until the Seventh All-Russian Congress of Soviets, December, 1919. *S"ezdy sovetov vserossiiskie i Soiuza SSR v postanovleniiakh i rezoliutsiiakh* (Moscow, 1935), pp. 129-30. The Fourth All-Ukrainian Congress of Soviets ratified it in May, 1920. *Istoriia sovetskoi konstitutsii*, pp. 137-38.

94. Order of the Revolutionary War Soviet, No. 1020, Batsell, *Soviet Rule in Russia*, p. 245. For an extensive account, based on archival materials, of the day-by-day growth of Russian influence in the Ukraine, see Kurshchyn, *Gosudarstvennoe sotrudnichestvo*, pp. 45-119.

95. Majstrenko, *Borot'bism*, pp. 119-23. See below, pp. 96-97.

96. Pipes, *Formation of the Soviet Union*, p. 144.

97. The three members of the secretariat were Kosior, Farbman (Rafail), and Drobnis. Popov, *Narys istorii KP(b) U*, p. 222.

98. The most critical faction was a group known as the Federalists under the leadership of H. F. Lapchyns'kyi. The Federalists denounced the Russian Bolsheviks for failing to develop strength in Ukrainian rural areas, for viewing the Ukraine as nothing but a larder to supply raw materials needed in Russia, and for ignoring the class war in the Ukraine. At a conference held in Gomel in November, 1919, the Federalists, joined by a more moderate group including Manuil'skii, Zatons'kyi, and Kosior, demanded that the Ukrainian Party Central Committee be re-established and greater authority given Ukrainian state and Party organs. *Ibid.,* pp. 210-13; Ravich-Cherkasskii, *Istoriia KP(b) U*, pp. 136-38.

99. "O sovetskoi vlasti na Ukraine" [On Soviet Power in the Ukraine], *VKP(b) v rezol.*, I, 324-26. A similar resolution was subsequently adopted by the Central Committe of the CP(b)U.

100. See above, p. 51.

101. The government consisted of Petrovs'kyi, Rakovskii, Zatons'-kyi, Manuil'skii, and two non-Bolsheviks who were added somewhat later — Grin'ko and Kachins'kyi. The party center included Rakovskii, Zatons'kyi, Kosior, Petrovs'kyi, and Manuil'skii. Ravich-Cherkasskii, *Istoriia KP(b) U*, p. 139. See also Majstrenko, *Borot'bism*, pp. 170-71.

102. Majstrenko, *Borot'bism*, p. 170.

103. Initially the new party called itself the Ukrainian Socialist Revolutionary Party (Borotbist). On August 6, 1919, the party merged with a segment of the Ukrainian Social Democratic Workers' Party and the new name was adopted. *Ibid.*, pp. 64-69, 124, 136-38; *Kommunisticheskii international*, Vol. I, Nos. 7-8 (1919), cols. 1111-12.

104. Early in 1919 Lenin recommended that the Borotbists be drawn into the Ukrainian government in order to broaden its base of support. His advice was not taken, and in March, 1919, the Ukrainian Bolsheviks at their Third Party Congress agreed in a formal resolution not only to exclude the Borotbists from the government, but also to reject any suggestions that they merge with the CP(b)U. On specific instructions from the Russian Bolsheviks, however, the first part of the decision was reversed, and Borotbists were drawn into the government. Majstrenko, *Borot'bism*, pp. 120, 124-25; Pipes, *Formation of the Soviet Union*, pp. 143, 147. Nevertheless Bolshevik hostility to the Borotbists remained. In a resolution of May, 1919, the Russian Bolsheviks denounced the Borotbists bitterly and suggested that their party would soon be liquidated. Majstrenko, *Borot'bism*, pp. 144-46. See also the exchange between Lenin and Bubnov at the Ninth Congress of the Russian Communist Party: *IX s''ezd RSDRP(b)*, p. 143; *Lenin*, XXX, 438-39.

105. *Lenin*, XXX, 171-72. At the same time Lenin insisted that he did not agree with parts of the program of the Borotbists and that he did not favor an alliance with them.

106. The letter is dated December 28, 1919. *Lenin*, XXX, 270-72. As an immediate result of the more moderate policy, two Borotbists were added to the Ukrainian government.

107. At the Ninth Congress of the Russian Communist Party (March-April, 1920) Lenin noted: "When we in the Central Committee spoke of maximum concessions to the Borotbists, we were laughed at and told that we were not being straight-forward; but one can attack directly only when one's enemy pursues a straight line. Once the enemy decides to zigzag and not follow a straight line, we must pursue and catch him at every turn. We promised the Borotbists maximum concessions, but on condition that they pursue a communist policy. In this way we proved that we are not guilty of the slightest intolerance. That our concessions were right was proved by the fact that all the better elements of the Borotbists have entered now into our Party. We have re-registered that party and instead of a Borotbist uprising which would have been inevitable we have brought into our Party, under our control and with our recognition,... the best of the Borotbists, while the rest have vanished from the political scene." *Lenin*, XXX, 438-39.

108. Specifically the Bolsheviks opposed Borotbist efforts to construct a separate Ukrainian Red Army and to gain admission to the Communist International as a distinct Ukrainian communist party. See Majstrenko, *Borot'bism*, pp. 172-82, 184-87; *Kommunisticheskii internatsional*, Vol. I, Nos. 7-8 (1919), cols. 1125-26; Vol. II, No. 9 (1920), cols. 1655-56; Kommunisticheskii internatsional, *Vtoroi kongress Kominterna iiul'-avgust 1920 g.* (Moscow, 1934), p. 603. (Hereafter, reports of Comintern Congresses are referred to only by number, as follows: *II kongress Kominterna.*)

109. Majstrenko reasonably estimates the membership of the CP(b)U at about 20,000 to 25,000 (at the time of the merger), and the membership of the Borotbists at about 5,000 to 15,000. Of the latter group Skrypnik estimated that 4,000 joined the CP(b)U, although Petrovs'kyi had noted earlier and probably more accurately that there were only 554 Borotbists who had become "responsible" members of the CP(b)U. Majstrenko, *Borot'bism*, pp. 203, 206. For a comparison of the composition of the two parties see: *ibid.*, pp. 203-8; Popov, *Narys istorii KP(b) U*, p. 225; the address of Blakytnyi, one of the Borotbist leaders, to the Fifth Conference of the CP(b) U, reproduced in part in *ibid.*, pp. 248-52.

110. Popov, *Narys istorii KP(b) U*, p. 225. Stalin also hailed the merger, declaring that since the Borotbists were largely representatives of the rural areas they would strengthen Bolshevik efforts to construct an alliance between the proletariat and the peasants. *Stalin*, IV, 304.

111. The first three meetings of the CP(b)U (1918-1919) were labelled as congresses. Beginning with the fourth, the meetings were called conferences, suggesting their subordination to the congresses of the Russian Communist Party. After 1925 — beginning with the IX Congress of the CP(b)U — the earlier term was reestablished; subsequently, both congresses and conferences were held by the Party in keeping with the Russian practice.

112. Ravich-Cherkasskii, *Istoriia KP(b) U*, pp. 150-51.

113. Popov, *Narys istorii KP(b) U*, p. 228.

114. In addition to Sapronov, the opposition group was led by Maksimovskii and Sosnovskii — both recent arrivals in the Ukraine — and by a group of Russians who had formerly been active in Ukrainian Party work — Farbman, Ol. Ivanov, Boguslavskii, and others. *Ibid.*, p. 226.

115. The new Central Committee included seventeen members: eight from the Sapronov opposition (Sapronov, Farbman, Ol. Ivanov, Gamarnik, Drobnis, Gamzii, V. Kossior, and Kharchenko); seven loyal Bolsheviks (Piatakov, who was no longer in the Ukraine, Petrovs'kyi, Zatons'kyi, Chubar', Voroshilov, Kviring, and Minin); two former Borotbists (Blakytnyi and Shums'kyi). Petrovs'kyi,

Chubar', and the two Borotbists immediately withdrew in protest. *Ibid.*, p. 232.

116. Only indirect reference to the question was made by Lenin and Krestinskii, although there was heated debate over the question of Party democracy and the principle of "one-man control." The Ukrainian delegation to the Congress presented a brief statement defending the Ukrainian decisions but agreeing to avoid discussion. See the addresses of Lenin, Krestinskii, and Volin in *IX s"ezd RSD RP(b)*, pp. 30-42, 222-23.

117. The new Central Committee consisted of eleven regular Bolsheviks (Rakovskii, Kosior, Manuil'skii, Petrovs'kyi, Artem, Zatons'kyi, Chubar', Iakovlev, Minin, and Kon) and two former Borotbists (Blackytnyi and Shums'kyi). *Ibid.*, p. 222; Popov, *Narys istorii KP(b) U*, pp. 233-34.

118. Popov, *Narys istorii KP(b) U*, pp. 233-34. See also the conforming resolution of the CP(b)U, "Instruktsiia TsK KP(b)U po pererehistratsii vsikh chleniv KP(b)U" [Instructions of the CC of the CP(b)U on Reregistration of all Members of the CP(b)U] (June 30, 1920), Komunistychna Partiia (bil'shovykiv) Ukrainy, Tsentral'nyi Komitet, Instytut istorii partii, Kyiv, *Istoriia KP(b) U v materialakh i dokumentakh*; 2 vols. (Kiev, 1933), II, 576-77.

119. Sapronov and other functionaries supporting him were withdrawn from the Ukraine by central authority. Popov, *History of the CPS U*, II, 87. By the time of the Fifth Conference of the CP(b)U (November, 1920) only about twenty delegates of 318 continued to attack central leadership *Ibid.*, pp. 238-46.

120. "The Congress unanimously endorses the efforts of the CEC and Sovnarkom of the Ukraine to strengthen the existing close union between the Ukrainian workers and peasants and their Russian brothers in the battle with enemies of Soviet Power. . . . [It] affirms that the UkSSR, preserving its independent state constitution, is a member of the All-Russian Socialist Soviet Federated Republic. . . . The Fourth All-Ukrainian Congress of Soviets, ratifying the agreement between the CEC's of the UkSSR and the RSFSR concerning the unification of the commissariats of war, finance, railroads, national economy, posts and telegraphs, and labor [the agreement of June 1, 1919] — entrusts to the future CEC to carry out and advance this same policy toward closer amalgamation. . . . [The Congress] looks forward with confidence to a future time when to the federation of the Soviet republics of Russia and the Ukraine, there will be added new allies, and a great international republic of Soviets will be formed." Kh. Rakovskii, *Otchet raboche-krest'ianskogo pravitel'stva Ukrainy IV-mu vseukrainskomu s"ezdu sovetov rabochikh, krest'ianskikh i krasnoarmeiskikh deputatov* (Kharkov, 1920), pp. 27-29. See also *Istoriia sovetskoi konstitutsii*, pp. 137-38.

121. "O vkliuchenii chlenov ukrainskogo TsIK v sostav VTsIK" [On the Inclusion of Members of the Ukrainian CEC in the Composition of the All-Russian CEC], *Istoriia sovetskoi konstitutsii*, p. 139.

122. "Workers'-Peasants' Treaty Alliance," Shapiro, *Soviet Treaty Series*, I, 83-84.

123. See above, pp. 50-51; *VKP(b) v rezol.*, I, 322, 324-25; Majstrenko, *Borot'bism*, p. 122; Rakovskii, *Otchet IV-mu s"ezdu*, pp. 22-23.

124. *Soviet Russia* (December 11, 1920), p. 571, quoted in Alfred L. P. Dennis, *The Foreign Policies of Soviet Russia* (New York, 1924), p. 187.

125. Statement of the Ukrainian Commissar of Foreign Affairs, V. I. Iakovlev, *Izvestiia*, August 13, 1922.

III. FEDERALISM AND UKRAINIAN CULTURAL NATIONALISM, 1921-1927

1. Stalin, *Marxism and the National Question*, p. 120.

2. *VKP(b) v rezol.*, I, 393.

3. Rakovskii, *Otchet IV-mu s"ezdu*, pp. 22-23.

4. See above, p. 87.

5. Popov, *Narys istorii KP(b) U*, p. 236.

6. Kh. Rakovs'kyi, "Novyi etap v radians'komu soiuznomu budivnytstvi" [New Stage in Soviet Union Construction], *Chervonyi shliakh*, II, No. 1 (January 1923), 69. For a recent Soviet statement on the question, see Kurshchyn, *Gosudarstvennoe sotrudnichestvo*, pp. 45-119, 142-44.

7. *XI s"ezd RKP(b)*, pp. 77-79. Skrypnik suggested that even the unification of the Communist Party as announced at the Eighth Party Congress was incorrect and that the right of the CP(b)U to independence including representation in the Communist International should be affirmed.

8. Popov, *Narys istorii KP(b) U*, pp. 261-70. A special Party meeting was held in May, 1921, and the Sixth Party Conference met in October. Popov notes that the Party was dominated by problems of internal organization and the New Economic Policy.

9. *Stalin*, V, 138.

10. *XI s"ezd RKP(b)*, pp. 121-24.

11. "Deklaratsiia ob obrazovanii Soiuza Sotsialisticheskikh Sovetskikh Respublikh" [Declaration on the Formation of a Union of Socialist Soviet Republics], *Istoriia sovetskoi konstitutsii*, pp. 234-35. See also Akademiia Nauk SSSR. Institut istorii, *Obrazovanie SSSR, Sbornik dokumentov, 1917-1924* (Moscow 1949), pp. 290-300. (Hereafter referred to as AN SSSR, *Obrazovanie SSSR.*) The resolution was adopted unanimously on December 13, 1922, by the

Seventh Congress of Soviets of the UkSSR. Apparently the resolution was in direct response to an instruction sent from Moscow. Walter R. Batsell, *Soviet Rule in Russia* (New York, 1929), p. 276.

12. "Ob osnovakh konstitutsii Soiuza Sotsialisticheskikh Sovetskikh Respublikh" [On the Fundamentals of the Constitution of the Union of Socialist Soviet Republics], *Istoriia sovetskoi konstitutsii* (December 13, 1922), pp. 237-39. Stalin, who was chairman of the drafting commission preparing a preliminary treaty of union, outlined the position of the commission on November 13. *Stalin*, V, 143-44, 411.

13. Pipes, *Formation of the Soviet Union*, p. 272.

14. *Ibid.*, pp. 272-78. See below, pp. 134-35.

15. At the Twelfth Congress of the RCP(b) Rakovskii stated, "Comrades, I assert that union construction has proceeded along an incorrect path. As is known to you, this is not only my opinion — it is also the opinion of Vladimir Il'ich." *XII s″ezd RKP(b)*, p. 534.

16. Kh. G. Rakovskii, "Otnosheniia mezhdu sovetskimi respublikami, Rossiia i Ukraina" (Relations between the Soviet Republics, Russia and the Ukraine), *Kommunisticheskii internatsional*, Vol. II, No. 12 (1920), cols. 2197-2202.

17. See note 178 in *Lenin* (3rd ed.), XXIV, 818-19.

18. See above, p. 90; Rakovskii's report to the Third All-Ukrainian Congress of Soviets, *Visti*, March 14, 1919.

19. Rakovskii, *Kommunisticheskii international*, Vol. II, No. 12, Cols. 2201-2202.

20. Rakovs'kyi, *Chervonyi shliakh*, II, No. 1, pp. 79-81, 83-85; Kh. H. Rakovs'kyi, *Piat' rokiv ukrains'koi radians'koi vlady* (Kharkov, 1923), pp. 7-9.

21. "As long as centralization means the concentration of power in the hands of one central organ and the transformation of all the masses of the population into obedient instruments for the execution of the orders of the central power, as long as centralization means the destruction of initiative, of economic, political and administrative self-help, . . . as long as centralization means that type of deadly, bureaucratic centralization that has been a synonym for injustice, then of course there is no greater enemy of Soviet power than centralization. . . . Against such centralization Communists must at all times battle resolutely." *Ibid.*, p. 82. See also pp. 70-84.

22. *XII s″ezd RKP(b)*, pp. 349-50, 531-34.

23. It has been suggested that Rakovskii, as one of Trotsky's close friends, was acting primarily in opposition to Stalin. Pipes, *Formation of the Soviet Union*, p. 278. This seems unlikely both in view of Trotsky's indifference to the national question and to Rakovskii's pleading, and in view of the uncertainty of Stalin's

position in the early months of 1923. See Edward Hallett Carr, *A History of Soviet Russia*; 4 vols. (New York, 1951-1954), IV, 268-85.

24. The treaty is included in *Stalin*, V, 396-401.

25. Ten of the representatives were from the RSFSR, three from the Ukraine, and one each from Belorussia and the Transcaucasian Federation. The Ukrainian delegates were probably Rakovskii, Skrypnik, and Manuil'skii. The commission was divided into six sub-commissions, each given responsibility for a portion of the draft. V. I. Ignat'ev, *Sovetskii stroi* (Moscow, 1928), pp. 29-31; AN SSSR *Obrazovanie SSSR*, pp. 339-42.

26. AN SSSR, *Obrazovanie SSSR*, p. 341.

27. *Stalin*, V, 143. Stalin had earlier agreed, however, that each minority nationality should be represented in the Union Central Executive Committee. *Lenin*, XXXIII, 335.

28. *Stalin*, V, 449.

29. Pipes, *Formation of the Soviet Union*, p. 278. The Council of Nationalities as established under the constitution comprised the membership of the Council of Nationalities Stalin had formed in 1921 as part of the RSFSR Commissariat of Nationality Affairs plus representatives from the three other republics.

30. AN SSSR, *Obrazovanie SSSR*, p. 342.

31. Ignat'ev, *Sovetskii stroi*, p. 32. The commission was enlarged on April 27 by the addition of ten new members — four from the RSFSR and two each from the Ukraine, Belorussia, and the Transcaucasian Federation. AN SSSR, *Obrazovanie SSSR*, p. 370.

32. *Stalin*, V, 425, 429. The commission was appointed by the Central Committee on February 24, 1923. Stalin was named chairman.

33. A majority of the members of the Central Committee of the CP(b)U supported Rakovskii. *XII s″ezd RKP(b)*, p. 607. Among the majority were Kviring, Skrypnik, Grin'ko, and probably Frunze and Petrovs'kyi. At the Twelfth Party Congress Rakovskii claimed to have the support of the entire Ukrainian delegation, which would have included at least eleven members of the Ukrainian Central Committee: A. Ivanov, Chubar', Frunze, Grin'ko, Kuznetsov, Kviring, Lebed', Manuil'skii, Petrovs'kyi, Skrypnik, and Ugarov. *Ibid.*, p. 603. Kviring subsequently reversed himself and declared his support for Stalin. *Ibid.*, p. 607.

34. *Ibid.*, p. 529.

35. *Ibid.*, pp. 460-62, 522-26, 528-34, 602-5.

36. *Ibid.*, pp. 603-5.

37. *Ibid.*, p. 606. The proposal was made to the Twelfth Party Congress and was defeated by a voice vote.

38. See *Stalin*, V, 342-43; Ignat'ev, *Sovetskii stroi*, p. 45. The suggestion was referred later to the constitutional commission of the Central Executive Committee.

39. *XII s"ezd RKP(b)*, pp. 460-61, 533-34.

40. The draft is given in Ignat'ev, *Sovetskii stroi*, pp. 123-28. A similar project was submitted by the Belorussian Republic. *Ibid.*, pp. 129-37.

41. Three classes of commissariats were established by the 1924 constitution: Union commissariats, operating under the exclusive jurisdiction of the Union government; Union-republic or directive commissariats, administering areas of concurrent jurisdiction; republic commissariats, functioning in areas exclusively within the jurisdiction of the republics. See below, pp. 77-78.

42. *Stalin*, V, 336.

43. See the brief exchange between Stalin and Rakovskii at the Fourth Conference of the Central Committee of the RCP(b). *Stalin*, V, 341.

44. *Stalin*, V, 313, 325, 419. Apparently Manuil'skii did not support Skrypnik and Rakovskii. *Ibid.*, p. 336.

45. Both Skrypnik and Grin'ko complained to the Twelfth Party Congress of the negative attitude toward the national question shown at the Seventh All-Ukrainian Party Conference. *XII s"ezd RKP(b)*, pp, 459-60. See below, pp. 105-6.

46. For Bolshevik statements denouncing federalism see *Lenin*, XX, 411; Vyshinsky, *Law of the Soviet State*, pp. 220-28; the references in Julian Towster, *Political Power in the USSR, 1917-1947* (New York, 1948), pp. 61-62. The Bolsheviks agreed to accept a federal system only after the Revolution and then only as a transitional form. In a resolution of March 23, 1919, the Eighth Congress of the Russian Communist Party declared that "the Party recognizes as one of the transition steps on the path to complete union, a federative union of the states, organized along Soviet lines." *VKP(b) v rezol.*, I, 295. For earlier statements see *Stalin*, IV, 8-9; *Lenin*, XXII, 135-36; XXVI, 435; XXVII, 130, 132, 180-82. See also *VKP(b) v rezol.*, I, 391-97; *II kongress kominterna*, p. 91.

47. *XII s"ezd RKP(b)*, pp. 349, 460-62, 523.

48. "The merging of the commissariats is a test for the Soviet apparatus: if this experiment were in practice to assume a great nation tendency, the Party would be compelled to adopt the most resolute measures against such a distortion, even to the extent of raising the question of annulling the merging of certain commissariats until such time as the Soviet apparatus has been properly re-trained, so that it will pay genuinely proletarian and genuinely fraternal attention to the needs and requirements of the small and backward nationalities." *Stalin*, V, 190. See also pp. 264, 313-26; *VKP(b) v rezol.*, I, 505.

49. *VKP(b) v rezol.*, I, 502-3, 505-6.

50. The constitution, including amendments adopted in 1925, is published in *Sistematicheskoe sobranie deistvuiushchikh zakonov SSSR* (Moscow, 1927), I, 3-15. A translation is given in Batsell, *Soviet Rule in Russia*, pp. 303-20.

51. The Ukrainian constitution as amended in 1925 and ratified in 1929 included sixteen articles dealing with these matters (Articles 18 to 33). The articles were identical with those previously written into the constitutuion of the RSFSR. For the republic constitutions see G. S. Gurvich, F. T. Ivanov, and V. Maksimovskii, *Sovetskoe gosudarstvennoe ustroistvo* (Moscow, 1930), pp. 245-303.

52. Under the republic constitutions adopted after 1924 the commissariats for internal trade and national minorities were eliminated.

53. In the period when the Central Executive Committee was not in session, its presidium was empowered to annul decisions of the republic councils of people's commissars and central executive committees and to suspend decisions of the republic congresses of soviets (Articles 31-32).

54. *Vtoroi s"ezd Sovetov SSSR. Stenograficheskii otchet* (Moscow, 1924), p. 106. (Hereafter, reports of USSR Congresses of Soviets are referred to only by number, as follows: *II S"ezd Sovetov SSSR.*) See also Skrypnik's defense of the RSFSR, *ibid.*, pp. 106-7.

55. *III s"ezd Sovetov SSSR* (May, 1925), p. 103. See also the report by Solodub, *ibid.*, pp. 132-34.

56. SSSR, Tsentral'nyi ispolnitel'nyi komitet, *Vtoraia sessiia tsentral'nogo ispolnitel'nogo komiteta SSSR, II sozyva. Stenograficheskii otchet* (Moscow, 1924), pp. 425-26. (Hereafter, reports of sessions of the USSR Central Executive Committee are referred to only by number of session and convocation, as follows: *II sessiia TsIK SSSR, II sozyva.*)

57. *Ibid.*, pp. 426-27.

58. *III sessiia TsIK SSSR, I zozyva*, pp. 7-25, 103-10.

59. *II sessiia TsIK SSSR, II sozyva*, pp. 305-10, 326-33, 333-35, 573-86.

60. *Ibid.*, pp. 424-28, 445-47, 467-71, 475-77, 616-23. See also *II sessiia TsIK SSSR, III sozyva*, pp. 616-24.

61. *S"ezdy Sovetov SSSR v postanovleniiakh i rezoliutsiiakh* (Moscow, 1939), pp. 57-63, 70, 71.

62. Vsesoiuznyi institut iuridicheskikh nauk ministerstva iustitsii SSSR, *Ocherki po istorii organov sovetskoi gosudarstvennoi vlasti* (Moscow, 1949), p. 125. (Hereafter referred to as VIIuN, *Ocherki po istorii.*) In November, 1925, the Commissariat was joined with the Commissariat of Foreign Trade, but no change in its Union-republic status was made.

63. *Ibid.*, p. 158.

64. See Chubar's criticism to the Fifteenth Party Conference (November, 1926) and Rykov's agreement on behalf of the Party leadership. *XV konferentsiia VKP(b)*, pp. 147, 263. See also Chubar's comment on a decision of the April Plenum of the Party Central Committee. *Ibid.*, p. 147.

65. *Lenin*, XX, 368-69, 372, 373, 377-78; XXI, 373, 374, 377.

66. *Lenin*, XX, 384, 410, 421; XXII, 307.

67. *Lenin*, XX, 384-85, 412; XXII, 140.

68. *Lenin*, XX, 383-84. See also pp. 382, 413.

69. *Lenin*, XX, 384, 422.

70. *Lenin*, XX, 407. See also p. 385.

71. *VKP(b) v rezol.*, I, 324-26. Contrast with an earlier statement minimizing the importance of nationalism in the Ukraine. *Lenin*, XXIX, 171-72.

72. Figures are for 1920. See Nikolai N. Popov, *Natsional'naia politika sovetskoi vlasti* (Moscow, 1927), p. 98. See also V. Zhebrovs'kyi, *Rist partii* (Kharkov, 1930), p. 86.

73. *Stalin*, V, 28. See also pp. 24, 27-29; *VKP(b) v rezol.*, I, 391-97.

74. *Stalin*, V, 24.

75. *Stalin*, V, 49.

76. The notes were dated December 30 and 31, 1922. They were first officially published in 1956: "K voprosy o natsional'nostiakh ili ob 'avtonomizatsii'" [On the Question of the Nationalities or of "Autonomization"], *Kommunist*, XXXIII, No. 9 (June, 1956), 22-26. A translation of a copy made by Trotsky is included in Pipes, *Formation of the Soviet Union*, pp. 273-77. See also Lenin's brief note of October 6, 1922. *Lenin*, XXXIII, 335.

77. See above, pp. 65-76; Pipes, *Formation of the Soviet Union*, pp. 271, 279-80.

78. *VKP(b) v rezol.*, I, 501-7. See also *XII s"ezd RKP (b)*; *Stalin*, V, 181-94, 236-80.

79. *VKP(b) v rezol.*, I, 504.

80. "Prakticheskie meropriiatiia po provedeniiu v zhizn' rezoliutsii XII s"ezda partii po natsional'nomu voprosu" [Practical Measures for Carrying Out the Resolution of the XII Congress of the Party on the National Question], *ibid.*, I, 540-41. See also *Stalin*, V, 291-341. The resolution was prepared by Stalin and endorsed by the Politburo of the Russian Communist Party.

81. *Stalin*, V, 318-19. The italics are mine.

82. *Kommunist*, XXXIII, No. 9, 26.

83. *Stalin*, V, 238-39, 244-45.

84. *Stalin*, V, 244-47.

85. "If the task of our Party lies in making Soviet power important to the masses, we must recognize that this can only be achieved by

making Soviet power understandable to the masses." *Stalin*, V, 319. See also pp. 293-94, 314, 319-21.

86. *Stalin*, V, 329-30.

87. The composition of the government as established on March 14, 1919, is given in *Visti*, March 15, 1919. At least eight of the principal members of the government, including Rakovskii, Podvoiskii, and Voroshilov, were opposed to a separate development for Ukrainian institutions.

88. *Visti*, January 3, 1919; Majstrenko, *Borot'bism*, p. 122; *Lenin* (3d ed.), XXIV, 818-19.

89. *Visti*, March 16 and May 7, 1919.

90. A Soviet source suggests that over half the members of the Communist Party were serving in the army and an additional large group were mobilized "on the labor front." H. P. Kravchenko, *Partiina orhanizatsiia Ukrainy v borot'bi za dal'she zmitznennia iednosti partii* (Kiev, 1954), p. 32. In October, 1920, 37,384 of the 73,113 Party members in the Ukraine were military personnel. *Ibid.*, p. 39.

91. Komunistychna Partiia (bil'shovykiv) Ukrainy, Tsentral'nyi Komitet, Instytut istorii partii, Kyiv. *Heroichnyi shliakh borot'by i peremog* (Kiev, 1950), p. 60. (Hereafter referred to as KP(b)U, TsK, *Heroichnyi shliakh*.)

92. *Visti*, February 27, 1930.

93. Popov, *Narys istorii KP(b)U*, pp. 232-33.

94. Cf. Vynnychenko's account in Parti Communiste Ukrainien (Groupe étranger), *La Révolution en Danger* (Vienna, 1921), pp. 16-26, with the Soviet account in *Bol'shaia sovetskaia entsiklopediia*; 1st ed. (Moscow, 1930), Vol. XI, col. 67. (Hereafter referred to as *BSE*; unless otherwise noted, references are to the first edition.) The latter states that Vynnychenko insisted on membership in the Politburo of the CP(b)U, a position that was refused him.

95. See the resolution adopted on September 21, 1920, "O vvedenii ukrainskogo iazyka v shkolakh i sovetskikh uchrezhdeniiakh" [On Establishing the Ukrainian Language in Schools and Soviet Institutions], Andrii Khvylia, *Natsional'nyi vopros na Ukraine* (Kharkov, 1926), pp. 121-22.

96. Popov, *Narys istorii KP(b) U*, p. 279.

97. See the decision of the Central Committee of the RCP(b), quoted in part in Majstrenko, *Borot'bism*, pp. 214-15.

98. Popov, *Narys istorii KP(b) U*, pp. 228-29.

99. See above, pp. 59-60.

100. Popov, *Narys istorii KP(b) U*, pp. 228-31, 247.

101. See above, n. 98, p. 340.

102. Popov, *Narys istorii KP(b) U*, n. 2, p. 232.

103. Ie. F. Girchak, *Na dva fronta v bor'be s natsionalizmom*; 2d ed. (Moscow, 1931), p. 35; Kravchenko, *Partiina orhanizatsiia Ukrainy*, p. 48.

104. Popov, *Narys istorii KP(b) U*, p. 247.

105. Zinoviev was supported by others at the Conference. See *ibid.*, p. 248; Ia. Iakovlev, "Proty novoi vylazky ukhyl'nykiv v bik ukrains'koho natsionalizmu" [Against the New Attack of Deviators on the Side of Ukrainian Nationalism], *Istoriia KP(b) U*, pp. 636-37.

106. Popov, *Narys istorii KP(b)U*, p. 248.

107. *Ibid.*, p. 250. See also the address of Comrade Bron', referred to on p. 251.

108. *Ibid.*, p. 247.

109. Molotov was elected to the Central Committee of the CP(b)U by the Fifth Conference and was subsequently chosen First Secretary of the Party—a post he held until March, 1921. Kravchenko, *Partiina orhanizatsiia Ukrainy*, p. 49.

110. The Ukrainian Party Council of May, 1921, endorsed the decisions of the Eighth Conference of the RCP(b). Popov, *Narys istorii KP(b) U*, p. 279; Majstrenko, *Borot'bism*, p. 216; Kravchenko, *Partiina orhanizatsiia Ukrainy*, pp. 110-12. The verification of Party membership in the Ukraine was accomplished in the period from July to October, 1921.

111. Skrypnik noted to the Twelfth Party Congress (April, 1923) that as a result of the purges in the Ukraine, only 118 of the 4,000 Borotbists who had initially entered the Party remained members. *XII s"ezd RKP(b)*, p. 524.

112. On the effects of the purge, see Popov, *Narys istorii KP(b) U*, pp. 266, 275-76, 280.

113. *Ibid.*, p. 270. Shums'kyi was then Ukrainian ambassador to Poland. Majstrenko, *Borot'bism*, p. 261. He was re-elected to the Central Committee in 1924. *Visti*, May 18, 1924.

114. Popov, *Narys istorii KP(b) U*, p. 280.

115. *Ibid.*, p. 281.

116. Lebed', *Sovetskaia Ukraina*, p. 29.

117. "We know theoretically that a battle of the two cultures [city and village] is inevitable. For us in the Uk., as a result of historical conditions, the culture of the city is Russian, the culture of the village is Ukrainian.... To set for ourselves the task to Ukrainize actively the Party, and necessarily also the workers class, ... will serve the interests of the cultural movement of reactionary forces since nationalization, that is the artificial dissemination of the Ukrainian language in the Party and workers' class under the present political, economic, and cultural relations between the cities and villages—means to adopt the lower culture

of the village in preference to the higher culture of the city." Girchak, *Na dva fronta*, pp. 20-21; Popov, *Narys istorii KP(b) U*, p. 281.

118. *Ibid.*

119. See above, pp. 90-91.

120. Popov, *Narys istorii KP(b) U*, pp. 281-82. See also Grin'ko's address to the Twelfth Congress, *XII s"ezd RKP(b)*, pp. 459-60. The faction was also silent at the Twelfth Congress.

121. See Skrypnik's address to the Twelfth Party Congress, *XII s"ezd RKP(b)*, p. 526.

122. *Ibid.*, p. 460. See also pp. 459-62, 522-26. Skrypnik noted as a typical example that following the Conference a high Party official, when addressed in Ukrainian, responded bluntly, "Speak to me in an intelligible language !" *Ibid.*, p. 526.

123. *Stalin*, V, 329-30.

124. Popov, *Narys istorii KP(b) U*, pp. 282-83; *XII s"ezd RKP(b)*, pp. 523-25.

125. *BSE*, Vol. LXI (1934), cols. 696-97; *Malaia sovetskaia entsiklopediia*, Vol. VII (Moscow, 1930), col. 168. (Hereafter referred to as *MSE*.)

126. See Carr, *History of Soviet Russia*, IV, 289-90.

127. See Chubar's statement in *Rechi na sobraniiakh izbiratelei v verkhovnyi sovet SSSR* (Moscow, 1938), pp. 80-86.

128. *BSE*, Vol. XXXII (1936), col. 131. Cf., however, his emphasis on the importance of the peasant question, E. Kviring, *Uroki gruzinskogo vosstaniia* (Kharkov, 1925), pp. 26-31.

129. See above, n. 33, p. 346.

130. E. Kviring, "Krutyi povorit chy rozhortannia popered'noi roboty" [A Sharp Change Or a Continuation of Previous Work], *Chervonyi shliakh*, II, Nos. 4-5 (1923), 107-12.

131. *XII s"ezd RKP(b)*, pp. 522-26.

132. John A. Armstrong, *Ukrainian Nationalism* 1939-1945 (New York, 1955), p. 13.

133. *Visti*, April 22, 1926.

134. *X s"ezd RKP(b)*, pp. 205-9.

135. Popov, *Narys istorii KP(b) U*, n. 1, p. 280.

136. "O merakh obespecheniia ravnopraviia iazykov i o sodeistvii razvitiiu ukrainskogo iazyka" [On Measures for Guaranteeing the Equality of Languages and on the Equal Development of the Ukrainian Language], quoted in Khvylia, *Natsional'nyi vopros*, pp. 115-16. See also *Visti*, October 8, 1924; May 20, 1925.

137. *Visti*, October 8, 1924.

138. *Visti*, August 29, 1924. See also the resolution on the press adopted by the Thirteenth Party Congress, *VKP(b) v rezol.*, I, 610-15.

139. "Pro zakhody terminovoho perevedennia povnoi ukrainizatsii radians'koho aparatu" [On Measures for the Decisive Achivement

of Full Ukrainization of the Soviet Apparatus] (April 30, 1925), *Visti*, May 20, 1925; Khvylia, *Natsional'nyi vopros*, pp. 123-28.

140. *Visti*, August 9, 1924.

141. *Ibid.* These figures probably exaggerate the use of Ukrainian. Cf. the figures given in August, 1925, which reported only 25 percent of the 653 higher schools teaching exclusively in Ukrainian and only 25 percent, partially. *Visti*, August 6, 1925.

142. *Visti*, August 9, 1924, and January 3, 1925.

143. "Postanova plenumu TsK KP(b)U pro ukrainizatsiiu" [Decision of the Plenum of the CC of the CP(b)U on Ukrainization], *Visti*, May 9, 1925. See also Khvylia, *Natsional'nyi vopros*, pp. 108-14.

144. *Stalin*, V, 294.

145. "Tezisy plenuma TsK i TsKK KP(b)U ob itogakh ukrainizatsii" [Theses of the Plenum of the CC and CCC of the CP(b)U on the Results of Ukrainization] (June 1926), *Visti*, June 15, 1926.

146. *Stalin*, IV, 10.

147. See above, p. 98.

148. *VKP(b) v rezol.*, I, 540-41; .*Stalin*, V, 309, 323.

149. The system was adopted for the Ukraine by a decision of the Eighth Ukrainian Congress of Soviets (January, 1924). The system was described as not only a method of defense but also a means of solidifying ties between workers and peasants. A. Butsenko, *Desiat' vseukrains'kykh z'izdiv rad* (Kharkov, 1927), p. 76.

150. The district was not conterminous with the Ukraine, but included also the Crimea. Its commander was the old Russian Bolshevik, Mikhail Frunze, a leading member of the Central Committee of the CP(b)U and ultimately (January to November, 1925), Commissar of Military Affairs for the USSR.

151. *Visti*, March 7, 1924; June 10, 1924.

152. *Visti*, May 9, 1925. See also December 31, 1925.

153. *Stalin*, V, 49.

154. See above, n. 117, pp. 351-52.

155. Popov, *Narys istorii KP(b) U*, p. 284.

156. "Postanova plenumu TsK KP(b)U pro ukrainizatsiiu" [Decision of the Plenum of the CC of the CP(b)U on Ukrainization], *Visti*, May 9, 1925.

157. *Visti*, November 29, 1925.

158. The three westernmost provinces in the Ukraine—Kiev, Volynia, and Podolia—reported to a governor general at Kiev. Pipes, *Formation of the Soviet Union*, pp. 4-5.

159. *Stalin*, V, 318-19.

160. Butsenko, *Desiat' vseukrains'kykh z'izdiv*, p. 85; Arsen Khomenko, *Natsional'nyi sklad liudnosty USRR* (Poltava, 1931), pp. 141-44; *XIV s"ezd VKP(b)*, p. 886.

161. *XIV s"ezd VKP(b)*, p. 886. See also his earlier report to the Kharkov guberniia committee, *Visti*, April 10, 1925.

162. Popov, *Narys istorii KP(b) U*, p. 286.

163. See the resolution of the Executive Committee of the Comintern, "Pro ukrains'ku komunistychnu partiiu" [On the Ukrainian Communist Party] (December 24, 1924), *Visti*, January 8, 1925. Cf. the resolution of the Comintern concerning the Borotbists wherein it was emphasized that "the Communist International demands that in every country there be only one Communist party." *Kommunist*, February 29, 1920.

164. *Vtoroi kongress kominterna*, pp. 411-12. The Party's membership was estimated at 100 to 500.

165. Popov, *Narys istorii KP(b) U*, p. 286; KP(b)U, TsK, *Heroichny shliakh*, p. 79.

166. "Pro ukrain'sku komunistychnu partiiu," *Visti*, January 8, 1925.

167. "Likvidatsiinyi z'izd livoi fraktsyi UKP" [Liquidating Congress of the Left Fraction of the UCP], *Visti*, March 12, 1925.

168. See for example the position taken by E. Kviring in *Uroki gruzinskogo*, pp. 34-36.

169. *Visti*, March 4, 1925.

170. "Pro ukrains'ku komunistychnu partiiu," *Visti*, January 8, 1925.

171. Popov, *Narys istorii KP(b) U*, pp. 304-5.

172. *Visti*, April 8, 1925.

173. Popov, *Narys istorii KP(b) U*, pp. 226-36, 240-46, 258-59, 265-69, 275-76, 290-91, 299-300, 304-5.

174. See the report given by Kaganovich to the Fifteenth Party Congress, *XV s"ezd VKP(b)*, pp. 137-38.

175. Soviet sources subsequently ascribed to Kaganovich a key role in the battle against Ukrainian nationalists. See his official biography in *BSE*, Vol. XXX (1937), col. 516.

176. See above, pp. 45-46.

177. *XIV s"ezd VKP(b)*, pp. 876-82. The proposal had first been presented by Skrypnik to the Twelfth Party Congress (April, 1923), but a decision had been postponed. *XII s"ezd RKP(b)*, pp. 606-607.

178. A. Andreev, presenting the report on changes in the rules, noted that the formation of a Russian Party and a Russian Central Committee in addition to the All-Union organizations would be a great danger to the Party. "But, comrades, has there been up to the present any necessity for the organization of a Russian Party? Has there been any need for the formation of a special Russian Central Committee?" There had not, Andreev declared, and a change of Party name did not now make these institutions necessary. *XIV s"ezd VKP(b)*, p. 881.

179. "A change in the name of the national parties would mean absolutely nothing, since our national party organizations exist basically under the same rules as the guberniia and oblast organizations, yet such a change of names of the separate national parties would of course inevitably weaken us politically;" and again, "in contrast to the moderate degree of decentralization in the structure of our Soviet Union, the Party remains a centralized, united Party from top to bottom." *Ibid.*, pp. 881-82. See also pp. 889-90.

180. *VKP(b) v rezol.*, II, 85.

181. In reply to objections, Kaganovich noted that the abolition of the guberniia Party committees had more than compensated for the centralizing trend of the new provisions. *XIV s"ezd VKP(b)*, pp. 883-87, 889-90.

182. *Stalin*, VIII, 150.

183. *XIII s"ezd RKP(b)*, pp. 44, 253-54.

184. *Ibid.*, p. 533. Molotov was especially disturbed because the workers' group within the CP(b)U then totaled 71 percent. Somewhat illogically, he also insisted on the importance of drawing peasants into the Party.

185. *VKP(b) v rezol.*, I, 589, 608-10, 612, 613, 620-21, 630-32.

186. *XIV s"ezd VKP(b)*, p. 119. Zinoviev was answered by four leaders of the CP(b)U, Postyshev, Petrovs'kyi, Medvedev, and Kaganovich. *Ibid.*, pp. 156-58, 166-69, 177-78, 233-34.

187. The leaders of the anti-Ukrainization faction were Dashkovs'kyi and Lobanov. See Popov, *Narys istorii KP(b) U*, pp. 299-300; *Visti*, December 10, 1925.

188. Postyshev, Petrovs'kyi, Medvedev, and Kaganovich took the floor to speak against Zinoviev; Chubar' introduced a resolution denouncing Kamenev; Kaganovich spoke against the opposition arguments of Kharitonov; S. Kosior supported the official report on Party rules. *XIV s"ezd VKP(b)*, pp. 156-58, 166-69, 177-78, 233-34, 716-17, 884-87, 890-92. See also Popov, *Narys istorii KP(b) U*, p. 294.

189. *III S"ezd Sovetov SSSR*, pp. 272-80.

190. See statements by Butsenko, Alekseeva, and Grin'ko, *ibid.*, pp. 281-86, 290-93.

191. *Ibid.*, p. 537.

192. *II sessiia TsIK, III sozyva*, pp. 392-446. Also reported in *Visti*, April 17, 1926.

193. *II sessiia TsIK, III sozyva*, pp. 458-68 ; *Visti*, April 18, 1926.

194. *II sessiia TsIK*, III *sozyva*, pp. 446-544. See especially the replies of Petrovs'kyi, Zatons'kyi, and Skrypnik, pp. 498-505, 512-18, 531-36. Also reported in *Visti*, April 18, 1926.

195. *II sessiia TsIK, III sozyva*, pp. 1072-78.

196. The resolution was somewhat equivocal, calling both for increased Ukrainization work and also for greater emphasis on minority rights. *Visti*, April 30, 1926.

197. See the pessimistic reports printed in *Visti*, November 11, 15, 17, 18, and 20, 1925, and the editorials of August 6 and December 3, 1925. According to the decision of the Ukrainian government of April 30, 1925, the program was to have been completed by January 1, 1926. *Visti*, May 20, 1925.

198. The foregoing is taken from Stalin's account, but there is no reason to question its accuracy. *Stalin*, VIII, 149-50.

199. *Ibid.*, VIII, 149-54. The letter is dated April 26, 1926.

200. See the June 18, 1925, resolution of the All-Union Central Committee, "O politike partii v oblasti khudozhestvennoi literatury" [On the Policy of the Party in the Area of Literature], *Pravda*, July 1, 1925.

201. George S. N. Luckyj, *Literary Politics in the Soviet Ukraine*, 1917-1934 (New York, 1956), pp. 41-65.

202. *Ibid.*, pp. 65-66, 92-102.

203. *Stalin*, VII, 139.

204. *Stalin*, VII, 138.

205. See the resolution of the Thirteenth Party Congress, "O pechati" [On the Press], *VKP(b) v rezol.*, I, 610-15.

206. *XII s"ezd RKP(b)*, pp. 459-62, 522-26; Mykola Skrypnyk, *Statti i promovy* (Kharkov, 1931), II, Part II, 15-25.

207. Girchak, *Na dva fronta*, p. 56.

208. *Stalin*, VIII, 153.

209. *Stalin*, VIII, 152-53.

210. *Stalin*, V, 35-36, 39 ; see also pp. 57-59.

211. *Stalin*, V, 187-89, 192, 247-48.

213. *VKP(b) v rezol.*, I, 504. See also *XII s"ezd RKP(b)*, p. 600 ; *Stalin*, V, 271. This phrase was not included in the original resolution but was adopted as an amendment accepted by Stalin.

212. Enukidze, in a report to the USSR Central Executive Committee in 1926, stated : "We cannot forget that our national policy, our national language and national culture can be developed to a significant degree on the basis of the culture and language of the Great-Russian people. Of course there are those in one or another of the republics who say that it can be developed independently, separately from the Russian language, cutting off these nations in an isolated way from the Great-Russian language and from the Great-Russian culture. This will never succeed. . . . Study of the Russian language and of the Russian culture is essential for us, and in the building of our Union as a whole we cannot take one step without assimilating the Russian language and its culture." *II sessiia TsIK, III sozyva*, pp. 1075-76.

214. *Stalin*, V, 319-20.

215. *Stalin*, VIII, 153-54.

216. Mykola Skrypnyk, *Dzherela ta prychyny rozlamu v KPZU* (Kharkov, 1928), pp. 13-14, 18. See also Girchak, *Na dva fronta*, pp. 97-99, 102.

217. Skrypnyk, *Dzherela to prychyny*, p. 23.

218. "Tezy TsK KP(b)U pro pidsumky ukrainizatsii" [Theses of the CC of the CP(b)U on the Results of Ukrainization] (June 15, 1926), *Visti*, June 15, 1926; *Ostanni partiini dokumenty z natzional'noi polityky KP(b)U* (Kharkov, 1927), pp. 1-16; a slightly altered Russian translation is found in Girchak, *Na dva fronta*, pp. 198-206.

219. The composition of the Central Committee as established six months earlier by the Ninth Conference of the CP(b)U is given in *Visti*, December 10, 1925. No members of the opposition, anti-nationalist group held leadership posts.

220. *XII s'ezd RKP(b)*, pp. 522-26 ; *XV konferentsiia VKP(b)*, pp. 143-51; Chubar's report to the Kharkov Okrug Committee of the CP(b)U, *Visti*, June 13, 1926. In contrast, see Zatons'kyi's report to the Ukrainian Komsomol (June, 1926) which followed Stalin's approach more closely. V. Zatons'kyi, *Natsional'na problema na Ukraini* (Kharkov, 1926), pp. 3-51; reprinted in part in A. Leites and M. Iashek, *Desiat' rokiv ukrains'koi literatury*; 2d ed. (Kharkov, 1930), II, 493-512.

221. For an earlier expression of similar views see the addresses of Zatons'kyi, Kaganovich, and Slavyn to the Fourth Conference of Party members of the Ukrainian Military District, *Visti*, April 22, 24, and 27, 1926.

222. See the letter written by Khvyl'ovyi, Dosvytnyi, and Ialovoi, dated December 1, 1926, Girchak, *Na dva fronta*, pp. 230-32. For statements on Shums'kyi's continued support of Khvyl'ovyi see *ibid.*, pp. 97-107; Shum'kyi's letter of confession, *Visti*, April 30, 1930.

223. See Soludub's address to the Ninth Conference of the CP(b)U (December, 1925) and Chubar's answering comments. (*Visti*, December 10, 1925.) See also Khvylia, *Natsional'nyi vopros*, pp. 85-87.

224. In addition to the June resolution on Ukrainization, see the July and September resolutions of the Central Committee on Ukrainization of the trade unions and of the theaters, *Visti*, July 6 and September 7, 1926. See also Chubar's report to the Fifteenth Conference of the VKP(b), *XV konferentsiia VKP(b)*, pp. 143-51.

225. See Zatons'kyi's report to a meeting of the Ukrainian Council of Workers among the National Minorities, *Visti*, January 11, 1927.

226. See Petrovs'kyi's address to the All-Ukrainian Council of Workers among the National Minorities, *Visti*, January 13, 1927.

227. See Girchak, *Na dva fronta*, p. 40; Chubar's report to the Kharkov Okrug Party Conference, *Visti*, January 13, 1927.

228. "Ob izbrashcheniiakh pri provedenii natsional'noi politiki" [On Perversions in the Carrying Out of the National Policy], *Bol'shevik*, III (December 31, 1926), 50-58; IV (January 1, 1927), 59-69. See also Lobanov's statement to the All-Ukrainian Council of Workers among the National Minorities, *Visti*, January 11, 1927.

229. *Visti*, March 6, 1927. Skrypnik became the new Commissar of Education.

230. Girchak, *Na dva fronta*, pp. 119-39.

231. For a discussion of the campaign against the Communist Party of the Western Ukraine and for resolutions and official documents see Girchak, *Na dva fronta*, pp. 119-39, 206-30, 235-38; *Visti*, July 5, 6, and 9, November 27, 1927; April 30, 1930; *Ostanni partiini dokumenty*, pp. 24-69; Skrypnyk, *Dzherela ta prychyny*; Ie. F. Hirchak, *Shums'kizm i rozlam v KPZU* (Kharkov, 1928); Skrypnyk, *Statti i promovy*, II, Part II, 80-103; *Kommunisticheskii internatsional v dokumentakh, 1919-1932* (Moscow, 1933), p. 767; *XV s″ezd VKP(b)*, pp. 648-49; Popov, *Narys istorii KP(b)U*, pp. 300-303.

232. Girchak, *Na dva fronta*, pp. 221-22; N. Lovitskii, "Ocherednye zadachi kommunisticheskoi partii Zapadnoi Ukrainy" [Future Tasks of the Communist Party of the Western Ukraine], *Kommunisticheskii internatsional*, X (August 13, 1928), 17-24; K. Danilovich, "III s″ezd KPZU" [Third Congress of the Communist Party of the Western Ukraine], *Kommunisticheskii internatsional*, X (November 30, 1928), 18-26.

233. See Shums'kyi's statement to the Comintern, CP(b)U, and All-Union Communist Party (April 30, 1930), Girchak, *Na dva fronta*, p. 238; *Visti*, April 30, 1930.

234. See Larin's address to the Fifteenth Party Congress (December, 1927), *XV s″ezd VKP(b)*, pp. 704-5. At the same meeting Bukharin, principal editor of *Bol'shevik*, agreed that Larin's accusations that the Ukrainization program was being guided by "Russophobes" and "Petliurists" should have been removed. He added, however, that the article was generally acceptable as a basis for discussion. *Ibid.*, p. 741.

235. *Visti*, January 13, 1927. See also Skrypnik's statement to the Union Central Executive Committee, *III sessiia TsIK, III sozyva*, pp. 58-59.

236. *Visti*, January 11, 1927.

237. *Visti*, March 9, 1927.

238. See above, n. 233.

239. *Visti*, April 19, 1927.

240. *Visti*, May 24, 1927.

241. "Zakon pro rivnopravnist' mov na Ukraini" [Law on the Equality of Languages in the Ukraine], *Visti*, July 8, 1927.

242. "Zaiava TsK KP(b)U do Vykonkomu Kominterna" [Declaration of the CC of the CP(b)U to the Executive Committee of the Comintern] (June, 1927), *Visti*, July 5, 1927. Also printed in Skrypnyk, *Dzherela ta prychyny*, pp. 108-123; *Ostanni partiini dokumenty*, pp. 35-46.

243. "Doklad tov. L. M. Kaganovycha pro robotu TsK KP(b)U" [Report of Comrade L. M. Kaganovich on the Work of the CC of the CP(b)U] (November 22, 1927), *Visti*, November 27 and 29, 1927.

244. At the July Plenum of the Central Control Commission of the All-Union Communist Party the status of Party work in the Ukraine was discussed. *Visti*, July 27, 28, and 30, 1927. Zinoviev accused Ukrainian leaders of carrying out Ukrainization in a "Petliurist" spirit. See Skrypnik's report to the Fifteenth Congress of the All-Union Communist Party, *XV s"ezd VKP(b)*, pp. 647, 648.

245. *XV s"ezd VKP(b)*, pp. 647-49. Kaganovich said nothing about Ukrainization, confining his remarks to the problem of Party opposition. *Ibid.*, pp. 131-40.

246. *Ibid.*, pp. 703-6. See also Bukharin's report to the Congress, *ibid.*, p. 741.

247. See the following comments by Ukrainian leaders on a work by V. A. Vaganian, *O natsional'noi kulture* [On National Culture]: Girchak, *Na dva fronta*, pp. 22-30; the address of Kaganovich to the Tenth Congress of the CP(b)U, *Visti*, November 27, 1927; A. Krinitskii, "K voprosu o natsional'noi kul'ture" [On the Question of National Culture], *Bol'shevik*, IV, No. 9 (May 1, 1927), 51-63; K. Tabolov, "O natsional'noi kul'ture, ob ukrainizatsii i o literaturnoi isterike Vaganiana i Larina" [On National Culture, on Ukrainization and on the Literary Hysterics of Vaganian and Larin], *Bol'shevik*, IV, Nos. 11-12 (June 15, 1927), 69-77.

248. Bukharin, commenting on the disagreement between Skrypnik and Larin, criticized Skrypnik for opposing legitimate attacks on excesses in the Ukrainization program and criticized Larin for failing to see the political consequences of his statements and the national hostilities they might arouse. *XV s"ezd VKP(b)*, p. 741.

IV. CENTRALIZATION AND THE DEMAND FOR UNIFORMITY.

1. The Union government had established in 1923 and 1924 a Central Scientific Institute of Agriculture and a Central Agricultural Bank. *S"ezdy Sovetov SSSR*, pp. 25, 57. See the recurring discussions on the Committees of Poor Peasants (*Komitety nezamozhnykh selian*):

Popov, *Narys istorii KP(b) U*, pp. 235, 276-77, 291-95; *VKP(b) v rezol.*, II, 40, 395; *XIV s"ezd VKP(b)*, pp. 166-68, 233-34.

2. VIIuN, *Ocherki po istorii*, p. 165. For a discussion of the right of the Union government to convene conferences of republic commissars, see *III sessiia TsIK SSSR, I sozyva*, pp. 22-25, 109.

3. Vladimir Gsovski, *Soviet Civil Law*; 2 vols. (Ann Arbor, 1949), I, 705, 706; II, 739, 740, 742.

4. VIIuN, *Ocherki po istorii*, p. 165; Vyshinsky, *Law of the Soviet State*, p. 407.

5. Gsovski, *Soviet Civil Law*, I, 710-11; II, 743.

6. VIIuN, *Ocherki po istorii*, pp. 165-66, 181; Vyshinsky, *Law of the Soviet State*, p. 407; *Istoriia sovetskoi konstitutsii*, p. 237. For Ukrainian opposition see *V S"ezd Sovetov SSSR*, Biulleten' XVII, p. 11. The authority of the republics was subsequently limited by the creation of Union Commissariats of Grain and Livestock Sovkhozes and of Produce Collection. VIIuN, *Ocherki po istorii*, p. 199.

7. VIIuN, *Ocherki po istorii*, pp. 165-68, 199. In 1934 the Union-republic commissariats of light industry were transformed into republic commissariats of local industry and a Union Commissariat of Light Industry.

8. *Ibid.*, p. 166; *Istoriia sovetskoi konstitutsii*, pp. 293-96, 330, 332.

9. VIIuN, *Ocherki po istorii*, p. 199; *Istoriia sovetskoi konstitutsii*, pp. 340-43.

10. See a report by A. I. Butsenko to the Fourth Congress of Soviets, *IV S"ezd Sovetov SSSR*, p. 201.

11. *Ibid.*, pp. 378-81.

12. *Ibid.*, p. 201.

13. *XV s"ezd VKP(b)*, pp. 893-94.

14. *III sessiia TsIK, IV sozyva*, pp. 118-23, 702-5, 711-14; *IV sessiia TsIK, IV sozyva*, Biulleten' VII, pp. 22-28.

15. Quoted in P. P. Postyshev, *Sovetskaia Ukraina—nesokrushimyi forpost velikogo SSSR* (Kiev?, 1933), p. 20; *Visti*, December 6, 1933. See also I. I. Zhagelev, "Skrypnyk proty SRSR, iak iedynoi soiuznoi derzhavy" [Skrypnik against the USSR, as a Single Union State], *Radians'ka Ukraina*, No. 1 (January, 1934), p. 21. Skrypnik's objection was presented to the Central Committee of the All-Union Communist Party. His protest was overruled, and he was apparently ordered, perhaps as a matter of Party responsibility, not to discuss the question before the Union Central Executive Committee. *IV sessiia TsIK, IV sozyva*, Biulleten' XVI, p. 21.

16. See the critical reports of two Ukrainian representatives Lesovik and Poloz to the February, 1927, meeting of the USSR Central Executive Committee, *III sessia TsIK, III sozyva*, pp. 678-85, 692-97.

17. *IV S'ezd Sovetov SSSR*, pp. 67-68.

18. *Ibid.*, pp. 68-70, 106-10, 160-62, 136-39, 198-201, 378-81, 426-30.

19. *XV s'ezd VKP(b)*, pp. 133-34.

20. *Ibid.*, pp. 887-92.

21. *Ibid.*, pp. 905-9.

22. "Do problemy ukrains'koi ekonomiky," *Bil'shovyk Ukrainy*, III, No. 2 (January, 1928), 46-72; III, No. 3 (February, 1928), 42-63. The article was not available to me. The following is based on commentaries in Andrii Richyts'kyi, *Do problemy likvidatsii perezhytkiv koloniial'nosty ta natsionalizmu* (Kharkov, 1928); Girchak, *Na dva fronta*, pp. 107-19. For a more moderate but similar statement see S. Sadvosov, "O natsional'nostiakh i natsionalakh" [On Nationalities and Nationals], *Bol'shevik*, V, No. 1 (January, 1928), 56-64.

23. "Proty ekonomichnoi platformy natsionalizmu" [Against the Economic Platform of Nationalism], *Bil'shovyk Ukrainy*, V, Nos. 5-6 (March, 1930), 54-69; V, No. 7 (April, 1930), 28-40. See also Volobuev's letter of November, 1928, to *Bil'shovyk Ukrainy*, reprinted in Girchak, *Na dva fronta*, pp. 234-35.

24. Girchak, *Na dva fronta*, pp. 234-35. Volobuev noted that he had first recanted in February almost immediately after the publication of his article.

25. In a report to the March Plenum (1928) of the Central Committee of the CP(b)U Kaganovich declared: "the statements of Volobuev follow ... the line of bourgeois restoration with us in the Ukraine. This is bourgeois chauvinism and we are exposing it for what it is." KP[b]U, TsK, *Heroichnyi shliakh*, p. 83. See also D. Lebed', "Vnimanie ideologicheskomu frontu" [Attention to the Ideological Front], *Bol'shevik*, V, No. 7 (April, 1928), 79-87.

26. *III sessiia TsIK, IV sozyva* (April, 1928), pp. 97-101, 118-23; *IV sessiia TsIK, IV sozyva* (December, 1928), Biulleten' IV, pp. 43-47; Biulleten' V, pp. 4-10; Biulleten' VI, pp. 1-7, 28-32; Biulleten' VII, pp. 22-28; *XVI konferentsiia VKP(b)* (April, 1929), pp. 47-51, 54-56; *V S'ezd Sovetov SSSR* (May, 1929), Biulleten' IV, pp. 3-6, 13-15; Biulleten' X, pp. 6-8; Biulleten' XI, pp. 22-25, 41-43; Biulleten' XVII, pp. 6-11.

27. *II sessiia TsIK, V sozyva*, Biulleten' VI, pp. 4-10.

28. *Ibid.*, Biulleten' VI, p. 9.

29. *Ibid.*, Biulleten' VI, pp. 10-12, 13-14, 22-26, 33-35; Biulleten' IX, pp. 4-12; Biulleten' X, pp. 2-8; Biulleten' XI, pp. 1-3; Biulleten' XII, pp. 19-21; Biulleten' XVI, pp. 20-22.

30. *Ibid.*, Biulleten' VI, pp. 32, 36-38; Biulleten' IX, pp. 12-14; Biulleten' XI, p. 1.

31. The Ukrainian budget was increased by fourteen million rubles; the control figures were approved without change. *Ibid.*, Biulleten' XIII, pp. 6-8; Biulleten' XVIII, pp. 8-13.

32. See the comments of Postyshev, Chubar', and Skrypnik, *XVI s"ezd VKP(b)*, pp. 107-8, 168, 243; *Visti*, June 10, 1930.

33. *XVI s"ezd VKP(b)*, pp. 169, 177.

34. *III sessiia TsIK, V sozyva*, Biulleten' XI, pp. 19-23; Biulleten' XIV, pp. 4-10. See also *II sessiia TsIK, VI sozyva*, Biulleten' XII, pp. 22-26.

35. See Kosta Tabolov, "Protiv linii natsional'noi demokratii" [Against the Line of National Dmocracy], *Bol'shevik*, V, No. 1 (January, 1928), 65-78.

36. See Chubar's address to the Sixteenth Conference of the All-Union Communist Party (April, 1929), *XVI konferentsiia VKP(b)*, pp. 47-51; Kosior's address to the Eleventh Congress of the CP(b)U (June, 1930), *Visti*, June 17, 1930.

37. *III S"ezd Sovetov SSSR*, pp. 232-33; *IV S"ezd Sovetov SSSR*, pp. 68, 107; *V S"ezd Sovetov SSSR*, Biulleten' X, pp. 6-8; Biulleten' XI, pp. 22-25; Biulleten' XVII, pp. 6-11.

38. See the addresses of Postyshev, Chubar', and Skrypnik to the Sixteenth Party Congress (June, 1930), *XVI s"ezd VKP(b)*, pp. 107-10, 165-69, 243. See also Petrovs'kyi's address to the USSR Central Executive Committee (April, 1931), *III sessiia TsIK, V sozyva*, Biulleten' XIV, 8.

39. See the comments of Butsenko and Chubar', *II sessiia TsIK III sozyva*, pp. 157, 408-9.

40. Richyts'kyi, *Do problemy likvidatsii*, p. 13.

41. See for example the report in *Visti*, March 7, 1928. See also the report of Kaganovich to the Sixteenth Party Congress (June, 1930), *XVI s"ezd VKP(b)*, p. 81.

42. "Nova polozhennia pro okrvykonkomy" [The New Situation Concerning the Okrug Executive Committee], *Visti*, December 2, 1928.

43. *Visti*, May 11, 1929. See also Stalin's report to the Sixteenth Party Congress (June, 1930), *Stalin*, XII, 345-46.

44. *Visti*, January 17, June 14 and 19, July 29, 1930; *XVI s"ezd VKP(b)*, pp. 165-68; V. Grossman, "Raion-oblast'," *Bol'shevik*, VII, No. 13 (July, 1930), 15-21.

45. *XVI s"ezd VKP(b)*, p. 83; *Visti*, January 17, June 14 and 19, July 16, 17, and 29, August 1, 5, 7, 9, 10, 12, 13, and 17, September 3, 5, 9, and 27, October 2, 9, and 21, 1930.

46. See Zaton'skyi's report of June, 1930, and the objections of Skrypnik and others, *Visti*, June 19, 1930. Cf., however, Skrypnik's discussion, *Visti*, August 5, 1930.

47. *Visti*, July 17 and 29, August 1, 9, and 12, 1930.

48. *XVI s"ezd VKP(b)*, pp. 167-68.

49. *Visti*, February 11, 1932. See the somewhat inaccurate account in Ark Abramov and A. Ia. Aleksandrov, *Partiia v rekonstruktivnyı period* (Moscow, 1934), p. 105.

50. *Visti*, February 10, 1932. The Donbass and the city of Mariupol' (Zhdanov) were momentarily given a separate status. In July, 1932, a Donbass oblast was formed. *Visti*, July 15, 1932.

51. *V S"ezd Sovetov SSSR*, p. 16; *XVI s"ezd VKP(b)*, p. 243.

52. *XV s"ezd VKP(b)*, pp. 828-34.

53. Tabolov, *Bol'shevik*, V, No. 1, 65-78; Lebed', *Bol'shevik*, V, No. 7, 79-87.

54. See Skrypnik's address to the Eleventh Congress of the CP(b)U, *Visti*, June 10, 1930; Postyshev's address to the Sixteenth All-Union Party Congress, *XVI s"ezd VKP(b)*, p. 108.

55. See Skrypnik's address to the Sixteenth All-Union Party Congress, *XVI s"ezd VKP(b)*, p. 243.

56. According to official figures the ethnic composition of the CP(b)U from 1922 to 1933 was as follows (figures in percent):

Year	Russians	Ukrainians	Jews	Others
1922	54	23	14	10
1924	48	33	14	5
1925	43	37	12	8
1927	28	52	—	21
1930	28	52	—	19
1931	25	58	—	17
1933	23	60	—	17

Ravich-Cherkasskii, *Istoriia KP(b) U*, pp. 241-42; Khvylia, *Natsional'nyi vopros*, p. 54; Vseoiuznaia Kommunisticheskaia Partiia (bol'shevikov), Tsentral'nyi Komitet, Organizatsionno-instruktorskii otdel, *Sostav VKP(b) v tsifrakh*, XI (Moscow, 1932), 90-96; *Visti*, November 27, 1927; June 16, 1931; *Pravda*, January 24, 1934. The official figures do not take into account the large number of non-Russians who had become Russified, adopting Russian as their primary tongue. If this group is classified as Russian, the Russian percentages are increased by 25 to 35 percentage points. Cf. the figures for trade union membership in *Visti*, January 20, 1927.

57. *Visti*, April 19, 1927; February 14, 1928; January 9, 1929; January 3 and May 24, 1930; Skrypnyk, *Statti i promovy*, II, Pt. 2, 104-28.

58. As late as 1929 there were virtually no Party organizations in the countryside. Official statements reported only one Party member per thousand rural inhabitants. In the sovkhozes there were less than three Bolsheviks in each farm unit. *VKP(b) v rezol.*, II, 395-96.

59. Skrypnyk, *Statti i promovy*, II, Pt. 2, 251-53, 374-79. According to Skrypnik, 1,300,000 new workers moved to the Donbass in the first two years of the Five- Year Plan. By 1930, 51.5 percent of the workers were Ukrainian although only 44 percent were able to speak the language. See also Kosior's address to the Fourteenth Kiev Okrug Party Conference (December, 1928), *Visti*, January 9, 1929.

60. See the observations of a Soviet defector, Victor Kravchenko, *I Chose Freedom* (New York, 1947), pp. 63-65.

61. The only materials available to me were: Tabolov, *Bol'shevik*, V, No. 1, 65-78; Lebed', *Bol'shevik*, V, No. 7, 79-87; Girchak, *Na dva fronta*, pp. 140-97; Skrypnyk, *Statti i promovy*, II, Pt. 2, 254-329; N. N. Popov, "Natsional'naia politika partii v period sotsialisticheskoi rekonstruktsii" [National Policy of the Party in the Period of Socialist Reconstruction], *Pravda*, October 31, 1929.

62. See Stalin's reply to comrades Meshkov, Kovalchuk, and others (March, 1929), *Stalin*, XI, 333-55. See also Luckyj, *Literary Politics*, pp. 142-44.

63. In December, 1925, the Ukrainian Politburo comprised Kaganovich, Petrovs'kyi, Chubar', Skrypnik, Radchenko, Rukhymovych, Klymenko, Zatons'kyi, and Kirkizh. *Visti*, December 13, 1925. By November, 1927, Rukhymovych, Klymenko, and Kirkizh had been transferred out of the Ukraine and Zatons'kyi shifted to the important post of chairman of the Central Control Commission. Their places were taken by Medvedev, Postyshev, and Semenov —all formerly candidate members of the Politburo—and by Lomov, a new-comer to the Ukraine. *Visti*, November 30, 1927.

64. *VKP(b) v rezol.*, II, 285; *Visti*, July 15, 1928.

65. *XV s"ezd VKP(b)*, p. 1320.

66. *Visti*, October 7, 1928. See also December 4, 1928. For an earlier statement see the address by Prykhod'ko—Skrypnik's assistant in the Education Commissariat—to a conference of trade union representatives, *Visti*, May 29, 1928.

67. See Kosior's report to the Fourteenth Kiev Okrug Party Conference (December, 1928), *Visti*, January 9, 1929; statements and reports by Skrypnyk, *Statti i promovy*, II, Pt. 2, 104-23, 142-43, 153-59, 229-34, 251-53, 254-73, 274-329, 347-73; *XVI konferentsiia VKP(b)*, pp. 81-82.

68. "Sostoianie ukrainizatsii v promyshlennykh okrugakh" [Status of Ukrainization in the Industrial Districts] (December 23, 1929), Girchak, *Na dva fronta*, pp. 239-42; "Postanovlenie biuro khar'kovskogo okruzhkoma KP(b)U ot 5/XII 1929 g." [Decision of the Bureau of the Kharkov Okrug Committee of the CP(b)U of December 5, 1929] (December 7, 1929), *ibid.*, pp. 242-45.

69. *XVI konferentsiia VKP(b)*, p. 81.

70. *Statti i promovy*, II, Pt. 2, 362-71.

71. *Ibid.*, pp. 352-53; *XVI konferentsiia VKP(b)*, p. 81.

72. Skrypnik estimated in 1929 that there were 1,100,000 Russified Ukrainians in the cities and 300,000 Russians who spoke Ukrainian. *Statti i promovy*, II, Pt. 2, 157.

73. *Ibid.*, pp. 113-17, 156-59.

74. The text of the indictment is available in *Visti*, February 2 to March 9, 1930. The records of the trial are available in *Visti*, March 11 to April 22, 1930.

75. *Visti*, February 26 and 27, April 22, 1930.

76. *Visti*, March 5, 1930.

77. *Visti*, March 1, 1930.

78. *Visti*, March 2 and 4, 1930.

79. *Visti*, March 8, 1930.

80. *Visti*, April 22, 1930. The sentences varied from two to ten years.

81. D. Ihnatiuk, *Ukrains'ka avtokefal'ne tserkva i Soiuz vyzvolennia Ukrainy* (Kharkov, 1930).

82. *Visti*, February 21, 1930.

83. *Visti*, May 25 and 27, June 5, 1930. See also Postyshev's report to the Sixteenth Party Congress (June, 1930), *XVI s"ezd VKP(b)*, p. 109.

84. Political Report of the Central Committee of the CP(b)U to the Eleventh Congress of the CP(b)U (June, 1930), *Visti*, June 17, 1930; Report to the Sixteenth Congress of the All-Union Communist Party (July, 1930), *XVI s"ezd VKP(b)*, pp. 178-79.

85. *Visti*, August 2, 1931; P. Liubchenko, "Ukrains'ki natsionalisty v borot'bi za restavratsiiu kapitalizmu" [Ukrainian Nationalists in the Battle for the Restoration of Capitalism], *Bil'shovyk Ukrainy*, V, Nos. 9-10 (May, 1930), 58-75.

86. Report to the Sixteenth Congress of the All-Union Communist Party (July, 1930), *XVI s"ezd VKP(b)*, p. 243; *Visti*, July 5, 1930. Skrypnik cautioned also against Russian efforts to do the same thing. "Kontr -revoliutsiine shkidnytstvo na kul'turnomy fronti" [Counterrevolutionary Wrecking on the Cultural Front], *Chervonyi shliakh*, VIII, No. 4 (April, 1930), 138-50; "Spilka Vyzvolennia Ukrainy" [Union for the Liberation of the Ukraine], *Bil'shovyk Ukrainy*, V, No. 8 (April, 1930), 11-24.

87. *Visti*, June 17, 1930.

88. *Stalin*, XII, 362-71; XIII, 3-8. Stalin had expressed similar views earlier (March, 1929) in a letter discussing the national question. "Natsional'nyi vopros: Leninizm," *Stalin*, XI, 333-55. The letter was not published at the time, and its contents were not widely known.

89. *Stalin*, XII, 362. Cf. Stalin's statement of 1923 on the similar effects of the adoption of the New Economic Policy, *Stalin*, V, 187.

90. "O sel'skom khoziaistve Ukrainy i o rabote v derevne" [On the Rural Economy of the Ukraine and on Work in the Countryside], *VKP(b) v rezol.*, II, 391-96.

91. See *Stalin*, XII, 274-80.

92. *Stalin*, XIII, 320-21.

93. *Visti*, June 17, 1930. See also the reports of the CP(b)U to the Union (December, 1930), Vsesoiuznaia Kommunisticheskaia Partiia (bol'shevikov), *Itogi ob″edinennogo plenuma TsK i TsKK VKP(b), Dekabr'* 17-21, 1930 (Leningrad, 1930).

94. *XVI s″ezd VKP(b)*, pp. 242-43; K. Tabolov, "Protiv velikorusskogo shovinizma v voprosakh natsional'noi kul'tury" [Against Great-Russian Chauvinism in Questions of National Culture], *Bol'shevik*, VII, No. 13 (July 15, 1930), 78-91; An. Senchenko, "Natsional'ne pytannia v period rozhornutoho sotsiialistychnoho nastupu na vs'omu fronti" [The National Question in the Period of the Development of a Socialist Offensive on a Wide Front], *Bil'shovyk Ukrainy*, V, No. 17 (September 15, 1930), 47-61; Skrypnyk, *Statti i promovy*, II, Pt. 2, 394-99; Mykola Skrypnyk, "Perebudovnymy shliakhamy [Along Reconstruction Paths], *Bil'shovyk Ukrainy*, VI, No. 12 (June 30, 1931), 13-36.

95. Tabolov, *Bol'shevik*, VII, No. 13, 78-91; A. Khvylia, "Proletariiat i praktychne rozhortannia kul'turno-natsional'noho budivnytstva" [The Proletariat and the Practical Development of Cultural-National Construction], *Bil'shovyk Ukrainy*, V, Nos. 13-14 (July 31, 1930), 38-55; T. Gorb, "Stanovyshche ukrains'koi liudnosty Kazakstanu" [The Status of the Ukrainian Population of Kazakhstan], *Bil'shovyk Ukrainy*, V, Nos. 19-20 (October, 1930), 60-66; Ie. Hirchak, "Boiovi problemy natsional'noi kul'tury" [Urgent Problems of National Culture], *Bil'shovyk Ukrainy*, VI, No. 5 (March 15, 1931), 51-62; M. Skrypnyk, "Zblyzhennia i zlyttia natsii za doby sotsiializmu" [The Consolidation and Unification of the Nation During the Period of Socialism], *Bil'shovyk Ukrainy*, VI, No. 8 (April 30, 1931), 17-30 ; Ie. Hirchak, "Za leninizm ! Proty kavts'kiianstva !" [For Leninism ! Against Kautskyism !], *Bils'hovyk Ukrainy*, VI, No. 11 (June 15, 1931), 28-42. See also numerous issues of *Visti*, June to December, 1930.

96. *Narys istorii Ukrainy* (Kharkov, 1922). The book's sixth printing was halted in 1929 by order of the Agitation-Propaganda Department of the Central Committee of the CP(b)U. See Kosior's address to the Eleventh Congress of the CP(b)U, *Visti*, June 17, 1930. See also Iavors'kyi, *Istoriia Ukrainy v styslomy narysi;* 2d ed. (Kharkov, 1928).

97. See Iavorskyi's report in *Trudy pervoi vsesoiuznoi konferentsii istorikov-marksistov* 28-XII-1928—4-I-1929; 2d ed. (Moscow, 1930), I, 426-35.

98. P. Gorin, "O roli proletariata v revoliutsionnom dvizhenii Ukrainy" [On the Role of the Proletariat in the Revolutionary Movement of the Ukraine], *Bol'shevik*, VII, No. 1 (January 15, 1930), 43-52; Mykola Skrypnyk, "Pomylky ta vypravlennia akademika M. Iavors'koho" [The Mistakes and Corrections of Academician M. Iavors'kyi], *Bil'shovyk Ukrainy*, V, No. 2 (January 31, 1930), 12-26.

99. Skrypnyk, *Statti i promovy*, II, Pt. 2, 111-12. An indication of his acceptability as late as 1928 was his election to the All-Union Academy of Sciences. *Visti*, October 10 and 11, 1928.

100. A. Khvylia, "Burzhuazno-natsionalistychna trybuna" [Bourgeois-Nationalist Tribune], *Bil'shovyk Ukrainy*, VI, No. 6 (March 31, 1931), 46-58.

101. See Kosior's report to the November Plenum of the Central Committee and Central Control Commission of the CP(b)U, *Visti*, December 2, 1933.

102. M. Redin, "Za bil'shovyts'kyi povorot u vykladanni istorii" [For a Bolshevik Transformation in the Teaching of History], *Bil'shovyk Ukrainy*, VI, No. 11 (June, 1931), 66-94.

103. Decision of the Central Committee of the CP(b)U, "Pro robotu ukrains'koho instytutu marksyzmu-leninizmu" [On the Work of the Ukrainian Institute of Marxism-Leninism] (June 23, 1931), *Ekonomist-Marksyst*, I, No. 1 (July-August 1931), 181-83.

104. Decision of the Central Committee of the All-Union Communist Party, "Pro pochatkovu i seredniu shkolu" [On the Beginning and Middle Schools], *Visti*, September 6, 1931. See also *Visti*, August 28, September 5, 17, 19, and 21, 1932.

105. Decision of the Central Committee of the All-Union Communist Party (April 23, 1932), quoted in Luckyj, *Literary Politics*, pp. 264-65. See also pp. 159-72.

106. *Visti*, July 18, 1932. See also June 15, 1932.

107. See the report by A. Khvylia to the Central Committee of the CP(b)U, "Pro stan na movnomu fronti" [On the Situation on the Language Front], *Visti*, May 1, 1933. See also the reports by Khvylia and Kilerog to a meeting of Ukrainian educators (June 27, 1933), *Visti*, June 30, 1933.

108. *Visti*, May 1, 1933.

109. *XVII s"ezd VKP(b)*, p. 199. See also p. 66. For earlier statements see the addresses of Postyshev and Kosior to the joint plenum of the Central Committee and Central Control Commission of the CP(b)U (November, 1933), Postyshev, *Sovetskaia Ukraina*, pp. 12-13; *Visti*, December 6, 1933; P. P. Postyshev and S. V. Kos-

sior, *Soviet Ukraine Today* (Moscow, 1934), p. 72; *Visti*, December 2, 1933. See also Abramov and Alexandrov, *Partiia*, pp. 195-96.

110. *XVII s"ezd VKP(b)*, p. 68.

111. Andrei Richyts'kyi, candidate of the Central Committee of the CP(b)U, was specifically mentioned. *Ibid.*, p. 70; KP(b)U, TsK, *Heroichnyi shliakh*, p. 86.

112. For a careful and detailed statement of the sympathies of Ukrainian nationalist writers for Ukrainian peasants, see Posty-shev's address of June 1935, "Puti ukrainskoi sovetskoi literatury" [Paths of Ukrainian Soviet Literature], *Pravda*, June 10, 1935.

113. *Visti*, February 14 and May 12, 1932.

114. See the decision of the Politburo and Central Control Commission, *Visti*, May 8, 1932.

115. "Postanova plenumu TsKK KP(b)U" [Decision of the Plenum of the Central Control Commission of the CP(b)Uj (July 9, 1932), *Visti*, July 16, 1932.

116. The meeting was labeled the Third All-Ukrainian Party Conference (July 6-9, 1932). The principal addresses to the Conference and its final resolution are printed in *Visti*, July 6-17, 1932.

117. *Visti*, July 14 and 15, 1932.

118. *Visti*, July 15, 1932.

119. In a Party procedure which was becoming steadily more common, the two leaders were "co-opted" to membership by the Ukrainian Central Committee and then elected to the executive bureaus. See the Central Committee decision, *Visti*, October 15, 1932.

120. The only high official affected by the appointments was V. A. Stroganov, who was dropped from the Orgburo and Party Secretariat. *Visti*, October 15, 1932.

121. See the brief biographies in *Visti*, October 15, 1932.

122. *Visti*, November 21 and 23, December 4, 1932.

123. *Visti*, December 11, 1932. For the Ukrainian response, see *Visti*, December 23, 1932, and numerous decisions published in December and the early months of 1933.

124. The resolution was not made public but was later discussed by Postyshev in his address to the joint plenum of the Central Committee and Central Control Commission of the CP(b)U (November 21, 1933). Postyshev, *Sovetskaia Ukraina*, p. 6.

125. *Visti*, January 4, 1933.

126. The number of collective farms in the Ukraine decreased from 35,000 in 1931 to 25,000 in 1932, and to 24,000 in 1933. See *Sotsialisticheskoe stroitel'stvo* (Moscow, 1934), pp. 159-60.

127. See for example William Henry Chamberlin, *Russia's Iron Age* (Boston, 1934), Ch. IV.

128. "Pro robotu na seli" [On the Work in the Countryside], *Visti*, January 17, 1933. Other reports to the plenum are printed in *Visti*, January 10-17, 1933.

129. *Visti*, January 17, 1933.

130. "Tseli i zadachi politicheskikh otdelov MTS i sovkhozov" [Aims and Tasks of the Political Departments of the MTS and State Farms] (January 11, 1933), *Pravda*, January 13, 1933; *VKP(b) v rezol.*, II, 524-31. See also the directive sent by Khataevich to all local and district Party organizations in the Ukraine, *Visti*, January 24, 1932.

131. The resolution was not initially made public, but was read by Kosior to a plenary session of the Central Committee of the CP(b)U on February 5, 1933. *Visti*, February 13, 1933.

132. Kosior remained First Secretary of the CP(b)U but gave little attention to Ukrainian Party work. The ousted leaders were Maiorov, Stroganov, and Terekhov.

133. *Visti*, May 24, 1933; Abramov and Aleksandrov, *Partiia*, p. 151; *XVII s"ezd VKP(b)*, pp. 140-43, 161-64, 573-76.

134. Postyshev and Kossior, *Soviet Ukraine Today*, pp. 11-12.

135. In January, 1934, Kaganovich noted in his report to the Seventeenth Party Congress that 5,581 Party workers had been sent into the Ukraine. *XVII s"ezd VKP(b)*, p. 531.

136. *Visti*, February 21, 1933. The new chief was V. A. Balitskii, who had held the post earlier but had been recalled for police work in Moscow. See Furer's address to the Seventeenth Party Congress, *XVII s"ezd VKP(b)*, p. 575.

137. *Visti*, March 5, 1933.

138. "Pro chystku partii" [On the Purge of the Party], *Visti*, April 29, 1933.

139. K. V. Sukhomlin noted in his report to the Twelfth Congress of the CP(b)U that 19.3 percent of Party members and candidates in the four oblasts where the purge had been completed— Donets, Kiev, Vinnitsa, and Odessa—had been expelled. In addition, 16.2 percent had been demoted to candidate or Party-sympathizer status. Of those expelled from the Party 27.5 percent were removed on charges of being enemy, class, or bourgeois elements. *Visti*, February 2, 1934.

140. According to Postyshev, in the approximately 500 raions of the Ukraine, 237 secretaries of Party committees, 249 chairmen of executive committees, and 158 chairman of Party control commissions were removed before October 1933. *Soviet Ukraine Today*, pp. 11-12.

141. A. Shlikhter, *Bor'ba s natsionalisticheskimi uklonami na sovremennom etape* (Kharkov, 1933), p. 83.

142. *Ibid.*, pp. 83-84.

143. See numerous decisions of the Central Committees of the All-Union Communist Party and CP(b)U, *Visti*, August 28, September 5, 17, 20, 23, and 27, 1932.

144. *Visti*, October 4, 1932.

145. *Visti*, March 11, 1933.

146. *Visti*, March 1, 1933. Skrypnik was replaced by Zatons'kyi.

147. Shlikhter, *Bor'ba s natsionalisticheskimi uklonami*, p. 84.

148. The Politburo comprised eighteen men: Balitskii, Cherniavs'-kyi, Chubar', Chuvyrin, Demchenko, Iakir, Khataevich, Kosior, Liubchenko, Petrovs'kyi, Postyshev, Popov, Sarkis, Shlikhter, Skrypnik, Sukhomlyn, Veger, Zatons'kyi. At least seven had been selected by central leaders and sent to the Ukraine. For an indication of the attitude of the majority of the Central Committee see the moderate decision of February 7, 1933, *Visti*, February 10, 1933.

149. "Narada z pytan' natsional'noi polityky partii" [Discussion on the Question of the National Policy of the Party], *Visti*, May 1, 1933. Ostensibly, the addresses were reports to the Central Committee of the CP(b)U. The addresses were given by N. N. Popov, Party secretary recently sent to the Ukraine from Moscow; V. Zatons'kyi, newly-appointed Commissar of Education; and A. Khyvlia, Deputy Commissar of Education.

150. *Ibid.*

151. Skrypnik's address to the Central Committee was not made public. The above is taken from Postyshev's account. *Visti*, June 22, 1933; *Pravda*, June 22, 1933.

152. *Ibid.*

153. *Visti*, July 3, 1933.

154. *Visti*, June 30, 1933.

155. *Visti*, July 6, 1933.

156. *Visti*, July 8 and 9, 1933.

157. *II sessiia TsIK SSSR, II sozyva*, p. 425. See also *III sessiia TsIK SSSR, I sozyva*, pp. 19-23.

158. *I sessiia TsIK SSSR, III sozyva*, pp. 1-10, 12-14; *II sessiia TsIK SSSR, III sozyva*, pp. 568-69, 616-24; *IV sessiia TsIK SSSR, IV sozyva*, pp. 19-26.

159. *II S″ezd Sovetov SSSR*, pp. 106-7, 424-27; *II sessiia TsIK SSSR, III sozyva*, pp. 616-24; *II sessiia TsIK SSSR, II sozyva*, p. 425; *IV sessiia TsIK SSSR, IV sozyva*, pp. 19-26.

160. *II sessiia TsIK SSSR, IV sozyva*, pp. 216-24. See also *V S″ezd Sovetov SSSR*, pp. 14-16; *III sessiia TsIK SSSR, V sozyva*, pp. 219-29; *XVI s″ezd VKP(b)*, p. 243; Skrypnyk, *Statti i promovy*, II, Pt. 2, 153-59.

161. Girchak, *Na dva fronta*, p. 6; Skrypnyk, *Statti i promovy*, II, Pt. 2, 270-72.

162. *Stalin*, XII, 371.

163. *Visti*, July 12 and 23, 1933.

164. *Visti*, July and August, 1933.

165. *Visti*, July 22, 1933.

166. See the decision of the Central Committee of the CP(b)U, *Visti*, August 10 and December 15, 1933.

167. *Visti*, January 12, 1934.

168. See the addresses of Popov and Kosior to a meeting on July 9, 1933, of Kharkov active Party workers (*Visti*, July 12 and 23, 1933); the resolutions of the Kiev and Odessa Party workers (*Visti*, July 17 and 22, 1933); the addresses of Kosior, Postyshev, Popov, and Liubchenko to the November Plenum of the Central Committee and Central Control Commission of the CP(b)U (*Visti*, December 2, 6, 10, and 11, 1933); the addresses of Zatons'kyi, Shlikhter, and Chubar' to the USSR Central Executive Committee, December 1933 - January 1934, (*IV sessiia TsIK SSSR, VI sozyva*, Biulleten' V, pp. 26-37; Biulleten' VI, pp. 14-18; Biulleten' VIII, pp. 29-36); Postyshev's report to the Kharkov Party Conference of January 10, 1934 (*Visti*, January 18, 1934); Postyshev's report to the Twelfth Congress of the CP(b)U (*Visti*, January 24, 1934); the reports of Postyshev, Khataevich, Shlikhter, and Kosior to the Seventeenth Congress of the All-Union Communist Party (*XVII s"ezd VKP[b]*, pp. 64-71, 76-79, 86-88, 197-201).

169. *Visti*, November 26, 1933; Postyshev and Kossior, *Soviet Ukraine Today*, p. 110.

170. Postyshev and Kossior, *Soviet Ukraine Today*, pp. 94-96.

171. *Ibid.*, p. 111.

172. *Ibid.*, pp. 50-57.

173. *Ibid.*, pp. 77, 90, 95-96, 99-100, 104, 112; *Visti*, July 12 and August 23, 1933.

174. Postyshev and Kossior, *Soviet Ukraine Today*, pp. 95-96.

175. *Visti*, July 12, 1933.

176. Postyshev and Kossior, *Soviet Ukraine Today*, p. 99.

171. *Visti*, July 12, 1933. See also June 30, 1933.

178. *XVII s"ezd VKP(b)*, pp. 76-79.

179. *Ibid.*, p. 32.

180. See especially a letter written by Stalin on December 12, 1930, praising Russia—its history, its revolutionary movement, its working class—as the model to be followed by the proletariat of other countries. *Stalin*, XIII, 23-27.

V. THE NEW LOYALTY AND NATIONAL RIGHTS, 1934-1944

1. The Politburo comprised the following: Balitskii, Demchenko, Zatons'kyi, Kosior, Petrovs'kyi, Postyshev, Sarkisov, Sukhomlin,

Khataevich, Chubar', Chuvyrin, and Iakir. Candidates were Shlikhter, Liubchenko, Cherniavs'kyi, Veger, and Popov, The four Party secretaries were Kosior, Postyshev, Popov, and Liubchenko. *Visti*, January 24, 1934.

2. The new appointees were Khataevich, Veger, and Popov; Postyshev and Zatons'kyi were re-appointees who had earlier served in the Politburo. The members and candidates dropped between 1930 and 1934 were Skrypnik, Kartvelishvili, Semenov, Stroganov, Servychenko, Terekhov, and Zaytsev.

3. Balitskii, Kosior, Postyshev, Sarkisov, Khataevich, Iakir, Veger, and Popov.

4. See Postyshev's report of March 29, 1934, to the plenum of the Kharkov City Committee (*Visti*, April 6, 1934) and his report of December 3, 1934, to a meeting of the Kiev Party organization (*Visti*, December 10, 1934).

5. *Ibid.*; *Visti*, May 12, 1934.

6. "O politotdelakh v sel'skom khoziaistve" [On the Political Departments in the Rural Economy], *VKP(b) v rezol.*, II, 620-26.

7. See Liubchenko's address of May 17, 1934, to a plenary session of the Central Committee of the Ukrainian Komsomol. *Visti*, May 26, 1934.

8. *Visti*, February 26, April 28, June 11, 21, and 22, July 23, October 23 and 24, December 10, 1934.

9. See Liubchenko's report of June 13, 1934, to the Central Committee of the CP(b) (*Visti*, June 21, 1934); his report to thé Seventh Congress of Soviets, January 30, 1935 (*VII s"ezd Sovetov SSSR*, Biulleten' III, pp. 7-16); Postyshev's report to the Kiev city Party committee, February 22, 1935 (*Pravda*, March 5, 1935). See also *Visti*, February 23, May 6, June 16, July 18, 1934.

10. *Visti*, June 21, 1934. See also Postyshev's report to the leadership of the Union of Soviet Writers of the Ukraine, *Visti*, June 10, 1935.

11. *Visti*, June 28, 1934. See also the reports of Zhdanov and Gorkii to the First All-Union Congress of Soviet Writers. Only Bukharin adopted a more moderate approach. A. Zhdanov, Maxim Gorky, and others, *Problems of Soviet Literature* (Moscow, 1935), pp. 9, 59-61, 212.

12. *Visti*, October 23, 1934; *Pravda*, March 5, 1935.

13. *Pravda*, March 5, 1935.

14. *Visti*, October 23, 1934.

15. *Visti*, October 23, 1934; *Pravda*, March 5, 1935.

16. *Pravda*, March 5, 1935.

17. P. P. Liubchenko, "Novaia stranitsa v istorii Ukrainy" [A New Page in the History of the Ukraine], *Pravda*, June 23, 1934; H. I. Petrovs'kyi, "Za novi peremohu sotsialystychnoi Ukrainy"

[Toward a New Victory of the Socialist Ukraine], *Radians'ka Ukraina*, X, No. 7 (July, 1934), 15-16.

18. P. P. Postyshev, "Kvitne i mitsnie industrial'no-kolhospna Ukraina" [April and the Powerful Industrial-Kolkhoz Ukraine], (Report to the Second Congress of Soviets of the Kiev Oblast, January 11, 1935), *Bil'shovyk Ukrainy*, X, Nos. 1-2 (January-February, 1935), 13-30; P. P. Postyshev, "Pidsumky perevirky partiinykh dokumentiv u KP(b)U i zavdannia partiinoi roboty" [Results of the Verification of Party Documents in the CP(b)U and Tasks of Party Work], *Bil'shovyk Ukrainy*, XI, No. 3 (March, 1936), 9-33; S. V. Kosior, "Zvit tsentral'noho komitetu KP(b)U XIII z'izdovi" [Report of the Central Committee of the CP(b)U to the Thirteenth Congress], *Visti*, June 4, 1937.

19. P. P. Postyshev, *Pravda*, March 5, 1935; P. P. Postyshev, *Bil'shovyk Ukrainy*, XI, No. 3, 9-33; "Pro stan partiinoi propahandy i agitatsii" [On the Status of Party Propaganda and Agitation], (Decision of the Central Committee of the CP[b]U, July 15, 1936), *Bil'shovyk Ukrainy*, XI, No. 7 (July, 1936), 1-4.

20. See the communications of the Commissariat of Internal Affairs, *Pravda*, December 4, 1934.

21. The resolution was not made public but was later referred to in other Party pronouncements. See Kommunisticheskaia Partiia Sovetskogo Soiuza, *Kommunisticheskaia Partiia Sovetskogo Soiuza v rezoliutsiiakh i resheniiakh s"ezdov, konferentsii i plenumov TsK (1898-1954)*, 3 vols. (7th ed.; Moscow, 1954), III, 279-80. (Hereafter referred to as *KPSS v rezol.*)

22. See *Report of Court Proceedings. The Case of the Trotskyite-Zinovievite Terrorist Centre* (Moscow, 1936); *Report of Court Proceedings. The Case of the Anti-Soviet Trotskyite Centre* (Moscow 1937); *Report of Court Proceedings. The Case of the Anti-Soviet Bloc of Rights and Trotskyites* (Moscow, 1938).

23. *Visti*, December 2, 1934.

24. *Visti*, August 15, 1936.

25. Postyshev, *Bil'shovyk Ukrainy*, XI, No. 3, 9-33.

26. See Stalin's report to the March, 1937, plenum of the Central Committee of the All-Union Communist Party (*Pravda*, March 29, 1937) and the reports of Kosior and Kudriavtsev to the Thirteenth Congress of the CP(b)U (May-June, 1937). *Visti*, May 30 and June 4 1937. See also *Pravda*, May 30, 1937.

27. *Pravda*, March 29, 1937.

28. The resolution was not made public but was discussed by Kosior, Khataevich, and Kudriavtsev at the Thirteenth Congress of the CP(b)U. *Visti*, May 30 and 31, June 4, 1937.

29. *Visti*, January 18, 1937. Ostensibly, Postyshev was removed because his duties as Second Secretary of the CP(b)U were too demanding to permit him to hold a second post.

30. Hryhory Kostiuk, *The Fall of Postyshev* (New York, 1954), pp. 20-22; A. Avtorkhanov, "Pokorenie partii" [Subjugation of the Party], *Posev*, VI, No. 45 (November 5, 1950), 14-16.

31. The debates of the plenum were not made public, but in 1956 Nikita Khrushchev discussed the work of the plenum in a closed address to the Twentieth Congress of the Communist Party of the Soviet Union. An unofficial transcript of Khrushchev's address is printed in the *New York Times*, June 5, 1956.

32. As Khrushchev later noted, "Attempts to oppose groundless suspicions and charges resulted in the opponent falling victim of the repression. This characterized the fall of Comrade Postyshev." *Ibid.*

33. M. M. Khataevich, Party chief of the Dnepropetrovsk oblast, was promoted to fill the vacancy. *Visti*, March 18, 1937. Postyshev was at first merely transferred to work in the Kuibyshev oblast of the RSFSR. *Visti*, March 20, 1937. It was not until January, 1938, that he was expelled as a candidate of the All-Union Politburo. *KPSS v rezol.*, III, 306.

34. *Visti*, March 17, 1937.

35. See Kosior's address to the Thirteenth Congress of the CP(b)U (May 27, 1937), *Visti*, June 4, 1937.

36. The Politburo comprised Gikalo, Zatons'kyi, Kosior, Kudriavtsev, Liubchenko, Petrovs'kyi, Popov, Pramnek, Sukhomlin, Khataevich, Shelekhes. Candidates were Sarkisov, Margolin, Veger, Cherniavs'kyi, and Shlikhter. Party secretaries were Kosior, Khataevich and Popov. *Visti*, June 4, 1937. The only changes after the dropping of Postyshev in March were the additions of Gikalo and Pramnek, and the exclusion of Iakir—former commander of the Kiev Military District—who was dropped with Tukhachevskii and other Army leaders.

37. *Pravda*, September 2, 1937; *Soviet Political Personalities: Seven Profiles* (New York, 1952), pp. 1-7. Liubchenko was replaced briefly by M. Bondarenko, then by M. M. Marchak, and finally (February 21, 1938) by D. S. Korotchenko. *Visti*, February 22, 1938.

38. *Visti*, January 28, 1938.

39. *KPSS v rezol.*, III, 306-15.

40. *Ibid.*, III, 306; *Visti*, January 28, 1938.

41. See Burmistenko's report to the Fourteenth Congress of the CP(b)U (June, 1938), *Visti*, June 21, 1938.

42. For reports on changes in oblast leadership see *Visti*, February 22 and 27, April 9, 17, and 28, May 30, June 5, 8, and 10, 1938.

43. See *Visti*, May 15 to June 13, 1938.

44. The three were M. D. Diukanov, P. R. Krivonos, and S. K. Timoshenko. Compare the listings in *Visti*, June 4, 1937, and June 20, 1938.

45. The Politburo was reduced to eight members and candidates. The members were Khrushchev, Burmistenko, Korotchenko, Timoshenko, Uspenskii, and Shcherbakov; candidates were Osipov and Zadionchenko. *Visti*, June 20, 1938.

46. See the addresses of Kosior and Kudriavtsev to the Thirteenth Congress of the CP(b)U (May-June, 1937), *Visti*, May 30 and June 4, 1937; the addresses of Khrushchev, Burmistenko, Zadionchenko ,and Korotchenko to the Fourteenth Congress of the CP(b)U (June, 1938), *Visti*, June 16 and 21, 1938.

47. See Chernov's testimony, *Report of Court Proceedings. The Case of the Anti-Soviet Bloc of Rights and Trotskyites.* See also Khrushchev's report to the Eighteenth Congress of the All-Union Communist Party (March 1939), *XVIII s"ezd VKP(b)*, p. 169.

48. *Report of Court Proceedings. The case of the Anti-Soviet Bloc of Rights and Trotskyites,* pp. 11-12, 67-71.

49. *Pravda*, December 29, 1937.

50. For an opposite view see Kostiuk, *Fall of Postyshev*, pp. 10-13.

51. See Stalin's report to the February-March Plenum of the All-Union Central Committee (March 5, 1937), *Pravda*, April 1, 1937; the editorial in *Visti*, May 9, 1937; the reports of Kosior and Kudriavtsev to the Thirteenth Congress of the CP(b)U (May-June, 1937), *Visti*, May 30 and June 4, 1937. See also an article by B. Vinogradov attacking Trotskyites in the Kharkov Party organization, *Visti*, August 18, 1936.

52. For example, the Kiev Party leadership was denounced for ignoring principles of intra-Party democracy and self-criticism and for selecting an excessive number of Party leaders by cooptation rather than by election.

53. Report to the Ninth Congress of the Ukrainian Komsomol (April 5, 1936), *Pravda* and *Visti*, April 11, 1936; *Molodniak*, X, No. 6 (May, 1936), 2-23.

54. Avtorkhanov, *Posev*, VI, No. 45, 14-16; VI, No. 50, 14-15. Vladimir Dedijer, *Tito* (New York, 1953), pp. 106-7.

55. Of the five members and candidates of the All-Union Politburo removed in 1938, all but one—Ezhov—were identified with the Ukraine: Kosior, Postyshev, Chubar', and Petrovs'kyi.

56. Avtorkhanov, *Posev*, VI, No. 50, 14-15. Khrushchev declared that these decisions were taken by Stalin alone without the agreement of any high Party body. *New York Times*, June 5, 1956.

57. *Pravda*, November 26, 1936. See also the earlier article by S. Dimanshtein, "Leninsko-stalinskaia natsional'naia politika i proekt novoi konstitutsii SSSR" [The Lenin-Stalin National Policy and

the Draft of the New Constitution of the USSR], *Bol'shevik*, XIII, No. 13 (July 1, 1936), 64-78.

58. See *Pravda*, October 4, 1937; *Visti*, June 9, 1938; N. Fominov, "Pobeda leninsko-stalinskoi natsional'noi politiki" [Victory of the Leninist-Stalinist National Policy], *Bol'shevik*, XV, No. 9 (May 1, 1938), 37-46; "Velikaia druzhba narodov SSSR" [The Great Friendship of the Peoples of the USSR], *Bol'shevik*, XV, No. 13 (July 1, 1938), 1-7.

59. *Visti*, June 8, 1938.

60 *Visti*, June 16, 1938. See also *Visti*, June 9, 1938.

61. *XVIII s"ezd VKP(b)*, pp. 170, 240.

62. See Articles 14, 20, 34, 35, 49f, 57-63, 68c, 79-88, 104, 115, 134-42.

63. SSSR. Verkhovnyi Sovet, *Vtoraia sessiia Verkhovnogo Soveta SSSR, I sozyva. Stenograficheskii otchet* (Moscow, 1938), pp. 649-74, 692-700. (Hereafter, reports of sessions of the USSR Supreme Soviet are referred to only by number of session and convocation, as follows: *II sessiia Verkh. Sovet, I sozyva.*) See above, pp. 82-83.

64. See Voroshilov's report to the Eighteenth Congress of the All-Union Communist Party (March, 1939), *XVIII s"ezd VKP(b)*, pp. 190-92. See also B. Leontiev, "Krasnaia armiia—internatsional'-naia armiia" [The Red Army—an International Army], *Revoliutsiia i natsional'nosti*, No. 2 (February, 1937), p. 48.

65. Zhdanov, *Problems of Soviet Literature*, p. 60.

66. M. Tulepov, "Leninsko-stalinskaia natsional'naia politika" [The Lenin-Stalin National Policy], *Partiinoe stroitel'stvo*, IX, No. 7 (April 1, 1937), 51. See also V. Kirpotin, "Russkaia kul'tura" [Russian Culture], *Bol'shevik*, XV, No. 12 (June 15, 1938), 60-63; "Rosiis'ka mova—nadbannia radians'kykh narodiv" [The Russian Language—Property of the Soviet Peoples], *Visti*, July 8, 1938; O. Nazarenko, "Bil'she uvahy vykladanniu rosiis'koi movy" [Greater Attention to the Study of the Russian Language], *Visti*, August 6, 1938.

67. Kirpotin, *Bol'shevik*, XV, No. 12, 47. See also B. Volin, "Velikii russkii narod" [The Great Russian People], *Bol'shevik*, XV, No. 9 (May 1, 1938), 26-36.

68. "Na pershomu z'izdi radians'kykh pys'mennykiv Ukrainy" [To the First Congress of Soviet Writers of the Ukraine], *Visti*, June 21, 1934.

69. Iu. Iosypchuk, "Pushkin i Shevchenko" [Pushkin and Shevchenko], *Visti*, February 10, 1937. See also Kirpotin, *Bol'shevik*, XV, No. 12, 59-60; numerous articles during the Shevchenko 125th anniversary celebrations, *Visti*, August 29 to November 20, 1938, and throughout 1939. For a similar discussion on the Ukrainian writer M. M. Kotsiubins'kyi see *Pravda*, September 17, 1939.

70. In a curious incident the Ukrainian publication *Sovetskaia Ukraina* emphasized Shevchenko's dependence on Russians by not-

ing that he was released from a Tsarist prison in 1857 at the prompting of the Russian democrats Chernyshevskii, Dobroliubov, and Nekrasov. *Pravda* subsequently denounced the article, observing, inaccurately, that the first was only two years old at the time, the second, only ten, and the third, only seventeen. *Pravda*, July 13, 1938.

71. See above, pp. 186, 197.

72. *Pravda*, October 4 and December 29, 1937. See also Pavlo Tychyna, "Pro movu nashykh hazet" [On the Language of our Newspapers], *Visti*, May 5, 1938.

73. See *Visti*, July 9, 1939. The new dictionary for the first time excluded the distinctive Ukrainian letter "h," retaining only the Russian "g."

74. *Visti*, January 1, 1938.

75. In 1941 *Visti* ceased publication. In 1943 *Komunist* was transformed into the Russian *Pravda Ukrainy*, while *Sovetskaia Ukraina* became the Ukrainian *Radians'ka Ukraina*.

76. See *Visti*, April 24, 1938.

77. See above, pp. 143-44.

78. See the criticism expressed in *Visti*, August 6, 1938; *Pravda*, February 10, 1941.

79. *Visti*, June 17, 1938.

80. Max Beloff, *The Foreign Policy of Soviet Russia*, 1929-1941 (London, 1949), I, 94, 101, 105; II, 58-59, 64.

81. Armstrong, *Ukrainian Nationalism*, pp. 28-29, 31-33, 42-43.

82. A. K. Uspenskii was dropped as head of the Ukrainian NKVD apparently in December, 1938, when his chief, N. I. Ezhov, was purged in Moscow; he was replaced by I. A. Serov, perhaps at Khrushchev's behest. In February, 1939, Orgburo member S. I. Usenko was replaced by Ia. A. Khomenko, elevated to the post of secretary of the Ukrainian Komsomol. By May, 1940, I. H. Lysenko was added to the Orgburo and appointed head of the Propaganda Section of the CP(b)U, apparently replacing N. N. Poliakov. Of the four other changes in top Ukrainian leadership two are unexplained (the dropping of A. V. Osipov and G. G. Teleshev and elevation of A. A. Epishev and M. S. Spivak), and two were clearly unrelated to the purge (the recall of Politburo member A. S. Shcherbakov to Moscow in July, 1938, and his replacement by L. R. Korniets; the selection of M. S. Hrechukha, apparently in July, 1939, to succeed Marshal S. K. Timoshenko on the Politburo). Of the 86 members of the Central Committee elected in June, 1938, 39 were replaced by May, 1940, a slightly larger number than could be explained by the normal rate of attrition. See John Armstrong, *The Soviet Bureaucratic Elite* (New York, 1959), pp. 24-26.

83. *II sessiia Verkh. Sovet, I sozyva*, pp. 242-47. See also the reports by Korotchenko, Burmistenko, and Khrushchev, pp. 26-34, 366-76, and 715-24.

84. From November, 1936, to January, 1938, only 4.018 members and 3,432 candidates were admitted to the CP(b)U. M. Kvasov, "Rost partorganizatzii Ukrainy" [Growth of Party Organizations of the Ukraine], *Pravda*, August 28, 1938.

85. A. Osipov, "Territorial'nye i kolkhoznye pervichnye partorganizatsii" [Territorial and Kolkhoz Primary Party Organizations], *Pravda*, September 30, 1938; A. S. Shcherbakov, "Aktivno otbirat' v partiiu luchshikh liudei" [Actively Draw into the Party the Best People], *Pravda*, October 4, 1938.

86. Report to the Fifteenth Congress of the CP(b)U, *Pravda*, May 18, 1940.

87. Newspaper and journal articles developing these themes are too numerous to permit a listing. For examples, see *Visti*, December 15-30, 1939; *Pravda*, January 14 and May 1, 1941; *Bol'shevik*, XVII, No. 1 (January, 1940); XVII, Nos. 15-16 (August, 1940), 28-42.

88. Armstrong, *Soviet Bureaucratic Elite*, pp. 115-17.

89. *Visti*, September 24, 28, and 29, November 2 and 9, 1939; *Pravda*, July 2, September 9 and 16, 1940. In the month of December alone 1,702 Party members were sent to the Stanislav and Lvov oblasts—two of the six oblasts formed in the Polish territories. See Armstrong, *Soviet Bureaucratic Elite*, p. 112.

90. *Pravda*, November 15, 1939.

91. *Visti*, December 9, 1939. For the changes in Bukovina and Bessarabia see *Stalinskoe plemia*, August 21, 1940.

92. Armstrong, *Soviet Bureaucratic Elite*, pp. 105-6.

93. Armstrong, *Ukrainian Nationalism*, pp. 65-69, 71-72.

94. *Ibid.*, pp. 71-72.

95. See especially *ibid.*

96. Aleksei Fedorov, *The Underground Committee Carries On* (Moscow, n.d.), p. 16. See Armstrong, *Soviet Bureaucratic Elite*, p. 128.

97. Armstrong notes that 3,600 Communists were dispatched to the Kiev oblast organization alone. *Soviet Bureaucratic Elite*, pp. 128-29.

98. Sidor Kovpak, *Vid Putivlia do Karpat* (Kiev, 1946).

99. See *Pravda*, July 16, 17, 21, 25, and 29, September 11, 1941; February 21, April 2, September 11, 1942; February 17, May 13 and 14, 1943; *Sovetskaia Ukraina*, September 16, 1941; December 25, 1942; *Komunist*, March 17, 1942; November 6, 1943.

100. *Pravda*, November 28, 1941. Other meetings were held in January, July, August, and December, 1942. *Pravda*, January 14, July 11, September 5, December 26, 1942; *Sovetskaia Ukraina*,

January 3, 1943; Akademiia nauk URSR. Instytut istorii i arkheologii Ukrainy, *Naukovi zapysky*, I (Ufa, 1943); *Ukraina byla i budet sovetskoi, vtoroi anti-fashistskii miting predstavitelei ukrainskogo naroda*, 30 *avgusta* 1942 (Saratov, 1942); *Dvadtsat'piat' let Ukrainskoi Sovetskoi Sotsialisticheskoi Respubliki* (Moscow, 1943).

101. See *Pravda*, January 5 and 7, July 17 and 21, 1941; December 25, 1942; February 17, October 3 and 20, 1943; *Sovetskaia Ukraina*, September 16, 1941; December 25, 1942.

102. AN URSR, IIAU, *Naukovi zapysky*.

103. *Pravda*, October 11, 1943. Similar awards honoring Russian military leaders were also established.

104. See the series of studies on Russian writers published in 1942 and 1943 under the title *Pisateli—patrioty velikoi rodiny;* 8 vols. (Moscow, 1942-43); see also works such as *Geroicheskoe proshloe russkogo naroda* (Moscow, 1943).

105. G. Vasetskii, "Nesokrushimoe edinstvo velikogo sovetskogo naroda" [Indestructible Unity of the Great Soviet People], *Bol'shevik*, XVII, No. 14 (July, 1941), 35-41; E. Genkina, "Lenin o bratstve i druzhbe narodov SSSR" [Lenin on the Brotherhood and Friendship of the Peoples of the USSR], *Bol'shevik*, XIX, No. 1 (January, 1943), 35-45.

106. See below, p. 249.

VI. THE CULMINATION OF NATIONAL RESTRICTIONS, 1944-1953

1. For an estimate of the damage suffered in the Ukraine during World War II see Mary Redmer and V. I. Wolpert, "Economic Rehabilitation in the Ukraine," Operational Analysis Paper No. 39, United Nations Relief and Rehabilitation Administration, European Regional Office (London, 1947). Mimeographed.

2. *Pravda Ukrainy*, October 13, 1944. See also November 21 and 25, December 10, 1944; July 2, 1946.

3. "O nedostatkakh v politicheskoi rabote sredi naseleniia zapadnykh oblastei USSR" [On Weaknesses in Political Work among the People of the West Oblasts of the Ukrainian SSR]. The resolution was not made public but was later discussed in Party meetings in the Ukraine. See *Pravda*, November 25, 1944; *Pravda Ukrainy*, November 21 and December 1, 1944.

4. *Pravda*, November 25, 1944; A Azizian, "Uspekhi leninsko-stalinskoi natsional'noi politiki" [Successes of the Lenin-Stalin National Policy], *Bolshevik*, XX, No. 2 (January, 1945), 36-47.

5. See Khrushchev's report to the Sixth Session of the Ukrainian Supreme Soviet (March, 1944), *Pravda*, March 16 and 17, 1944; *Pravda Ukrainy*, October 8, November 16, December 10, 1944;

Pravda, October 15, 1945; "Ob ideino-politicheskoi rabote partiinykh organizatsii v sovremennykh usloviiakh" [On the Ideological-Political Work of Party Organizations under Contemporary Conditions], *Bol'shevik*, XX, Nos. 17-18 (September, 1945), 1-10.

6. See Part VII of Khrushchev's report to the Sixth Session of the Supreme Soviet, *Pravda*, March 17, 1944; *Pravda*, October 15, 1944; *Pravda Ukrainy*, October 21 and November 16, 1944; M. Mitin, "Pobeda ideologii druzhby narodov nad ideologiei zverinogo natsionalizma fashistov" [Victory of the Ideology of the Friendship of Peoples over the Ideology of the Bestial Nationalism of the Fascists], *Pravda Ukrainy*, December 5, 1944; A. Beletskii, "Shevchenko i Franko o russkoi kul'ture" [Shevchenko and Franko on Russian Culture], *Pravda Ukrainy*, December 7, 1944; *Pravda*, December 14, 1944; *Pravda Ukrainy*, December 24, 1944; February 23 and May 9, 1945.

7. For the legal enactments see *Constitution of the USSR as Amended by the 1st, 2nd, 3rd, 6th, 7th and 8th Sessions of the Supreme Soviet of the USSR* (Washington, D.C., 1945), pp. 30-31.

8. *X sessiia Verkh. Sovet SSSR, I sozyva*, pp. 270-71.

9. See *ibid.*, pp. 271-73 and above, pp. 114-15. According to Molotov national military formations were then in existence for Lithuanians, Latvians, Esthonians, Georgians, Azerbaidzhani, Armenians, Kazakhs, and some others. *Ibid.*, p. 271.

10. *Ibid.*, pp. 313-14.

11. Edward R. Stettinius, Jr., *Roosevelt and the Russians: the Yalta Conference* (New York, 1949), p. 187. See also p. 173.

12. Stalin declared to Roosevelt: " You know there are two parts of Russia that have been completely devastated. Every building is gone, every farm house, and there are millions of people living in these territories—and it is very important from the point of view of humanity—and we thought, as a gesture, they ought to be given something as a result of this coming victory. They have had very little civilization. One is the Ukraine, and the other is White Russia. We all felt—not any of us coming from there in the government— we think it would be fitting to give them a vote in the Assembly. In these two sections, millions have been killed, and we think it would be very heartening—would help to build them up—if we could get them a vote in the Assembly." Samuel I. Rosenman (ed.). *The Public Papers and Addresses of Franklin D. Roosevelt* (New York, 1950), XIII, 610-11.

13. *Pravda Ukrainy*, March 29, 1945.

14. See especially *Pravda Ukrainy*, April 8 and 11, 1945. Compare with typical articles published in 1938 and 1939 when an opposite position was taken. *Pravda*, September 23 and 27, October 24, November 16, 1938.

15. "Vystuplenie tovarishcha I. V. Stalina na prieme v Kremle v chest' komanduiushchikh voiskami Krasnoi Armii" [Statement of Comrade I. V. Stalin at a Reception in the Kremlin in Honor of the Commanders of the Troops of the Red Army], *Bol'shevik*, XX, No. 10 (May, 1945), 1-2.

16. Chechens, Ingush, Kalmyks, Balkars, Karachai, and Crimean Tatars. The Volga Germans had earlier (1941) been removed. New York *Times*, November 30, 1945, p. 2; June 27, 1946, p. 4; June 17, 1956. For the brief official statements on these changes see *Pravda*, June 26 and 28, 1946. See Khrushchev's secret address to the Twentieth Party Congress. *New York Times*, June 5, 1956.

17. See "Russkii narod—rukovodiashchaia sila sredi narodov nashei strany" [The Russian People—the Leading Force among the Peoples of Our Country], *Bol'shevik*, XX, No. 10 (May, 1945), 3-12.

18. New York *Times*, June 5, 1956.

19. See Armstrong, *Ukrainian Nationalism*, pp. 130-64.

20. See numerous *emigré* publications: *Istoriia ukrains'koho viis'ka* (2d ed.; Winnipeg, 1953), pp. 712-819; Petro Mirchuk, *Ukrains'ka povstans'ka armiia, 1942-1952* (Munich, 1953), pp. 87-319; *The Ukrainian Insurgent Army in Fight for Freedom* (New York, 1954); Oleh Martovych, *Ukrainian Liberation Movement in Modern Times* (Edinburgh, 1951), pp. 128-66; *UPA in Western Europe* (2d ed.; New York, 1948); *Ukrainian Resistance* (New York, 1949), pp. 131-37.

21. An amnesty was offered Ukrainian partisans in 1944, but it was conditioned on an absolute renunciation of nationalist ties. *Pravda*, March 17, 1944. See also *Pravda Ukrainy*, December 10, 1944.

22. *Pravda*, March 17, 1944; *Pravda Ukrainy*, November 16 and December 10, 1944.

23. The eight retaining high posts were Khrushchev, Korotchenko, Korniets, Hrechukha, Spivak, Epishev, Kolybanov, and Serdiuk. The seven who did not return to the Ukraine but were transferred to Party work elsewhere or were dropped from the Party were Burmistenko, Serov, Lysenko, Khomenko, Zadionchenko, Liubavin, and Kvasov. For data on the Central Committee covering a somewhat longer period see Armstrong, *Soviet Bureaucratic Elite*, pp. 24-26.

24. Fedorov, Mishchenko, Serdiuk, Markov, Matiushyn, Spivak, Gaevoi, Mel'nikov, Churaev, Hrushets'kyi, Senin, Begma, Slon', Kompanets, Horobets, Gorenkov. Not all remained in the same oblasts; some were promoted from other work. See also *ibid.*, pp. 134-35.

25. On May 3, 1945, twenty-eight of the Ukraine's leaders were awarded highest honors for their wartime activities. *Pravda Ukrainy*, May 4, 1945. Earlier (February, 1945), nearly 80 percent of the regional leaders of the Ukraine had been granted lesser awards. *Pravda Ukrainy*, February 3 to 12, 1945.

26. Khrushchev had been promoted to full membership in March, 1939. *Pravda*, March 11, 1939.

27. *Pravda*, February 6, 1944. Korniets became Vice-President of the Council of People's Commissars.

28. *Pravda*, July 14, 1944. From February to July, 1944, Oleksandr Korniichuk, prominent Ukrainian playwright, had served as Commissar of Foreign Affairs. *Pravda*, February 6, 1944.

29. *Pravda Ukrainy*, September 27, 1944. See *Pravda Ukrainy*, March 9, 1947.

30. N. S. Khrushchev, "O nekotorykh voprosakh vnutripartiinoi raboty" [On Some Questions of Intra-Party Work], *Pravda Ukrainy*, June 8, 1946.

31. Armstrong, *Soviet Bureaucratic Elite*, p. 17.

32. *Pravda Ukrainy*, August 8, 1944.

33. "Vsemerno povyshat' uroven' partiino-politicheskoi raboty" [To Improve Continuously the Level of Party-Political Work], *Pravda Ukrainy*, December 1, 1944. See also *Pravda Ukrainy*, December 7, 1944; Armstrong, *Soviet Bureaucratic Elite*, pp. 114-22.

34. See Khrushchev's report to the Thirteenth Plenum of the Central Committee of the CP(b)U (August 15-17, 1946), "Uluchshit' podbor, rasstanovku i vospitanie kadrov" [To Improve the Selection, Assignment, and Training of Cadres], *Pravda*, August 23, 1946.

35. *Ibid.*; *Pravda Ukrainy*, July 6, 1946.

36. Komunistychna Partiia (bil'shovykiv) Ukrainy, Tsentral'nyi Komitet, *Rezoliutsii plenumu tsentral'noho komitetu KP(b) U, 28 liutoho - 2 bereznaia 1946 r.* (Kiev, 1946). (Hereafter, reports of plenary sessions of the Central Committee of the CP[b]U are referred to only by number, as follows: *X plenum TsK KP[b]U.*) *XI plenum TsK KP(b) U*; *XII plenum TsK KP(b) U*; *Pravda Ukrainy*, August 18, 1946. See also *Pravda Ukrainy*, March 3, 5, and 6, May 19, 21, 22, and 23, June 8, July 6, 11, 13, 14, and 21, 1946; "O politicheskoi raboti v derevne" [On Political Work in the Countryside], *Bol'shevik*, XXIII, Nos. 13-14 (July, 1946), 1-9.

37. See especially the resolution of the Tenth Plenum of the Central Committee, "Pro stan vnutripartiinoi roboty v dnipropetrovs'kii, poltavs'kii i drohobyts'kii oblasnykh partiinykh orhanizatsiiakh" [On the Status of Intra-Party Work in the Dnepropetrovsk, Poltava, and Drogobych Oblast Party Organizations], *X plenum TsK KP(b) U*, pp. 31-45; *Pravda Ukrainy*, June 8, 1946; *Pravda*, August 23, 1946.

38. "Pro pidsumky 1945 sil's'kohospodars'koho roku i pidhotovsku do vesnianoi sivby 1946 roku" [On the Results of the 1945 Agricultural Year and on Preparation for the Spring Sowing of 1946], *X plenum TsK KP(b) U*, pp. 7-30.

39. See the Central Committee resolutions of July, 1946, *XII plenum TsK KP(b) U.* See also the resolution of May, 1946, *XI plenum TsK KP(b) U*, pp. 7-33.

40. See above, n. 20, p. 381.

41. See below, pp. 257-67.

42. *XII plenum TsK KP(b) U*, pp. 3-6.

43. *Pravda*, August 23, 1946. See also the decision of the All-Union Central Committee, "O podgotovke i perepodgotovke rukovo-diashchikh partiinykh i sovetskikh rabotnikov" [On the Training and Retraining of Leadership Party and Soviet Workers], (August 2, 1946), *KPSS v rezol.*, III, 476-84.

44. "O merakh pod"ema sel'skogo khoziaistva v poslevoennyi period" [On Measures for Raising the Rural Economy in the Post-War Period], *KPSS v rezol.*, III, 502-50.

45. Kaganovich was a member of the All-Union Politburo; Patolichev was one of the secretaries of the All-Union Communist Party. *Pravda Ukrainy*, March 5, 1947.

46. Decisions of the Fourteenth Plenum of the Central Committee of the CP(b)U, *Pravda Ukrainy*, March 4, 1947.

47. See the decisions of the Fifteenth and Sixteenth Plenums of the Central Committee of the CP(b)U, *Pravda Ukrainy*, March 19 and 23, June 29, 1947; "Shiroko razvernut' politicheskuiu raboty v derevne" [Widely To Develop Political Work in the Countryside], *Bol'shevik*, XXIII, No. 6 (March, 1947), 1-8.

48. P. A. Naidenov, first secretary of the Dnepropetrovsk oblast. *Pravda Ukrainy*, November 23, 1947. The other secretary removed was H. P. Pinchuk of the Trans-Carpathian oblast.

49. A sterner view of the role played by Kaganovich in the Ukraine was given by Kal'chenko. In June, 1957, when Kaganovich was ousted from central Party leadership, Kal'chenko accused him of having "slandered and offended Party personnel in every way, discrediting many honest and devoted Party people and trampling on their dignity.... Had Kaganovich not been recalled from the Ukraine in time, he would have done tremendous damage to the Communist Party of the Ukraine and the Ukrainian people." *Pravda*, July 5, 1957. See also *Radians'ka Ukraina*, October 20, 1961.

50. See the resolution of the Eighteenth Plenum of the Central Committee of the CP(b)U (March, 1948), *Pravda Ukrainy*, March 14, 1948.

51. Decisions of the Sixteenth Plenum of the Central Committee of the CP(b)U (December 26, 1947), *Pravda Ukrainy*, December 27, 1947.

52. *Pravda Ukrainy*, July 25, 1947.

53. See Mel'nikov's report to the November plenum of the Dnepropetrovsk oblast committee, *Pravda Ukrainy*, November 23, 1947.

54. "O zhurnalakh *Zvezda* i *Leningrad*," *KPSS v rezol.*, III, 485-88.

55. "O repertuare dramaticheskikh teatrov i merakh po ego uluchsheniiu" [On the Repertoire of Dramatic Theaters and Measures for its Improvement]·(August 26, 1946), *ibid.*, III, 489-94; "Ob opere 'Velikaia druzhba' V. Muradeli" [On the Opera "Great Friendship" by V. Muradeli] (February 10, 1948), *Sovetskaia muzyka*, XII, No. 1 (January, 1948), 3-8. "O kinofil'me 'Bol'shaia zhizn'"' [On the Film "Great Life"] (September 4, 1946), *Bol'shevik*, XXIII, No. 16 (August, 1946), 50-53. See also three statements by A. A. Zhdanov: *Doklad o zhurnalakh "Zvezda" i "Leningrad"* (Moscow, 1952); *Vystuplenie na diskussii po knige G. F. Aleksandrova "Istoriia zapadnoevropeiskoi filosofii"* (Moscow, 1947); *Vstupitel'naia rech' i vystuplenie na soveshchanii deiatelei sovetskoi muzyki v TsK VKP(b)* (Moscow, 1952).

56. *KPSS v rezol.*, III, 487. See also Zhdanov, *Doklad o zhurnalakh*, pp. 17-21.

57. See Marc Slonim, *Modern Russian Literature, from Chekhov to the Present* (New York, 1953), pp. 407-35; Ernest J. Simmons (ed.), *Through the Glass of Soviet Literature, Views of Russian Society* (New York, 1953), pp. 3-26.

58. Zhdanov, *Vstupitel'naia rech'*, pp. 8-11, 20-22. See also Andrey Olkhovsky, *Music under the Soviets, the Agony of an Art* (New York, 1955), pp. 49-52, 151-57.

59. See above, pp. 184-87, 212-13.

60. "Respublikanskoe soveshchanie po voprosam propagandy" [Republic Meeting on Questions of Propaganda], *Pravda Ukrainy*, June 29, 1946.

61. For the most complete criticism, see "Ob 'Ocherke istorii ukrainskoi literatury'" [On the "Outline of the History of Ukrainian Literature"], *Pravda Ukrainy*, June 30, 1946. See also Khrushchev's address to the Thirteenth Plenum of the Central Committee of the CP(b)U, *Pravda*, August 23, 1946; the decision of the Thirteenth Plenum, *Pravda Ukrainy*, September 1, 1946; *Pravda Ukrainy*, July 23, 1946; *Pravda*, September 2, 1946; *Pravda Ukrainy*, September 21, 1946. For a general account of developments in the period see Danylo Lobai, *Neperemozhna Ukraina* (Winnipeg, 1950).

62. See S. Kovalev, "Ispravit' oshibki i osveshchenii nekotorykh voprosov istorii Ukrainy" [To Correct Mistakes in the Presentation of Some Questions of the History of the Ukraine], *Pravda Ukrainy*, July 23, 1946; N. N. Petrovs'kyi, "Protiv burzhuazno-natsionalisticheskoi 'shkoly' Grushevskogo" [Against the Bourgeois-Nationalist "School" of Hrushevs'kyi], *Pravda Ukrainy*, July 25, 1946; *Pravda Ukrainy*, September 21, 1946; January 29 and October 3, 1947; K. Litvin, "Ob istorii ukrainskogo naroda" [On the History of the Ukrainian People], *Bol'shevik*, XXIV, No. 7 (April, 1947), 41-56.

63. *Pravda Ukrainy,* August 20, October 12 and 16, 1946; August 2, 1947; *Pravda,* July 4, 1947.

64. See the criticism of *L'vovskaia Pravda* (*Pravda Ukrainy,* August 20, 1946); Khrushchev's comments on *Pravda Ukrainy* and *Radians'ka Ukraina* in his report to the Thirteenth Plenum of the Central Committee of the CP(b)U (*Pravda,* August 23, 1946); the denunciations of the satirical journal, *Perets'* (*Pravda,* August 24, 1946; *Pravda Ukrainy,* September 26, 1946); the Ukrainian Central Committee decision on the literary journal, *Vitchyzna* (*Pravda Ukrainy,* October 5, 1946); the Ukrainian Central Committee decision abolishing the Party journals, *Partrobitnyk Ukrainy* and *Propagandyst i agitator,* and re-establishing the journals *Bil'shovyk Ukrainy* and *Partiine zhyttia* (*Pravda Ukrainy,* November 2, 1946); Korniichuk's comments on Ukrainian journals (*Pravda,* July 4, 1947).

65. *Pravda,* September 2, 1946; July 4, 1947; *Pravda Ukrainy,* August 20 and December 26, 1946; January 29, August 2 and 28, November 20, 1947; December 2, 7, 8, 9, 10, 11, and 29, 1948; February 8, 1949.

66. See the decision of the Ukrainian Central Committee, *Pravda Ukrainy,* October 12, 1946.

67. See the decision of the Ukrainian Central Committee, *Pravda Ukrainy,* May 25, 1948.

68. See I. D. Nazarenko's address to a general meeting of the Division of Social Sciences of the Ukrainian Academy of Sciences, *Pravda Ukrainy,* September 21, 1946.

69. See the government list published in *Pravda Ukrainy,* March 9, 1947.

70. U.S., Congress, House of Representatives, *Favoring the Extension of Diplomatic Relations with the Republics of Ukraine and Byelorussia,* Hearing before the Special Subcommittee of the Committee on Foreign Affairs, U.S. House of Representatives, 83d Cong., 1st Sess., on H. Con. Res. 58, July 15, 1953 (Washington, 1953), p. 77.

71. *Pravda Ukrainy,* June 30, July 23, August 8, October 5, 1946; January 29, July 4, August 2, 1947.

72. *Pravda Ukrainy,* October 5, 1946.

73. *Pravda Ukrainy,* February 8, 1949; see also the attack on V. Cherednychenko, *Pravda,* September 2, 1946.

74. *Pravda,* September 2, 1946. See also *Pravda Ukrainy,* June 29, 1946; *Pravda,* August 23 and 29, 1946; *Radians'ka Ukraina,* August 21, 1946.

75. *Pravda Ukrainy,* September 21, 1946. The italics are mine.

76. "O zhurnale satiry i iumora 'Perets',' iz postanovleniia TsK KP(b)U" [On the Journal of Satire and Humor "Perets'," from the Decision of the Central Committee of the CP(b)U], *Pravda Ukrainy,* September 26, 1946.

77. *Pravda Ukrainy*, June 30, 1946, quoting Stalin, *Marxism and the National-Colonial Question*, p. 151.

78. See the Central Committee decision on the journal, *Perets'*. *Ibid.*

79. *Pravda Ukrainy*, July 2, 1946.

80. *Lenin*, XX, 8-10.

81. *Pravda Ukrainy*, June 30, 1946; October 3, 1947.

82. A. Korneichuk, "Nekotorye problemy razvitiia ukrainskoi literatury" [Some Problems in the Development of Ukrainian Literature], *Pravda*, July 4, 1947.

83. *Pravda Ukrainy*, June 29, 1946.

84. Korneichuk, *Pravda*, July 4, 1947.

85. See for example Iu. S. Kobylets'kyi, *Obraz I. V. Stalina v ukrains'kii radians'kii literaturi* (Kiev, 1950).

86. M. Ruzin, "O ser'eznykh politicheskikh oshibkakh v shkol'nykh uchebnikakh" [On Serious Political Mistakes in School Textbooks], *Pravda Ukrainy*, December 30, 1947.

87. N. N. Petrovs'kyi, "Protiv burzhuazno-natsionalisticheskoi 'shkoly' Grushevskogo" [Against the Bourgeois-Nationalist "School" of Hrushevs'kyi], *Pravda Ukrainy*, July 25, 1946.

88. A. Korneichuk, "Literatura Sovetskoi Ukrainy pered velikim iubileem" [The Literature of the Soviet Ukraine before the Great Anniversary], *Pravda Ukrainy*, August 2, 1947.

89. *Pravda Ukrainy*, October 3, 1947.

90. *Pravda Ukrainy*, June 30, 1946.

91. *Pravda Ukrainy*, July 23, 1946.

92. *Pravda Ukrainy*, August 2, 1947.

93. See Manuil'skii's report to the Sixteenth Congress of the CP (b)U (January, 1949), Komunistychna Partiia (bil'shovykiv) Ukrainy, *XVI z'izd komunistychnoi partii (bil'shovykiv) Ukrainy, 23-28 sichnia 1949 r. Materialy z'izdu* (Kiev, 1949), p. 74. (Hereafter referred to as *XVI z'izd KP[b] U*.) See also *Pravda Ukrainy*, February 19, 1949.

94. *XVI z'izd KP(b) U*, pp. 73-74.

95. "Plenum pravleniia Soiuza pisatelei Ukrainy" [Plenum of the Directorate of the Union of Writers of the Ukraine], *Pravda*, March 5, 1949.

96. Arn. Chikobava, "O nekotorykh voprosakh sovetskogo iazykoznaniia" [On Some Questions of Soviet Philology], *Pravda*, May 9, 1950.

97. See *Pravda*, May 9, 16, 23, and 30, June 6, 13, and 27, July 4, 1950.

98. Stalin's first two statements were printed in *Pravda*, June 20 and July 4, 1950. Subsequently they were reprinted with three additional statements in *Marksizm i voprosy iazykoznaniia* (Moscow, 1950). An English translation is available: Joseph Stalin, *Marxism and Linguistics* (New York, 1951).

99. Stalin, *Marxism and Linguistics*, p. 11.
100. *Ibid.*, p. 22.
101. See above, pp. 178-79.
102. Stalin, *Marxism and Linguistics*, p. 28.
103. *Ibid.*, pp. 45-46.
104. A. E. Mordinov, "O razvitii iazykov sotsialisticheskikh natsii v SSSR" [On the Development of the Languages of the Socialist Nations in the USSR], *Voprosy filosofii*, IV, No. 3 (1950), 82-85.
105. See *ibid.*, pp. 93-95.
106. The percentage of west Ukrainian peasant households included in collectives in the years 1948 to 1951 was as follows:

January 1, 1948	9.6 percent
January 1, 1949	49.0
July 1, 1950	92.7
July 1, 1951	95.2

Akademiia nauk USSR, Institut ekonomiki, *Ocherki razvitiia narodnogo khoziaistva Ukrainskoi SSR* (Moscow, 1954), p. 524.
107. "O sostoianii i merakh ulushcheniia massovopoliticheskoi raboty sredi gorodskogo i sel'skogo naseleniia" [On the Status and Measures for Improvement of Mass-Political Work among the City and Rural Population], *Pravda Ukrainy*, May 18, 1949.
108. Direct accounts of the Central Committee session or its decisions are not available. See later references in *Pravda*, October 14, 1950; *Pravda Ukrainy*, February 21 and August 11, 1951.
109. See especially the report of the September, 1950, Plenum of the Lvov oblast committee, *Pravda*, September 30, 1950; I. Grushevs'kyi, "Ideologicheskaia rabota sredi intelligentsii" [Ideological Work among the Intelligentsia], *Pravda*, October 14, 1950; the report of the Lvov oblast Party conference of February, 1951, *Pravda Ukrainy*, February 21, 1951.
110. "Bol'she neprimirimosti k nedostatkam v partiinoi i khoziaistvennoi rabote" [More Ruthlessness toward Shortcomings in Party and Economic Work] (Report of the February Party conference of the Lvov oblast), *Pravda Ukrainy*, February 21, 1951.
111. *Ibid.* See also Armstrong, *Soviet Bureaucratic Elite*, p. 115.
112. *Pravda*, September 30, 1950.
113. *Ibid.*; *Pravda*, October 14, 1950.
114. "Protiv ideologicheskikh izvrashchenii v literature," *Pravda*, July 2, 1951.
115. "Liubi Ukrainu," *Zvezda*, XXVIII, No. 5 (May, 1951), 128-29.
116. See the report of a July Party meeting in the Union of Soviet Writers of the Ukraine, "Reshitel'no i do kontsa iskorenit' ideologicheskie izvrashcheniia v literature" [Decisively and Finally To Root Out Ideological Perversions in Literature], *Pravda Ukrainy*, July 14, 1951.

117. *Pravda Ukrainy*, July and August, 1951.

118. *Pravda Ukrainy*, December 18, 1949.

119. In eight instances new secretaries were appointed; in six cases secretaries were shifted from one oblast to another.

120. *Pravda*, July 2, 1951.

121. The resolution was not made public but was described in *Pravda*, July 13, 1951, and in *Pravda Ukrainy*, July 14, 1951.

122. V. Shamovskii, "Partorganizatsii L'vova perestraivaiut rukovodstvo ideologicheskoi rabotoi" [Party Organizations of Lvov are Reorganizing Leadership of Ideological Work], *Pravda Ukrainy*, August 11, 1951.

123. Oblasts in which changes are known to have been made include Odessa, Zaporozh'e, Voroshilovgrad, Zhitomir, and Stanislav. Changes were also made in the same period in the Kherson, Poltava, Kirovograd, and Vinnitsa oblasts.

124. For four oblasts the figures were as follows:

Ternopol'	33 percent
Dnepropetrovsk	30
Zhitomir	25
Lvov	21

"Plenum TsK KP(b) Ukrainy" [Plenum of the Central Committee of the CP(b) of the Ukraine], *Pravda*, June 2, 1952.

125. *Pravda Ukrainy*, April 5, 1952.

126. *Pravda Ukrainy*, May 30, 1952.

127. *Ibid*. See also reports of oblast plenary sessions in *Pravda Ukrainy*, June 7, 11, 12, 21, and 27, 1952.

128. Kiev, Zaporozh'e, Kirovograd, Vinnitsa, Rovno, Ternopol', Drogobych, Zakarpat'skaia, and Chernovtsy. Earlier, in the summer of 1952, changes had been made in the Poltava, Zhitomir, Lvov, and Izmail oblasts.

129. L. G. Mel'nikov, "Otchet Tsentral'nogo Komiteta KP(b)U" [Report of the Central Committee of the CP(b)U], *Pravda Ukrainy*, September 25, 1952. See also reports to the Congress by Bazhan, Korniets, Serdiuk, Hrushets'kyi, and Nazarenko, *Pravda Ukrainy*, September 26, 27, and 28, October 2, 1952; "Protiv retsidivov burzhuaznogo natsionalizma" [Against Relapses of Bourgeois Nationalism], *Pravda Ukrainy*, October 3, 1952; F. Enevich, "Ser'eznye nedostatki zhurnala 'Kommunist Ukrainy'" [Serious Weaknesses of the Journal "Kommunist Ukrainy"], *Kommunist*, XXIX, No. 20 (November, 1952), 108-13; "Za novyi pod'em ideologicheskoi raboty" [For a New Raising of Ideological Work], *Pravda*, December 28, 1952; Pavlo Tychina, "Ivan Franko—neprimirimyi borets protiv ukrainskogo burzhuaznogo natsionalizma" [Ivan Franko—Uncompromising Warrior against Ukrainian Bourgeois Nationalism], *Pravda Ukrainy*, January 10, 1953; "O natsionalisticheskikh pisaniiakh D.

Kosarika" [On the Nationalist Writings of D. Kosarik], *Pravda Ukrainy*, January 11, 1953.

130. Harrison E. Salisbury, *American in Russia* (New York, 1955), pp. 140-58.

VII. THE NEW LEADERSHIP, 1953-1957

1. See Salisbury, *American in Russia*, pp. 170-74.

2. *Pravda Ukrainy*, April 11, 1953. At the same time, the Ministry of State Security was absorbed into the Ministry of Internal Affairs. Similar steps were taken in the other Union republics.

3. *Pravda Ukrainy*, May 6, 1953.

4. "Plenum TsK KP Ukrainy" [A Plenum of the Central Committee of the CP of the Ukraine], *Pravda Ukrainy*, June 13, 1953.

5. Mel'nikov's place on the Bureau of the Central Committee was taken by the Ukrainian playwright O. I. Korniichuk who, in the previous week, had been named First Deputy Chairman of the Ukrainian Council of Ministers. *Ibid.*

6. See reports of plenary sessions of the Party committees in the Lvov, Stanislav, Drogobych, Ternopol', Volynia, Zakarpatskaia, Izmail, and Chernovtsy oblasts. *Pravda Ukrainy*, June 18, 19, 20, and 26, 1953.

7. "Uluchshit' rukovodstvo razvitiem ekonomiki i kul'tury v zapadnykh oblastiakh Ukrainy" [To Improve Leadership in the Development of the Economy and Culture in the Western Oblasts of the Ukraine], *Pravda Ukrainy*, June 26, 1953.

8. G. Gaponchuk, "Uluchshit' lektsionnuiu propagandu" [To Improve Lecture Propaganda], *Pravda Ukrainy*, June 21, 1953.

9. *Pravda Ukrainy*, June 26, 1953.

10. Gaponchuk, *Pravda Ukrainy*, June 21, 1953.

11. *Zaria Vostoka*, April 15 and 16, 1953. Beria's role in the Georgian changes was suggested by V. M. Bakradze in his report to the Georgian Supreme Soviet (*ibid.*) and in an editorial in *Zaria Vostoka*, April 29, 1953. See also the changes in Latvia reported in *Pravda*, June 28, 1953.

12. *Zaria Vostoka*, April 16, 21, and 29, May 5, 1953.

13. That Khrushchev remained the dominant influence in the Ukraine is suggested by the few changes in Party leadership made after Beria's removal. Only two shifts were reported in the Party press: O. I. Korniichuk was added to the Bureau of the Communist Party of the Ukraine; K. Z. Lytvyn, newly appointed Minister of Culture, was dropped as Second Secretary of the Lvov oblast. *Pravda Ukrainy*, June 13 and 18, 1953.

14. *Pravda*, July 10, 1953. See also the reports by Korniichuk and Semenenko in *Pravda Ukrainy*, July 11, 1953, and the editorials and reports in *Pravda Ukrainy*, July 12 and 14, 1953.

15. See below, p. 294.

16. *Pravda Ukrainy*, July 16, 1953. Meshik was subsequently executed with Beria.

17. *Pravda Ukrainy*, August 18, 1953.

18. *Pravda Ukrainy*, September 13, 1953.

19. *Pravda Ukrainy*, September 19, November 24 and 25, 1953. The changes were made in the Sumy, Chernigov, and Chernovtsy oblasts. This was the first mention of Komiakhov, and his background is unknown.

20. The most important changes were made in January, 1954, when M. S. Hrechukha was shifted from the Presidency of the Presidium of the Ukrainian Supreme Soviet to Vice-Chairman of the Council of Ministers; D. S. Korotchenko was dropped as Chairman of the Council of Ministers and named to Hrechukha's post; N. T. Kal'chenko was promoted to replace Korotchenko. *Pravda Ukrainy*, January 16, 1954.

21. *Pravda*, February 27, 1954.

22. *Ibid.*; *Pravda Ukrainy*, February 28, 1954. The two chief economic motivations were the uniting of the iron and steel centers near Kerch in the Crimea with those of the Donbass in the Ukraine and the completion of an irrigation system designed to draw water from the southern Ukraine to the dry steppes of the northern Crimea.

23. See Kyrychenko's address to a Kiev election meeting, *Pravda*, March 10, 1954. See also *Pravda Ukrainy*, February 27 and 28, 1954.

24. *BSE*, Vol. LIX (1935), cols. 816-18.

25. *Pravda Ukrainy*, January 12, 1954.

26. *Pravda Ukrainy*, January 17, 1954.

27. A. M. Puzanov, "Doklad Predsedatelia Soveta Ministrov RSFSR na Iubileinoi sessii Verkhovnogo Soveta RSFSR 29 maia 1954 goda" [Report of the President of the Council of Ministers of the RSFSR to the Jubilee Session of the Supreme Soviet of the RSFSR, May 29, 1954], *Pravda*, May 30, 1954.

28. See the proclamation of the USSR government and Party leadership to the government of the RSFSR, *Pravda*, May 30, 1954.

29. *Pravda*, May 23, 1954; see also May 22-31, 1954.

30. See also the list and discussion in Armstrong, *Soviet Bureaucratic Elite*, pp. 147-51.

31. The ethnic composition of the Party was reported at the Fifteenth (May, 1940) and Nineteenth (January, 1956) Congresses as follows:

	1940	1956
Ukrainians	63.1 percent	74.2 percent
Russians	19.1	25.0
Others	17.8	.8

Pravda, May 18, 1940; V. Holub, "Konspektyvnyi narys istorii KP-(b)U" [Concise Outline of the History of the CP(b)U], *Ukrains'kyi zbirnyk*, IX (1957), 136. The remarkable decrease in Party members from ethnic groups other than Russian and Ukrainian suggests a reclassification of these groups. There are indications these figures are not accurate. For more recent, conflicting figures—which also seem unreliable—see "Kommunisticheskaia partiia Ukrainy v tsifrakh," [The Communist Party of the Ukraine in Figures], *Partiinaia zhizn'*, No. 12 (June, 1958), pp. 57-59.

32. I. Kravtsev, "Leninskaia natsional'naia politika i ee osushchestvlenie na Ukraine" [Leninist National Policy and its Realization in the Ukraine], *Pravda Ukrainy*, December 25, 1956. Ukrainians constituted 66.2 percent, 65.3 percent, and 67.8 percent of the delegates to the Seventeenth, Eighteenth, and Nineteenth Congresses of the Communist Party of the Ukraine in 1952, 1954, and 1956. *Pravda Ukrainy*, September 26, 1952; March 26, 1954; *XIX z'izd KPU*, p. 99.

33. *Pravda Ukrainy*, December 25, 1956.

34. According to the preliminary census figures of 1959, 76.1 percent of the population of the Ukraine was ethnically Ukrainian. *Pravda*, February 4, 1960.

35. "Naveki vmeste" [Forever United], *Pravda*, January 18, 1954. See also Kal'chenko s statement in *Izvestiia*, January 16, 1954.

36. *Pravda Ukrainy*, March 24, 1954. Kyrychenko was referring specifically to the Organization of Ukrainian Nationalists (OUN). See also his speech of March 9, 1954 (*Pravda Ukrainy*, March 10, 1954) and the editorial in *Pravda Ukrainy*, February 23, 1954.

37. *Pravda Ukrainy*, May 23, 1954. See the article by Iosif Krutii, "O puchinakh moego razryva s ukrainskimi natsionalistami" [On the Causes of My Break with Ukrainian Nationalists], *Pravda*, May 19, 1954; also Kyrychenko's harsh statement to the Twentieth Congress of the Communist Party of the Soviet Union (February, 1956), *XX s'ezd KPSS*, I, 143-44.

38. *Pravda Ukrainy*, January 12, 1954; A. Kasimenko, "Istoricheskoe znachenie vossoedineniia Ukrainy s Rossiei" [Historic Importance of the Reunion of the Ukraine with Russia], *Pravda*, May 16, 1954.

39. *V. I. Lenin o natsional'nom i natsional'no-kolonial'nom voprose* (Moscow, 1956).

40. *Kommunist*, XXXIII, No. 9, 22-26. See above, pp. 89-90.

41. Z. Levina and A. Romanova, "Velikaia rol' V. I. Lenina v organizatsii Soiuza Sovetskikh Respublik" [The Great Role of V. I. Lenin in the Organization of the Union of Soviet Republics], *Pravda*, July 11, 1956.

42. H. Emel'ianenko, "Lenins'ki pryntsypy natsional'noi polityky KPRS" [Leninist Principles on the National Policy of the Communist Party of the Soviet Union], *Komunist Ukrainy*, XXXII, No. 10 (October, 1956), 49-61.

43. M. Iovchuk, "Leninizm-vysshee dostizhenie russkoi i mirovoi kul'tury" [Leninism—the Highest Achievement of Russian and World Culture], *Kommunist*, XXXII, No. 1 (January, 1955), 23-28.

44. *Ibid.*; *Literaturnaia gazeta*, November 10 and 15, 1955; P. Fedoseev, "Sotsializm i patriotizm" [Socialism and Patriotism], *Kommunist*, XXX, No. 9 (June, 1953), 12-28.

45. N. S. Khrushchev, "Otchetnyi doklad Tsentral'nogo Komiteta Kommunisticheskoi Partii Sovetskogo Soiuza XX s″ezdu partii" [Informational Report of the Central Committee of the Communist Party of the Soviet Union to the Twentieth Congress of the Party], *XX s″ezd KPSS*, I, 87.

46. Levina and Romanova, *Pravda*, July 11, 1956.

47. *Kommunist*, XXXIII, No. 9, 22-26.

48. New York *Times*, June 5, 1956.

49. Kravtsev, *Pravda Ukrainy*, December 25, 1956; S. Kazakov, "Chto chitat' ob internatsional'nom vospitanii trudiashchikhsia" [What To Read on the International Development of the Working People], *Partiinaia zhizn'*, No. 12 (June, 1955), pp. 71-78.

50. *XX s″ezd KPSS*, II, 422.

51. P. G. Tychyna, *Pravda Ukrainy*, August 8, 1953. Tychyna noted that of the 30,000 schools in the Ukraine nearly 3,000 were being conducted in the Russian language. Other figures were given by Lytvyn who reported the following on the percentage of students of Ukrainian background in the higher schools:

1929 —	51.8 percent	1949 —	55.6 percent
1938 —	54.2	1950 —	57.9
1946 —	51.8	1951 —	59.1
1947 —	53.5	1952 —	59.9
1948 —	53.8	1953 —	62.7

K. Z. Litvin, *Rastsvet kul'tury sovetskoi Ukrainy* (Kiev, 1954), pp. 36, 38. The figure for 1953 is for candidates of the higher schools.

52. Litvin, *Rastsvet kul'tury*, p. 68.

53. Kravtsev, *Pravda Ukrainy*, December 25, 1956.

54. See above, pp. 288-89.

55. The discrepancy in the totals was not explained but was presumably accounted for by schools for which information was not available.

56. See above, n. 31, p. 390. In 1956 only 0.4 percent of the total copies of newspapers printed in the Ukraine were in languages other than Ukrainian or Russian. Kravtsev, *Pravda Ukrainy*, December 25, 1956.

57. Litvin, *Rastsvet kul'tury*, p. 32.

58. The figure is roughly confirmed by the 1959 census which indicated that of the Soviet Union's 36,981,000 Ukrainians, 87.6 percent considered Ukrainian their native tongue. *Pravda*, February 4, 1960. Since pressures for abandoning Ukrainian would be much greater in the non-Ukrainian republics—with the possible exception of the Moldavian SSR—it seems reasonable that a slightly larger percentage, perhaps 90 percent, of Ukrainians inside the Ukrainian SSR would have continued accepting Ukrainian as their primary language.

59. Aram Khatchaturian, "O tvorcheskoi smelosti i vdokhnovenii" [On Creative Boldness and Inspiration], *Sovetskaia muzyka*, XVII, No. 11 (November, 1953), 7-13; Il'ia Erenburg, "O rabote pisatelia" [On the Work of a Writer], *Znamia*, XXIII, No. 10 (October, 1953) 160-83; "Pravo i dolg teatra" [Right and Duty of a Theater], *Pravda*, November 27, 1953; V. Pomerantsev, "Ob iskrennosti v literature" [On Sincerity in Literature], *Novyi mir*, XXIX, No 12 (December, 1953), 218-45; D. Shostakovich, "Radost' tvorcheskikh iskanii" [The Joy of the Creative Search], *Sovetskaia muzyka*, XVIII, No. 1 (January, 1954), 40-42.

60. *Sovetskaia muzyka*, XVIII, No. 1, 40-42.

61. November 27, 1953.

62. A. Surkov, "Pod znamenem sotsialisticheskogo realizma" [Under the Banner of Socialist Realism], *Pravda*, May 25, 1954; V. Ermilov, "Za sotsialisticheskii realizm" [For Socialist Realism], *Pravda*, June 3, 1954; "Glavnaia zadacha sotsialisticheskogo realizma—vozbuzhdenie revoliutsionnogo miroponimaniia" [The Chief Task of Socialist Realism Is To Arouse Revolutionary Understanding], *Pravda*, June 18, 1954; "Za dal'neishii pod'em sovetskoi literatury" [For a Further Improvement of Soviet Literature], *Kommunist*, XXXI, No. 9 (June, 1954), 12-27. See also earlier statements in *Pravda*, January 6, 1954, and *Literaturnaia gazeta*, January 30, 1954.

63. Surkov, *Pravda*, May 25, 1954.

64. "Za tesnuiu sviaz' literatury i iskusstva s zhizn'iu naroda" [For a Close Tie between Literature and Art and the Life of the People], *Pravda*, August 28, 1957.

65. *Ibid.*

66. *Ibid.* Shostakovich seconded Khrushchev's comments: "It seems to me that abusive epithets leveled at workers in Soviet culture must be eliminated forever." ("Po puti, ukazannomu partiei" [Along the Path Laid Down by the Party], *Sovetskaia musyka*, XXI, No. 10 [October, 1957], 10.)

67. A. M. Pikman, "O bor'be kavkazskikh gortsev s tsarskimi kolonizatorami" [On the Battle of Caucasian Mountaineers with Tsarist Colonizers], *Voprosy istorii*, No. 3 (March, 1956), pp. 75-84; S. K. Bushuev, "O kavkazskom miuridizme" [On Caucasian Muridism], *Voprosy istorii*, No. 12 (December, 1956), pp. 72-79. See, however, the criticism in *Kommunist*, XXXIV, No. 4 (March, 1957), 17-29, where *Voprosy istorii* is charged with adopting a "liberal" attitude.

68. Kazakov, *Partiinaia zhizn'*, No. 12, pp. 71-78; A. A. Surkov, "O sostoianii i zadachakh sovetskoi literatury" [On the Status and Tasks of Soviet Literature], *Literaturnaia gazeta*, December 16, 1954.

69. O. I. Kyrychenko, "Otchet Tsentral'nogo Komiteta KP Ukrainy" [Report of the Central Committee of the CP of the Ukraine], *Pravda Ukrainy*, January 19, 1956; Kravtsev, *Pravda Ukrainy*, December 25, 1956.

70. P. Petrenko, "Nova knyga z istorii ukrains'koi radians'koi literatury "[New Book on the History of Ukrainian Soviet Literature], *Komunist Ukrainy*, XXX, No. 3 (March, 1955), 64-72.

71. Kravtsev, *Pravda Ukrainy*, December 25, 1956; *XX s″ezd KPSS*, I, 90.

72. Kravtsev, *Pravda Ukrainy*, December 25, 1956. See also Khatchaturian, *Sovetskaia muzyka*, XVII, No. 11, 7-13.

73. *XX s″ezd KPSS*, I, 38. The quotation is from *Lenin*, XXIII, 58.

74. "Pust' zdravstvuet nerushimaia bratskaia druzhba nashikh narodov" [Hail the Indestructible Brotherly Friendship of Our Peoples] *Pravda*, July 12, 1957.

75. B. Gafurov, "Druzhba narodov—istochnik sily sovetskogo gosudarstva" [Friendship of Peoples Is the Source of the Strength of the Soviet State], *Pravda*, August 15, 1955; K. Dubyna, "Pro formy perekhodu riznykh krain do sotsializmu" [On the Methods of the Transition of Various Countries to Socialism], *Komunist Ukrainy*, XXXI, No. 4 (April, 1956), 31-42.

76. Emel'ianenko, *Komunist Ukrainy*, XXXII, No. 10, 49-61.

77. *XX s″ezd KPSS*, I, 90-91.

78. *Lenin*, XXI, 86, quoted in *ibid.*

79. M. Tikhomirov and others, "Nauchnyi trud po istorii Ukrainy" [Scientific Work on the History of the Ukraine], *Pravda*, April 18, 1954.

80. *Pravda Ukrainy*, October 10, 27, 29, 30, and 31, November 2, 1954.

81. Surkov, *Literaturnaia gazeta*, December 16, 1954; Petrenko, *Komunist Ukrainy*, XXX, No. 3, 64-72; Emel'ianenko, *Komunist Ukrainy*, XXXII, No. 10, 49-61; Kravtsev, *Pravda Ukrainy*, December 25, 1956.

82. Kravtsev, *Pravda Ukrainy*, December 25, 1956.

83. Gafurov, *Pravda*, August 15, 1955; *XX s"ezd KPSS*, I, 40, 87.

84. *XX s"ezd KPSS*, I, 91.

85. *Partiinaia zhizn'*, No. 24 (December, 1956), p. 69; "Sovetskii apparat upravleniia—vazhnoe orudie kommunisticheskogo stroitel'stva" [Soviet Administrative Apparatus—Important Arm of Communist Construction], *Kommunist*, XXXIII, No. 17 (November, 1956), 3-16.

86. G. Shitarev, "Demokraticheskii tsentralizm i rukovodiashchaia deiatel'nost' partiinykh organov" [Democratic Centralism and the Leadership Work of Party Organs], *Kommunist*, XXX, No. 18 (December, 1953), 51-66.

87. *Pravda*, March 21, 1954.

88. Included in the latter group were the Ministries of Justice, Automotive Transport and Highways, Urban and Rural Construction, and Building Materials Industries.

89. "Ob izmenenii praktiki planirovannia sel'skogo khoziaistva" [On Revising the Practice of Planning Agriculture], *Pravda*, March 11, 1955.

90. *XX s"ezd KPSS*, I, 88.

91. *Ibid.*, I, 90. See also Kravtsev, *Pravda Ukrainy*, December 25, 1956.

92. V. Chuistov, "Leninskii printsip demokraticheskogo tsentralizma v upravlenii khoziaistvom" [The Leninist Principle of Democratic Centralism in the Administration of the Economy], *Pravda Ukrainy*, February 7, 1957. Kal'chenko reported that in the Soviet Union as a whole nearly 10,000 enterprises were shifted in the period from 1954 to 1957. "Rech' tov. N. T. Kal'chenko" [Speech of Comrade N. T. Kal'chenko], *Pravda Ukrainy*, February 8, 1957.

93. *Pravda Ukrainy*, February 8, 1957.

94. *Pravda*, March 30, 1957; see also May 8 and 11, 1957.

95. *Pravda Ukrainy*, May 31 and June 1, 1957.

96. *Pravda*, May 24, 1957.

97. *Pravda*, February 12, 1957. For the corresponding changes in the Ukraine see *Pravda Ukrainy*, March 17, 1957.

98. *Pravda Ukrainy*, August 29, 1957.

99. See above, pp. 80-83.

100. *Pravda,* May 8, 1957.

101. *Pravda Ukrainy*, August 29, 1957.

102. Gafurov, *Pravda*, August 15, 1955.

103. *XX s"ezd KPSS*, I, 89-90.

104. Gafurov, *Pravda*, August 15, 1955.

BIBLIOGRAPHY

Only items referred to in the text or of direct relevance to the study are included. Newspaper articles are not listed except where they are of special interest.

Most items are available at the Library of Congress. Other items are to be found in the Russian collections of one of the following: New York Public Library; Hoover Library of War, Peace, and Revolution, Stanford University; Columbia University Libraries; University of Chicago Libraries. A few items were used in the Lenin Library in Moscow and are not available outside the Soviet Union.

PUBLIC DOCUMENTS
RECORDS OF PARTY CONGRESSES, CONFERENCES, AND PLENARY SESSIONS

KOMMUNISTICHESKAIA PARTIIA SOVETSKOGO SOIUZA: KPSS (Communist Party of the Soviet Union).

Until the Eighth Congress (March-April, 1919) the Party bore the name Rossiiskaia Sotsial-Demokraticheskaia Rabochaia Partiia (bol'shevikov): RSDRP(b) (Russian Social-Democratic Workers' Party [Bolshevik]). From the Eighth to the Fourteenth Congress (December, 1925) the Party was designated Russkaia Kommunisticheskaia Partiia (bol'shevikov): RKP(b) (Russian Communist Party [Bolshevik]). From the Fourteenth to the Nineteenth Congress (October, 1952) the Party was named Vsesoiuznaia Kommunisticheskaia Partiia (bol'shevikov): VKP(b) (All-Union Communist Party [Bolshevik]).

Kommunisticheskaia Partiia Sovetskogo Soiuza v rezoliutsiiakh i resheniiakh s"ezdov, konferentsii i plenumov TsK, 1898-1954 (The Communist Party of the Soviet Union in Resolutions and Decisions of Congresses, Conferences, and Plenums of the Central Committee, 1898-1954). 3 vols. 7th ed. Moscow, 1954.

Vsesoiuznaia Kommunisticheskaia Partiia (bol'shevikov) v rezoliutsiiakh s"ezdov, konferentsii i plenumov Ts. K., 1898-1935 (All-Union Communist Party [Bolshevik] in Resolutions of Congresses, Conferences, and Plenums of the Central Committee, 1898-1935). 2 vols. 5th ed. Moscow, 1935.

Protokoly VI s″ezda RSDRP(b), 26 iiulia - 3 avgusta, 1917 g. (Minutes of the Sixth Congress of the RSDWP [b], July 26 - August 3, 1917). Moscow, 1919.

Protokoly VIII s″ezda RSDRP(b), mart-aprel' 1919 g. (Minutes of the Eighth Congress of the RSDWP [b], March-April, 1919). Moscow, 1919.

Protokoly deviatogo s″ezda RKP(b), 29 marta - 4 aprelia 1920 g. (Minutes of the Ninth Congress of the RCP[b], March 29 - April 4, 1920). Moscow, 1920.

Desiatyi s″ezd RKP(b). Protokoly, mart 1921 g. (Tenth Congress of the RCP[b]. Minutes, March, 1921). Moscow, 1933.

Odinnadtsatyi s″ezd RKP(b), mart-aprel' 1922 g. (Eleventh Congress of the RCP[b], March-April, 1922). Moscow, 1936.

Dvenadtsatyi s″ezd Rossiiskoi Kommunisticheskoi Partii (b), 17-25 aprelia 1923 g. Stenograficheskii otchet (Twelfth Congress of the Russian Communist Party [b], April 17-25, 1923. Stenographic Record). Moscow, 1923.

Trinadtsatyi s″ezd Rossiiskoi Kommunisticheskoi Partii (b), Stenograficheskii otchet, 23-31 maia 1924 g. (Thirteenth Congress of the Russian Communist Party [b]. Stenographic Record, May 23-31, 1924). Moscow, 1924.

XIV s″ezd Vsesoiuznoi Kommunisticheskoi Partii (b). Stenograficheskii otchet, 18-31 dekabria 1925 g. (Fourteenth Congress of the All-Union Communist Party [b]. Stenographic Record, December 18-31, 1925). Moscow, 1926.

Rykov, A. I., (ed.). *Ob itogakh ob″edinennogo plenuma TsK i TsKK VKP(b), 14-23 iiulia 1926* (On the Results of the Joint Plenum of the Central Committee and Central Control Commission of the All-Union Communist Party [b], July 14-23, 1926). Moscow, 1926.

XV konferentsiia Vsesoiuznoi Kommunisticheskoi Partii (b), 26 oktiabria - 3 noiabria 1926 g. Stenograficheskii otchet (Fifteenth Conference of the All-Union Communist Party [b], October 26 - November 3, 1926. Stenographic Record). Moscow, 1927.

XV s″ezd Vsesoiuznoi Kommunisticheskoi Partii (b), 2-19 dekabria 1927 g. Stenograficheskii otchet (Fifteenth Congress of the All-Union Communist Party [b], December 2-19, 1927. Stenographic Record). Moscow, 1928.

XVI konferentsiia Vsesoiuznoi Kommunisticheskoi Partii (b). Stenograficheskii otchet, 23-29 aprelia 1929 g. (Sixteenth Conference of the All-Union Communist Party [b]. Stenographic Record, April 23-29, 1929). Moscow, 1929.

Itogi noiabr'skogo plenuma TsK VKP(b), 10-17 noiabria 1929 g. (Results of the November Plenum of the Central Committee of the All-Union Communist Party [b], November 10-17, 1929). Leningrad, 1929.

XVI s″ezd Vsesoiuznoi Kommunisticheskoi Partii (b), 26 iiunia - 13 iiulia 1930 g. Stenograficheskii otchet (Sixteenth Congress of the All-Union Communist Party [b], June 26 - July 13, 1930. Stenographic Record). Moscow, 1930.

Itogi ob″edinennogo plenuma TsK i TsKK VKP(b), dekabr'17-21, 1930 (Results of the Joint Plenum of the Central Committee and Central Control Commission of the All-Union Communist Party [b], December 17-21, 1930). Leningrad, 1930.

Itogi plenuma TsK VKP(b), 11-15 iiunia 1931 g. (Results of the Plenum of the Central Committee of the All-Union Communist Party [b], June 11-15, 1931). Leningrad, 1931.

XVII konferentsiia Vsesoiuznoi Kommunisticheskoi Partii (b), 30 ianvaria - 4 fevralia 1932 g. Stenograficheskii otchet (Seventeenth Conference of the All-Union Communist Party [b], January 30 - February 4, 1932. Stenographic Record). Moscow, 1932.

XVII s″ezd Vsesoiuznoi Kommunisticheskoi Partii (b), 26 ianvaria - 10 fevralia 1934 g. Stenograficheskii otchet (Seventeenth Congress of the All-Union Communist Party [b], January 26 - February 10, 1934. Stenographic Record). Moscow, 1934.

XVIII s″ezd Vsesoiuznoi Kommunisticheskoi Partii (b), 10-21 marta 1939 g. Stenograficheskii otchet (Eighteenth Congress of the All-Union Communist Party [b], March 10-21, 1939. Stenographic Record). Moscow, 1939.

Gruliow, Leo (ed.). *Current Soviet Policies. The Documentary Record of the 19th Communist Party Congress and the Reorganization after Stalin's Death.* New York, 1953.

XX s″ezd Kommunisticheskoi Partii Sovetskogo Soiuza, 14-25 fevralia 1956 goda. Stenograficheskii otchet (Twentieth Congress of the Communist Party of the Soviet Union, February 14-25, 1956. Stenographic Record). 2 vols. Moscow, 1956.

Gruliow, Leo (ed.). *Current Soviet Policies II, The Documentary Record of the 20th Communist Party Congress and Its Aftermath.* New York, 1957.

KOMMUNISTICHESKAIA PARTIIA UKRAINY (Communist Party of the Ukraine)

Until the Nineteenth Congress of the Communist Party of the Soviet Union (October, 1952) the Party bore the name, Kommunisticheskaia Partiia (bol'shevikov) Ukrainy: KP(b)U (Communist Party [Bolshevik] of the Ukraine: CP[b]U). Ukrainian works are published under the name, Komunistychna Partiia Ukrainy.

Kommunisticheskaia partiia Ukrainy v rezoliutsiiakh i resheniiakh s″ezdov i konferentsii, 1918-1956 (The Communist Party of the Ukraine in the Resolutions and Decisions of its Congresses and Conferences, 1918-1956). Kiev, 1958.

Pervyi s"ezd Kommunisticheskoi Partii (b) Ukrainy, 5-12 iiulia 1918 g. (First Congress of the Communist Party [b] of the Ukraine, July 5-12, 1918). Kharkov, 1923.

Ostanni partiini dokumenty z natsional'noi polityky KP(b) U (Recent Party Documents on the National Policy of the CP[b]U). Kharkov, 1927.

Rezoliutsii plenuma Tsentral'nogo Komiteta KP(b) U, 9-10 iiulia 1946 g. (Resolutions of the Plenum of the Central Committee of the CP[b]U, July 9-10, 1946). Kiev, 1946.

Rezoliutsii plenuma Tsentral'nogo Komiteta KP(b) U, 14-18 maia 1946 g. (Resolutions of the Plenum of the Central Committee of the CP[b]U, May 14-18, 1946). Kiev, 1946.

Rezoliutsii plenumu Tsentral'noho Komitetu KP(b) U, 28 liutoho - 2 bereznia 1946 r. (Resolutions of the Plenum of the Central Committee of the CP[b]U, February 28 - March 2, 1946). Kiev, 1946.

XVI z'izd komunistychnoi partii (bil'shovykiv) Ukrainy, 23-28 sichnia 1949 r. Materialy z'izdu (XVI Congress of the Communist Party [Bolshevik] of the Ukraine, January 23-28, 1949. Materials of the Congress). Kiev, 1949.

XVII z'izd komunistychnoi partii (bil'shovykiv) Ukrainy, 23-27 veresnia 1952 r. Materialy z'izdu (XVII Congress of the Communist Party [Bolshevik] of the Ukraine, September 23-27, 1952. Materials of the Congress). Kiev, 1953.

XVIII z'izd komunistychnoi partii (bil'shovykiv) Ukrainy, 23-26 marta 1954 r. Materialy z'izdu (XVIII Congress of the Communist Party [Bolshevik] of the Ukraine, March 23-26, 1954. Materials of the Congress). Kiev, 1954.

XIX z'izd komunistychnoi partii (bil'shovykiv) Ukrainy, 17-21 sichnia 1956 roku. Materialy z'izdu (XIX Congress of the Communist Party [Bolshevik] of the Ukraine, January 17-21, 1956. Materials of the Congress). Kiev, 1956.

Plenum Tsentral'nogo Komiteta, 1959. Stenograficheskii otchet (Plenum of the Central Committee, 1959. Stenographic Record). Kiev, 1959.

KOMMUNISTICHESKII INTERNATSIONAL (Communist International)

Kommunisticheskii internatsional v dokumentakh, 1919-1932 (The Communist International in Documents, 1919-1932). Moscow, 1933.

Vtoroi kongress Kominterna, iiul'-avgust 1920 g. (Second Congress of the Comintern, July-August, 1920). Moscow, 1934.

Piatyi vsemirnyi kongress Kommunisticheskogo Internatsionala, 17 iiunia - 8 iiulia 1924 g. (Fifth World Congress of the Communist International, June 17 - July 8, 1924). 2 vols. Moscow, 1925.

RECORDS OF SOVIET CONGRESSES AND SESSIONS

S"ezdy Sovetov vserossiiskie i Soiuza SSR v postanovleniiakh i rezoliutsiiakh (Congresses of Soviets of the All-Russian and Union of Soviet Socialist Republics in Decisions and Resolutions). Moscow, 1935.

S"ezdy Sovetov SSSR v postanovleniiakh i rezoliutsiiakh (Congresses of Soviets of the USSR in Decisions and Resolutions). Moscow, 1939.

s"ezdy sovetov sssr. stenograficheskie otchety (Congresses of Soviets of the USSR. Stenographic Records)

I S"ezd Sovetov SSSR. Stenograficheskii otchet (December 30, 1922). Moscow, 1923.

Vtoroi S"ezd Sovetov SSSR... (January 26 - February 2, 1924). Moscow, 1924.

Tretii S"'ezd Sovetov SSSR... (May 13-20, 1925). Moscow, 1925.

4 S"ezd Sovetov SSSR... (April 18-23, 1927). Moscow, 1927.

5 S"ezd Sovetov SSSR... (May 20-28, 1929). Moscow, 1929.

6 S"ezd Sovetov SSSR. Stenograficheskii otchet i postanovleniia. (March 8-17, 1931). Moscow, 1931.

7 S"ezd Sovetov SSSR. Stenograficheskii otchet i postanovleniia. (January 28 - February 6, 1935).

sssr. tsentral'nyi ispolnitel'nyi komitet. sozyv... stenograficheskii otchet (USSR. Central Executive Committee. Convocation... Stenographic Report)

I sozyv (First Convocation)

I-ia sessiia tsentral'nogo ispolnitel'nogo komiteta SSSR. Stenograficheskii otchet (First Session of the Central Executive Committee of the USSR. Stenographic Record, December 30, 1922). Moscow, 1923.

Vtoraia sessiia TsIK SSSR... (July 6, 1923). Moscow, 1923.

Tret'ia sessiia TsIK SSSR... (November 6-12, 1923). Moscow, 1924.

II sozyv (Second Convocation)

Pervaia sessiia TsIK SSSR... (February 2, 1924). Moscow, 1924.

2 sessiia TsIK SSSR... (October 17-29, 1924). Moscow, 1924.

3 sessiia TsIK SSSR... (March 3-7, 1925). Moscow, 1925.

III sozyv (Third Convocation)

1 sessiia TsIK SSSR... (May 21, 1925). Moscow, 1925.

2 sessiia TsIK SSSR... (April 12-25, 1926). Moscow, 1926.

3 sessiia TsIK SSSR... (February 14-25, 1927). Moscow, 1927.

IV sozyv (Fourth Convocation)

Pervaia sessiia TsIK SSSR... (April 27, 1927). Moscow, 1927.

2 sessiia TsIK SSSR... (October 15-20, 1927). Moscow, 1927.

3 sessiia TsIK SSSR... (April 11-21, 1928). Moscow, 1928.

4 sessiia TsIK SSSR... (December 3-15, 1928). Moscow, 1928.

V sozyv (Fifth Convocation)

2 sessiia TsIK SSSR... (November 29 - December 8, 1929). Moscow, 1929.

3 sessiia TsIK SSSR... (January 4-12, 1931). Moscow, 1931.

VI sozyv (Sixth Convocation)

2 sessiia TsIK SSSR. Stenograficheskii otchet i postanovleniia (December 22-28, 1931). Moscow, 1931.

4 sessiia TsIK SSSR. Stenograficheskii otchet i postanovleniia (December 28 - January 4, 1934). Moscow, 1934.

VII sozyv (Seventh Convocation)

2 sessiia TsIK. Stenograficheskii otchet (January 10-17, 1936). Moscow, 1936.

3 sessiia TsIK. Sbornik biulletenei (January 11-13, 1937). Moscow, 1937.

SSSR. VERKHOVNYI SOVET. STENOGRAFICHESKIE OTCHETY (USSR.
Supreme Soviet. Stenographic Records)

I sozyv (First Convocation)

Pervaia sessiia Verkhovnogo Soveta SSSR. Stenograficheskii otchet (First Session of the Supreme Soviet of the USSR, Stenographic Record) (January 12-19, 1938). Moscow, 1938.

Vtoraia sessiia Verkh. Soveta SSSR... (August 10-21, 1938). Moscow, 1938.

Tret'ia sessiia Verkh. Soveta SSSR... (May 25-31, 1939). Moscow, 1939.

Vneocherednaia chetvertaia sessiia Verkh. Soveta SSSR... (August 28 - September 1, 1939). Moscow, 1939.

Vneocherednaia piataia sessiia Verkh. Soveta SSSR... (October 31 - November 2, 1939). Moscow, 1939.

Shestaia sessiia Verkh. Soveta SSSR... (March 29 - April 4, 1940). Moscow, 1940.

Vos'maia sessiia Verkh. Soveta SSSR... (February 25 - March 1, 1941). Moscow, 1941.

Desiataia sessiia Verkh. Soveta SSSR... (January 28 - February 1, 1944). Moscow, 1944.

Odinnadtsataia sessiia Verkh. Soveta SSSR... (April 24 - April 27 1945). Moscow, 1945.

II sozyv (Second Convocation)

Zasedaniia Verkhovnogo Soveta SSSR (Pervaia sessiia). Stenograficheskii otchet (Meetings of the Supreme Soviet of the USSR [First Session]. Stenographic Record) (March 12-19, 1946). Moscow, 1946.

Zasedaniia... (*Vtoraia sessiia*)... (October 15-18, 1946). Moscow, 1946.

Zasedaniia... (*Tret'ia sessiia*)... (February 20-25, 1947). Moscow, 1947.

Zasedaniia... (*Chetvertaia sessiia*)... (January 30 - February 4, 1948). Moscow, 1948.

BOOKS AND ARTICLES

Abramov, Ark and A. Ia. Aleksandrov. *Partiia v rekonstruktivnyi period* (The Party in the Reconstruction Period). Moscow, 1934.

Akademiia nauk SSSR. Institut istorii. *Obrazovanie SSSR, Sbornik dokumentov, 1917-1924* (Formation of the USSR, Collection of Documents, 1917-1924). Moscow, 1941.

Akademiia nauk URSR. Instytut istorii Ukrainy. *Istoriia Ukrainy, korotkyi kurs* (History of the Ukraine, Short Course). Kiev, 1941.

Akademiia nauk URSR. Instytut istorii i arkheologii Ukrainy. *Narys istorii Ukrainy* (Outline of the History of the Ukraine). Ufa, 1942.

—— *Naukovi zapysky* (Scientific Notes). 2 vols. Ufa, 1943-1946.

Akademiia nauk USSR. Institut ekonomiki. *Ocherki razvitiia narodnogo khoziaistva Ukrainskoi SSR* (Notes on the Development of the National Economy of the Ukrainian SSR). Moscow, 1954.

Alekseenko, A. G. *Gorodskie sovety Ukrainskoi SSR (1917-1920 gg.)* (City Soviets of the Ukrainian SSR [1917-1920]). Kiev, 1960.

Allen, W. E. D. *The Ukraine.* Cambridge, 1941.

Antonov-Ovseenko, V. A. *Zapiski o grazhdanskoi voine* (Notes on the Civil War). 2 vols. Moscow, 1924-1933.

Armstrong, John A. *The Politics of Totalitarianism.* New York, 1961.

——. *The Soviet Bureaucratic Elite: a Case Study of the Ukrainian Apparatus.* New York, 1959.

——. *Ukrainian Nationalism 1939-1945.* New York, 1955.

Avtorkhanov, A. "Pokorenie partii" (Subjugation of the Party), *Posev,* VI, No. 45 (November 5, 1950), 14-16; VI, No. 50 (December 10, 1950), 14-15.

Azizian, A. K. *O rabote I. V. Stalina "Marksizm i natsional'nyi vopros"* (On the Work of J. V. Stalin "Marxism and the National Question"). Moscow, 1949.

——. "Uspekhi leninsko-stalinskoi natsional'noi politiki" (Successes of the Leninist-Stalinist National Policy), *Bol'shevik,* XX, No. 2 (January, 1945), 36-47.

Bakshiev, D. *Tsentralizm i demokratizm bol'shevistskoi partii* (Centralism and Democracy in the Bolshevik Party). Moscow, 1948.

Batsell, W. R. *Soviet Rule in Russia.* New York, 1929.

Beloff, Max. *The Foreign Policy of Soviet Russia, 1929-1941.* 2 vols. London, 1949.

Besarabov, M. A. and V. M. Chupryna. *Komunistychna partiia Ukrainy v borot'bi za razvitok kolhospnoho vyrobnytstva v 1938-1941 rr.* (The Communist Party of the Ukraine in the Battle for the Development of Kolkhoz Production in 1938-1941). Lvov, 1959.

Boiko, I. *Velyki sotsialistychni peremohy ukrains'koho narodu* (The Great Socialist Victories of the Ukrainian People). Kiev, 1948.

Bol'shaia sovetskaia entsiklopediia (Great Soviet Encyclopedia). 65 vols. 1st ed. Moscow, 1926-1939.

Bol'shaia sovetskaia entsiklopediia (Great Soviet Encyclopedia). 50 vols. 2d ed. Moscow, 1940-1957.

Borodin, A. A. and P. P. Bachinskii. "Kompartiia Ukrainy v bor'be za osushchestvlenie reshenii VIII s"ezda partii" (The Communist Party of the Ukraine in the Battle for the Realization of the Decisions of the Eighth Congress of the Party), *Voprosy istorii KPSS*, IV, No. 1 (1960), 71-90.

Bortsov, B. P., N. N. Lipovchenko, and Ia. E. Paskho. "K osveshcheniiu voprosa ob obrazovanii KP(b) Ukrainy i ee taktiki v 1918 godu" (Toward the Clarification of the Question of the Formation of the CP[b] of the Ukraine and its Tactics in 1918), *Voprosy istorii KPSS*, IV, No. 3 (1960), 65-89.

Bosh, Evgeniia. *God bor'by* (Year of Battle). Moscow, 1925.

—— *Natsional'noi pravitel'stvo i sovetskaia vlast' na Ukraine* (National Government and Soviet Power in the Ukraine). Moscow, 1919.

Bunyan, James and H. H. Fisher. *The Bolshevik Revolution 1917-1918.* Palo Alto, 1934.

Bushuev, S. K. "O kavkazskom miuridizme" (On Caucasian Muridism), *Voprosy istorii*, No. 12 (December, 1956), 72-79.

Butsenko, A. *Desiat' vseukrains'kykh z'izdiv rad* (Ten All-Ukrainian Congresses of Soviets). Kharkov, 1927.

Carr, Edward Hallett. *A History of Soviet Russia.* 4 vols. New York, 1951-1954.

Chamberlin, William Henry. *Russia's Iron Age.* Boston, 1934.

—— *The Ukraine, a Submerged Nation.* New York, 1944.

Chernenko, Níkolai B. *Bor'ba KP za vosstanovlenie promyshlennosti i konsolidatsiiu rabochego klassa Ukrainy v 1921-1925 gg.* (Battle of the C. P. for the Development of Industry and the Consolidation of the Workers' Class of the Ukraine in 1921-1925). Kiev, 1959.

Chubar', Vlas Iakovlevich. *Sovetskaia Ukraina, doklad v presidiume TsIK Soiuza SSR 5-go dekabria 1924 goda* (Soviet Ukraine, Report in the Presidium of the Central Executive Committee of the Union SSR, December 5, 1924). Kharkov, 1925.

Constitution of the U.S.S.R. as Amended by the 1st, 2nd, 3rd, 6th, 7th, and 8th Sessions of the Supreme Soviet of the U.S.S.R. Washington, D.C., 1945.

Dedijer, Vladimir. *Tito.* New York, 1953.

Dennis, Alfred L. P. *The Foreign Policies of Soviet Russia.* New York, 1924.

Dimanshtein, S. "Leninsko-stalinskaia natsional'naia politika i proekt novoi konstitutsii SSSR" (The Lenin-Stalin National Policy and the Draft of the New Constitution of the USSR), *Bol'shevik*, XIII, No. 13 (July 1, 1936), 64-78.

Dmytryshyn, Basil. *Moscow and the Ukraine. 1918-1953.* New York, 1956.

Dobb, Maurice. *Soviet Economic Development since 1917.* New York, 1948.

Dobrin, Samuel. "Soviet Federalism and the Principle of Double Subordination," The Grotius Society, *Transactions for the Year 1944, Problems of Peace and War*, Vol. XXX. London, 1945.

Donii, N. R. "Obrazovanie Kommunisticheskoi partii Ukrainy" (Formation of the Communist Party of the Ukraine), *Voprosy istorii KPSS*, II, No. 3 (1958), 33-49.

Dubyna, K. "Pro formy perekhodu riznykh krain do sotsializmu" (On the Methods of the Transition of Various Countries to Socialism), *Komunist Ukrainy*, XXXI, No. 4 (April, 1956), 31-42.

Dvadtsat'piat' let Ukrainskoi Sovetskoi Sotsialisticheskoi Respubliki (Twenty-five Years of the Ukrainian Soviet Socialist Republic). Moscow, 1943.

Emel'ianenko, S. "Lenins'ki pryntsypy natsional'noi polityky KPRS" (Leninist Principles on the National Policy of the CPSU), *Komunist Ukrainy*, XXXII, No. 10 (October, 1956), 49-61.

Entsyklopediia Ukrainoznavstva (Encyclopedia of Ukrainian Information). 3 vols. Munich, 1949.

Erenburg, Il'ia. "O rabote pisatelia" (On the Work of a Writer), *Znamia*, XXIII, No. 10 (October, 1953), 160-83.

Eudin, X. J. "Soviet National Minority Policies, 1918-1921," *The Slavonic and East European Review*, XXI (November, 1943), 31-55.

Fedenko, Panas. *Ukraina pislia smerty Stalina* (The Ukraine after the Death of Stalin). Munich, 1956.

Fedorov, Aleksei. *The Underground Committee Carries On.* Moscow, n.d.

Fedoseev, P. "Sotsializm i patriotizm" (Socialism and Patriotism), *Kommunist*, XXX, No. 9 (June, 1953), 12-28.

Fominov, N. "Pobeda leninsko-stalinskoi natsional'noi politiki" (Victory of the Leninist-Stalinist National Policy), *Bol'shevik*, XV, No. 9 (May 1, 1938), 37-46.

Gafurov, B. "Druzhba narodov—istochnik sily sovetskogo gosudarstva" (Friendship of Peoples Is the Source of the Strength of the Soviet State), *Pravda*, August 15, 1955.

Gaponchuk, G. "Uluchshit' lektsionnuiu propagandu" (To improve Lecture Propaganda), *Pravda Ukrainy*, June 21, 1953.

Genkina, E. "Lenin o bratstve i druzhbe narodov SSSR" (Lenin on the Brotherhood and Friendship of the Peoples of the USSR), *Bol'shevik*, XIX, No. 1 (January, 1943), 35-45.

Girchak, Ie. F. *Na dva fronta v bor'be s natsionalizmom* (On Two Fronts in the Battle with Nationalism). 2d ed. Moscow, 1931.

Gorin, P. "O roli proletariata v revoliutsionnom dvizhenii Ukrainy" (On the Role of the Proletariat in the Revolutionary Movement of the Ukraine), *Bol'shevik*, VII, No. 1 (January 15, 1920), 43-52.

Gratz, Gustav and Richard Schuller. *The Economic Policy of Austria-Hungary during the War in Its External Relations*. New Haven, 1928.

Grossman, V. "Raion-oblast'," *Bol'shevik*, VII, No. 13 (July, 1930), 15-21.

Gsovski, Vladimir. *Soviet Civil Law*. 2 vols. Ann Arbor, 1949.

Gurvich, G. S. *Osnovy sovetskoi konstitutsii* (Foundations of the Soviet Constitution). Moscow, 1926.

Gurvich, G. S., F. T. Ivanov and V. Maksimovskii. *Sovetskoe gosudarstvennoe ustroistvo* (Soviet State Construction). Moscow, 1930.

Hirchak, Ie. "Boiovi problemy natsional'noi kul'tury" (Urgent Problems of National Culture), *Bil'shovyk Ukrainy*, VI, No. 5 (March 15, 1931), 51-62.

——. *"Shums'kizm i rozlam v KPZU* (Shums'kyism and the Break in the Communist Party of the Western Ukraine). Kharkov, 1928.

——. "Za leninizm! Proty kavts'kiianstva!" (For Leninism! Against Kautskyism!), *Bil'shovyk Ukrainy*, VI, No. 11 (June 15, 1931), 28-42.

Hirnyi, P. "Antiradians'ki plany ukrains'koi natsionalistychnoi kontr-revoliutsii na Zakhidnii Ukraini" (Anti-Soviet Plans of The Ukrainian Nationalist Counter-Revolution in the Western Ukraine), *Bil'shovyk Ukrainy*, X, No. 3 (March, 1935), 22-36.

Holub, V. "Konspektyvnyi narys istorii KP(b)U" (Concise Outline of the History of the CP[b]U), *Ukrain'skyi zbirnyk*, IX (1957), 31-137.

Horb, T. "Stanovyshche ukrains'koi liudnosty Kazakstanu" (Situation of the Ukrainian Population of Kazakhstan), *Bil'shovyk Ukrainy*, V, Nos. 19-20 (October, 1930), 60-66.

Hryshko, Vasyl. *Experience with Russia*. New York, 1956.

Iakubovskaia, S. I. *Ob''edinitel'noe dvizhenie za obrazovanie SSSR (1917-1922)* (The Unif'cation Movement behind the Formation of the USSR [1917-1922]). Moscow, 1947.

Iaroshenko, Andriy O. *Komunistychna partiia Zakhidnoi Urkainy— orhanizator i kerivnyk revoliutsiyno-vyzvol'noi borot'by trudiash- chykh zakhidnoukrains'kykh zemel'* (The Communist Party of the West Ukraine—Organizer and Leader of the Revolutionary-Libera- tion Battle of the Workers of the West Ukrainian Land). Kiev, 1959.

Iavors'kyi, Matvii. *Istoriia Ukrainy v styslomu narysi* (History of the Ukraine in Brief Outline). 2d ed. Kharkov, 1928.

———. *Narys istorii Ukrainy* (Outline of the History of the Ukraine). Kharkov, 1922.

Ignat'ev, V. I. *Sovetskii stroi* (Soviet Building). Moscow, 1928.

Ihnatiuk, D. *Ukrains'ka avtokefal'na tserkva i Soiuz vyzvolennia Ukrainy* (The Ukrainian Autocephalous Church and the Union for the Liberation of the Ukraine). Kharkov, 1930.

Iovchuk, M. "Leninizm—vysshee dostizhenie russkoi i mirovoi kul'- tury" (Leninism—Highest Achievement of Russian and World Culture), *Kommunist*, XXXII, No. 1 (January, 1955), 23-28.

Istoriia gosudarstva i prava Ukrainskoi SSR (1917-1958 gg.) (History of State and Law of the Ukrainian SSR [1917-1958]). 3 vols. Kiev, 1959.

Istoriia sovetskoi konstitutsii v dekretakh i postanovleniiakh sovetskogo pravitel'stva, 1917-1936 (History of the Soviet Constitution in the Decrees and Decisions of the Soviet Government, 1917-1936). Moscow, 1936.

Istoriia ukrains'koho viis'ka (History of the Ukrainian Army). 2d ed. Winnipeg, 1953.

Iurchenko, Oleksandr T. *Lenin i utvorennia Komunistychnoi partii Ukrainy* (Lenin and the Formation of the Communist Party of the Ukraine). Kiev, 1958.

Kazakov, S. "Chto chitat' ob internatsional'nom vospitanii trudiash- chiksia" (What to Read on the International Development of the Working People), *Partiinaia zhizn'*, No. 12 (June, 1955), pp. 71-78.

Kharitonov, V. L. "Bor'ba bol'shevikov Ukrainy za sozdanie oblast- noi organizatsii (1914 g.-iiul' 1917 g.)" (Battle of the Bolsheviks of the Ukraine for the Creation of a Regional Organization [1914- July, 1917]), *Voprosy istorii KPSS*, V, No. 1 (Jan.-Feb., 1961), 111-20.

Khatchaturian, Aram. "O tvorcheskoi smelosti i vdokhnovenii" (On Creative Boldness and Inspiration), *Sovetskaia muzyka*, XVII, No. 11 (November, 1953), 7-13.

Khomenko, Arsen. *Natsional'nyi sklad liudnosty USRR* (National Composition of the Population of the UkSSR). Poltava, 1931.

Khrushchev, Nikita S. "O nekotorykh voprosakh vnutripartiinoi raboty" (On Some Questions of Intra-Party Work), *Pravda Ukrainy*, June 8, 1946.

———. "Text of Speech on Stalin by Khrushchev, as Released by the State Department," *New York Times*, June 5, 1956, pp. 13-16.

———. "Za tesnuiu sviaz' literatury i iskusstva s zhizn'iu naroda" (For a Close Tie between Literature and Art and the Life of the People), *Pravda*, August 28, 1957.

Khvylia, A. *Natsional'nyi vopros na Ukraine* (The National Question in the Ukraine). Kharkov, 1926.

———. "Burzhuazno-natsionalistychna trybuna" (Bourgeois-Nationalist Tribune), *Bil'shovyk Ukrainy*, VI, No. 6 (March 31, 1931), 46-58.

———. "Proletariiat i praktychne rozhortannia kul'turno-natsional'noho budivnytstva" (The Proletariat and the Practical Development of Cultural-National Construction), *Bil'shovyk Ukrainy*, V, Nos. 13-14 (July 31, 1930), 38-55.

Kirpotin, V. "Russkaia kul'tura" (Russian Culture), *Bol'shevik*, XV, No. 12 (June 15, 1938), 47-63.

Klimko, Mykhailo S. *Vos'ma konferentsiia KP(b) U* (Eighth Conference of the CP[b]U). Kiev, 1959.

Kommunisticheskaia Partiia (bol'shevikov) Ukrainy. *Piat' let: sbornik statei i vospominanii* (Five Years; Collection of Articles and Memoirs). Kharkov, 1922.

"Kommunisticheskaia partiia Ukrainy v tsifrakh" (The Communist Party of the Ukraine in Figure), *Partiinaia zhizn'*, No. 12 (June, 1958), 57-59.

Komunistychna Partiia (bil'shovykiv) Ukrainy. Tsentral'nyi Komitet. Instytut istorii partii, Kyiv. *Heroichnyi shliakh borot'by i peremoh* (Heroic Path of Battle and Victory). Kiev, 1950.

———. *Istoriia KP(b) U v materialakh i dokumentakh* (History of the CP [b]U in Materials and Documents). 2 vols. Kiev, 1933.

Komunistychna Partiia (bil'shovykiv) Ukrainy. Tsentral'nyi Komitet. Kul'tpropviddil. *Borot'ba za radians'ku Ukrainu* (Battle for the Soviet Ukraine), Kharkov, n.d.

Komunistychna partiia—natkhnennyk i orhanizator sotsialistychnykh peretvoren' v zakhidnykh oblastiakh URSR (The Communist Party —Inspirer and Organizer of Socialist Reconstruction in the West Oblasts of the UkSSR). Kiev, 1960.

Konovalov, Mykhailo A. *Borot'ba KP U za zmitsnennia soiuzu robitnykiv i selian v period razhornutoho nastupu sotsializmu po us'omu frontu (1930-1936 rr.)* (The Battle of the CPU for Strengthening the Union of Workers and Peasants in the Period of the Large-Scale Drive for Socialism on a Broad Front [1930-1936]). Kiev, 1959.

Konstitutsii Sovetskikh Sotsialisticheskikh Respublik (Constitutions of the Soviet Socialist Republics). Moscow, 1937.

Kosior, S. V. *Statti i promovy, 1933-1936* (Articles and Statements, 1933-1936). Kiev, 1936.

Kostiuk, Hryhory. *The Fall of Postyshev.* New York, 1954.

Kovalevs'kyi, M. *Opozytsiini rukhy v Ukraini i natsional'na polityka SSSR (1920-1954)* (The Opposition Movement in the Ukraine and the National Policy of the USSR [1920-1954]). Munich, 1955.

Kovpak, Sidor. *Vid Putivlia do Karpat* (From Putivl' to the Carpathians). Kiev, 1946.

Kozybovs'kyi, F. *Burzhuazna istoriia material'noi kul'tury na posluhakh fashyzmu* (The Bourgeois History of Material Culture in the Service of Fascism).

Kravchenko, H. P. *Partiina orhanizatsiia Ukrainy v borot'bi za dal'she zmitsnennia i ednosti partii* (The Party Organization of the Ukraine in the Battle for the Further Strengthening of the Unity of the Party). Kiev, 1954.

Kravchenko, Victor. *I Chose Freedom.* New York, 1947.

Kravtsev, I. "Leninskaia natsional'naia politika i ee osushchestvlenie na Ukraine" (Leninist National Policy and Its Realization in the Ukraine), *Pravda Ukrainy,* December 25, 1956.

Kuchabs'kyi, Vasyl'. *Bol'shevyzm i suchasne zavdannia ukrains'koho zakhodu* (Bolshevism and the Current Task of Ukrainian Work). Lvov, 1925.

Kultyshev, S. S. "Rost riadov partii v 1945-1950 gg." (Growth of the Ranks of the Party in 1945-1950), *Voprosy istorii KPSS,* II, No. 2 (1958), 57-72.

Kulykovs'kyi, M. S. "Radians'ka konstytutsiia—vtilennia lenins'koi natsional'noi polityky" (The Soviet Constitution—Embodiment of the Leninist National Policy), *Radians'ka Ukraina,* XI, No. 7 (July, 1935), 8-16.

Kurshchyn, V. M. *Gosudarstvennoe sotrudnichestvo mezhdu Ukrainskoi SSR i RSFSR v 1917-1922 gg.* (State Cooperation Between the Ukrainian SSR and the RSFSR in 1917-1922). Moscow, 1957.

Kurshchyn, V. M. and N. R. Donii. "Obrazovanie Kom. Par. Uk." (Formation of the Communist Party of the Ukraine), *Voprosy istorii KPSS,* II, No. 3 (1958), 33-49.

Kviring, E. *Uroki gruzinskogo vosstaniia* (Lessons from the Georgian Uprising). Kharkov, 1925.

——. "Krutyi povorit chy rozhortannia popered'noi roboty" (A Sharp Change or a Continuation of Previous Work), *Chervonyi shliakh,* II, Nos. 4-5 (1923), 107-12.

Ladreit de Lacharriere, Guy. *L'Idée Fédérale en Russie de Riourik a Staline (862-1945).* Paris, 1945.

Lawrynenko, Jurij. *Ukrainian Communism and Soviet Russian Po-*

licy toward the Ukraine, an Annotated Bibliography, 1917-1953.
New York, 1953.

Lebed', Dmitrii. *Sovetskaia Ukraina i natsional'nyi vopros za piat' let*
(The Soviet Ukraine and the National Question During Five
Years). Moscow, 1924.

——. "Vnimanie ideologicheskomu frontu" (Attention to the Ideological Front), *Bol'shevik*, V, No. 7 (April, 1928), 79-87.

Leites, A. and M. Iashek. *Desiat' rokiv ukrains'koi literatury* (Ten
Years of Ukrainian Literature). 2 vols. 2d ed. Kharkov, 1930.

Lenin, V. I. *Selected Works.* 12 vols. New York, 1935-1939.

——. *Sochineniia* (Works). 30 vols. 3d ed. Moscow, 1928-1936.

——. *Sochineniia* (Works). 35 vols. 4th ed. Moscow, 1941-1951.

——. "K voprosy o natsional'nostiakh ili ob 'avtonomizatsii'" (On
the Question of the Nationalities or of "Autonomization"), *Kommunist*, XXXIII, No. 9 (June, 1956), 22-26.

Leontiev, B. "Krasnaia armiia—internatsional'naia armiia" (The Red
Army—an International Army), *Revoliutsiia i natsional'nosti* (February, 1937), pp. 45-53.

Lepeshinskii, P. (ed.). *Istoriia VKP(b) v s″ezdakh* (History of the
All-Union Communist Party [b] in Congresses). Kharkov, 1928.

Levina, Z. and A. Romanova. "Velikaia rol' V. I. Lenina v organizatsii Soiuza Sovetskikh Respublik" (The Great Role of V. I. Lenin
in the Organization of the Union of Soviet Republics), *Pravda*,
July 11, 1956.

Likholat, A. V. *Razgrom natsionalisticheskoi kontrrevoliutsii na
Ukraine (1917-1922 gg.)* (Destruction of the Nationalist Counter-
Revolution in the Ukraine [1917-1922]). Moscow, 1954.

Litvin, K. Z. "Ob istorii ukrainskogo naroda" (On the History of the
Ukrainian People), *Bol'shevik*, XXIV, No. 7 (April, 1947), 41-56.

——. *Rastsvet kul'tury sovetskoi Ukrainy* (Blossoming of the Culture
of the Soviet Ukraine). Kiev, 1954.

Liubchenko, P. *Stalinskaia konstitutsiia i Sovetskaia Ukraina* (The
Stalin Constitution and the Soviet Ukraine). Moscow, 1936.

——. "Ukrains'ki natsionalisty v borot'bi za restavratsiiu kapitalizmu" (Ukrainian Nationalists in the Battle for the Restoration of
Capitalism), *Bil'shovyk Ukrainy*, V, Nos. 9-10 (May, 1930), 58-75.

Lobai, Danylo. *Neperemozhna Ukraina* (The Invincible Ukraine).
Winnipeg, 1950.

Low, Alfred D. *Lenin on the Question of Nationality.* New York,
1958.

Luckyj, George S. N. *Literary Politics in the Soviet Ukraine. 1917-
1934.* New York, 1956.

Maiorov, M. *Iz istorii revoliutsionnoi bor'by na Ukraine* (From the
History of the Revolutionary Battle in the Ukraine). Kiev, 1922.

Majstrenko, Iwan. *Borot'bism, a Chapter in the History of Ukrainian
Nationalism.* New York, 1954.

Makohon, A. *Politosvitnia robota sered natsmenshostei na seli* (Political-Educational Work among the National Minorities in the Countryside). Kharkov, 1927.

Malaia sovetskaia entsiklopediia (Small Soviet Encyclopedia). 10 vols. Moscow, 1928-1931.

Malitskii, A. (ed.). *Sobranie sovetskikh konstitutsii i konstitutsionnykh aktov* (Collection of Soviet Constitutions and Constitutional Acts). Kharkov, 1928.

Manuil'skii, D. Z. and S. S. Dukel'skii (eds.). *Delo chlenov Tsentral'nogo Komiteta Ukrainskoi Partii Sotsial.-Revoliutsionerov* (Trial of Members of the Central Committee of the Ukrainian Party of Socialist-Revolutionaries). Kharkov, 1921.

Marcuse, Herbert. *Soviet Marxism, a Critical Analysis.* New York, 1958.

Margolin, Arnold D. *From a Political Diary.* New York, 1946.

Markov, S. F. *Otechestvennaia voina ukrainskogo naroda protiv germanskikh interventov v 1918* (The Fatherland War of the Ukrainian People Against the German Interventionists in 1918). Moscow, 1941.

Martovych, Oleh. *Ukrainian Liberation Movement in Modern Times.* Edinburgh, 1951.

Mazepa, I. "Ukrainia under Bolshevist Rule," *The Slavonic Review*, XII (1933-1934), 323-46.

Meyer, Alfred G. *Leninism.* Cambridge, 1957.

Miliukova, Nina O. *Borot'ba Komunistychnoi partii Ukrainy za pidvyshchennia kul'turno-tekhnichnoho rivnia robitnychoho klasu (1928-32 gg.)* (Battle of the Communist Party of the Ukraine for the Raising of the Cultural-Technical Level of the Workers' Class [1928-1932]). Kiev, 1960.

Mints, Isaak and E. Gorodetskii (eds.). *Dokumenty o razgrome germanskikh okkupantov na Ukraine v 1918 godu* (Documents on the Destruction of German Occupation Forces in the Ukraine in 1918). Moscow, 1942.

Mirchuk, Petro. *Ukrains'ka povstans'ka armiia, 1942-1952* (Ukrainian Insurgent Army, 1942-1952). Munich, 1953.

Misov, Leonid D. *U borot'bi za pidnesennia partiinoi robotu. Z praktyky robotu part. orhanizatsii Drohob., L'vivs'koi, Stanisl. ta Ternop. obl. URSR* (Concerning the Battle for the Strengthening of Party Work. From the Practical Work of the Party Organizations of the Drogobych, Lvov, Stanislav, and Ternopol Oblasts of the UkSSR). Lvov, 1957.

Mordinov, A. E. "O razvitii iazykov sotsialisticheskikh natsii v SSSR" (On the Development of the Languages of the Socialist Nations in the USSR), *Voprosy filosofii*, IV, No. 3 (1950), 82-85.

Nykolyshyn, S. *Kul'turna polityka bil'shevykiv i ukrains'kyi kul'-*

turnyi protses (Cultural Policy of the Bolsheviks and the Ukrainian Cultural Process). N.p., 1947.

"Ob ideino-politicheskoi rabote partiinykh organizatsii v sovremennykh usloviiakh" (On the Ideological-Political Work of Party Organizations under Contemporary Conditions), *Bol'shevik*, XX, Nos. 17-18 (September, 1945), 1-10.

"Ob opere 'Velikaia druzhba' V. Muradeli" (On the Opera "Great Friendship" by V. Muradeli), *Sovetskaia muzyka*, XXII, No. 1 (January, 1948), 3-8.

"O kinofil'me 'Bol'shaia zhizn'" (On the Film "Great Life"), *Bol'shevik*, XXIII, No. 16 (August, 1946), 50-53.

Oktiabr' v Ekaterihoslave (October in Ekaterinoslav). Dnepropetrovsk, 1957.

Olkhovsky, Andrey. *Music under the Soviets, the Agony of an Art.* New York, 1955.

"O politicheskoi raboti v derevne" (On Political Work in the Countryside), *Bol'shevik*, XXIII, Nos. 13-14 (July, 1946), 1-9.

Parti Communiste Ukrainien (Groupe étranger). *La Révolution en Danger.* Vienna, 1921.

Pavlov, P. "Razgrom Sovnarkoma Ukrainy" (Destruction of the Sovnarkom of the Ukraine), *Narodnaia Pravda*, No. 4 (June, 1949), pp. 16-18.

Petrenko, P. "Nova knyga z istorii ukrains'koi radians'koi literatury" (New Book on the History of Ukrainian Soviet Literature), *Komunist Ukrainy*, XXX, No. 3 (March, 1955), 64-72.

Petrovskii, D. *Revoliutsiia i kontr-revoliutsiia na Ukraine* (Revolution and Counter-Revolution in the Ukraine). Moscow, 1920.

Petrovskii, N. N. *Vossoedinenie ukrainskogo naroda v edinom ukrainskom sovetskom gosudarstve* (Reunification of the Ukrainian People in a Single Ukrainian Soviet State). Moscow, 1944.

Petrovs'kyi, H. I. "Za novi peremohu sotsialistychnoi Ukrainy" (Toward a New Victory of the Socialist Ukraine), *Radians'ka Ukraina*, X, No. 7 (July, 1934), 15-16.

Pidzharyi, Fedir D. *Komunistychna partiia Ukrainy v borot'bi peremohu kolhospnoho ladu* (The Communist Party of the Ukraine in the Battle for the Victory of the Kolkhoz System). Kiev, 1960.

Pikman, A. M. "O bor'be kavkazskikh gortsev s tsarskimi kolonizatorami" (On the Battle of Caucasian Mountaineers with Tsarist Colonizers), *Voprosy istorii*, No. 3 (March, 1956), 75-84.

Pipes, Richard. *The Formation of the Soviet Union.* Cambridge, 1954.

Pitsiura, Dmitro I. *Orhanizatory mas. Z praktyky robotu sil's'kikh raikomiv partii* (Organizers of the Masses. From the Practical Work of the Rural Raion Committees of the Party). Lvov, 1959.

Podgornyi, N. "Sovetskaia Ukraina v bratskoi sem'e narodov SSSR"

(The Soviet Ukraine in the Fraternal Family of the Peoples of the USSR), *Kommunist*, XXXI, No. 8 (May, 1954), 12-26.

Polons'ka-Vasylenko, N. D. *Ukrains'ka akademiia nauk* (The Ukrainian Academy of Sciences). Part 1. Munich, 1955.

Pomerantsev, V. "Ob iskrennosti v literature" (On Sincerity in Literature), *Novyi mir*, XXIX, No. 12 (December, 1953), 218-45.

Popov, N. N. *Narys istorii Komunistychnoi Partii (bil'shovykiv) Ukrainy* (Outline of the History of the Communist Party [Bolshevik] of the Ukraine). Kharkov, 1928.

——. *Natsional'naia politika sovetskoi vlasti* (The National Policy of Soviet Power). Moscow, 1927.

——. *Oktiabr' na Ukraine* (October in the Ukraine). Kiev, 1934.

——. *Outline History of the Communist Party of the Soviet Union*. 2 vols. Moscow, 1934.

——. "Natsional'naia politika partii v period sotsialisticheskoi rekonstruktsii" (National Policy of the Party in the Period of Socialist Reconstruction), *Pravda*, October 31, 1929.

Postyshev, P. P. *Sovetskaia Ukraina—nesokrushimyi forpost velikogo SSSR* (The Soviet Ukraine—Indestructible Outpost of the Great USSR). [Kiev], 1933.

——. "Kvitne i mitsnie industrial'no kolhospna Ukraina" (April and the Powerful Industrial-Kolkhoz Ukraine), *Bil'shovyk Ukrainy*, X, Nos. 1-2 (January-February 1935), 13-30.

——. "Pidsumky perevirky partiinykh dokumentiv v KP(b)U i zavdannia partiinoi roboty" (Results of the Verification of Party Documents in the CP[b]U and Tasks of Party Work), *Bil'shovyk Ukrainy*, XI, No. 3 (March, 1936), 9-33.

Postyshev, P. P. and S. V. Kossior. *Soviet Ukraine Today*. Moscow, 1934.

"Pro stan partiinoi propagandy i agitatsii" (On the Status of Party Propaganda and Agitation), *Bil'shovyk Ukrainy*, XI, No. 7 (July, 1936), 1-4.

"Proty ekonomichnoi platformy natsionalizmu" (Against the Economic Platform of Nationalism), *Bil'shovyk Ukrainy*, V, Nos. 5-6 (March, 1930), 54-69; V, No. 7 (April, 1930), 28-40.

Rabinovich, C. E. *Vserossiiskaia voennaia konferentsiia bol'shevikov 1917 goda* (All-Russian Military Conference of Bolsheviks, 1917). Moscow, 1919.

Radians'ke budivnytstvo na Ukraini v roku hromadians'koi viiny (1919-1920). Zbirnyk dokumentiv (Soviet Construction in the Ukraine in the Years of the Civil War [1919-1920]. Collection of Documents). Kiev, 1957.

Radkey, Oliver Henry. *The Election to the Russian Constituent Assembly of 1917*. Cambridge, 1950.

Rafes, M. *Dva goda revoliutsii na Ukraine* (Two Years of Revolution in the Ukraine). Moscow, 1920.

Rakovskii, Kh. G. "Novyi etap v radians'komu soiuznomu budivnytstvi" (New Stage in Soviet Union Construction), *Chervonyi shliakh*, II, No. 1 (January, 1923). 69-88.

——. "Otnosheniia mezhdu sovetskimi respublikami, Rossiia i Ukraina" (Relations between the Soviet Republics, Russia and the Ukraine), *Kommunisticheskii internatsional*, Vol. II, No. 12 (1920), cols. 2197-2202.

Rakovskii, Kh. H. *Otchet raboche-krest'ianskogo pravitel'stva Ukrainy IV-mu vseukrainskomu s"ezdu sovetov rabochikh, krest'ianskikh i krasnoarmeiskikh deputatov* (Report of the Workers'-Peasants'Government of the Ukraine to the Fourth All-Ukrainian Congress of Soviets of Workers', Peasants', and Red Army Deputies). Kharkov, 1920.

——. *Piat' rokiv ukrains'koi radians'koi vlady* (Five Years of Ukrainian Soviet Power). Kharkov, 1923.

Ravich-Cherkasskii, M. *Istoriia Kommunisticheskoi Partii (b-ov) Ukrainy* (History of the Communist Party [Bolshevik] of the Ukraine). Kharkov, 1923.

Rechi na sobraniiakh izbiratelei v verkhovnyi sovet SSSR (Speeches to Meetings of Voters in the Supreme Soviet of the USSR). Moscow, 1938.

Redin, M. "Za bil'shovyts'kyi povorot v vykladanni istorii" (For a Bolshevik Transformation in the Teaching of History), *Bil'shovyk Ukrainy*, VI, No. 11 (June, 1931), 66-94.

Redmer, Mary and V. I. Wolpert. "Economic Rehabilitation in the Ukraine," Operational Analysis Paper No. 39, United Nations Relief and Rehabilitation Administration, European Regional Office. London, 1947. (Mimeographed.)

Report of Court Proceedings. The Case of the Anti-Soviet Bloc of Rights and Trotskyites. Moscow, 1938.

Report of Court Proceedings. The Case of the Anti-Soviet Trotskyite Centre. Moscow, 1937.

Report of Court Proceedings. The Case of the Trotskyite-Zinovievite Terrorist Centre. Moscow, 1936.

Reshetar, John S. *The Ukrainian Revolution, 1917-1920.* Princeton, 1952.

Riadnina, U. *Bil'shovyts'ki orhanizatsii Ukrainy v Zhovtnevii revoliutsii* (Bolshevik Organizations of the Ukraine in the October Revolution). Kiev, 1958.

Richyts'kyi, Andrii. *Do problemy likvidatsii perzhytkiv koloniial'nosty ta natsionalizmu* (On the Problem of the Liquidation of Survivals of Colonialism and Nationalism). Kharkov, 1928.

Rosenman, Samuel I. (ed.). *The Public Papers and Addresses of Franklin D. Roosevelt*. Vol. XIII. New York, 1950.

Rudnev, V. *Ukrains'ki burzhuazni natsionalisty—ahentura mizhnarodnoi reaktsii* (Ukrainian Bourgeois Nationalists—Agents of International Reaction). Kiev, 1955.

"Russkii narod—rukovodiashchaia sila sredi narodov nashei strany" (The Russian People—the Leading Force among the Peoples of Our Country), *Bol'shevik*, XX, No. 10 (May, 1945), 3-12.

Rybalka, Ivan K. *Vidnovlennia Radians'koi vlady na Ukraini (1918-1919 rr.)* (Establishment of Soviet Power in the Ukraine [1918-1919]). Kiev, 1957.

Rysakoff, A. *The National Policy of the Soviet Union*. New York, 1932.

Sadovs'kyi, V. *Natsional'na polityka sovetiv na Ukraini* (The National Policy of the Soviets in the Ukraine). Warsaw, 1937.

Sadvosov, S. "O natsional'nostiakh i natsionalakh" (On Nationalities and Nationals), *Bol'shevik*, V, No. 1 (January, 1928), 56-64.

Salisbury, Harrison E. *American in Russia*. New York, 1955.

Schapiro, Leonard. *The Communist Party of the Soviet Union*. New York, 1959.

Senchenko, An. "Natsional'ne pytannia v period rozhornutoho sotsiialistychnoho nastupu na vs'omu fronti" (The National Question in the Period of the Development of a Socialist Offensive on a Wide Front), *Bil'shovyk Ukrainy*, V, No. 17 (September 15, 1930), 47-61.

Shapiro, Leonard (ed.). *Soviet Treaty Series*. 2 vols. Washington, D.C., 1950.

Sherstiuk, Fedir Iu. *Partiine budivnytstvo na Ukraini v 1926-1929 rr.* (Party Construction in the Ukraine in 1926-1929). Kiev, 1960.

"Shiroko razvernut' politicheskuiu raboty v derevne" (Widely To Develop Political Work in the Countryside), *Bol'shevik*, XXIII, No. 6 (March, 1947), 1-8.

Shitarev, G. "Demokraticheskii tsentralizm i rukovodiashchaia deiatel'nost' partiinykh organov" (Democratic Centralism and the Leadership Work of Party Organs), *Kommunist*, XXX, No. 18 (December, 1953), 51-66.

Shlikhter, A. *Bor'ba s natsionalisticheskimi uklonami na sovremennom etape* (The Battle with Nationalist Deviations in the Current Period). Kharkov, 1933.

———. *Klassovaia bor'ba na sele i partiia* (Class Battle in the Rural Areas and the Party). Kharkov, 1927.

Shmorhun, Petro M. *V. I. Lenin i bil'shovyts'ki orhanizatsii na Ukraini* (V. I. Lenin and Bolshevik Organization in the Ukraine). Kiev, 1960.

Shostakovich, D. "Po puti, ukazannomu partiei" (Along the Path Laid Down by the Party), *Sovetskaia muzyka*, XXI, No. 10 (October, 1957), 10.

——. "Radost' tvorcheskikh iskanii" (The Joy of the Creative Search), *Sovetskaia muzyka*, XVIII, No. 1 (January, 1954), 40-42.

Simmons, Ernest J. (ed.). *Through the Glass of Soviet Literature, Views of Russian Society.* New York, 1953.

Sistematicheskoe sobranie deistvuiushchikh zakonov SSSR (Systematic Collection of Laws in Force in the USSR). Vol. I. Moscow, 1927.

Sizonov, K. P. "Dobyty reshtky kontrrevoliutsiinoho trots'kizmu ta natsionalizmu na fronti radbudivnytstva i prava" (To Destroy the Survivals of Counter-Revolutionary Trotskyism and Nationalism on the Front of Soviet Construction and Law), *Radians'ka Ukraina*, X, No. 11 (November, 1934), 30-37.

——. "Radians'ka konstytutsiia—vtilennia radians'koi demokratii i lenins'koho internatsionalizmu" (The Soviet Constitution—Embodiment of Soviet Democracy and Leninist Internationalism), *Radians'ka Ukraina*, X, No. 12 (December, 1934), 37-46.

Skrypnyk, Mykola. *Dzherela ta prychyny rozlamu v KPZU* (Sources and Causes of the Break in the Communist Party of the Western Ukraine). Kharkov, 1928.

——. *Statti i promovy* (Articles and Statements). Vol. II, Part 2. Kharkov, 1931.

——. "Kontr-revoliutsiine shkidnytstvo na kul'turnomy fronti" (Counter-Revolutionary Wrecking on the Cultural Front), *Chervonyi shliakh*, VIII, No. 4 (April, 1930), 138-50.

——. "Perebudovnymy shliakhamy" (Along Reconstruction Paths), *Bil'shovyk Ukrainy*, VI, No. 12 (June 30, 1931), 13-36.

——. "Pomylky ta vypravlennia akademika M. Iavors'koho" (Mistakes and Corrections of Academician M. Iavors'kyi), *Bil'shovyk Ukrainy*, V, No. 2 (January 31, 1930), 12-20.

——. "Spilka vyzvolennia Ukrainy" (Union for the Liberation of the Ukraine), *Bil'shovyk Ukrainy*, V, No. 8 (April, 1930), 11-24.

——. "Zblyzhennia i zlyttia natsii za doby sotsiializmu" (The Consolidation and Unification of the Nation during the Period of Socialism), *Bil'shovyk Ukrainy*, VI, No. 8 (April 30, 1931), 17-30.

Slonim, Marc. *Modern Russian Literature, from Chekhov to the Present.* New York, 1933.

Solovei, D. *Holhota Ukrainy* (The Golgotha of the Ukraine). Part 1. Winnipeg, 1953.

——. "Natsional'na polityka partii i uriadu SSSR v Ukraini u svitli deiakykh nainovishykh faktiv" (The National Policy of the Party and Government of the USSR in the Ukraine in the Light of Certain Recent Facts), *Ukrains'kyi zbirnyk*, VI (1956), 109-95.

Sosiura, Volodymyr. "Liubi Ukrainu" (Love the Ukraine), *Zvezda*, XXVIII, No. 5 (May, 1951), 128-29.

Sova, H. *Do istorii bol'shevyts'koi diisnosty* (On the History of Bolshevik Reality). Munich, 1955.

"Sovetskii apparat upravleniia—vazhnoe orudie kommunisticheskogo stroitel'stva" (Soviet Administrative Apparatus—Important Arm of Communist Construction), *Kommunist*, XXXIII, No. 17 (November, 1956), 3-16.

Soviet Political Personalities: Seven Profiles. New York, 1952.

Stalin, Iusef V. *Marksizm i voprozy iazykoznaniia* (Marxism and the Linguistics Question). Moscow, 1950.

——. *Sochineniia* (Works). 13 vols. Moscow, 1946-1951.

——. *Statti i promovy pro Ukrainu* (Articles and Statements on the Ukraine). Kiev, 1936.

Stalin, Joseph V. *Marxism and Linguistics.* New York, 1951.

——. *Marxism and the National and Colonial Question.* New York, [1935].

Stettinius, Edward R., Jr. *Roosevelt and the Russians: the Yalta Conference.* New York, 1949.

Struve, Gleb. *Soviet Russian Literature 1917-1950.* Norman, Oklahoma, 1951.

Suprunenko, Nikolai I. *KP—vdokhnovitel' i rukovoditel' bor'by ukrainskogo naroda za sozdanie i uprochenie Ukrainskogo Sovetskogo gosudarstva* (C.P.—Inspirer and Leader of the Battle of the Ukrainian People for the Creation and Consolidation of the Ukrainian Soviet State). Kiev, 1954.

——. *Velika zhovtneva Sotsialistychna revoliutsiia na Ukraini* (The Great October Socialist Revolution in the Ukraine). Kiev, 1948.

Surkov, A. A. "O sostoianii i zadachakh sovetskoi literatury" (On the Status and Tasks of Soviet Literature), *Literaturnaia gazeta*, December 16, 1954.

——. "Pod znamenem sotsialisticheskogo realizma" (Under the Banner of Socialist Realism), *Pravda*, May 25, 1954.

Svetlanin, A. "Taina sobytii 1937-1938 godov" (Mystery of the Events of 1937-1938), *Sotsialisticheskii Vestnik*, XXIX, No. 3 (March, 1949), 47-49.

Tabolov, Kosta. "Protiv linii natsional'noi demokratii" (Against the Line of National Democracry), *Bol'shevik*, V, No. 1 (January, 1928), 65-78.

——. "Protiv velikorusskogo shovinizma v voprosakh natsional'noi kul'tury" (Against Great-Russian Chauvinism in Questions of National Culture), *Bol'shevik*, VII, No. 13 (July 15, 1930), 78-91.

Towster, Julian. *Political Power in the USSR, 1917-1947.* New York, 1948.

Trotsky, Leon. *The History of the Russian Revolution*. New York, 1932.

Trudy pervoi vsesoiuznoi konferentsii istorikov-marksistov 28-XII-1928 - 4-I-1929 (Transactions of the First All-Union Conference of Marxist-Historians, December 28, 1928 - January 4, 1929). Vol. I. 2d. ed. Moscow, 1930.

Tsamerian, I. *O proizvedeniiakh I. V. Stalina "Marksizm i natsional'-nyi vopros": "Natsional'nyi vopros i leninizm"* (On the Works of I. V. Stalin, "Marxism and the National Question" and "The National Question and Leninism"). Moscow, 1951.

Tsentral'noe statisticheskoe upravlenie SSSR, otdel demografii. *Trudy* (Works). Vol. XX: *Itogi vsesoiuznoi gorodskoi perepisi 1923 g.* (Results of the All-Union Urban Census of 1923). Moscow, 1924.

Tsentral'noe statisticheskoe upravlenie SSSR, otdel perepisi. *Vsesoiuz-naia perepis' naseleniia 1926 goda* (All-Union Census of Population of 1926). Vol. XI. Moscow, 1927.

Tulepov, M. "Leninsko-stalinskaia natsional'naia politika" (Leninist-Stalinist National Policy), *Partiinoe stroitel'stvo*, IX, No. 7 (April 1, 1937), 44-54.

Ukraina byla i budet sovetskoi, vtoroi anti-fashistskii miting pred-stavitelei ukrainskogo naroda, 30 avgusta 1942 (The Ukraine Has Been and Will Be Soviet, Second Anti-Fascist Meeting of Representatives of the Ukrainian People, August 30, 1942). Saratov, 1942.

Ukraine. Ministerstvo vyshoi osvity URSR. *Iz istorii Komunistychnoi partii Ukrainy* (From the History of the Communist Party of the Ukraine). Kiev, 1959.

Ukraine. Narodnyi komisariiat osvity USRR. *Stan i zavdannia kul'-turnoho budivnytstva na Ukraini* (Status and Task of Cultural Construction in the Ukraine). Kharkov, 1927.

Ukraine. Narodnyi komissariat vnutrennikh del. *Okruga i raiony U.S.S.R.* (Okrugs and Raions of the Uk.S.S.R.). Kharkov, 1923.

Ukraine. Tsentral'ne statystychne upravlinnia. *Korotki pidsumky perepysu naselennia Ukrainy 17 hrudnia roku 1926* (Short Summary of the Census of the Population of the Ukraine, December 17, 1926). Kharkov, 1928.

L' Ukraine Sovietiste, Quatre Années de Guerre et de Blocus. Berlin, 1922.

The Ukrainian Insurgent Army in Fight for Freedom. New York, 1954.

Ukrainian Resistance. New York, 1949.

Ukrains'ka zahal'na entsykl'opediia (Ukrainian General Encyclopedia). 3 vols. Lvov, 1938.

UPA in Western Europe. 2d ed. New York, 1948.

U.S. Congress. House of Representatives. *Favoring the Extension of Diplomatic Relations with the Republics of Ukraine and Byelo-russia.* Hearing before the Special Committee of the Committee on Foreign Affairs, U.S. House of Representatives, 83d Cong., 1st Sess., on H. Con. Res. 58, July 15, 1953. Washington, D.C., 1953.

U.S. Department of State. *Papers Relating to the Foreign Relations of the United States, 1918. Russia.* Vols. I and II. Washington, D.C., 1931.

V. I. Lenin o natsional'nom i natsional'no-kolonial'nom voprose (V. I. Lenin on the National and National-Colonial Question). Moscow, 1956.

Vasetskii, G. "Nesokrushimoe edinstvo velikogo sovetskogo naroda" (Indestructible Unity of the Great Soviet People), *Bol'shevik*, XVII, No. 14 (July, 1941), 35-41.

"Velikaia druzhba narodov SSSR" (GreatFriendship of the Peoples of the USSR), *Bol'shevik*, XV, No. 13 (July 1, 1938), 1-7.

Voitsekhivs'kyi, Iu. O. "Peromohy lenins'ko-stalins'koi natsional'noi polityky partii" (Victories of the Leninist-Stalinist National Policy of the Party), *Radians'ka Ukraina*, XI, No. 6 (June, 1935), 15-19.

Volin, B. "Velikii russkii narod" (The Great Russian People), *Bol'-shevik*, XV, No. 9 (May 1, 1938), 26-36.

Vsesoiuznaia Kommunisticheskaia Partiia (bol'shevikov). *Spra-vochnik partiinogo rabotnika* (Reference Book for the Party Worker). Vols. V, VI, VIII, and IX. Moscow, 1924-1935.

Vsesoiuznaia Kommunisticheskaia Partiia (bol'shevikov). Tsentral'-nyi Komitet. Organizatsionno-instruktorskii otdel. *Sostav VKP(b) v tsifrakh* (Composition of the All-Union Communist Party [b] in Figures). Vol. XI. Moscow, 1932.

Vsesoiuzna Komunistychna Partiia (bil'shovykiv). Tsentral'nyi Ko-mitet. *Pytannia partiino-orhanizatsiinoi roboty* (The Question of Party-Organization Work). Kiev, 1945.

Vsesoiuznyi institut iuridicheskikh nauk ministerstva iustitsii SSSR. *Ocherki po istorii organov sovetskoi gosudarstvennoi vlasti* (Notes on the History of Organs of Soviet State Authority). Moscow, 1949.

Vyshinsky, Andrei Y. *The Law of the Soviet State.* New York, 1948.

"Vystuplenie tovarishcha I. V. Stalina na prieme v Kremle v chest' komanduiushchikh voiskami Krasnoi Armii" (Statement of Comrade I. V. Stalin to a Reception in the Kremlin in Honor of the Com-manders of the Troops of the Red Army), *Bol'shevik*, XX, No. 10 (May, 1945), 1-2.

Weinreich, Uriel. "The Russification of Soviet Minority Languages," *Problems of Communism*, II, No. 6 (1953), 46-57.

Weinstein, Harold R. "Land Hunger and Nationalism in the Ukraine, 1905-1917," *Journal of Economic History*, II (May, 1942), 24-35.

——. "Language and Education in the Soviet Ukraine," *The Slavonic Review*, XX (1941), 124-48.

Wheeler-Bennett, John W. *The Forgotten Peace, Brest Litovsk.* New York, 1939.

"Za dal'neishii pod″em sovetskoi literatury" (For a Further Improvement of Soviet Literature), *Kommunist*, XXXI, No. 9 (June, 1954), 12-27.

Zatons'kyi, V. P. *Natsional'na problema na Ukraini* (The National Problem in the Ukraine). Kharkov, 1926.

——. *Natsional'no-kul'turnoe stroitel'stvo i bor'ba protiv natsionalizma* (National-Cultural Construction and the Battle against Nationalism). Kharkov, 1934.

Zhagelev, I. I. "Skrypnyk proty SRSR, iak iedynoi soiuznoi derzhavy" (Skrypnyk against the USSR, as a Single Union State), *Radians'ka Ukraina*, No. 1 (January, 1934), 11-24.

Zhdanov, A. A. *Doklad o zhurnalakh "Zvezda" i "Leningrad"* (Report on the Journals "Zvedza" and "Leningrad"). Moscow, 1952.

——. *Vstupitel'naia rech' i vystuplenie na soveshchanii deiatelei sovetskoi muzyki v TsK VKP(b)* (Introductory Speech and Statement to Contemporary Workers in Soviet Music in the Central Committee of the All-Union Communist Party [b]). Moscow, 1952.

——. *Vystuplenie na diskussii po knige G. F. Aleksandrova "Istoriia zapadnoevropeiskoi filosofii"* (Statement on the Discussion of the Book by G. F. Aleksandrov "History of West European Philosophy"). Moscow, 1947.

Zhdanov, A., Maxim Gorky, and others. *Problems of Soviet Literature.* Moscow, 1935.

Zhebrovs'kyi V. *Rist partii* (Growth of the Party). Kharkov, 1930.

PERIODICALS

Bil'shovyk Ukrainy (Bolshevik of the Ukraine). After November, 1952, the journal appeared under the title, *Komunist Ukrainy*. Kiev, monthly. 1930-31; 1935-36; 1955-57.

Bol'shevik (Bolshevik). After November, 1952, the journal appeared under the title, *Kommunist*. Moscow, semiweekly. April, 1924 - December, 1957.

Chervonyi shliakh (The Red Path). Kharkov, monthly. 1923-36.

Letopis' revoliutsii (Annals of the Revolution). Kharkov, bimonthly. 1922-28.

Komunist (Communist). Kiev, daily. October, 1940 - December, 1943.

Molodniak (Youth). After 1937 the journal appeared under the title, *Molodyi bil'shovyk* (Young Bolshevik). Kiev, monthly. 1936; 1938-40.

Pravda (Truth). Moscow, daily. 1934-57.

Pravda Ukrainy (Truth of the Ukraine). Kiev, daily. August-December, 1944; February, 1945 - April, 1950; January, 1951 - December, 1957.

Radians'ka Ukraina (Soviet Ukraine). Kiev, monthly. 1934-39.

Sovetskaia Ukraina (Soviet Ukraine). Kiev, daily. September-October, 1941; April, 1942; November, 1942 - March, 1943.

Ukrains'kyi zbirnyk (Ukrainian Collection). Munich, irregular. 1954-57.

Visti Vseukrains'koho Tsentral'noho Vykonavchoho Komitetu (News of the All-Ukrainian Central Executive Committee). Kharkov, daily. February-May, 1919; January, 1924 - June, 1929; January, 1930 - December, 1934; April, 1936 - June, 1937 ; January, 1938 - December, 1939.

Voprosy istorii KPSS (Questions of the History of the CPSU). Moscow, bimonthly. 1957-1961.

INDEX